Greater Love

Michael Kendrick

Published by Michael Kendrick
© Michael Kendrick 2007

FOREWORD

"Greater Love Hath No Man Than This, That A Man Lay Down His Life For His Friends."

During research for my earlier book: 'Fifty Good Men And True' about the Famous Fifty, I was contacted by a good many folk enquiring as to whether their relatives were among the aforementioned number. My answer was invariably in the negative, however, I felt so infused by the tender glow of such memories, that it seemed a criminal shame not to commit them to book form.

Within these pages you will find familiar names: some being related to the Fifty, whilst others come from particularly distinguished local families. Incredibly so, three entries received valour awards that cannot be bettered! It is my firm conclusion that every subject within the wealth of pages within this book is worthy of entry, and I feel extremely proud to have the opportunity of presenting them.

I sincerely hope that readers will savour the contents; the pages overflow with memorable events of young men who enlisted into a bestial war of attrition, of which the likes could never have been imagined: World War 1. A large proportion never returned to home shores: stricken petals from a flower of a generation returning to the dust from whence they came. I thank Providence for the storylines; many survivors remaining both mentally and physically scarred for life. To sacrifice or risk one's mortality for the sake of others has to be the pinnacle of devotion to our Creator, there cannot be a 'Greater Love'!

Michael Kendrick.
2007

DEDICATION

I dedicated my first book: 'Fifty Good Men And True' to my dear grandfather, Charles Hatter, who was one of their number, and without his inspirational memories the book would never have been written. Copies of that book now rest in the National Archives for the benefit of present and future generations.

My second book; 'Epitaph For The Few' was dedicated to a now departed friend, Wing Commander C. F. 'Bunny' Currant D.S.O. D.F.C. and bar, Croix de Guerre. Without his encouragement and confidence in me, I would never have written poems about my heroes. I urged him to approach the Poet Laureate for an anthology, but he always replied that he wanted a genuine 'Friend of The Few' to deliver the goods.

This third book is dedicated to a very dear lady, a lady who rarely complains despite suffering from childhood setbacks and a debilating illness for over twenty years. Without the blessing and support of my wife, Beryl (nee Hare): the love of my life, for eternity, my best friend, I would never have undertaken writing any of the aforementioned. Beryl has always insisted that whatever the circumstances, I had to continue researching and writing about earlier generations of our countrymen: so that they would never be forgotten.

So it is now written: 'Greater Love', dedicated to my dear wife, Beryl.

A fourth book will be released later: 'Sons and Daughters', similar in make up to the above but relating to World War 2. I will not be writing another book on World War 1; I would like readers to understand that I look upon those two books as a dedication towards the history of my dear hometown and county; it has genuinely been a labour of love.

Michael Kendrick.

CONTENTS

CONTENTS

Preface by DAVID TAYLOR M.P.

NORTH WEST LEICESTERSHIRE

Having awaited Michael Kendrick's first book with great anticipation and been duly rewarded, I was delighted to be asked to contribute a few opening words to his third, which is as moving and fascinating as its W.W.1 predecessor.

It is very easy in these days when the atrocities of war have become global and much publicised, in spite of the conviction in 1914 that "this lot" would be the one to end them all, to forget the intrinsic local nature of its impact. The author describes the fathers, brothers and sons who manifested immense bravery and in too many cases, made the ultimate personal sacrifice, to uphold values and ways of life which have been held dear for generations. The families on record in Michael's book with the words, like Bill Barney's sister "I never saw him again," it is for them and for us to reflect on the endurance and the courage of these patriots.

This book is in direct contrast with that feeling of distance and detachment the men in it were all local to the area where I was born and brought up, Ibstock, Ellistown, Hugglescote, Donington le Heath many of their homes are still there in the heart of the community. And, of course, that is what they were the heart of the community, ripped out for a greater task colliers, railwaymen, teachers ordinary men called to service and nation as a matter of personal conviction and choice.

Their names are still among us with their descendants, the Moores, the Emmersons, the Kendricks, the Wykes, all with largely unsung heroes in their family trees. But unsung no longer, now that this book has brought their stories and their heroism into the light for public scrutiny. Here is presented an opportunity for the present and future inhabitants of their villages (as well as the wider audience they deserve) to appreciate the lives and actions of those who, indeed, showed a greater love.

David Taylor

ACKNOWLEDGEMENTS

Yet again I have been honoured and privileged to work with some extremely knowledgeable and communicative local people in the preparation of this, my third book.

Dear friends, Denis Baker, who trawls and fact finds, and Martin Bird: a magician relating to computer techniques, have provided immeasurable assistance, as has Melanie Pollard.

I express my sincere gratitude to David Taylor: a very busy member of parliament, for finding the time to submit an excellent preface, also to my dear sister, Maureen Jarvis, for proofreading.

Over the last five years I have visited many homesteads, and all have provided a warm welcome. Nearly all have displayed a profound eagerness: a deep, caring love ensuring that their ancestors' lives and military histories are recorded for later generations.

Once again, I am indebted to the Coalville Times for their excellent archives and continuing assistance. The same applies to bookshops, especially local ones that have sold earlier books by the hundreds, and, never forgetting, the purchasers, and I hope they are pleased by my efforts.

Finally, I would like to mention that my local books are as much a social study as exposing the bare details of warfare, and my singular intent is to express pity for those poor souls who lost their lives as a result of military barbarity.

The content of this book never ceases to amaze me. I hasten to add that I have simply compiled the information, the quality lies within the subject material. It is quite voluminous because, without exception, every item submitted has been published, and I believe the folk of Leicestershire and beyond will be stunned by the quality of the subjects within. I hope that this book, like: 'Fifty Good And True', will pass to the National Archive.

Charles Hatter can be seen top right.

WALKING IN GRANDFATHER'S FOOTSTEPS

Grandfather was a frontline soldier during the First
World War.
A mere lad of twenty years when volunteering for
the Army Corps.
Tough training and manoeuvres at Luton forged a
force hard and keen.
Long icy nights neath canvas in the snowy winter of
nineteen-fourteen.

February 1915 bore a Channel crossing to
Le Havre from Southampton.
Trenches near Armentieres and Messines saw action
with rifle and gun.
Yon Ypres Salient where death was commonplace by
gas, shell or gunshot.
Hill 60 mocking that notorious trench, numbered as
50: a real hot spot!

Sanctuary Wood wasn't a haven in an embattled
Flanders' countryside.
Now a shady glade and old trenches proffer an
experienced guide.
Was it coincidence that my soles trod prints of
military boot steps?
Grandfather: July 1915 and me in July 1985 in
those same depths.

Possibly a time-gap of three score and ten years are
of significance.
If he'd perished my soul would be empty and of no
consequence.

Could it be in those earthworks at some wearying
hour he saw me?
Perhaps I am capable of unlocking his past with a
genetic key.
Did he hear a cheery whisper or a fleeting notion
passed to him?
These I offered whilst in a vaguely familiar trench
as lights grew dim.
"Your grandson will walk in your footprints in
seventy years hence."
I took the twisty trail aware that I'd never have to
suffer his events.

I wandered back and forth in those frontline
excavations in deepest thought.
At rest by a flooded dugout I scanned fields where
once he valiantly fought.
Thank you grandfather, especially your endeavours
for King and Country.
Thank you grandmother, especially for a mother
who gave birth to me!

I bade a goodbye to Flanders' lace and welcomed
the chalky cliffs of Dover.
I didn't walk alone in foreign fields: someone
helped me and watched over.
Grandfather was a frontline soldier during the First
World War.
A mere lad of twenty years when he volunteered for
the Army Corps.

Grandfather: **Charles Hatter**, 1/5th Battalion,
Leicestershire Regiment 1914-19.

Michael Kendrick

ISAAC WILLIAM BANCROFT

Little is known of Isaac's parents: his father was employed as a 'headman' at Bardon Stud Farm, near Coalville, and it is believed that both of his parents came from the village of Tonge; situated ten kilometres (six miles) northwest of Loughborough, Leicestershire.

Private Isaac Bancroft with Esther on his knee. His wife, Leah with baby, George. Taken during Christmas leave 1914.

Isaac, born in 1890 at Tonge, had two other brothers, James (Jim) and Thomas (Tom).

I understand that the family moved to Bardon while the siblings were young, and when Isaac left school he took employment at Bardon Hill Quarry. The remaining pinnacle of the aged rugged hill is still the highest point in the county: standing tall at over nine hundred feet.

The mildly natured young man married local girl, Leah Smith, in 1910, and they settled down in a cosy, rented, terraced house: strictly reserved for employees at 27, Old Row, Bardon.

Isaacs' brother, Jim, loved the outdoor life and for seventeen years he was the gardener for a Leicester family by the name of Brucianni. Of Italian race, they owned a successful bakery and coffee shop, and to this day enjoy a lot of custom. Jim never married.

The other brother, Tom married Coalville girl, Lucy; unfortunately he died in the most tragic of circumstances in a rock fall at nearby Stanton-under-Bardon Quarry.

By September 1914, Isaac was the proud father of Esther, a two-and-a-half years old girl, and, George, a ten-month old baby. He travelled the short distance to enlist at Coalville, and was ultimately posted to the 7th Leicestershire Battalion. He had some leave around Christmas 1914, see photograph. (For Isaac's Battalion experiences please read those of Tom Wood).

After three-and-a-half years on the Western Front he was demobilised and returned home in 1919. Leah was shocked by his physical condition and mental health, and in those bleak times there was little chance of a speedy recovery with a wife and two children to support. He returned to the quarry, but finances were dire, and he was desperate for an improved wage, especially upon seeing that pre-war colleagues of reserved occupations had received promotions. He applied for the job of hostler at Desford Colliery and was successful, although it meant a round trip of twenty-kilometre (twelve miles) walk, but that was not unusual in the Twenties. The Everard family, who owned the quarry and lived at Bardon Hall, had no alternative but to ask him to vacate his house. It has passed through generations: the day of the move; it was snowy and frostily cold as Isaac, still rather weak, loaded the family's few possessions onto a horse drawn dray and set off for Coalville. Leah's mother, a widow, had sold her property and with the revenue had bought two small houses in Waterworks Road, Coalville. Isaac and family lived in one house while mother-in law lived next door. A further son, Kenneth was born there in 1920.

In the war some of Isaac's toes were frostbitten: not bad enough for amputation, nevertheless the blood flow was poor, and for several years Leah and her mother massaged them daily.

In 1923 a hostler's job became available at nearby Snibston Colliery, and apparently the Snibston pit ponies benefited enormously: like his father he had a way with horses.

The manager at that colliery was Jabez Emmerson, one of the Famous Fifty and 'skipper' at the local Toc-H. (See later notes on Jabez).

Around 1925, Isaac and his family moved to 224, Bardon Road, where his interests included keeping pigs, chickens, and ferrets. I have been told that at long last Isaac and Leah found contentment; they had always been devoted to one another. Isaac became a real countryman at heart, and he had finally (after decades) recovered physical fitness and mental contentment: only the occasional W.W.1 nightmare. For two decades life could not have been better as they enjoyed the delights of family life and the happy marriages of George and Esther.

Along came World War 2: the sad deaths of local Service personnel, followed by the tragic illness and passing of Esther in 1944

Soon this depression was replaced when Ken married a delightful Belgium girl. The years trickled by and Isaac retired from work; he enjoyed many happy hours in his garden and spent even longer sitting by an open fire with his wife: reminiscing, watching television and enjoying family activities.

The old soldier, like so many of his old pals, enjoyed a drink. Weekly, and for many years, he caught the bus to his local public house: 'The Birch Tree' at Bardon. Veterans found that a drink and a chat helped them to forget the horrors of World War 1.

The 23rd June 1969 had been a gorgeously warm summer's day. That evening, as always when leaving the house, he hugged and kissed Leah in their front room, closed the front door and prepared to cross the road to the bus stop, just opposite. He was so looking-forward to a cool and refreshing pint of beer. Isaac exchanged a smile and a wave to Leah, turned, and whilst crossing the road was in collision with a car! His wife ran out immediately in a heartbroken and badly shocked state: an ambulance was called.

The seventy-nine year old was rushed to hospital, but he died from severe internal injuries just three days later: June 26th. At the inquest the car-driver said that he failed to see Mr. Bancroft because he had been blinded by the glare of the setting sun! The sun had certainly set on Leah's life, and Isaac was buried near to their blissful first home, at St. Peter's Churchyard, Bardon, just as his red garden roses were in full bloom.

Their son, George, said that as a boy he couldn't recall his father: *"He was away most of my early years fighting on the Western Front."* As a teenager, George, took-up an apprenticeship at Mellor Bromley, Leicester. He travelled by bus to the company, and during one of those trips he started a conversation with a young lady, his future wife, Edith, who was working at Dryad Ltd, on High Cross Street, Leicester. Edith was born at Carlisle, but her family moved south and for numerous years her father worked at Coleman's Ironmonger Shop, Coalville. They were married in 1938 and for many years lived at 178A, Bardon Road, Coalville. George was secretary of Coalville 'Toc-H' for twenty-five years. A few of his many friends were: 'Skipper' Jabez Emmerson, Ted Gaston, who repaired

224 Bardon Road, Coalville; the home of Isaac and Leah Bancroft. In the foreground is the bus stop post where Isaac was killed.

The grave of Isaac and Leah Bancroft, Saint Peter's Church, Bardon.

George Bancroft, shortly before he passed away in 1999.

television sets for Coleman's Shop, Frank Pollard, a builder, Ken Darby, schoolteacher, Ken Maddox and Dick Smith, both policemen, 'Puzzles' Smith, a maths teacher at Coalville Grammar School. A friend whose name was linked to tragedy was Harry Spencer. His mother completely lost the will to live after the death of her husband during W.W.1. It was reported that whilst he was shaving in the trenches, a large shell suddenly exploded, and the shock made him twitch and cut an artery.

George Bancroft passed away in 1999, aged 86 years: his ashes were scattered on his parents' grave, St. Peter's Churchyard, Bardon.

Kenneth fought during World War 2 and landed on the beaches on 'D'-Day, the 6th June 1944. He married a Belgium girl, Martha, whom he met in Antwerp during the military advance. After demobilisation in England he sent for Martha and they married shortly afterwards, moving in to next door: 222, Bardon Road. They had a son Colin and a daughter, Liliane. For most of his life he was a miner at Desford Colliery, where his father had worked just after W.W.1. When Isaac died they lived on Gwendolyn Road, Leicester; and took Leah in to look after until she died on 12th April 1979, aged 88 years. She was buried with her beloved husband. Ken died at sixty-six years in 1986 and also rests in St. Peter's. In 2004 Martha was still living at Leicester.

Esther married well-known rugby player, Louis Stokes, who was in the Royal Air Force in World War 2. She died of tuberculosis at Markfield Sanatorium in 1944, aged thirty-three years: again asleep in St. Peter's Churchyard.

'Tiger', Frederick Edwin, was tragically killed in an accident in the mill at Bardon Hill Quarry on the 24th April 1919: five months after the armistice. The son of Elizabeth Neale, he was twenty-seven and is buried in Woodhouse Churchyard. My thanks to Edith Bancroft, George's wife, who is now in her nineties.

WILLIAM BARNEY

Arthur Barney was born in 1868 and his future wife, Georgina Sherratt, in 1869. Arthur was employed as a miner at South Leicestershire Colliery, Ellistown, and initially they settled down in the village of Moira, a few kilometres southwest of Ashby de la Zouch.

William was always known as Bill, and he was born at Moira on the 10th July 1894. He was one of eight children, Timothy, Frank, Georgina, Arthur, Mary, Sarah and Alice. Around the turn of the century the family moved to 8, Cumberland Road, Ellistown, with the family worshipping at St. Christopher's Church in the village.

Upon finishing his education at the local school,

Bill joined his father at South Leicestershire Colliery and though only a young man was treated with a good deal of respect, there was something of the leader about him. He decided to broaden his horizons, and at Coalville in 1912 he enlisted into the Fifth Leicestershire Battalion as a territorial soldier, service number 1240. Continuing on a similar theme, in July1914, Bill passed interviews and was all set to receive basic training within the Metropolitan Police Force; unfortunately, the start of the Great War meant this had to be cancelled. It was considered that it would only be a temporary measure, for everyone said the war would be over by Christmas!

On the 4th August 1914, Bill was with his

Lance Corporal William Barney in 1914.

Battalion at the annual training camp at Bridlington, and following mobilisation they entrained from Loughborough for Luton, where he received promotion to Lance Corporal.

Bill's youngest sister, Alice, could recall Bill having a spell of leave in late 1914. *"A Travelling Picture Show was pitched-up on 'the-top-field' at Ellistown (now the site of Vince Foster's upholstery factory), and Bill took me there and paid for me to go in. He looked so smart in his uniform, but we knew he had to return to his unit. He picked me up and kissed me goodbye and I never saw him again."*

As mentioned in my earlier book, in the spring of 1915 the Battalion created a 'Tunnelling Section'. At this time they were in shallow trenches opposite to Spanbroekmolen (Hill 76), on the Messines Ridge, Belgium. Lieutenant Aubrey Moore of 'D' Company was ordered to recruit and take charge, because by profession in civilian life he was a qualified mining surveyor. The task of this section of some forty men was to counter-mine the Germans, who were digging beneath the 46th North Midland Division's frontline trenches. Their aim was to eliminate the enemy's tunnels by detonating mines near them, and this they did with a degree of success. The Lieutenant only accepted volunteers and most had colliery experience, and Bill was ideally suited. He was in excellent company and worked alongside such fine men as Jabez and William Emmerson, Bill Cowley and Cecil Hurley. The Battalion War Diary explained

that after one detonation, Lieutenant A. Moore and Private W. Barney went deep below the ground to assess the damage they had inflicted on a German sap. The two of them had to be carried out by stretcher and almost died from inhaling noxious fumes.

Shortly afterwards the Battalion moved to the dreaded Ypres Sector, where Bill would have been very active underground digging and shoring up tunnels deep beneath the salient. One cannot imagine the horrors of this job or the appalling conditions the men endured. Often, hand-to-hand fighting resulted when opposing tunnellers clashed in the bowels of the earth, also, if one side detected the other they blew-up the gallery, the men too. Medals were soon issued for such outstanding bravery, but not soon enough for Bill. It is recorded that he was killed on the late evening of the 30th June 1915, mortally wounded in the head. The Battalion had only just returned to the frontline trenches during the dark hours of 29/30th June after a hike over familiar ground, namely Shrapnel Corner, alongside Zillebeke Lake, Maple Copse, and Sanctuary Wood to Trench 50. Over the next two-three months many men of the Battalion were to die at this infamous spot, and accompany Bill to a final resting place in Sanctuary Wood Cemetery.

Several of his pals wrote to his parents, explaining that he had been sniped in the head and had died swiftly. He would have been twenty-one years of age on the 10th July 1915.

Before the war Lance Corporal (later sergeant) William Cave had lived just two doors down from the deceased, and he wrote the following letter to Bill's parents.

'Dear Mr. & Mrs. Barney, I am writing to let you know that William was killed on Wednesday night, June 30th at quarter past nine. Alfred Burton was with him, and just before he was shot he was asking how everyone was getting on back home. He did not suffer much and he died thirty minutes later. His last words were to thank those who had bandaged his wound. The following night they asked me to bury him because he was my mate, and I said I would and did! He was buried in full uniform and we covered him with a blanket so that no dirt could touch his face. Forty

of us stood over his grave and prayed for him. I made a cross and put it over his grave and as long as I'm in the area I will care for it. We all miss him but just remember that he died for King and country.'

Sergeant Cave was sniped whilst in charge of a wiring party in No-Man's-Land on the 28th December 1917.

Corporal John Hall wrote a letter:

'I am sorry to write that your son, William, has been killed in action. He was with me at the time and we were just talking about what we would do when we got leave when he was shot through the head. We all miss him, we always will and he was a good soldier, willing to do anything that was asked. I don't think there was a more popular N.C.O. in the Company than 'Tim' we always called him that name. I am writing to you on behalf of the rest of the boys. I know he was buried decently, William Cave saw to that. We are nearly all Coalville and District lads in this part of the trench and we look out for each other. Alf Burton was also with him at the time. We offer our deepest sympathy.'

Corporal John Hall was killed at the Charge of the Hohenzollern Redoubt on the 13th October 1915.

Alfred Burton sent a similar letter, also Lance Corporal F. Smith of Nailstone Wood.

Private Alfred Burton died in action on the 17th August 1917. All four are remembered on the Coalville Clock Tower Memorial.

I took a photograph of Bill's grave. It is situated

The grave of William Barney at Sanctuary Wood Cemetery.

in a corner of Sanctuary Wood Cemetery, and a red rose was in full bloom adjacent to where he lies. (Bill's grave reference is 1V. T.5. and all the graves around him are men from Leicestershire).

His mother died in 1938 and his father in 1949, neither could afford to visit their son's grave, few could from this area. Pleasingly, all of the other seven children survived to marry and have happy and contented lives. There are too few people in the twenty-first century who appreciate the sacrifice of men such as Bill Barney.

Lance Corporal William Barney's name can be read on the Coalville Clock Tower War Memorial and also on the Memorial Tablet within St. Christopher's Parish Church.

Many thanks to Constance Foster, daughter of Bill's sister, Alice.

I also thank Constance for telling me of her father's eldest brother, Walter Hill.

WALTER HILL

Walter was born in 1896 at Hugglescote, and at the time of his enlistment at Coalville was residing at nearby Donington-le-Heath. He was the son of Henry and Elizabeth Hill who lived at Forest House Farm, Battleflat, Bardon Hill, near Coalville.

Walter, service number 15744, was in the 7th Battalion of the Leicestershire Regiment, which has already been written about. Together with the 6th, 8th and 9th Battalions it formed the 110th Brigade, part of Kitchener's New Army.

All the training was based upon the intention of punching a massive hole in the German positions at a selected position in France. With success it would allow a mobile war of which the Allies were confident of achieving victory. The area for the thrust was a place of rural beauty often frequented by Parisian holidaymakers before the war. The first day of the battle, 1st July 1916, resulted in the death of twenty thousand of Kitchener's men, plus nearly forty thousand being wounded, and the location was known as the Somme.

Walter was badly wounded on the 14th July 1916 in the area of Bazentin le Petit Wood. He was sent down the line to the 36th Casualty Clearing Station at Heilly only to die on Friday 21st July 1916. Walter's is buried close by at Heilly Station Cemetery, Mericourt-L'Abbe, Somme in France. His grave reference is II.C.6.

Walter was twenty years of age when he died.

ROSES AT SANCTUARY WOOD CEMETERY

Dear roses, so majestic in stance alongside pristine-
pure headstones.
Is it just coincidence that you are red and not the
grey of hidden bones?
A floral tribute to young veins flushed with vital
life-giving corpuscles.
Short lives, youthful memories, the ruinous power of
military muscles.

Dear roses, you reach to the heavens above a skirt
of dewy green foliage.
Is it simply chance that serene stems and greenery
whisper a message?
Homeland's pastures and tossed leather-balls onto
willow-bats at cricket.
Short lives, youthful memories, mossy human frames
lost under a thicket.

Dear roses, so potent a perfume that rarefies the air
in which you dwell.
Were you created to proffer such a service for
buried occupants who fell?
Such valeting vapours wouldn't have sufficed
mustard gas or cordite.
Short lives, youthful memories, sacrificial sons
believing duty was right.

Dear roses, soon an autumnal chill will spill blood
red petals to earth.
Does only Nature decide when petals fall or when
time's ripe for new birth?
Flowers from a generation decayed to dust and
failed to scatter their seed.
Short lives, youthful memories, we all pray that
such souls have been freed.

I was inspired by the grave of Lance Corporal Bill Barney to write the above poem and dedicate it to him and his family circle. Its essence befits all who are buried in the corner of a foreign field.

Michael Kendrick

Bill's grave is second
from the left.

WILLIAM BEES V.C.

William was born on the 12th September 1872 at Loughborough, a market town in northwest Leicestershire, some twelve kilometres (eight miles) northeast of Coalville. He was the son of William and Jane Bees and he was educated at the town's Board School.

Following a variety of jobs William decided his life required a touch of adventure, and the seventeen year old enlisted at Normanton Barracks on the 7th March 1890, as a regular soldier into the 1st Battalion of the Nottingham and Derbyshire Regiment.

The soldier certainly saw life, and one of his many battles was involved in the 1897-98 Tirah Campaign in India's Northwest Frontier, taking pride in receiving the clasped medal. Tirah is a dangerous mountainous tract lying between the Khyber Pass and Khanki Valley, and when the Afridi took to weapons in a continuation of their religious struggle (Jihad), they captured the Khyber posts and forts near Peshawar. In the fiercest struggle since the 2nd Afghan War, 40,000 British and Indian troops were rushed to the Tirah. The troops overcame opposition at Dargai and entered the Miranzai Valley to regain control of the area.

No doubt William received leave and returned to his hometown to speak of the horrors of a 'Holy War'; certainly the newspapers reported in graphic detail a war that later captured the imagination of many a young boy whilst reading his treasured Boy's Own Book of Great Adventures.

In 1899, continued conflict between British Imperial policies and the Boers' (descendants of original Dutch immigrants) national individualism, flared into a bloodbath of a war. Sixty years earlier Boers had trekked northwards into the wilderness to escape from British rule, establishing homes on the Transvaal and Orange Free State, independent republics, and subject to certain British treaty rights. However, British annexations followed them, and problems really escalated when gold was discovered in the Transvaal. British citizens poured in to hopefully claim a share: President Kruger, a 'South Africa for the Boers' (only) man, treated them oppressively!

Private William Bees circa 1900.

British troops were rushed to the area, however, the Boers proved to be tough and elusive fighters and the early part of the conflict witnessed several British disasters. By 1900 Lord Roberts and Lord Kitchener got the upper hand but the struggle continued until 1902.

In the autumn of 1901, William Bees was in the Western Transvaal and under the command of Colonel Kekewich, famed as a defender of Kimberley during a long siege. Private Bees was in a party of troops combing the area of Magaliesberg, an area of caves and ravines where women and children were in refuge. On the afternoon of the 29th September 1901, Colonel Kekewich and 1,000 soldiers of the Derbyshire, Scottish Horse and Yeomanry Regiments pitched camp at Moedwil Farm, by the river Selens. That night the Boer's commander, Koos De la Rey, sent the bulk of his force to conceal themselves in the rocks and bushes by the river. A pre-dawn patrol spotted the Boers, and in the following confusion of flying bullets, and stampeding British horses, a fierce battle lasted for ninety minutes. The British suffered severe casualties and it was during this battle that William distinguished himself.

The British troops rallied and with use of the bayonet the Boers suffered severe losses and decided upon a steady withdrawal.

The London Gazette of the 17th December 1901 announced his award of the Victoria Cross.

On the 30th September 1901 at Moedwil, Private Bees was one of a Maxim-gun detachment, which suffered heavy casualties, six out of the nine men being hit. Hearing his wounded comrades asking for water, Private Bees went forward under heavy fire to a spruit held by the Boers about 500 yards ahead of the men, and brought back a kettle filled with water. In doing this he had to pass within 100 yards of some rocks also held by the enemy and the kettle he was carrying was hit by several bullets.

Lord Kitchener, then Commandant at Rustenburg pinned the V.C. onto the newly promoted Corporal William Bees on the 30th July 1902.

Charles William Bees, father's friend, William Bees V.C. and Lillian Elizabeth Bees circa 1914-15.

As a result of his service in South Africa, William also received the Queen's Medal with three bars and the King's medal with two bars. He retired from the Army on the 18th September 1902.

When William returned to northwest Leicestershire he was treated as a celebrity, indeed Mary Bradford, a famous song-writer was inspired to compose a ballad: 'The Old Kettle' a very popular music-hall song of the day.

On the 25th April 1903, the thirty one year old married local girl, Sarah, at All Saint's Church, Loughborough, and the couple had two children: Charles William (Billy) on the 25th March 1904 and Lillian Elizabeth on the 28th June 1907.

Following a spell of civilian life, Corporal Bees re-enlisted into Kitchener's Army in October 1914. Sadly his health failed and was discharged. Undeterred he joined his old Regiment, and remained with the Sherwood Foresters at Whitburn, Sunderland until he was transferred to the Durham Light Infantry, with whom he received postings at Blythe and South Shields. He was again transferred to Class W for mining, and after serving 133 days with the Colours was described as being of 'good character.' Yet again he re-enlisted on the 30th January 1918 into the Royal Army Service Corps, and was eventually transferred to the Army Reserve and subsequently demobilisation on the 6th February 1919.

That year William took his wife and children to live at 78, Margaret Street, Coalville. Jobs were difficult to find, especially for a forty-seven year old with few skills outside of the Military. The Coalville Urban District Council offered him employment as a road-sweeper, and he gladly accepted the employment, never one wanting to idle.

Naturally, William was a well-known and respected figure on his rounds, and he was an active member with the Salvation Army, playing the drum in their local band.

Although he had friends in high places Generals, Baronets, Members of Parliament, and Garden Parties at Buckingham Palace, he was just as much at home when sitting with pals and enjoying a pint of beer in Coalville's Public Houses, especially at the Snibston New Inn.

Colossal grief struck the family during the spring of 1925, when twenty-year old Billy Bees lost his life in an accident whilst working at Stableford's Wagon Works. He was appallingly crushed between a wagon and buffer on the 24th April 1925: quickly dying from his injuries! William and Sarah suffered another tragedy two years later when their twenty years old daughter, Lillian died from natural causes on the 2nd October 1927. Earlier she had married Bruce Hammonds and had given birth to a daughter, Lillian (Joyce). William and Sarah were to bring-up

Sarah and William Bees at Coalville Railway Station, with their grand daughter, Lillian (Joyce). They are about to depart in response to an invitation to a V.C.'s Dinner at the House of Lords, November 1929.

The family home, 78 Margaret Street, Coalville.

their baby granddaughter.

A ray of sunshine entered their lives when they were both invited to the House of Lords on the 9th November 1929. The Prince of Wales (later King Edward Vlllth) presented him with a copy of 'The Legion Book'. William joked with the future king and offered to make him a gift of a puppy whippet bitch; from a dog he had for several years. The Prince could not accept the kind gesture but wrote William a charming letter of thanks. Shortly afterwards a stranger called and bought the puppy for the huge sum of £5.00. (A 'princely sum' indeed!)

A horrendous and utterly distasteful state of affairs hit the newspapers in April 1938. A Police Court at Coalville chaired by Mr. H. J. Ford, with magistrates Mrs. Everard, Mr. E. Orton, Mrs. J. Smith and Mr. A. Dolman sat in judgement of William, who was accused of keeping a dog without a licence. The old-age pensioner said he was waiting for his pension before he could afford to pay the amount. He added that he was very sorry to cause an offence but the dog was old and ill and did not want

to destroy it, but would soon be buying a licence. The chairman was unmoved and said he was guilty: could not make an exception, even though William was an old soldier! William retaliated by saying he did not expect preferential treatment. He was fined seven shillings and sixpence. He offered to pay at one shilling a week and the bench accepted. Ironically the dog had produced the puppy offered (bought) by the Prince of Wales.

The case produced a public outcry, with many asking how our country could allow a Victoria Cross holder to fall on such hard times. He received money from many parts of Britain and an anonymous benefactor paid for the licence. The Royal British Legion stepped in and awarded him a life pension of ten shilling (fifty new pence) per week.

The publicity also encouraged a woman then living in Rugby, to return William's King's Medal, which she claimed to have found in a Coalville Street.

Almost certainly the upset and stress damaged William's health because he only claimed £2 from the Legion: dying at his home on Monday the 20th June 1938, aged sixty-six years.

His death was reported in the Coalville Times on the 24th June 1938, with Sarah stating that she had received many messages of sympathy, including a telegram from local Member of Parliament, Sir William Edge.

William was buried at London Road Cemetery, Coalville, on Saturday the 25th June 1938. The streets were lined as thousands of people paid admiration and respect as the cortege slowly wheeled passed.

Heading the procession were officers and men of the Sherwood Foresters and the 5th Leicestershire Territorials, with the Hugglescote Band playing the 'Dead March.' The coffin was shrouded by a Union Jack, and sitting upon that a cushion, on which were placed his many medals. A standard hearse (efforts to obtain a gun carriage and a firing party were unsuccessful), carried it. Close behind were family mourners, representatives of the Royal British Legion and the Salvation Army, and road staff of the Coalville Urban District Council. Sir William Edge was present and defrayed the cost of the band.

The cortege passed the Municipal Offices, its

The grave of William Bees, his wife, Sarah and their granddaughter, Lillian Boysen.

flag at half-mast, and the Reverend W. A. Martyr conducted the service at Christ Church. The brave old soldier was laid to rest near to his son and daughter: a bugler sounded the 'Last Post' and 'Reveille.'

At the annual dinner of the Old Comrades Association at Derby on the 15th October 1938, Sarah Bees handed over her late husband's medals to his old regiment. Also present were four ex-members wearing their Victoria Crosses: Brigadier C. E. Hudson, Sergeant J. Upton, Corporal F. Greaves and Corporal E. A. Egerton.

In a voice wavering with emotion Mrs. Bees said:

"I am proud to be with you all this evening and prouder still to present my husband's Victoria Cross and medals to the Regiment. My husband was always proud to be a Forester, and I make this presentation knowing I am carrying out his wishes. He was a proper rough diamond, as many of you know, but his heart was in the right place, and he would never see a comrade without a meal and shelter. In our thirty-five years of married life he has given food and shelter to comrades on many an occasion and a whip round for their benefit and, perhaps, gone round with them to find a job."

Major General Sir F. B. Morris, Colonel of the Regiment, said he had the honour to accept the Cross and medals of so gallant soldier on behalf of the Regiment. He did so with particular pleasure because Corporal Bees was in his Company at Tirah, forty-one years earlier. He added that the medals were noble gifts and would always be treasured in the Regiment in memory of a gallant soldier. The medals were placed in the officers' mess.

In return, Mrs. Bees received a set of miniature medals, which she added she would be proud to wear on appropriate occasions. When the dear lady passed away on the 4th January 1957, aged eighty-one years, the medals were buried with her.

In March 1996 Coalville people yet again flocked to remember William Bees V.C. His grave was refurbished and rehallowed by the Chaplain of the Royal British Legion, Reverend Joe Hart, and wreathes were laid by Mrs. Lillian (Joyce) Boysen (William's granddaughter), the Sherwood Foresters, and Councillor Alfie Smith (chairman of the N.W. Leicestershire District Council.) The Sherwood Foresters played the 'Last Post.'

The Coalville Times reported the above ceremony on the 22nd March 1996 and added that Peter Boysen (great grandson) said: *"I am very proud. Of course I never met him, but its nice to have him remembered after such a long time."*

Sadly, since that date, Mrs Boysen has passed away: on the 14th February 2001, aged seventy-four years, she is buried with her grandparents.

Before attempting to write this essay I trundled along many of Coalville's roads, imagining William pushing his brush in all weathers along the gutter ways. Certainly I am not decrying the importance of such a job: it is vital for our welfare, but do feel an occupation more befitting his famed social standing should have been offered. It says a lot for his humane qualities that for eighteen years this sociable, compassionate and kindly man hand-swept all manner of waste from our streets. It does not say a lot for the way our Country treated brave men in times past, notably post World War 1: a 'Land Fit For Heroes!'

I am very grateful to Phil Ellis of the North West Leicestershire District Council for supplying and consenting for me to use such estimable information.

THE OLD KETTLE

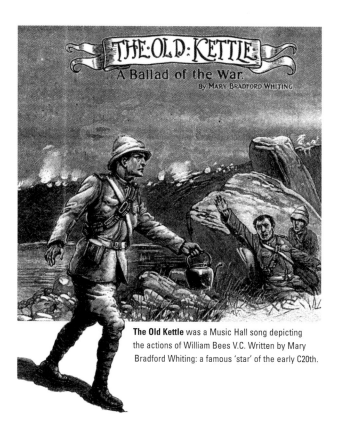

The Old Kettle was a Music Hall song depicting the actions of William Bees V.C. Written by Mary Bradford Whiting: a famous 'star' of the early C20th.

"What! Part with that old kettle?"
She said, and her eyes grew dim;
"If I'd come to my very last farthing
I wouldn't part with him!
You say that it's battered and rusty,
A piece of old iron, no more;
Worth? Well, perhaps three half pence
At a second hand dealer's store!"

"But to me that old iron kettle
Has a worth that can never be told,
A value that could not be greater
If it had been made of gold.
So I've hung it over the mantel
And there it shall ever stay,
And pass to my children's children
When I come to my dying day."

"For out in the rush of battle
The boy that I love so dear,
Was left with his wounded comrades,
Alone, and with no help near.
The enemy guarded the river'
Their shot was dropping still,
And the little band crept closer
In the grass of the wind-swept hill."

"I'd give the world for some water!"
Said one poor lad with a sigh,
Jo sprang to his feet from the cover,
For he saw this old kettle hard by.
"Lie down again, man," said his comrade;
"If you go they will shoot you dead!"
"I'll die or I'll get you that water!"
Was all that the brave boy said.

"So down he went to the river,
Right close to the enemy track,
He dipped the kettle, and filled it,
And brought it safely back.
The bullets whizzed around him,
Fired by the sleepless foe;
They made those dents in the kettle,
But God preserved my Jo!"

"And when the King, God bless him!
Heard what my boy had done,
He sent a cross and ribbon,
And said it was nobly won.
So the sign of his Sovereign's honour
Is shining on his breast;
But I've got the poor old kettle,
And I think I like it best!"

"And when above my mantel
Its battered sides I see,
Nothing the world could offer
Would look so fair to me;
For it tells that love and pity
Shone clear through those clouds of strife,
It's not a piece of old iron,
It's the price of a precious life!"

(The kettle was in fact a
soldier's mess tin.)

With thanks to Lesley Hale.

GRAVE TALES FROM FLANDERS
(PASSCHENDAELE 1917)

Trenches that bite deeply into the shell-churned, battle scarred earth.
Arteries of life amidst desolation, no poppies near the many watery graves.
Only the rats grow fat on a diet of fetid meat recycled into a rodent birth.
Pity the poor infantry as they battle in hell while saluting heavenly braves.

Blessed troops, thirsty, hungry, lousy, encrusted by mud, layer upon layer.
It's of no protection, nor insulation, but is of uniform colour and abounds.
Steely bullets cool in flight, red-hot on explosion; perhaps a final prayer.
Metallic and alien, a projectile buried in organs and muscular surrounds.

The Generals stress the supreme, steadfast qualities of our fighting men.
Mothers endure childbirth, their labours replenish the fallen for future wars.
Demons invite necessity; do we not have to fight to survive or die as men?
Don't women provide the vital lifeblood and yolk for our nation's cause?

Yes, they were all milked as 'babes in arms', sleeping in cots so passively.
At such a time hearts were strong, bodies weak and lungs fresh of breath.
What came of the soldiers of Passchendaele who waged war so actively?
Hearts were strong, weary of body and lungs filled by the stench of death!

All were divinely created, cynically rearranged: amorphous and grotesque.
Will the dead, as spiritual beings, venture down a winding old English lane?
Could they observe the oaks, willows and flowery meadows so picturesque?
Tear-stained Bibles testify eternally of loved soldier boys never seen again.

And still the Devil warps the reasoning power and conscience of politicians.
Oh, why did that slippery serpent reduce immortal life to mere vestigial tissue?
Grave tales of Flanders where life's as flimsy as a flame on live ammunitions!
Explosions and the energy is spent, bodies join the Paschendaele death queue.

Ghouls offer a sardonic welcome to new military recruits for continued pleasure.
Skeletal remains chatter on the barbed wire in the bleak winds of war that blow.
No poppy petals, only flimsy flakes of human skin drift as confetti to a measure.
Always consider the immortal names scribed on Rolls of Honour that are on show.

No dispersal, yet, of the iniquitous dark clouds that rain blood on life's innocent.
How many more headstones need to be sculptured, how many more roses weeping?
How many churchyard memorials and telegrams of death still need to be sent?
An autumn sun brightens a mossy head stone, an epitaph: 'Simply a babe sleeping'!

Michael Kendrick
Autumn 1980

PHILIP ERIC BENT V.C. D.S.O.

To me the stunning photograph of Philip Bent encapsulates and epitomises the very finest qualities that were evident in the 'lost flower of a generation.' I detect a strong character with positive determination, quiet confidence - not arrogance and a focussed mind. It is clearly apparent that he was the possessor of great inner strength, a leader of men, a man to inspire those around him, and his eyes disclose compassion, for it is known he cared deeply for his men. It is on that note that I proudly present this essay in my book.

Philip Bent was born at Halifax in Nova Scotia, on the eastern seaboard of Canada on the 3rd January 1891. He was of English ancestry and it is sad to

Lieutenant Philip Bent of the 9th Leicestershire Battalion, 1915.

report that records on either side of the Atlantic appear to indicate that the eventual death of his mother ended the family branch-line. Readers may wonder why I have included a man of Canadian birth in a book relating to Leicestershire soldiers of the Great War. Two details allow me to 'adopt' such a valorous soldier into my humble book. Firstly, he attended the famous Grammar School at Ashby de la Zouch between 1904 and 1907 and, secondly, he won his Victoria Cross and Distinguished Service Order (DSO) whilst serving with the Leicestershire Regiment.

The frontage of the famous old Grammar School House at Ashby de la Zouch. For several years this was home for pupil, Philip Bent and also that of his young Housemaster, Bernard Vann. Both of the above men were to be awarded the Victoria Cross during the Great War of 1914-18.

Built in 1657 the Grammar School had about twenty boarders and forty day boys at that time, and whilst a boarder Philip was made head-boy after displaying virtuous qualities and academic ability. He was particularly fond of boxing and cricket and felt very much at home in the school and also around the historical market town. Among his school friends were Aubrey Moore, later Captain Moore MC of the Fifth Leicestershire Battalion, Jabez Emmerson, later Captain Emmerson DCM of the Seventh Leicestershire and Frederic (no k) Scott, later Captain Scott MC of the Sixth Leicestershire. All of then served in the same Brigade at various times during the war.

Philip's friendship with Aubrey Moore, a man of distinguished ancestry, continued after his schooldays and they spent a few holidays together at Weymouth where Philip had relations.

In January 1909 Philip was admitted as a cadet to H.M.S. 'Conway' and served until December 1910 when he was assessed as 'very good'. He was awarded a badge as Senior Cadet Captain of Port Main and described as very popular and a stout boxer (silver medallist). Shortly afterwards as 2nd Mate he spent a period aboard H.M.S. 'Vimeira'. Little is known until 1912 when he was living at St. Leonard's-on-Sea, near to Hastings in East Sussex. For reasons unknown he returned to academia, and began studies at Edinburgh University.

At the outbreak of the Great War he enlisted as a private soldier into 'A' Company, 1st City of Edinburgh Battalion, Royal Scots Regiment, and based at Edinburgh Castle. Displaying his customary loyalty and love of Leicestershire he asked for a transfer to join the Tigers, and did so at Bourley Camp, just outside of Aldershot in the autumn of 1914. Initially allocated to the 7th Battalion, he was commissioned on the 5th December 1914 and as a 2nd Lieutenant was appointed in command of number 2 platoon of 'A' Company, the 9th Battalion. His Ashby de la Zouch Grammar School friend, 2nd Lieutenant Frederic Scott was in the 9th also. The Battalion, together with the other three service battalions, six, seven and eight, were involved in individual training and also squad and platoon drills. All four battalions were composed of new and keen volunteer recruits. Departing from glorious golden autumnal warmth, the rage of winter encouraged bitterly cold conditions for the troops under canvas, and just before Christmas the Battalion entered a barrack block at Aldershot following a spate of deaths from viral pneumonia.

In March 1915 the above four battalions were grouped together as the 110th Brigade within the 37th Division, and placed under the command of Sir Guy Bainbridge. Soon the 9th Battalion was billeted at New Romney in Kent, and in April the Brigade met-up at Perham Down on the Salisbury Plain for final training. On the 29th July 1915 the Brigade embarked for France, the 9th Battalion aboard SS. 'St. Seiriol' that departed from Folkestone docks in complete darkness and silence, destination Boulogne and the Western Front.

The Brigade saw action in the Kemmel Sector of Flanders, Monchy-au-Bois just to the north of Gommecourt on the Somme in France, the Battle of

Lieutenant Philip Bent with some of his men at Perham Down. Circa April 1915.

Bazentin Ridge, Guedecourt, the Hohenzollern Redoubt of 1916, Fontaine-les-Croisilles of May 1917 before participation in the Battle of Paschendaele in the autumn of 1917.

Philip was promoted to full lieutenant on the 20th March 1916 and whilst in the trenches in the Bienvillers - Bailleulmont Sector was **mentioned in despatches.**

On April 1916 he wrote a letter to his mother, Sophia Bent:

'Life in the trenches this winter has not been very pleasant, owing to the excessive bad weather, which has made our trenches into canals and forced our dug-outs to fall in. However, the last week has been glorious, sunshine and good northwesterly winds; so we are all hoping that the worst of the weather is over. Everything is very quiet with us, a few hours bombardment and an occasional bombing escapade make up our daily routine.'

On the 7th July 1916 a further promotion made it Captain Bent, and he fought in the horrendous Battle of Bazentin le Petit. With casualties among senior field officers severe he was once again promoted on September 1st, and it was Major Bent who led his troops into battle on the Somme at Guedecourt on September 25th. He distinguished himself with several acts of bravery, and his men took their officer to heart, knowing that he cared immensely for their well-being. Philip was also highly focussed when required and possessed tremendous stamina and drive, indeed, an inspirational soldier to all those around him. It was also noted that he often led

from the front, which inevitably meant he was wounded on several occasions! One particularly bad wound in the autumn of 1916 was to his neck, forcing him to stay at Base Hospital for ten days, before he insisted on returning to his men.

On the 26th September 1916, Philip, 25 years of age was made Acting Lieutenant Colonel, and Gazetted Temporary Lieutenant Colonel on the 1st February 1917, ante-dated to 26th October 1916.

On the 22nd May 1917 he was again **mentioned in despatches** and on the 4th June was awarded the **Distinguished Service Order** (D.S.O.) for displaying outstanding bravery and leadership during a critical time in a battle.

In the autumn of 1917 Philip wrote to his old shipmates on H.M.S. *'Vimeira'*, explaining the conditions of life on the Western Front.

On the night of the 30th September 1917 the 110th Brigade entered the later stages of the Battle of Paschendaele, in the Ypres Sector of Belgium. I am informed that a combination of casualties to senior officers in the Battalion and pure ability, Philip, still only twenty-six years old, qualifies as the youngest ever Lieutenant Colonel (Acting) in the British Army to this day!

Philip, now commander of the 9th Battalion led his men along the duckboard track to the frontline, situated within the shattered remnants of Polygon Wood. The area was a quagmire (see photograph) and to stray from the boards meant death to any heavily laden soldier who fell into the deep mud-filled shell craters!

The area had witnessed fighting for several years; indeed soldiers of the 2/5th Leicestershire Battalion had attacked the Wood only four days earlier, September 26th, and was only finally captured by an Australian Battalion two days later.

The troops of the 8th and 9th Battalions moved to the right-hand sector of Polygon Wood, and in one or two instances were able to occupy captured German pillboxes. The 8th held the left-hand position and the 9th were to the right (see map). They dug themselves in as best they could, and all was peaceful during the first part of the evening. Philip sent out one or two patrols to reconnoitre No Man's Land in the hope of gathering some information. It was a particularly bitter, cold night and the troops lay

Polygon Wood in the Ypres Salient, September 1917.

in shallow mud filled trenches. The 6th and 7th Battalions were well back in the 'Wood' and in reserve.

At 4.40 am on the 1st October 1917 the Germans opened-up with an immense artillery barrage, and followed up with smoke shells to make night vision even poorer. Large numbers of determined German storm-troops hit and pushed back the 8th Battalion, who sustained severe casualties. Powerful and successive waves of troops then attempted to breach the 9th Battalion's position.

A captured German pillbox at Polygon Wood, September 1917.

David Kelly was the Brigade's Intelligence Officer: *'A great counter attack was launched by the Germans to recapture Polygon Wood. It was accompanied by the heaviest shelling I had ever encountered; a series of barrages, distributed in depth over several miles of ground and maintained, with only occasional short lulls! The enemy had also concentrated all available reserves of troops - now greatly swollen by the Russian collapse opposite us. I heard of one dramatic incident from the Adjutant of the 9th Battalion concerning Colonel Bent, their*

commanding officer. The colonel was in a pillbox when a runner came in saying that an SOS had gone up from the reserve company. It is recorded that Philip Bent said: "Then we had better get on", and went forward with his headquarter personnel. Collecting the reserve company and everyone available the colonel led a brilliant counter-attack, and was only struck down at the moment of victory. His last words were "Go on Tigers" as he waved his men forward with his pipe in hand!" This very gallant officer was so devoted to his work. If he was granted ten days leave he would be back within five!'

Lieutenant Colonel Philip Bent D.S.O. received a machine-gun bullet through the temple and died instantly. His body was never found; it was either blown to pieces in the continuing barrage or consumed by the sucking, glutinous pools of mud. Thanks to his inspired leadership the position and hence the Line, which looked to be collapsing, was held and the Brigade moved to Wardrecques later in the month.

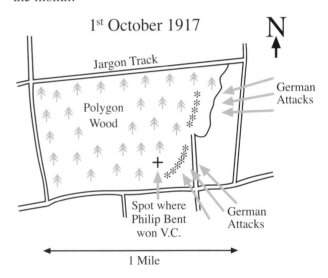

Map of Polygon Wood showing the positions of the 8th and 9th Leicestershire Battalions on the early morning of 1st October 1917.. The cross marks the spot where Colonel Philip Bent was killed.

The Victoria Cross is the world's most coveted medal for bravery, and only 1,350 men have received the award. The medal is cast in bronze from the cannons captured at Sevastopol in the Crimean War. **Colonel Philip Bent was gazetted for the award on the 11th January 1918.**

The account of the deed: *On the 1st October 1917 east of Polygon Wood, Zonnebeke, Belgium, when the situation was critical owing to the confusion caused by a heavy enemy attack and the* intense artillery fire, Lieutenant Colonel Bent collected a platoon that was in reserve and together with men from other companies and various regimental details, he organised and led them forward to the counter attack, which was successful and the enemy was checked. The coolness and magnificent example of the colonel resulted in the securing of a portion of the line essential to subsequent operation, but he was killed whilst leading a charge.

Philip's name can be read on the Tyne Cot Memorial Wall at Paschendaele, near Ypres and also on a memorial outside St. Alban's Church, Hindhead, Surrey. It is on the latter memorial because his mother was residing there at the time.

David Kelly, in his marvellous 1930 book: '39 Months With The Tigers', paints a characteristic picture of what the soldier of that battle looked like, *'Long strings of these weary mud-bedraggled 'animals' plodding along the greasy shell-swept tracks.'*

The letter that Philip wrote to his old companions aboard H.M.S. 'Vimeira' was delivered to them shortly after his death was announced.

On the 6th October 1917 Captain S. Tooth of the 9th Battalion wrote:

'It is with deepest sympathy that I have to recount that Lieutenant Colonel P. E. Bent D.S.O. fell in action on the 1st October 1917 whilst leading a most gallant attack. The Regiment was heavily attacked at dawn; the first two waves were beaten off but the third succeeded. The Colonel immediately led a counter attack with the remnants of the Battalion. Utterly regardless of his own life he went ahead of the men, waiving his revolver and shouting "Forward The Tigers". The attack was a brilliant success and the enemy were driven back, but at the moment of victory the Colonel was struck by a bullet and killed instantaneously.

It was the finest act possible, and undoubtedly saved the day. We feel the loss of the Colonel more than words can say, for he was beloved by all the ranks. I am very proud to have had the privilege of knowing such a fine Christian gentleman, whose memory will live forever in the history of this Regiment!'

Hugh F. Sawbridge, Chaplain of the 9th Battalion wrote the following:

> *Thelnetham Rectory.*
> *Diss.*
> *Norfolk.*
> *24th October 1917.*

Dear Mrs. Bent,

'I am so sorry I have been so long in writing, as I so much wanted to try to express to you how very greatly we all feel for you in your great sorrow.

Colonel Bent's death has been a very great blow to us, and we have lost one whom we all loved, respected and admired. It was difficult to realise he was so young, his character was so strong and his influence and power so great.

You cannot imagine how much it meant to me as Chaplain, to have a Colonel who was so good a churchman and Christian, and who was always so ready to help me in my work.

There is no doubt he made and kept the Battalion wonderfully efficient. He always would have everything ship-shape, and the men loved him for it.

He had a great pride in his old platoon (No2), the platoon he came out to France with. There are quite a number of them still left, and I know them very well, a splendid set of fellows and they often talk of the days when the colonel was their platoon commander, and speak of all he used to do for them, and how at first they thought he was rather strict, but how they soon saw how much they were learning and how smart and efficient they were getting.

It was the same when he got command of a Company, and then the full Battalion. He made everyone proud to the unit to which they belonged, and proud of their own efficiency, and he made everyone by his example and enthusiasm want to work to keep up and improve their reputation.

Two things especially I have repeatedly heard about him from the men during the two years I have been with the Battalion. He was absolutely tireless and absolutely fearless, and I can vouch for the truth of both.

You have already heard how he gave his life at

Polygon Wood. But I must tell you again what we all think. That his quick appreciation of the situation and his prompt action saved the Wood, and had he not acted so at a critical moment, the great victory of October 4th could never have taken place.

Some of our Division on our right were retiring during a strong German counter attack. Our men were doubtful as to what they should do. It was impossible, of course, to leave the right flank 'in the air', and some began to retire. Directly the Colonel heard what was happening, he collected all the men round headquarters and formed them into a supporting force, and went forward to the frontline, rallying all of the men and telling them exactly what to do. Very little ground had been lost; he got the line straight and stopped the German counter attack. As one of the men put it to me, they have a way of summing up what they mean in a short sentence: "He died an absolute hero!"

I only wish I could express to you how much I feel, and how much we all feel for you, as you can understand a little at any rate, what our loss must mean to you, his mother.

What a tremendous share the Mothers of England are having in the Great Sacrifice that is being made today.

May our heavenly Father, Who knows what it means to give an only Son in the greatest of all causes, bless and comfort you, and give you the strength to bear your great sorrow.

I am,
Yours very sincerely,
HUGH F. SAWBRIDGE,
Chaplain,
9th Battalion Leicestershire Regiment.'

Mrs Sophia Bent was living at Bristol when she travelled to Buckingham Palace to collect her son's Victoria Cross at the Investiture on the 2nd March 1918. In 1923 she decided to pass on the medal so it could have a permanent resting place at Ashby Grammar School, where Philip had such great happiness (see letter). His dress-sword was also placed in the Lady Chapel of the town's Parish

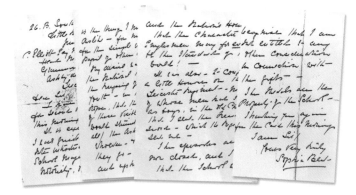

Sophia Bent's letter to Ashby de la Zouch Grammar School in 1923, expressing her wish that the Victoria Cross be kept there.

Church of St. Helen. The Army Museum at Halifax, Nova Scotia has the 1915 picture of Philip, together with his Cadet Captain's Badge and the silver medal he won for boxing on H.M.S. 'Conway'.

Philip's sword was stolen from the Church several years ago, and it is hoped that one day a suspicious purchaser may appreciate the sentiment involved and return it to its rightful place.

The Memorial to Philip Bent at Ashby de la Zouch Grammar School.

Only recently, and thanks to housemaster, John Williams, has the old boarding Grammar School House unveiled a permanent memorial to Philip (see photograph). The original medal was loaned to The Leicestershire Regimental Museum in 1970; however, a splendid wooden replica made from the fabric of the old school provides some justice. John Williams is a highly intelligent man and not prone to exaggeration, however, he can find no explanation as to what occurred at the unveiling ceremony. John and the town's dignitaries were stunned when the school's lights went out, precisely when he announced that Philip would be pleased with the showing of a fifteen-minute film dedicated to him! In addition an old sash window rattled loudly! John could not recall such a power failure before or the window rattling. Clive Jones, chairman of the school governors stood up to make a speech, and the window started rattling again; it had to be physically held to stop the noise! An electrician arrived and checked the three-phase fuse box, then pushed it back in, and when he calmly stating that he couldn't find any problems, all the lights came back on! The town did not have a power cut!

John Williams said, "*Certainly Philip Bent is with us today. We must remember he has no known grave and therefore, this is HIS memorial service at his old school.*"

John continued that the school has changed very little since Philip's time, and remarked that when the present day pupils watched the film as part of Armistice Week, many were moved to silence and humility.

Not only can the Leicester Road Grammar School feel enormously proud of Philip Bent, amazingly, they can claim another Victoria Cross holder, Bernard Vann, a housemaster between the years 1906-7. Whilst at Ashby he played football for Derby County as an amateur.

Lieutenant Colonel Bernard William Vann V.C., M.C. and Bar, Croix de Guerre with Palm

Bernard William Vann

He was born at Rushden, Northamptonshire on the 9th July 1887. His father, Alfred George Collins M.A. was headmaster of Chichele College at Higham Ferrers. He was educated at Chichele College and following his eighteen months at Ashby went to Jesus College, Cambridge, where he won a hockey blue. He took his degree in 1910 and was ordained deacon in 1912, becoming Chaplain and assistant master at Wellingborough School and at the outbreak of war applied for an army chaplaincy. After waiting for some time he grew impatient and applied for a commission as a frontline soldier in the 8th Battalion of the Sherwood Foresters, 46th North Midland Division. As a 2nd Lieutenant he showed his outspoken and freethinking attitude with a heated-argument with the Army Commander, General Allenby!

He was awarded the **Military Cross** in 1915 for his reassurances during an enemy flame-thrower attack, and in 1916 was promoted to Captain and then Major.

During September 1916 and in agony suffering from neuritis caused by his many wounds, he led a successful trench raid and killed several of the enemy. For this action he received a bar to his MC.

In February 1916 the French awarded him the **Croix-de-Guerre with Palm**, and in October was promoted to Acting Lieutenant Colonel of the full Battalion.

Receiving some overdue leave he married his fiancée, Doris Victoria Beck, in St. Paul's at Knightsbridge, and they had a son born on the 2nd June 1919.

By late 1918 Acting Lieutenant Colonel Vann was in command of the 6th Battalion. Already the holder of a Military Cross and bar he was to win the coveted Victoria Cross by the following act of valour, his Citation reads: *He led his Battalion with great skill across the Canal Du Nord through a very thick fog and under fire from field and machine-guns. On reaching the high ground above Bellenglise, the whole attack was held up by fire of all descriptions from the front and right flank. Realising that everything depended on the advance going forward with the creeping barrage Lieutenant Colonel Vann rushed up to the firing line and with the greatest gallantry led the line forward. By his prompt action* and absolute contempt for danger the whole situation changed, the men were encouraged and the line swept forward. Later he rushed a field gun single handed and knocked out three of the detachment. The success of the day was in no small degree due to the splendid gallantry and fine leadership displayed by the officer.

The award was gazetted on the 14th December 1918.

Having been wounded on at least eight occasions, on the 3rd October 1918, just four days after winning the Victoria Cross and five weeks before the end of the war he was instantaneously killed by a sniper's bullet. He was hit just after leading his men to victory against a strong enemy position. He was buried the same day and lies in Bellicourt British Cemetery in France.

His widow collected his medal from King George V at Buckingham Palace on the 26th November 1919. His Victoria Cross and other medals are on display in the Regimental Museum at Nottingham castle.

The following appreciation of Lieutenant Colonel Vann appeared in 'The Times'

As a brother officer I would like an opportunity to put on record a few reminiscences of a very gallant soldier. I can think of him only as a fighter, not merely against the enemy on the field, but a fighter against everything and everybody that was not an influence for good on his men. Sometimes the strength of his personality and the force of his convictions drove him up against 'authority', but he had no fear for himself, and nothing on earth would have moved him to do what he felt to be wrong. I remember his outspoken expressions to our Army Commander, General Allenby, who, however, never forgot him and always enquired kindly about him! He had extraordinary courage and tenacity. Buried and badly bruised by a trench mortar in 1915 he dug himself out and helped to dig others out. He was in bed for days afterwards but refused to go down the line. He was wounded severely at the Hohenzollern Redoubt in October 1915, and kept up an incessant bombing fight until ordered by the Brigadier to withdraw. Following his bar to his MC he was forcibly sent to England for hospitalisation for several months with neuritis. He was physically very strong, and his prowess at

football led to him winning most matches for his battalion side.

He had no time for slackers in any walk of life, but he always inspired others by his courage and energy. His Canadian widow will rejoice in the fact that her husband's gallantry has been recognised by the highest possible award.

(Unnamed)

A relative of mine, 2nd Lieutenant Arthur Newberry Choyce of Hugglescote served with and under Philip Bent until being wounded in May 1917.

My wife and I have visited the locations where Philip and Bernard were killed. They led by example, and lost their lives for the greater love of their men and their country.

Many thanks to housemaster, John Williams, of Ashby Grammar School and Nick Hudson, Editor of the Coalville Times.

Captain S. Tooth wrote earlier that it was an honour to have known such a fine Christian gentleman as Philip Bent. I too feel honoured to have acquainted myself with his memory and had the privilege to write an account about such a virtuous and honourable man. The same applies to his magnificent ex-tutor.

Rear of the old Grammar School.

KILLED IN ACTION

Soon they will return to earth, to the clay from whence they came.
Killed-in-action: warm blood spilt and bones of lifeless frame.
Jack was eighteen, with the posture of his father: mother's features.
A grammar school lad and well liked by all the teachers.

They sleep the sleep of eternity, and all three were far from thirty.
Jimmy's khaki's blooded and dirty; girls found his blue eyes flirty.
Enlisted at sixteen, nodded to eighteen, and reached it come death.
A ruptured body yelled out for mother with a dying breath.

The Devil rejoiced: attempted claims of images to God's likeness.
Johnny was twenty-four, at home a daughter and a wife called Bess.
Earlier he had sent them a letter, he was fine and in the pink.
He lay in agony before asking a dead comrade for a drink.

Johnny, Jimmy and Jack left daisy meadows and a village home.
Three close cousins now sleep forever in a Flemish poppies loam.
Three mothers unable to speak; dark curtains left drawn for a week.
Every eleventh-of-the-eleventh three silver-haired sisters weep.

Michael Kendrick.

ALFRED BURTON

George Burton was born in 1861 and his future wife, Stella Hudson in 1864. They married and set-up home on Deacon's Lane at Ibstock, a village four kilometres (two-three miles) south of Coalville, with son, Alfred, being born in 1896, one of fourteen children. Firstborn Ada was 1890, George William (Bill) 1892, James 1894, Sarah in 1899, John 1901, Arthur 1902, and May, Alice, Edith, Lucy and Sally. Two children died at birth.

Alfred Burton aged about 16.

A few years before the Great War the family moved to a property on the Ibstock Road at nearby Ellistown.

Alfred enlisted at Coalville into the Fifth Leicestershire Battalion around October 1914, service number 241335. The only photograph available shows a tall young man of about sixteen years, and on the back he has written: *"To Bill and Annie with love"*. Bill, was an elder brother, a collier at Desford Colliery and Annie was his wife.

Without doubt Alfred was in the trenches of the Ypres Salient in June of 1915, because he sent a letter to the parents of Lance Corporal William Barney offering sympathy, and explaining how his friend was sniped. A letter sent at the same time by Corporal Cave tells of how Alfred was with Bill just before he was sniped. Alfred experienced the majority of the main battles, namely Ypres, the Charge at the Hohenzollern Redoubt, Vimy Ridge, the Somme and Fosse 3 at Lens.

On the 15th August 1917 the Battalion was stationed in the St. Elie Left Sector, just to the north of Loos. The troops were marching in fours to the frontline for a full-battalion trench raid against Hulluch. Whilst passing Mansion House Dump, near to Vermelles, a large German shell exploded amongst 'B' Company. Eleven men were killed outright, fourteen suffered from serious shrapnel wounds and shell shock. Fergus Bonser of Loughborough, and Walter Pettit, one of the Famous Fifty from Ellistown were both killed in this incident.

The main objective of the trench raid was to detract attention from Hill 70, nearer to Loos, where the Canadians were to mount an offensive at precisely the same time. In addition the Fifth Battalion received orders to destroy a heavy trench mortar called, 'Goose', and to assess the extent of enemy tunnelling. A requirement of any raid was to capture several prisoners for interrogation purposes. As the summer sun faded, Alfred and his comrades blackened their faces in preparation, and would have been pleased to see that it was a moonless night. They knew of the task involved and what was expected of them, and the sergeants issued tots of syrupy rum, strong naval rum that helped to stiffen morale. I can assure readers our troops were never tipsy, but my grandfather told me it was potent stuff and 'revved you up.' On the 16th August 1917, at 10.30 pm our men were waiting for the officers' whistles to blow. At 10.58 pm the soldiers of the Fifth Battalion went over the top and followed a creeping barrage. There was a total inky-darkness and heavy cloud meant there was not even starlight, and when the barrage ceased communication could only be made by voice. They were delayed by No-Man's-Land being badly cratered, it had been fought over many times, and remnants of thick German wire proved troublesome. Eventually the Battalion overrun the German frontlines and fought their way to the enemy's third set of trenches, killing some and using Mills bombs on dugouts and tunnels. The war diary stated that a good quantity of enemy troops escaped by means of tunnels. Demolition parties then destroyed 'Goose' and other items. At the Battalion Headquarters a 'listening set' overheard the German Company Commander exclaiming: *"We are being attacked - frontline penetrated, - second-line wrecked, - third line entered, - send up two sections at once!"*

The Germans launched heavy counter attacks and Private Lilley with his Lewis gun was outstanding, so too Sergeant William Growdridge with his bayonet. (William, from Hinckley, was to be killed by a mortar bomb on 12th January 1918).

By 2.00 am on the morning of August 17th the troops regrouped and retired to their frontlines.

The War Diary reported: *'Captain Marriott ('B' Company) was killed, 2nd Lieutenant Plumer and seven men were never seen again, three men were taken prisoner and fifty one other ranks were wounded.'*

It is mentioned in the essay regarding Aubrey Moore that Captain Charles Shields ('D' Company) lost a leg with the other badly wounded in this raid.

It was in the early hours, when the counter-attack was at its most vicious, and hand to hand fighting was at its worse, that Private Alfred Burton lost his life. His body was never located, and it is possible that an enemy bombing party killed him, numbers of whom formed the first wave of the counter attack. He was just twenty-one years of age.

The Battalion did not assess the raid as a success. No prisoners were taken and little information was gained considering the losses received. It did not help when the signal flares failed to work, and runners had to be sent out to order a retirement, but finally on a positive note the raid helped the Canadian offensive.

Other local men who were killed during this raid: Charles Batson of Ashby de la Zouch, Percy Grant of Quorn and John Haynes of Loughborough. Private Alfred Burton's name is etched on the Loos Memorial Cemetery Wall and also on the Coalville Clock Tower Memorial.

Many thanks to Alfred's nephew, George Burton, son of John Burton. George also states that his uncle Jim (James) had a metal leg fitted up to his hip, but he is unsure whether this was a result of a war wound.

Inscribed on the Memorial Wall at Loos Cemetery the name of Alfred Burton. Also the name of Charles Cavendish, one of the Famous Fifty.

EDWARD CHAPMAN

The following information was gleamed from a copy of an old diary written by Edward. It details his personal memories of World War 1. I feel very fortunate that his daughter-in-law, Mrs Lillian Chapman, kept a copy after Edward's descendents took the original diary to Canada. Two photographs are shown, one when he was a private during the war, the other as an amiable 'lollipop-man' ensuring the safety of children crossing a busy road. I would have liked to have met Edward, and I am informed that he loved his country and the good folk in it.

Private Edward Chapman in 1914. He fought with Lieutenant Francis Barr in the 1/4th Leicestershire Regiment.

The War Diary Of Lance Corporal Edward Chapman

I enlisted in Leicester during September 1914, and alloted into the 2/4th Battalion of the Leicestershire Regiment, into what was called 'Athlete Company'. I was in training until 8th January 1915, when, with others I was picked for a draft to make up the strength of the 4th (1/4th) Battalion, and was sent to join them at Luton. I left Leicester by train and was billeted in private houses in Luton. I did various duties and a firing course and then left for Bishops Stortford, where we did some fieldwork and then moved on to Dunstable for firing, etc. We then returned to Bishops Stortford and I was inoculated twice and vaccinated. Two doctors then examined us to see if we were fit for overseas service. Passed O.K. On February 28th entrained for Southampton and on arrival we were told there was no boat ready for crossing, and so we had to march to a rest camp. Weather rough and raining all the time but on March 2nd we marched back to the docks and embarked on the troopship, 'Queen Empress', and had a decent crossing escorted by a destroyer. Arrived at Le Havre in France and marched to a railways station where we had a good meal. Each man was then issued with two-days rations, sheepskin coats, etc, and then bundled into cattle trucks, twenty-six to twenty-eight in each truck. After two days we arrived at the Belgium town of Cassel. We were billeted in large barns and stayed there until March 7th. Orders were received for us to march to Zuytpeene, about six kilometres (four miles) west where we were again billeted in barns. Whilst there we did various training duties, and when on parade a letter was read to us by our commanding officer, informing us of death penalties and No1 Field punishment for desertion and looting, etc! Our captain said he sincerely hoped nothing of that kind would happen amongst his men. We saw some men doing roadwork under armed guard, and poor devils they surely looked down and out! All of them had done something wrong.

On March 9th the whole Division marched east to Strazeele, a distance of about eighteen kilometres (twelve miles). On the way we saw some of our observation balloons and one of our aeroplanes dashing around, most interesting. We were reviewed by General Sir Horace Smith-Dorrien. He complimented us on our smartness and also the way we marched, considering the very bad roads. After a few days rest we marched to Sailly sur la Lys, about twelve kilometres (eight miles) southeast. There we found English troops in billets, and saw a 15 inch Howitzer gun in action firing from an armoured train. Orders came through for us to 'stand to' as we would be in reserve for the big battle of Neuve Chappele. We then went to nearby Bao St. Maur where we did some repair work to our trenches, and the whole time the Germans were shelling us heavily. On March 16th we marched the short distance to Steenwerk and had some bayonet practice. We had a fairly decent time with some good barns and we obtained from the farmhouses some meat, egg, chips, bread and butter and coffee for about twenty cents! We then marched nine kilometres (six miles) southeast to Armentieres, and then a short trip to the trenches at Le Bizet. We spent two days under instruction from the 1st King's Own and the 2nd Essex Battalion. We received our first casualties on Palm Sunday morning from a German sling bomb (whizz-bang).

We then proceeded fifteen kilometres (ten miles) northwest to Dranoutre where we found plenty of houses and estaminets, so stocked up before we went into the Line. We did periods of frontline, support and reserve and were then relieved and stayed in 'bivvies' (bivouac tents) in a large field concealed from the enemy by a large hill (Kemmel). Very nice scenery and in a wood close by we could hear a nightingale sing every night, it was lovely. When out of the Line we used to repair our clothes, and sometimes had new ones if classed as unfit. We were told that we would soon get a rest when Kitchener's Army was trained!

We left Dranoutre and the weather became very bad, raining in torrents and no billets were available so we slept in hedge bottoms with our waterproofs, there were plenty of grouse about.

At daybreak we saw some Belgium soldiers making trenches, dugouts and barbed-wire entanglements. This was at a front called the Ypres Salient. We used to go into trenches (35 and 50) between Hooge and Hill 60 for frontline, support and reserve and then go back to an area known as Railway Dug-Outs, by a railway embankment. We had some rough times and a large number of casualties. We stopped some months there and then went to Dickebusch, just outside of Ypres where we had some huts. We had to clean ourselves up as General Plummer came to inspect us. He told us we had done some very good work, and that we would be moving to another very hot part of the Line, where there will probably be some hand-to-hand fighting. On 2nd October 1915 we were issued with two-days rations and entrained for Gonneham, forty-five kilometres (thirty miles) south west of Ypres and in the French coalmining area. Our billet was a music hall. We did some field exercises including bomb throwing (Mills bomb). We entrained for Hesdigneul, a few kilometres from Bethune. A large aeroplane station was there, and we saw two large enemy aeroplanes that our airmen had brought down. Orders came that we hand in our bayonets to be sharpened, and we had new issues of gas masks and smoke helmets. Afterwards we did some practice attacks and a Divisional general watched us. We were then told to place all of our valuables in our packs and to leave them in a barn, which would be left under guard until we returned from the trenches. Our aeroplanes had taken photographs of the position we were to take and we were told as such. The following morning we moved off in fighting order, rations in haversacks and waterproof sheets rolled and strapped to our backs. We stopped for dinner, and then for tea and each hour until we reached the front at about midnight and relieved the Irish Guards. This position was known as the Hohenzollern Redoubt, Fosse 8, with the strongpoint Big Willie. We had been told to be sure to have a look over the trench at daybreak and to figure the lay of the land, but the trenches were so full we could barely move, and ate our breakfast ration as best we could. Some of the Guards remained to watch the attack. We were told when the bombardment would start and when the first wave would go over. Our own barbed wire had been cut leaving gaps for us to go through. At midday on the 13th October 1915, the barrage started from left to right flank and gas was used where possible. The Boche soon weighed things up and started thick and heavy causing us plenty of casualties. Promptly at 2.00 pm our Colonel Martin (who was near to us with watch in hand) shouted as loudly as he could for the first wave to go over the top, "God speed and the best of luck".

I believe every man did his best, killed and wounded were in large numbers! I got wounded in the left leg and while I was trying to unwind my puttee Jerry had a pop at me and hit me in the left arm (muscle)! I crawled back as best I could to our frontline trench and managed to get some help, and was taken down our communication trench to a First Aid Dressing Station. This was just a large dugout. I was told that from 12.00 noon to 4.00 pm some two *thousand odd injured had passed through the station. I went to Vermelles on a stretcher, and I was attended to again.*

After lying there for some time I was taken by a Red Cross motor to Bethune.

We saw some Jerry wounded and not long afterwards we had to be moved again as the Germans were shelling very heavily, it was not comfortable. The Red Cross took us to the railway station and we were taken to Etaples. Here we stayed at No 24 Canadian Hospital (a wounded General was there) and then from Calais on the S.S. Brighton Hospital Ship to Dover. We were put on a Red Cross train and taken to Nottingham, then in cars to Bagthorpe Military Hospital. Had a good time there and when about right, I went along with others to Clipstone for six weeks convalescence. I was looked after well and enjoyed some good entertainment, and when I returned to Nottingham they gave me a pass and a warrant for ten days sick leave. I went to dear old home and enjoyed myself not half!!

I returned to Nottingham and reported to the 3rd Line Headquarters where I was put in billets in a schoolroom in Calton Street.

January 1916 onwards

I was informed that I was now attached to the 3/4th Battalion Reserve. Some of the Battalion were with me at Calton Street School, some at the Eagle Works and the rest at St. Lukes. I did a few light duties and was then ordered to attend a medical board where I passed out as A1. I did heavier duties and attended the same board only to be told I was temporarily unfit because the wound in my arm had broken out again! I was selected with others to do a light duty on Midland and Great Central Railway in Leicester and billeted at home. Very unfortunately I was taken ill with influenza and was admitted to the Leicester Military Base Hospital. Upon discharge I returned to Nottingham where I was detailed for fatigues on the rifle range until I attended another medical board where I was passed as A1 for active service. I was given fresh kit and sent home for a short leave. Whilst at home I received a telegram ordering me to return immediately as a new draft were preparing to depart. The draft paraded at King Edward's Park and was inspected by Colonel Sarson who said a few words of

encouragement to the men. On April 19th we were ordered to entrain for Catterick Bridge (Scottish Camp) in North Yorkshire. On arrival we were put into well-constructed huts, and did fatigue work. We also cleaned the Wesleyan Institute and Church of England huts ready for a service. On April 26th I was on-guard at the Main Entrance Headquarters. Two days later I was picked out for a composite draft to go to Ireland to be ready at anytime when wanted! May 1st - trench digging, then unloading coal at California Camp. Then went on a 'sniping course'. June 9th - on guard-duty at the District Court Martial as part of fatigue. On July 18th ordered to be an officer's servant. August 9th - another medical inspection and again passed out as A1! On August 20th I was warned that our Draft might be sent to Ireland. October 19th - admitted into Hipswell Hospital with an impetigo discharge. Later I was given a warrant to entrain at Richmond Station for Louth in Lincolnshire. I was put into billets in the local paper-mill. Once again I was passed fit for a Draft and Colonel Murray inspected us. At 8.30 am we entrained for Folkestone. On December 23rd the weather was too bad for a crossing, but on the 25th December we had a Christmas Dinner as then embarked for Calais. From there we marched to an infantry base depot.

January 1917

On the 8th January 1917 we were told we would be joining the 5th (1/5th) Battalion Leicestershire Regiment. We entrained and finally arrived at Bienvillers and were billeted in huts and dugouts. This spot was a few kilometres from Gommecourt, on the northern sector of the Somme where the Battalion attacked on the 1st July 1916.

The weather was very bad, it snowed heavily. During January 23rd - 29th we were in the trenches on the Monchy-au-Bois Front.

March 1917

March 3rd - 17th at nearby Hannescamps. Spent quite a bit of time having to repair roads around Fonquevillers and Gommecourt where Jerry had blown them up. We were then given a spot of leave at Souastra. On March 28th after a spell south of Amiens, we marched to Saleux and entrained for the north. Passing through Doullens we arrived at Lillers and marched to Lairs, eighteen kilometres (twelve miles) through driving heavy rain. We arrived at our billets absolutely wet through. The weather improved and we played some football, etc.

April - December 1917

After two or three days we marched to Annequin, near Bethune. I had a pass and looked around Bethune Cathedral, it was lovely inside and I also went to a picture-show held in the Municipal Theatre. On April 19th we left for the Lens Front, stopping on the way at Noeux les Mines and Bully Grenay. We were on the outskirts of Lens, a large city about fifteen kilometres (ten miles) south west of Bethune. We were in the trenches there and threw many Mills bombs. We took some Jerry prisoners, and the enemy liked his gas in this area, having to have our gas-helmets on and off continually. This was a hot spot and we had many casualties with Jerry sending over all manner of shells. In July I suffered with a bit of gas and had to spend a short time at St. John Ambulance Hospital, Etaples.

On one occasion we had taken our usual proceedings for 'stand to' when a shell burst and shrapnel hit five others and me. The stretcher-bearers came and dug us out, and when things quietened down we were taken to an Advanced Dressing Station. From there Red Cross motors took us to No18 Casualty Clearing Station where we had a good meal, and then by Red Cross train onto Boulogne Hospital. Eventually I went for convalescence and had to have my eyes syringed twice daily by an eye specialist. I improved and took a pass to visit Boulogne, having a lovely time in nice weather.

I returned to my unit in October 1917 and they had moved north to St Elie Left Sector near to Loos. Soon after my arrival we moved to some trenches near to Hill 70, and then marched to Verquin. We then had eighteen days on the La Bassee Front. We came out and marched to Beuvry, a few kilometres south east of Bethune for six days rest. It was Christmas time and we had a very good Christmas dinner and we all enjoyed ourselves!

January 1918 onwards

Not long afterwards I had some 'Blighty' leave. I entrained for Boulogne feeling very excited, over to Folkestone and on to London. I went to a Salvation Army Centre for a good bath and spent the night in a nice bed. The following day I visited my sister in Edgware and then caught the train for Leicester. I got home about dinnertime and I don't need to say I had the very best time possible.

When I returned the 5th Battalion were now in the Cambrin Right Sector, just to the south of St Elie Left. As spring approached in 1918 we were in the Bethune area at Gorre and Essar, a relatively quiet spot, missing most of the German Spring Offensive. As the year progressed we had battles at places like Pontruet near to St. Quentin, a good ninety kilometres (sixty miles) south east of Bethune. One of our officers, Lieutenant Barrett, deservedly won the Victoria Cross.

On the 29th September 1918 we broke through the Hindenburg Line at Bellenglise and thrust to Magny la Fosse. We had to dig large graves there afterwards after the Staffords had a rough time in a sunken road.

Later everything went quiet and we were ordered to go forward only to find the Germans had evacuated. We carried on until Jerry spotted us and he opened fire with all sorts of shells including gas. I got hit by a piece of shrapnel in the chest and was sent down the line to No 47 Casualty Clearing Station, then onto hospital in Rouen and finally to No11 Convalescent Depot. I was detailed for the job of 'Post Corporal' I was discharged and returned to the 5th Battalion via Busigny, about twenty-seven kilometres (fifteen miles) north west of Bellenglise. The following day I was taken by motors to Le Chateau where I found the 5th Battalion in billets.

A Severe Struggle

The 5th Leicestershire achieved further distinction in the battle of Riquerval Wood. On October 11th strong patrols of the 4th Battalion advanced along the Bohain to Aisonville road. Later in the day the 5th Battalion, who had relieved their sister battalion, made determined attempts to penetrate into Riquerval Wood. This attack was pressed home with no little skill and at first met with some success, as the leading patrols pushed some distance into the outer fringes of the wood! The principal success was achieved by the Headquarters Staff of the Battalion, who established themselves in a house on the western edge of the southern lobe of the wood. The companies on either side of the Headquarters' Staff were driven back by the enemy and so they were left isolated. The Staff put up a good fight and managed to hold on to the outskirts of the wood and the captured house. For some time, units sent up to relieve them could not do so as they were pinned down. In the end a strong enemy counter attack drove them out of the wood and down the Bohain Road, where relief was effected. It was an incident in the fluctuations of the struggle and proved the tenacity of our men. The 5th like the 4th, 'were ever in the fight' and in the later phases when considerable resistance was encountered in the advance from Catillon to Saines du Nord, they overcame and won through!

I was put on guard duty at our headquarters and later was part of a draft of men selected to do some demolishing.

On February 14th 1919 I travelled to Busigny and entrained to a rest camp at Dieppe. Shortly I embarked from that port and it took twenty-six hours sailing to arrive at Tilbury Docks. I entrained for camp at Grantham where I handed over my equipment and caught the train for Leicester. I was once again a civilian after four and a half years in the military.

Extract from Leicester Mercury of October 1915

'Mrs. C. Chapman, wife of Private E. Chapman at 23, Newly Street, Leicester, has received news that her husband was wounded at the charge of the 13th October. He is now in Nottingham Hospital. Private Chapman has a bullet in the calf of his left leg and also a bullet wound in the muscle of his left arm. In a brief letter to his wife he says 'it was a big' but the boys did all they were asked to do. In civil life Private Chapman works at T. Brown and Co, Boot and Shoe Manufacturers, Leicester.'

The Cost Of It

By Edward Chapman.
The whole story of the 46th Division is splendid. Great deeds cost much. The severity of the fighting, in which the Division has been engaged during the war, is best seen from an examination of the casualty list.

The **total losses** between February 1915 and November 1918 are as follows:
Killed 275 officers and 3,475 other ranks.
Wounded 1,104 officers and 21, 285 other ranks.
Missing 123 officers and 1,502 other ranks.
Total = 1,502 officers and 28, 067 other ranks.
Such figures as these speak for themselves.

Edward Chapman.

Edward Chapman 'the colonel' escorting school children accross a busy road during an active retirement. (Circa 1970s).

Author's Comment

As I immersed myself into Edward's fascinating and highly factual account, I noticed a copy of a report from Lichfield Record Office, dated 28th October 1915. It describes the wounds that he received at the Charge of Hohenzollern Redoubt as being 'severe'! Afterwards I noticed another form: 'Soldier's Demobilisation Account', where the monetary value regarding back pay, etc, is itemised. I retain a strong appreciation of Edward's sacrifice and endurance during the war, and feel grieved that there is a deduction of £1. By the standards of today it is equivalent to £40. He had to pay, or as the form states, he was debited for the value of his military greatcoat! Edward asked if he could keep it, he had little other suitable clothing after four years on the Western Front, and I consider such debiting as indeed 'severe'!

Following the death of his wife, Edward went to live with his son, Norman, and his wife, Lily, at 187, Kingsway, Braunstone Town, near Leicester. The veteran died on 25th March 1982 at Nuffield Nursing Home at Leicester, at the age of ninety-four years. Alongside Norman, he also left a son, George, who lives in Southampton, and a daughter, Lillian at Loughborough.

A cutting from a Canadian newspaper states: *'Many friends of Southampton and Port Elgin will recall 'The Colonel' on his visits to Canada. He was recognised until his death as the oldest surviving member of the old Leicester 'Tiger' Battalion of World War 1.'*

Many thanks to Mrs Lillian Chapman for the opportunity to publish her father-in-law's war diary and photographs. Without the communication and support of Alwyne Watson none of the above information would have been published. Please see his photograph alongside the grave of Lieutenant Francis Tarr who also served with Edward's Battalion.

Alwyne Watson at the grave of Lt. F. Tarr. 1/4 Leics. Leicester Rugby and England star.

ARTHUR NEWBERRY CHOYCE

Arthur was born in 1893 in one of the Breach Cottages or 'Ten Row' as it was sometimes known. It is a homely huddle of small terraced dwellings with relatively large front gardens that, to this day, face onto Central Road, Hugglescote. The latter is a very old village that once had a community spirit all of its own, however, like so many other surrounding villages it now appears as a suburb of Coalville Town.

Apart from his military service in the Great War, Arthur always lived at Hugglescote, and indeed died in his only other residence, namely 177, Ivanhoe Cottages, almost opposite to where he was born. During his short life of forty-three years he was to achieve a considerable literary prominence, in fact he is still regarded, and will always be so as Leicestershire's Great War Poet. The Royal Leicestershire Regimental Museum at Leicester has his photograph and several of his books on display.

His father, Benjamin Choyce, was a carpenter who worked for South Leicestershire Colliery at Ellistown and also Snibston Colliery at Coalville. His mother, Mary Ann (nee Newberry) was from a long established Hugglescote family, and the couple had six children. I understand that his mother's side had evolved from wealthy farming stock, with relatives including a senior military officer, and an academic who was a master at a leading central-England public school. In his book Arthur describes his mother's typical family traits as: *"Loquacious, a daring independence, a shrewdness and foresight, and a brilliance in argument (especially when in the wrong, which, to do her justice, she seldom was.")*

It pleases me enormously to write that my grandmother, Hetty Selina Hatter (nee Palmer), from another well established family was a cousin of Arthur's. It may be a coincidence but since my teenage years I have written poetry on a wide variety

2nd Lieutenant Arthur Newberry Choyce of the 9th Leicestershire Battalion, 1916.

of subjects, including the Great War. The necessity to write comes from an inner drive. Some artists paint a scene and modify it to their personal outlook; I try to **describe** a scene, whether picturesque or emotional (usually both are entwined). I have mentioned the above details not to enhance or promote myself; it is enough to write that I consider fame to be a fleeting and superficial notion! Nevertheless, conversely, I feel I must fulfil my object and do justice to a Hugglescote gentleman of genuine quality. I find it also helps that my grandparents knew him well and liked him, including his eccentricities. My grandfather, Charles Hatter, one of the Famous Fifty, was in Arthur's class at the local Church School, and they resided almost opposite each other for most of Arthur's life. Also when Arthur was a teacher he taught my parents. My mother, Betty Kendrick (nee Hatter) thought he was wonderful and visited the poor man on his deathbed, whereas my father, Les, was of the opinion that he was too much of a disciplinarian with the boys and said: "*He even kept his bandolier hanging on the side of the blackboard!*"

Arthur's early years were typical of life within a close-knit coal-mining community. There was ample love but little wealth, and always the threat of a

father's death whilst excavating in the gritty seams of the earth. Clearly this hung heavily in his thoughts after the Whitwick Colliery Mining Disaster of 1898, the worst in Leicestershire. (An excellent book: 'Banded Together' provides an account from the Whitwick Historical Society Group). In his 1931 anthology, the poem: 'Day Shift' touches upon how a father was woken by his wife at six, only to return from pit at twelve with a broken back, quite dead!

Arthur was also very spiritually aware and spent many hours in worship, and deep discussion with Cannon Broughton at St. John The Baptist Church.

His latent ability and potential was spotted, and upon leaving St. John The Baptist Church School he received a scholarship to Market Bosworth Grammar School. Every school day he walked to Hugglescote Station to catch the steam train to Bosworth Station. To arrive at the quaint market town he then had an idyllic one-mile stroll through delightful countryside to the famous Dixie School. During these walks and others his young mind absorbed many of the wonders of nature and which are later revealed in his poems.

Arthur wrote about his early life living in 'The Breach Cottages in Hugglescote'

His fascinating semi-biographical novel: 'Lips at the Brim', initially describes his early life in 'Breach Cottages' or 'Ten Row' as he refers to them. He colourfully describes their long front gardens and little pigsties to the rear, housing: "*Some of the finest specimens with curly tails, all being fattened up for Christmas.*" Using fictitious names Arthur described most of the characters that lived on the row, and no doubt the Palmers are included under some guise in his delightful book. I will not venture down that avenue apart from reassuring readers that neither my grandmother nor great-aunt was '*Sarah Jane Pratt, a dirty, gawky redhead, all legs and teeth!*'

Following school Arthur's first position was as

a pupil-teacher under the headmastership of Mr. J. Massey at Bridge Road School, Coalville. For his efforts he received a token salary of half a crown per week. (12$^1/_2$ new pence).

Between the years 1911-14 he is regularly mentioned in the local press, items such as stage routines, pantomimes, plays or involvement with social functions in the Hugglescote Church School Rooms. He was an excellent dancer and orator and raised money in aid of the Church Lads' Brigade, the School and the Women's Unionists. Included in these activities were friends such as Victor Woolley (later one of the Famous Fifty), Cyril Walton and Amos Jarvis.

ON STAGE: Amos Jarvis. Victor Woolley. Arthur Choyce. Cyril Walton in early 1914.

Arthur continued his studies at evening class, and, when he passed the Royal Society of Arts Examination in Advanced French his marks were the highest in Leicestershire, including Leicester! For his efforts he was warmly congratulated by the matriculation of London University. Also, his poetry was regularly published in national magazines such as Nash's, Country Life and Pearsons. His poems not only depicted life in a mining village, but also his dear love of the flora and fauna of the countryside.

In September 1913 he enrolled as a student at Nottingham University. He was not always one to conform to dress or behaviour, and in defiance wore a pair of pink socks made from his sister's stockings for the Freshers' Ball. His time at university was somewhat stormy, not helped by his poetic temperament and inheriting many of his mother's character traits. His approach to life was 'live and let live', and he detested the attitudes of some of the lecturers with their pettiness and enforcement of university rules. He often rebelled when some of his friends, to his mind, were being treated harshly. He could be very succinct in such matters, and I am told he had an excellent speaking voice and was engagingly eloquent. Another aspect of Arthur's character was his extreme sensitivity. His stock answer for such criticism was: "*Are not all poets?*" Arthur was a compassionate man and easily empathised with the problems of others, and was blessed with a loyal and supportive disposition. He disliked arrogance and was prone to challenging such, hence some of his problems at university, but he also had some wonderful friends there.

On 15th March 1914 his father died, and in spite of his spiritual strength felt he no longer wanted to continue his studies, especially when in August some of his old school friends enlisted into the Forces. In his book he paints the cemetery scene: "*I sat on the red clay of the recently piled-up mound of my father's grave in the peaceful, shadowy churchyard, and stared at the fading wreaths of flowers. I took a single*

Published in 1930 'Lips at the Brim' is a semi-biographical book recalling Arthur Newberry's early life in 'Ten Row', his time at University and service during World War 1.

Mary Ann Choyce (mother) and 2nd Lieutenant Arthur Choyce of the Ninth Leicestershire Battalion. 1916.

red rose from my coat and placed it on the soil. This was my first distinct reminder that life is one tale of broken ties, of tears that follow swiftly and enviously on the heels of every snatched joy."

His devoted mother persuaded him of the vital importance of continuing his education, and so he compromised by joining the University Training Corps, and furthered his studies. He completed his course in 1915 with distinctions in English, History and Mathematics.

Arthur immediately enlisted as a private into the Royal Fusiliers and found basic training an anathema to his temperament, believing it to be soul destroying. He nevertheless won through and joined the Leicestershire Regiment and was soon commissioned as a 2nd Lieutenant in the Ninth Battalion, 110 Brigade. One of his brother officers was William Bent! As a frontline officer Arthur displayed considerable bravery in leading his men in the 1916 Battles of Bazentin Ridge and Guedecourt on the Somme, and in late 1916, early 1917, at Hohenzollern Redoubt in the Loos Sector. (This was where the Fourth and Fifth Leicestershire Battalions fought and suffered so heavily in October 1915). Then, on the 3rd May 1917, Arthur led his section on a frontal attack during the Battle of Bullecourt, on the Hindenburg Line.

The Ninth Battalion's offensive faced Fontaine Les Croisilles, and two waves of two lines attacked at night. They advanced bravely, but a heavy barrage and machine-gun fire hit them.

Losses were sixty-seven other-ranks, and only four of the sixteen officers were unscathed, and 2nd Lieutenant Newberry Choyce was one of them.
He wrote some excellent poetry in the trenches of France and Flanders, and his 1917 publication: 'Crimson Stains' revealed the horrors he witnessed. His poem: '**Destiny**', written two days after the above battle epitomises his Christianity and humanity.

> *A Dead boy lies in the sunlight,*
> *His cold lips say to me,*
> *How safe though tiredly trod,*
> *The path of Destiny,*
> *Still wanders through a troubled night*
> *To God.*

(Morning. 5th May 1917. Fontaine Croisilles).

German machine-gunners await the advance of enemy infantrymen.

A similar attack to that described above was made on the night of June 15th. The Ninth Battalion was advancing along communication trenches to the frontline to support the Eighth Battalion, when a furious German counter-barrage confronted them, and they received forty casualties! During the ferocious battle Arthur and some of his section must have joined the Eighth Battalion's attack, because he was badly wounded in the left arm by a bullet, and spent a reported twenty hours in a shell hole before

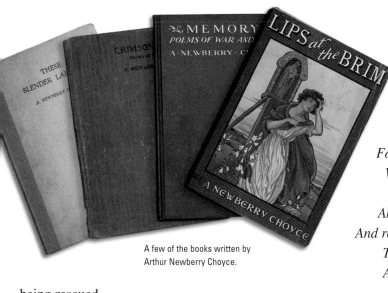

A few of the books written by
Arthur Newberry Choyce.

Memory

I know a lone spot on the Arras road
Where I shall hardly bear to walk again
For fear of waking those great souls I loved,
Who struggled to a death of piteous pain.

Ah! I should hear their laughter on the way,
And round my heart their boyish sighs would creep;
Till I must long to leave the rushing world
And steal away to join them in their sleep.

For only they who tread the tortured path
Of those torn roads where swaying poplars sigh,
Can dream how God could give no greater bliss
Than this hushed peace beneath the sad French sky.

I know a lone spot on the Arras road
That murmurs with the moan of Memory's pain.
And I should grieve my heart with stifled sobs
If I could bear to walk that road again.

being rescued.

He was hospitalised at Boulogne, then invalided home and finally sent to Blackpool for a period of convalescence.

On the 19th October 1917 the Coalville Times highlights his book: 'Crimson Stains', and proudly printed a few of his poems. It also congratulated him on the exalted idealism so prevalent in his poems, which they considered so worthy of the allies' cause.

His fighting days were over, but his qualities of leadership and his ability to inspire others was recognised. To this end he was invited by Lord Reading to visit the United States of America. He toured as 'Leicestershire's Soldier Poet' with the objective of boosting America's war contribution in men, money and ships. He lectured and recited his poems to huge audiences at Colorado Springs, Pueblo, Birmingham (Alabama), Denver, Kansas, Wyoming, Salt Lake City, St. Louis, Arkansas, Illinois, Utah, Nashville, Atlanta and sites in North Carolina. Typical was the response of the 'Birmingham News': "*He has amazingly good powers of description... a keen sense of humour... a deep inspiring earnestness... spiritual understanding, noted soldier lecturer, etc.*" The press at St. Louis: "*Lieutenant Choyce is credited with being the most graphic and stimulating war-talker that has ever visited St. Louis.*" Whilst in America the John Lane Company of New York and London published his 'Memory Poems of War and Love', in 1918. In this book I read what I consider to be one of his greatest war poems, top draw stuff!

When Arthur returned to Great Britain he left many friends behind who had entertained him in America. He had put Hugglescote on the 'map', because on his trek around the States, he carried a business card, as was the custom of the day, it read:

Mr. A. Newberry Choyce,
The Leicestershire Regiment.
Hugglescote.
Leicestershire.

Whilst a full-time teacher at Bridge Road School at Coalville other publications followed. In 1921: 'Glinting Dandelions', 1924: 'These Slender Larches' and 'Love Poems', 1930 his semi-autobiographical story: 'Lips at the Brim' and finally in 1931: 'Not Until Gilboa'.

For all of his success he never lost his footing in life, and never became self important and continued to live until the remainder of his days in his humble terraced cottage.

On the 11th April 1932 Arthur was appointed to the post of Headmaster of Snibston Primary School, and he remained in this post for five years until his premature death. He developed an abdominal growth

Snibston School where Arthur Newberry Choyce was headmaster.

some said it resulted from his war experiences and he was whisked to a London hospital to receive treatment. Initially he appeared to improve, but the death of his mother on the 25th January 1937 deeply moved him, and a few weeks later he developed pneumonia and died on the 2nd February 1937, aged only forty-three years.

The funeral service at his beloved St. John The Baptist Church was of a semi-military nature. Besides relatives and numerous friends, senior members from the Leicestershire Regiment attended, and his coffin was draped with a union jack. The Church was packed, the village streets were lined with people as Arthur made one final trip down Station Road, and he lies buried close to where the old station was: "Every school day he walked to Hugglescote Station to catch the steam train to Bosworth Station. To arrive at the quaint market town he then had an idyllic one-mile stroll through delightful countryside to the famous Dixie School. His young mind absorbed all of the wonders of nature!"

Mr. M. Haddock, principal of the Technical College wrote in the Coalville Times: *"In his passing*

'Sacred to the memory of Arthur Newberry Choyce. Poet. Lieutenant in the Leicestershire Regiment. Headmaster of Snibston School.'
(He lies buried alongside his father, died 1915 and his mother, died 25/3/37 aged 83 at Hugglescote Cemetery.)

this town has lost one of its finest sons, and one who adorned it in a real way!"

Arthur lies buried alongside his mother and father. I pay visits to his grave and place a poppy cross upon it every Remembrance Day.

'I've seen some fathers who are great and wise,
My father was as simple as could be.
I pity you you never touched his hand
Or you could never cease to envy me.'
(Extract from his poem: My Father's obituary
March 13th 1914).

As a final epitaph it must be recorded that Arthur was so proud to have served with and under Colonel P. Bent VC in the 9th Leicestershire Battalion.

Many thanks to Molly Donaldson of the Coalville 150 Group, and to relatives of mine.

Arthur Newberry Choyce 'In sincerity'

Born in a two-up two down cottage in the old village of Hugglescote. From being a child he was always very aware of the vibrancy of life and the environment to which he found himself. A scholar, a poet, a headmaster and an officer who served in the Great War. He died at the tragically early age of forty- three years. One of Hugglescote's finest.

PERCY WILLIAM CLIFF

Around the turn of the century I was taking some camera shots of the Coalville Clock Tower Memorial, when a name caught my attention. For some unknown reason I instantly knew that he had died as a teenager, and also felt quite certain that I would receive information about his service career.

In the spring of 2005, whilst promoting an earlier book at a military convention, a lady approached me and stated that she was the granddaughter of Percy Cliff. My mind flashed back five years; and informed her that I had been expecting Percy's information. The lady, Mrs. Janet Cartlidge seemed quite shocked, especially so when

Percy William Clifff

realising that Percy had not occurred in my research. Clearly, the following essay was intended to appear in this book, and I am delighted that is the case.

The 1901 census reveals that Joseph Cliff was the head of the household at 3, Mammoth Road, Coalville. He was born in the county of Staffordshire in 1866, and his occupation was that of a coalminer: almost certainly working at the nearby Whitwick Colliery. His wife, Mary Ann, was the same age, however this was her second marriage (nee Latham, nee Curtis). From her earlier marriage she had two daughters: thirteen-year-old Minnie (Latham) and eleven year old, Florence (Latham). Percy Cliff was born on the 21st March 1899, and there followed a second son, Joseph, who was born in 1906.

hewer's loader.

For a few years Percy toiled manfully in the dark and dank mine passages. With his extremely pleasant and kind-hearted attitude he enjoyed the companionship of many close friends, and enjoyed frequent walks taking the air and enjoying the picturesque Charnwood Forest.

I shudder when I think of the environment that colliery lads had to endure. Readers know of boy chimney sweeps in early Victoriana; I would do that than labour deep below ground and be involved with heaving and shovelling lumps of coal onto trucks. Indeed, a sad sign of the age: often there was little or no alternative work available.

By the summer of 1917 the fighting forces of

Mary Ann Cliff, mother of Percy circa 1914

Maud Haywood, soon to be wife of Percy Cliff

The Cliff family worshipped at Christ Church, Coalville, and Percy was baptised there on the 14th May 1899. Without doubt the children were educated at the adjacent Church School, with Percy receiving his Labour Certificate in 1912. He followed his father into Whitwick Colliery and trained as an underground roadman, later becoming a coal-

Britain and her Empire had suffered appalling losses, notably so her troops at the Battle of the Somme. Conscription had been ongoing since March 1916; however, the necessity for fit men was insatiable, often senior officers toured collieries hoping to entice young men (in reserved occupations) to enlist.

In June 1917, a few months after Percy's

The only babyhood photograph of Lavinia Cliff. 1921 aged four years.

The wedding of Eric Boot and Lavinia Cliff. 1939.

eighteenth birthday, the colliery manager called for a selection of men to line-up in front of two Leicestershire Regimental Officers. Percy was invited (he was picked out) to join the Colours and considered that the only honourable option was to accept!

He enlisted at Coalville, service number 48332, and posted into the 2/5th Leicestershire Battalion. He was to undertake many months of training, but was allowed a few days home leave in late July 1917. Before his enlistment invitation he had been smitten, falling totally in love with local girl, twenty-year-old, Maud Haywood. She was born on the 30th October 1897 at Thringstone, believed to be on Talbot Lane, and was baptised on the 10th July 1898 at St. Andrew's Parish Church. Upon leaving school she was employed by a local hosiery manufacturer.

Youthful hormones and the unpredictability of love meant that the twosome had to marry: doing so on the 22nd December 1917. The ceremony took place at Ashby de la Zouch Registry Office and the couple took to their marital home of 1, Brook Terrace, Thringstone. On the marriage certificate Percy wrote his home address as 6, Melbourne Street, Coalville.

On the 13th April 1918, Maud gave birth to daughter, Lavinia. It also coincided with a spot of leave for Percy prior to returning to the horrors of the Western Front.

Subsequently the heartbreaking day of departure arrived. It is often recalled within the family circle how he carried his new born child to Coalville Central Station. Lavinia was dressed in all white: wore a satin bonnet and was draped in a shawl

Eric Boot with his wife, Lavinia, and three years old daughter, Janet. Taken at Spring Hill, Whitwick in 1946.

for warmth. Maud, together with most of the family, was at the misty railway station for an embracing and extremely tearful farewell.

In late January 1918 the 1/5th Battalion was numerically weak, so much so that the 2/5th Battalion became non-operational: its troops topping-up the aforementioned battalion as well as their sister battalion, the 1/4th.

Percy crossed the Channel and joined the 1/5th Battalion in their trenches at Gorre and Essars, two villages that straggled the Bethune Canal of northern France. Action was relatively light, the main concerns being gas and the occasional barrage: Charles Cavendish, one of the Famous Fifty was killed there.

In September 1918, Percy was involved in the dawn attack at Pontruet: losses were heavy and it was in this battle that Lieutenant Barrett was badly wounded and was awarded the Victoria Cross.

The 1/5th Battalion, as part of the 46th North Midland Division, won glory as they succeeded in

The marriage of Janet Boot and Raymond Philip Cartlidge. 1960.

punturing the 'impregnable' Hindenburg Line at Bellenglise on the 29th September 1918. It was becoming apparent to frontline troops that the war was in its final phase; and naturally many troops became extra cautious after surviving for years. On the 1st November 1918 the Battalion left Fresnoy and marched to Becquigny, arriving at mid-day (all in the northeast of St. Quentin in northern France). They found some good billets within the village, and in the evening were informed of an order to attack German positions on the Sambre-Oise Canal. (The 1st Leicestershire Battalion had attacked these positions, but were taken out of the frontline on the 30/31st October of the same year).

On November 2nd the officers rode out to Morlain and onto Ribeauville to reconnoitre the enemy defences. I believe Percy accompanied these officers, perhaps he tended their horses or acted as a scout, whatever, he met his death at the tender age of nineteen years. It is consoling to know that the following day's attack was successful and many prisoners were taken.

I feel it is more than likely he was scouting in No-Man's-Land and was sniped. His body was never found, possibly destroyed in the following day's barrage, but pleasingly his name is commemorated on the 5th Panel of the Vis-En-Artois Memorial on the Arras to Cambrai Road. The Memorial bears the names of 9, 820 soldiers with no known graves: all killed in the Picardy and Artois advance extending from the 8th August 1918 to the Armistice of 11th November 1918.

Private Percy Cliff's name appears on the Christ Church Memorial Panel, a brass Memorial Plaque in the Council Offices, and on the Coalville Clock Tower Memorial. A certified copy of the entry of death confirms that he perished whilst serving with the 1/5th Leicestershire Battalion.

I grieve for all who died in warfare, but surely the suffocate clouds of sadness and despair that affected the family of a teenage father, young wife and baby girl must have been intolerable!

Percy's mother, Mary Anne Cliff, was devastated by his death and was comforted by taking care of his medals, a commemorative scroll, photographs, etc: having them framed, see photograph.

Maud Cliff, fortunately, had a strong personality and set about supporting Lavinia. Following a lengthy period of mourning she took a second husband, William (Bill) Burton from Limby Hall, Swannington. For a while they lived at Belton, a village five kilometres northeast of Coalville, with Lavinia attending school there. Later the Burtons returned to Whitwick and had five more children, Albert their eldest, May, Ida, Mary and Kathleen.

Maud was a naturally jolly person, and often

The sons of Raymond and Janet Cartlidge: Steve, Nigel and Glen. Taken in 1993.

Janet Cartlidge with framed memorial of her Grandfather, Percy William Cliff.

Harry Boot, was a coalminer.

Eric and Lavinia settled down to married life at 7, North Street, Whitwick, with the marriage being blessed with the birth of Janet on the 2nd May 1942.

Janet was living with her parents at 99, Hall's Lane in the same village, when, at the age of eighteen years she married twenty-four years old Raymond Philip Cartlidge, a painter and decorator who lived at 77, Glenmore Avenue, Shepshed. They have three sons, Steve, Nigel and Glen, with Nigel looking very much like Percy.

Maud's daughter, Kathleen is still alive, residing at her Thringstone home whilst step-sister, Lavinia, now nearly ninety years of age, is in care at: 'The Meadows' within the same village.

Many thanks to Janet Cartlidge for providing all

accompanied her husband into: 'Polly Burton's' (now: 'The Three Horse Shoes'). It is said that she gave a very fair rendition of: 'Take Me Home Again Kathleen.' The plucky lady died from cancer at home on the 17th July 1962, at the early age of sixty-four years. Bill died a few years later.

After the war Percy's half sister, Minnie, emigrated to the United States of America and settled at Philadelphia. Her stepbrother, Joseph, when he was twenty years of age, decided to follow her to the States and stayed with her

Lavender offers a sweet fragrance to visitors of the Memorial Wall at Vis-En-Artois. Percy Cliff is remembered on Panel 5.

for a time, eventually settling in an apartment in New York City for many decades. His niece, Lavinia, wrote to him for a long time until his letters suddenly stopped, the grim reaper.

Twenty-one years old, Lavinia Cliff, (it is rumoured that 'Lavinia' was the name of a ship that Percy travelled on) married twenty-three years old Eric Boot at St. John The Baptist Church, Whitwick on the 3rd June 1939. The certificate shows that she was living with her parents at 79, Talbot Road, Whitwick. Eric was employed as an engineer's fitter.

Two of the Famous Fifty, Sam Boot and Edgar Boot may be distantly related to Eric. His father,

of the above fascinating information. She hopes to visit the Memorial at Vis-En-Artois. "*I am very proud to own memorabilia that was awarded to my grandfather, but I am more proud of the man. He may have died before my birth but I have come to love what I have been told about him. I am a direct relative and his blood flows through my veins: he gave his life for his country he sacrificed his life for our freedom!*"

My grandfather, Charles Hatter served in the same Battalion, the 1/5th, and I feel he must have known Percy.

FAREWELL MY LOVE

His wounds healed and once again in his prime:
"Farewell my Love."
A distance on and a wave for the very last time:
"Farewell My Love."

Spring's soothing sun rose over the hill to view
A verdant valley fragrant with hawthorn perfume.
Sighing she waved a pretty hanky of white/ blue,
With prayers and desires upon his return soon.

They met on a gentle July evening's village fair,
He bought a gypsy ring and gave it her for luck.
The following year and marriage vows to share,
And tender kisses aside a prudent babbling brook.

His officer took him aside for immediate leave,
"Go home now lad and be with your dear wife.
Your first-born is to be called Charlie I believe.
All's not well and the doctor fears for her life."

On the bed she lay with face ashen and drained:
"Farewell My Love."
Again she whispered though far from her prime:
"Farewell My Love."

Michael Kendrick

ERNEST CROSS AND WILLIAM SETCHELL

Private Ernest Cross of the Royal Electrical and Mechanical Engineers. Circa 1915.

Thomas Cross, born on the 1st December 1851, lived a happy and fruitful life with his wife, Hannah, at 91, North Street (now 122 Central Road, and later added the adjacent property, 124 to their property at Hugglescote.) They had three children: Ada (born on the 2nd December 1885), Ernest (on the 14th March 1892), and Nellie (15th July 1898).

The children all attended Hugglescote Baptist Chapel and School where Mr. Fellows was the headmaster.

When Ernest left school at the age of thirteen his first job was assisting a Mr. Lawrence, who owned a general store at Ellistown. A few years later Ernest left to undertake a carpenter's apprenticeship at Orton and Dalby on Forest Road, Hugglescote. Having qualified he thoroughly enjoyed crafting wood and remained with the firm until shortly after

the outbreak of the war. On applying for enlistment into the Army, they decided that because of his carpentry skills he would be allocated to the Royal Electrical and Mechanical Engineers (R.E.M.E.). Officially: Service number: 204350, No1 Section, 477 Field Company, South Midland Royal Engineers, 48th Division.

Whilst training he sent several postcards to his family showing the bridge over the river Medway at Rochester in Kent and the 'canvas camp' on the North Down's Way where they were billeted.

R.E.M.E. was involved in many aspects of warfare, and besides the obvious they constructed and demolished bridges, supplied lighting and pumping apparatus, repaired roads, laid counter-

Private William Setchell of the 5th Leicestershire Battalion. Circa 1912

Ada Cross with Ernest and baby Nellie. Circa 1900.

65, Crescent Road, Hugglescote. The home of Ernest and Florrie Cross and where Raymond was born. X marked.

mines, erected signposts and location boards, et cetera.

Private Ernest Cross was only 5 feet 2½ inches tall but was well built, had a good brain and possessed a very strong Christian Faith. The latter, especially, contributed towards helping him through a difficult war, serving on the Western Front in France and Belgium and also on the North Italian Front. After the Armistice he saw the Catacombs in Rome and also attended a festival of music by Banda Dei RR. Carabinieri, Banda Della Guardia Repubblicana, Banda Americana and the Banae Riunite Della Guardia Reale Ingese.

On his return to England he returned to his old job at Orton and Dalby and often reflected on his four years of service, so much so that he wrote down some of the instances that had made a profound affect upon him.

On the 21st October 1922, Ernest married twenty-seven years old, Florrie Setchell, who lived at 29, Highfield Street at Coalville. (The Setchell family was originally from March in Lincolnshire: now Cambridgeshire).

The couple settled down to married life at 65, Crescent Road at Hugglescote having a son, Raymond, born on the 16th March 1926 after a difficult birth. (Raymond served in World War 2, as we shall read of in Book 4: 'Sons and Daughters.')

His wife, Florrie (Floss), had an elder brother, John William Setchell (born 1892), who preferred to be called, Bill, and attended the Wesleyan School on Belvoir Road, Coalville, where his headmaster was Mr. Frith.

Around 1908 Bill enlisted at Ashby de la Zouch into the 5th Leicestershire Battalion, service number 1077, and a little later married local girl, Maggie,

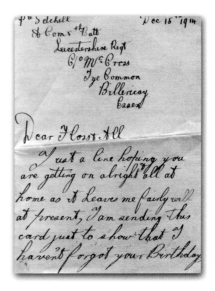

A letter from Private William Setchell whilst at Sawbridgeworth on the 15th December 1914 to his sister, Floss and All. Floss married Ernest Cross in 1922.

living on Highfield Street and having a son, Charlie.

As a territorial soldier, Bill Setchell was with his Battalion at the annual training camp at Bridlington when the Great War started.

Bill would have known all of the Coalville and District Territorial soldiers and every one of the Famous Fifty, especially the Hugglescote lads.

Bill, at Sawbridgeworth on the 15th December 1914 wrote to his sister, Florrie (Floss):

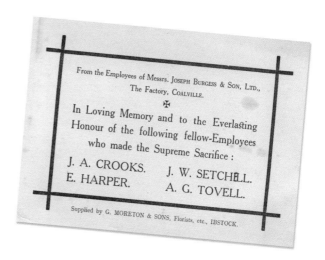

> *Pte. W. Setchell*
> *A Company 5th Battalion*
> *Leicestershire Regt.*
> *15th December 1915.*

C/O Mr. Cross.
Tye Common
Billericay
Essex.

Dear Floss and All,
Just a line hoping you are getting on alright and all those at home, as it leaves me fairly well at present. I am sending this card to show that I haven't forgot your Birthday. I may not be able to send another again as we never know what might happen between now and next year. I went to London on Saturday and saw your Uncle and All and I saw the baby boy and he is a bonny chap. I got back at 1.00 o'clock on Sunday morning and it wasn't half dark. They are getting on alright, and I am hoping to be in Coalville next Friday night, if not I shall be home for Christmas. The trenches* are full of water, 4 feet deep and we can't work in them. How is my mother getting on, is she any better? I think I have said all this time. Wishing you will have a happy Birthday as I don't think I shall.
With love from your brother, Bill.

* The Battalion had already been trained on the construction of trenches, and where possible time was spent in them to adapt to their hardships prior to the real thing. C/O a Mr. Cross was coincidental.

At some time during his service on the Western Front, Bill was wounded, and upon recovery was returned to another unit: a frequent occurrence. So it was that Pte. William Setchell was with the King's

Own Royal Rifles (K.O.R.R.) and serving in the same battalion as Captain Anthony Eden. The captain was in Flanders at the age of eighteen, an Adjutant at nineteen and a Brigade Major at twenty. Following W.W. 2 he became prime minister of our country. The K.O.R.R. Battalion detrained at Caestra and marched to billets in a farm near Meteren, and from there occupied the southern flank of the Ypres Salient, opposite the Bois Carre and just to the south of St. Eloi. Bill was killed in these trenches on the 29th February 1917, possibly from shellfire. A card from his employees: Messrs. Joseph Burgess & Sons Ltd was sent to his wife: 'In Loving Memory and to the Everlasting Honour of the following fellow-Employees who made the Supreme Sacrifice':

J. A. CROOKS. E. HARPER.
J.W.SETCHELL. A.G.TOVELL.

James Arthur Crooks, a Coalville man, was killed fighting with the 8th Leicestershire Battalion on the 15th July 1916. His name can be read on St. John the Baptist Church Memorial Plaque, Hugglescote. Archie Tovell was killed on the 1st

Thomas and Hannah Cross in their later years.

FOURTH STAGE : THE 4TH OCTOBER, 1917 (4/10)

A map taken from Ernest's 1920 copy of Illustrated Michelin Guides: Ypres and the Battle of Ypres.

February 1917, serving with the Machine-Gun Corpse; he was a great friend of Thomas Robson, one of the Famous Fifty. Ernest Harper M.M. was with the 7th Leicestershire when he lost his life on the 10th October 1917, and was almost certainly the brother of Jack Harper, another of the Famous Fifty.

William Setchell was twenty-five years of age when he met his death in the bitterly cold winter of 1916-17, and on the bloodstained ground of the Ypres Salient! Little is known what happened to his wife, Maggie, but their son, Charlie, was brought up with the help of several relatives, notably his auntie Florrie. Charles fought in World War 2.

All four of the above soldiers' names can be read on the Coalville Clock Tower War Memorial.

During World War 2, Ernest and Florrie took care of evacuee, Irene Hill, who had her photograph taken in 1944, and gave it to them with love. She later married another evacuee, Donald Underhill,

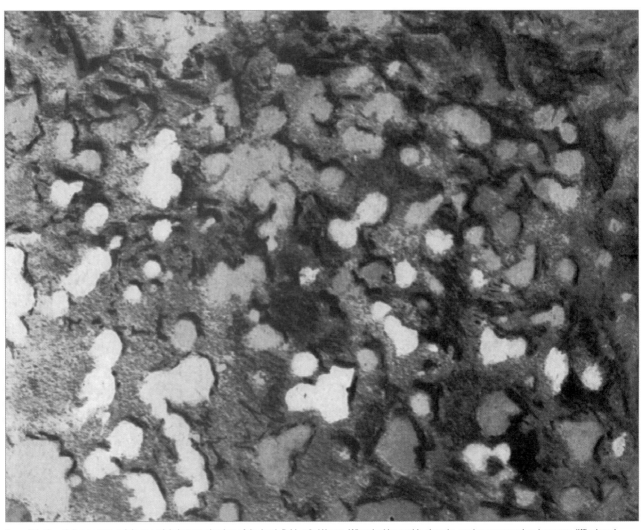

Incredible though it may appear, it is an aerial photograph taken of the battlefield at 3rd Ypres. When looking at this view the reader can associate how very difficult and dangerous it must have been for Ernest Cross and his pals when erecting posts during their night-time vigils.

Ernest Cross' sister, Nellie. Born in 1898. Like so many young women of her generation, she remained a spinster after the deaths of nearly one million men in W.W.1. She was described as very pretty and with a loving personality. Circa 1916.

Ernest and Florrie Cross took care of an evacuee during World War 2. The photograph sends love, and shows, Irene Hill, in 1944.
Irene married another Hugglescote evacuee named, Donald Underhill.

who was living on the Ashburton Road opposite to the Council School.

Besides taking care of Irene, Florrie also sold war bonds for the government and engaged herself in other voluntary work. During the war she received a signed certificate from Queen Elizabeth in appreciation of the service she was rendering.

The couple were fortunate in that their only son, Raymond, survived a perilous time around Arnhem in Holland in 1945, and were thrilled by his wedding to Kathleen Wharmby on the 1st April 1950. They had the pleasure of three grandchildren, Robert (born 1951), David (1955) and Sheila (1959)

It is sad to write that Florrie (Floss) died on the 14th October 1964, only sixty-nine years of age.

His elder sister, Ada, married Jesse Cooper and had two sons. She died on the 4th July 1967, aged eighty-two years.

Ernest Cross' love of the Hugglescote Baptist School grew as did his religious faith and he spent a large part of his life reading the Bible, until the old soldier 'faded away' on the 4th May 1969 at the age of seventy-seven.

Nellie, a very attractive and sociable girl

Florrie Setchell with her nephew, Charles. Circa 1916

A bridge that sapper Ernest Cross helped to construct in the Great War.

became a victim of our country loosing nearly one million young men, she never married! She spent a large chunk of her life supporting herself by working for Messrs. Joseph Burgess and Sons on Belvoir Road, Coalville. It was the same factory where her brother in law, Bill Setchell, had worked before mobilisation. Nellie departed on the 5th April 1985, aged eighty-six years.

My thanks to Raymond and Kathleen Cross. By coincidence they live in the house that was once occupied by Walter Handford (and wife/daughter), one of the Famous Fifty.

The MEMOIRS of ERNEST CROSS

Private Ernest Cross
No1 Section
477 Field Company
South Midland Royal Engineers
48th Division
Sign - White Diamond.

Incidence while on Active Service

A fight in the Air

It was towards the end of August or early September 1917 in the Ypres Sector of Belgium. I was in billets on the Canal bank to the left (east) of Ypres. We were in a second line of dugouts with our infantry in those on the Canal path. We had returned from our shift work up the Line at the end of the day. When in the dugout I heard a commotion in the air, it was aeroplanes and very low, then someone outside shouted that there was a scrap on. I rushed out into the entrance trench and was just in time to see a German fighter plane; it was chasing one of our scout planes. Ours was nothing more than a lost kite compared to the other, it had no defence weapons what so ever. This German plane could only fire from the tail with a machine-gun, so the pilot had to manoeuvre round until it got into a favourable position for firing. Each time the German was ready to fire from the tail with its machine-gun, our scout plane would do a stunt of suddenly falling or turning sideways or other such movements. This continued for sometime until it looked as though the German had him beaten. All of a sudden some bullet-fire rang out from the Canal path just in front of me, and the German plane began to fall!

I quickly climbed up the back of the trench I was in and looking over saw one of our troops with a Lewis gun he had just fired. He had rested the gun on a mate's shoulder to take aim and fire. Immediately the scout plane swooped down over him and shouted:

"Thank you, you've saved my life!"

The German plane fell some short distance away and I did not go to see it. One of my section went and said the pilot had been shot through the head. It was said that the Lewis gunner got a month's special leave, but he could have been court-martialled for firing without orders. The German pilot was an ace with a number of Allied planes (about 30) to his credit. The kill was posted up on our Royal Engineers' Company board. I cannot remember the pilot's name but it can be checked up on Army Records.

Courage on the Battlefield
Passchendaele: 3rd Ypres:
31st July - 15th November 1917.

No1

It was in the week following the 4th October 1917 that I was in a party of sappers with an officer. We had the job of naming various points and concrete pillboxes up at the Front in the Pilkem, Langemarck and Poelcappelle area in the Ypres Sector. We started at about 7.30 pm and finished about 5.30 am, having to walk all the way from our billets on the Canal bank, about eight kilometres (five miles) each way. A party of men numbering a dozen or more would start off with boards painted with letters to indicate the place names.

Some boards had one stake while others had two attached to them so they could be driven into the ground.

As each board was driven in that man had to re-join the company working further back until the last six were reached. I was in this party every night, with the exception of one, which was my weekly rest period. The six sappers with our officer, a 2nd Lieutenant Lightbody of No1 section, then moved forward as a party whether a man had a board or not. It was then that we knew we were approaching No-Man's-Land; there were no continuous trenches only slit trenches here and there. Also there were either fortified shell holes with machine-guns, sand bagged outposts or captured concrete Pillboxes. Our officer always had his right hand on the holster of his revolver; in the other hand he carried his map, flashlight and compass.

We were of course in battle-dress order with haversack, water bottle, two gas-masks, a rifle with 120 rounds of ammunition and tools of some kind (shovel, hammer) for driving the boards in the ground.

As we went forward sometimes our officer would take two sappers with him and go either to the left or right, so fixing boards that he had left behind.

Every now and again German star shells would light up all the area around and we would have to stand still until they died down. It was a very weird experience to stand there as in broad daylight with a painted board on your shoulder; also we were often caught in the shellfire of our own or the enemy's guns and sometimes both.

The early nights of that week were done, but later on a brilliant moon shone when the weather was good. It was on a very dark night when our party searched a concrete Pillbox, it was being used as a battalion headquarters, and our officer went inside to get some information and direction from the officer in charge. We were left mixed up with their infantry standing about, and I saw a wounded man on a stretcher and a number standing about. I was

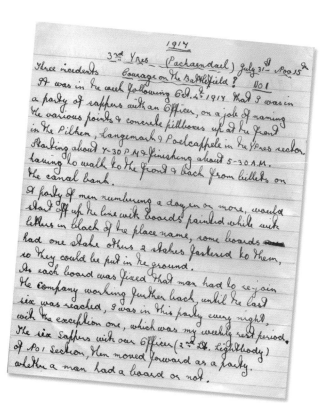

A page entitled: 'Courage on the Battlefields' relating to 3rd Ypres or Passchendaele from Ernest Cross' Memoirs of various incidents during the Great War.

startled by being gripped by the tunic collar and shook by a very excited company sergeant major, who looked as though he had had a double rum ration! He asked me who I was and to what company I belonged! I replied Royal Engineers. He then asked two or three more in our party, and I realised he was trying to get four men of the same company as the wounded man to carry him to the back area. I found that the C.S.M. had managed to get two of the same company but as he was trying to find others they slipped off into the dark. They probably did so because of the grave condition of the wounded man. At last he managed to get four men and they lifted the stretcher and set off on their journey. They had not gone far before being caught in a terrific barrage and (doubted) but often wondered if they got to journey's end.

No2. A Kindness Shown

On another night in the same week it was getting to the end of our shift and only two boards were to be fixed. I had the very last one and a territorial before the war carried the other; our Division was a territorial one. This man was the oldest in the party, at least twice my age and very strongly built, making two of me being only 5 feet $2^{1}/_{2}$". I was one of the smallest men in the section and probably the Company. He was a man I feared and when drunk he could be the very devil. He was that bad tempered that he had no real mate; even those who knew him most could not take to him much. Yet on this occasion when his turn came to fix his board, which was at a Pillbox, I was standing behind him. He immediately turned around to me and said: "Hear now, I can see you are about done in so give me that board!" He took it and fixed it at the last place in the Line that night.

There was no doubt that I was showing signs of exhaustion after carrying the board and other equipment for many hours over shell torn ground. The battlefield was thick mud and littered with debris of all kinds. By the time he helped, my mates would have been without a board to carry for a long time. It was at that instant that I saw Christ in the Devil, or else a splash of the Devine in mortal man!

No3. A Helping Hand.

It was the same week again and we had gone well up to the Front. It was difficult to tell how far away we were from the enemy because there were no continuous lines of trenches. Our officer asked a gun-crew in a shell hole where the frontline was and they did not know. That went to show how fluid the positions were at that time, for our infantry were attacking at dawn every day. It was early morning and there was brilliant moonlight when we arrived at a certain position, it appeared to me to lie in an open space with nothing rising from out of the ground. I could just see the last Pillbox to the rear. When our officer took two men with him to the left to fix a board at another Pillbox we were left to await their return. The enemy put down a barrage and also strafed our frontline. They then put it further forward for quite a distance and repeated it all at regular intervals. We stood watching until it came close to us and then took a dive for a shell-hole. They were all filled with water and so I flung my board down and lay on top of it. Just in front were the remains of a hedge. As I lay there I could hear all these shells whizzing over and dropping splinters, especially when they exploded near to me. After the barrage passed to the rear we got up and made sure everyone was all right, and then dived down when the barrage got near again. It happened while I was lying in that shell-hole and when it had quietened down. I peered up and saw two figures approaching, one had his head bandaged and the other a leg. They had their arms around each other for support and when they saw me they asked if I had a drink to spare. I offered them my water bottle and then they asked the way to the rear. I pointed to the Pillbox behind me because I knew no other way. They said they had been trying to get to the rear for a long time and that they must have been going around in circles. They said they were hiding in daytime and moving at night. I watched as they set off and then realised they were going around in a circle from where they should. I shouted to tell them, which was probably a foolish thing to do not knowing my position for certain. Anyway they corrected their path and were nearly at the Pillbox when the enemy put down a terrific barrage. I (doubt it) but I will never know if they reached safety.

Other Incidents during that week of October 1917 at Passchendaele

No1

On another night I had the last board to fix yet again. We arrived at what looked like a sandbag dugout and trench, the last but one board had been fixed and the rest stayed behind with a party of three going forward. The officer went inside to get some information from the infantry officer in charge and we talked in a whisper to the trench sentry, asking whether they saw anything of the enemy while on duty. He said they did and that if we looked over the parapet towards a stump of a hedge one crawling around on reconnaissance. We looked over and my mate saw him move, I didn't! We asked the sentry why he didn't fire and he said he was under orders not to as it would give their position away, and they were due to go 'over-the-top' in about an hour.

Then both officers came out of the dugout and I was close enough to hear the infantry officer say: "You take my tip and dump the board here tonight and come tomorrow night. I am sure the Pillbox is not in our hands now, it exchanged hands a few times during the day and Jerry has it now!" Our officer was still determined to find out as it was his duty to fix the board there, but we were relieved when he decided to dump it. Neither my mate nor me wanted a military medal so we returned to the rest and back to the Canal bank. Later we found out the Pillbox was in German hands at that time.

No2

One night our officer and two men went up to the left to fix the last board before we returned to the Canal bank. This time I was left with the others and we sheltered in a long narrow Pillbox that was unoccupied. Not far away was a river whose flow had widened by shelling. It always seemed a long time while we waited for the officer and men to return, and what would we do if he failed to return? It was a fearful thought for nobody else could guide us back. Now this night we had an Irishman with us and his nerve began to crack, what with the wailing of the awful shelling we had to endure. The man's eyes stuck out and began to role and he said he was leaving the Pillbox. We had great difficulty in trying

to contain him and thankfully by the time the others came back he had calmed down. We set off to the rear and came across the swollen river, and while we attempted to cross it Jerry put down another heavy barrage, shells falling thick and fast around us. Our officer ordered us to return and take shelter in the Pillbox and we just about made it. The river was called: The Steenbeek, I think. We then had to get back to our frontlines as quickly as possible or we'd be caught by our own infantry's attack, which was due at dawn. It was said that our work was privileged because we could get back in darkness before the battle was fought!

No3

It may have been one of the nights I have already mentioned. We were in single file and getting very close to the frontline, and it was a full moon and very clear. We came to an area where the day before there had been fierce fighting and the dead just lay where they had fallen. Germans and men of a Scottish Division, they had kilts on, were mixed up together as far as one could see. The ground was so very thickly covered with the dead that we had difficulty in not stumbling over them as we picked our way forward. I was walking next to our officer when he turned round and said to me: "Sapper Cross, I have never seen so many dead in my life!" It was possibly the same night as we walked over the battlefield because I was following the officer then. He suddenly went into a bogged shell-hole, which went up to one of his knees. I helped him out and he said: "You hold these—a map, compass and flashlight", and he got out but was covered in slime.

No4

It was in August 1917 at Passchendaele when I was working on a road in the back area, but for most of the time was under shellfire. We often had to dive into a shell-hole on one or other side of the road although that often gave little protection from flying splinters. Suddenly we were caught up in very heavy shelling: 9.2s from the German artillery. By the shriek of the first shell we knew we did not have time to take cover, so just lay in the mud on the road and nine of these shells fell close to us. It was a most fearful experience, lying close to the ground.

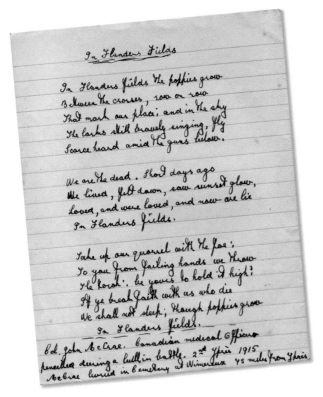

The final page in Ernest Cross' Memoirs of the Great War.

I could hear the fuses of the shells starting to go off in the ground and finally the full explosion with the feeling that the earth was opening up. All the debris then fell on us and it partly buried me. After getting up I could see I was standing on almost the edge of a large crater and looking for my mates, no one was injured, it was a real miracle! The shells had fallen between us and the nature of the soft ground had saved us, the explosives had not spread out as usual but had gone up in a 'V' shape.

A short distance away an officer sat there as calm as a cucumber, he had sat it all out, but this was the first time I had completely lost control of my nerves. Each time I heard a shell coming, which was not long after one another, I felt I was helplessly drawn up into just a blob, and this nine times in all.

On the Italian Front between December 1917 and January 31st 1919

No1. Early July 1918
After a spell up the Line in which we were caught in the Austro-German attack on the 15th June 1918 we had gone to the town of Aryignano for a period of rest. We were billeted on a street off the main square of the town, and near to an old school that was being used as a hospital. Opposite to our billets was a house with two daughters about my age and one was called Mary (Faggiana Maria); with my pals we spent many a happy hour there.

Many months afterwards when the Italian Armistice had been signed we rested at a village about twelve miles from where they lived. I borrowed one of the Company's cycles and went to see Mary again. I had to cycle back in the dark with no lamps and no moon to help me, and what a ride it was! For many miles there was an unfenced railway on my left and quite a good river flowing parallel on my right with only the odd boulder keeping me from falling in. Oh, what a sensation when meeting vehicles with headlights on, being temporary blinded, so I had to hope for the best and steer straight on. Anyway I was lucky to be able to see Mary and her sister and have a good time.

Mary said that in the period of leaving the town and also revisiting there was that terrible Spanish Flu epidemic sweeping through the area. They tried to make me understand what an awful havoc of death it had made in the town, especially the street where we had been billeted.

In Aryignano we had orders to move once more to the frontline on the Asiago Plateau and we spent three months there and finally left the sector. From there we went to the Piave Front just west of Venice, and marched there at night because of the terrific heat during the day. We had a days rest in some farm buildings but again we started at about 7.30pm, and by that time I had been on guard duty for twenty-four hours. Just before we paraded to start, the guards were told to march with their own section because there were no prisoners. After falling in, our Company was inspected before moving off. I then heard our C.S.M. shout for the guard to fall out and go to the front of the parade. We were ordered to take charge of one soldier who was drunk; I did not know him because he was from another section of the Company, but he was hefty, well built and Irish.

The Company turned into the main road and started on its march, we did not know our destination. We took up our position at the back of the column with the prisoner between two of us with fixed bayonets. The Company's transport always followed about two hours later in their column, resting every two hours against our one. We had not marched far before it was very difficult to see, and our prisoner was staggering from one side to the other. We told him to get a move on but with no response and so touched him with our bayonet and nothing again. It was really dark and we began to lose contact with our column and soon we lost sight and out of hearing with them. Our corporal was in a stew, not knowing our destination.

We at last came to a side road on our left (it was all open country), and decided to wait for our transport, which was due in two hours. We sat on the verge of the side road with our prisoner sprawled out and asleep, we hoped he would sleep the booze off. It must have been about midnight when we heard the rumble of our transport approaching. The corporal ordered me to wake him up, but I could not arouse him and before I could get him going the column had passed by the end of the side road. Eventually we got 'Paddy' onto the main road but just as before he was walking very slowly and still staggering, we could not make him alter. Suddenly, he straightened up and started running for all he was worth and soon caught up with our transport, we were left behind. He caught up with the rear truck of our transport column, hauled himself in and dropped to the bottom! Our corporal was now in an even bigger sweat than ever for it was an offence in itself to climb into a truck without permission. How could we get him out? I believed that nothing short of a Mill's bomb would have done it!

We decided to report him to Captain Briggs, the officer in charge of the column, and I was sent to find him but it was difficult to see the way ahead. I eventually met him when he was coming down the road on horseback. I saluted the captain and informed him of our trouble. He said: " Oh well, let him stay there till morning!" I returned to my corporal and like fools we brought up the rear and we could only stop every two hours for a rest.

We arrived at a camp in a field at about 8.00am and Paddy was put on a charge, but we never found out what his sentence was. What a performance!

At the back of Ernest's book he has written out Colonel John McRae's excellent poem: 'In Flanders Fields.'

In Flanders fields the poppies blow
Between the roses, row on row
That mark our place; and in the sky
The larks, still bravely singing, fly
Scarce heard amid the guns below.

We are the Dead. Short days ago
We lived, felt dawn, saw sunset glow,
Loved and were loved, and now we lie
In Flanders fields.

Take up our quarrel with the foe:
To you from failing hands we throw
The torch; be yours to hold it high.
If ye break faith with us who die
We shall not sleep, though poppies grow
In Flanders fields.

Sleep well Ernest Cross.

THE EMMERSON BROTHERS

In my earlier book I wrote at length about William and Jabez Emmerson, two brothers who were members of that exclusive little band of pals, the Famous Fifty. Their father, Alfred Barratt Emmerson, was the manager at Ellistown Colliery. Alfred's brother, Jay (actual name: Jabez) was the manager of nearby Bagworth Colliery.

The full Emmerson family circle was highly respected, not least because of their leadership during the Whitwick Mining Disaster of 1898.

Jay and his wife had three sons, Joseph, Alfred, and William. They also had a daughter, Mary, and all four possessed fine qualities that should have ensured them happy and successful lives.

Joseph was the first-born in 1890, the location is unknown, but from an early age lived with his

Private Alfred Emmerson.
Dated the 11th December 1914. Fourth Leicestershire Battalion.

2nd Lieutenant Joseph Emmerson in mid-1915.
Fourth Leicestershire Battalion.

parents in the 'White House' at Bagworth. Following grammar school he qualified as a colliery surveyor, and was employed locally. Cutting a dashing figure, the twenty-four year old, service number 3012, enlisted at Coalville in mid-September 1914, being allocated to the Fourth (1/4th) Leicestershire Battalion. He embarked for France with this battalion in March 1915, and rapidly reached the rank of 2nd Lieutenant; with his leadership and bravery profiting a '**Mentioned in Despatches**'. Undoubtedly the worst clash that this battalion fought in was the Charge of the Hohenzollern Redoubt, on the 13th October 1915. Its location is a few kilometres to the north of the mining town of Loos: northern France, and the charge was part of the oozing wound called the Battle of Loos. Prior to the attack our artillery bombarded the German fortifications, which were deep, extensive and well serviced. The redoubt teemed with machine-guns; a counter barrage and asphyxiating gas also played a role. For two days battle raged and included vicious hand-to-hand fighting. The Fourth Leicestershire Battalion suffered appalling losses, twenty officers and four hundred and fifty-three other ranks! 2nd Lieutenant Joseph Emmerson was last seen alive leading his men on a bayonet-charge to a second-line trench on the afternoon of the 13th October 1915. His body was never found and his name is remembered with honour on the Loos Memorial, Panel 42-44. He was unmarried and just twenty-five years of age.

Alfred was named after his uncle and was born on the 20th October 1892. Again very bright, he attended the celebrated Ashby de la Zouch Grammar School along with his two aforementioned cousins. On leaving school he qualified as a teacher and was assistant schoolmaster at Bagworth School when war was declared. He enlisted, service number 3011, at Coalville with his brother into the Fourth Leicestershire Battalion and likewise embarked for France in March 1915. This is verified by the 1915 war diary kept by his cousin, Jabez, who writes that on the 13th March 1915 he sees both Joseph and Alfred, and again on the 12th April 1915 when he comments about seeing the pair in a neighbouring barn and having a chat and a sing song.

Alfred, at the front, wrote a letter to his headmaster in early 1915 and asked him to recite it to

Home of the Emmerson's: the White House at Bagworth in 1898.

his former pupils.

Bagworth School.   *Alfred Emmerson.*
March 1915.   *4th Leicestershire*
                               Battalion.
                               France.

Dear Mr. Williams,

We are very busy indeed. We are 'right in it', except for being in the trenches, and we will soon be in those! We are living in a barn, but you have no idea how comfortable it is, and we also have a café attached, so we are all right. Even as I write the ground continually shakes due to the percussion of the big guns. One of the biggest out there is only one hundred yards away and its thunder is great. It gives one huge crack-half bang-and even in the barn you can feel the rush of air as the shock waves travel.

We are quite used to it now. Some German shells have been bursting in the air nearby. Yesterday we saw a lovely sight, an aeroplane being fired at by big guns. It was an English plane and the daring of the pilot was great. He circled round and then dived and rose out of range and so on. The flashes of the bursting shells (shrapnel) and the smoke that looked like small puffs of cotton wool against the blue sky, made a very pretty picture. At night the whole district is illuminated by flashes from guns, searchlights and fireballs. The latter float in the air and are like electric lamps.

They are thrown by the Germans to illuminate the whole area and so prevent British soldiers from entering or leaving the trenches. Of course the old soldiers tell us many hair-raising yarns, but we take the proverbial grain of salt with them. You would no doubt like to know how we live, well you wouldn't recognise me. My hair is off, shaved almost, and after my usual flowing mane you can guess how I look. I have had to grow a moustache, my clothes are no longer immaculate, and they are dirty and greasy. My boots are covered in mud and dirt and I've had to use my handkerchief for a month. We eat and drink out of the same vessel, a mess tin which we carry everywhere. The outsides are black, like a gypsy's pot, with being on fires but we contrive to keep the inside clean. We have knives and forks. We have bacon for breakfast, 'pontoon' soup for dinner, jam for tea and cheese for supper. When we don't have bread we use biscuits, hard like dog biscuits! Our dining tables are our knees and we sit on the ground or straw. If we travel a long way we use cattle trucks, each truck holding forty men, but for journeys under twenty miles we march. We carry all our belongings on our backs, except blankets and fur coats. We do carry towels, comforters, change of underclothing, shirt, socks, overcoat, and any other 'luxury' you wish to carry. It all weighs about seventy pounds but after twenty miles it feels like double! We know nothing of outside affairs except for the occasional newspaper. We know nothing of the progress of the war! The wildest rumours float about, but there is a gentleman known as the 'censor' who stops me from telling you too much.

We have just received orders to move again. We are only given five minutes notice so we have to skip about. The local people here are peasant class, very little money and no too clean. The children, of course, cannot attend school at the moment, and they seem to spend a lot of time on the manure heap and scream and shout like Red Indians. They have picked up many English phrases and delight in repeating them over and over again. You cannot believe the difference in life between France and England at the moment.

Best wishes,

Alfred Emmerson. (Private).

The entire letter was published in the Coalville

The War Memorial at Bagworth Parish Church.

Times on the 2nd April 1915. Alfred was particularly careful to euphemise with phrases such as 'comfortable barns' and the beauty of shells exploding in a blue sky. Clearly the sight of the English aeroplane thrilled him and later in the war requested a transfer to the Royal Flying Corpse.

Alfred received swift promotions with the Fourth Battalion and was offered a cadetship for officer training. During this period of officer training he married his fiancée, Maggie, who came from Shenton, near to Nuneaton, Warwickshire. Alfred duly received his commission as a 2nd Lieutenant and on the 30th September 1915 was posted to the Fifth Leicestershire Battalion. The Fourth and the Fifth were sister battalions and accompanied each other during the war. As mentioned, on the 13th October 1915, at the Charge of the Hohenzollern Redoubt, the Fourth Battalion was in the first attacking wave, and Alfred knew this and would have been within one hundred yards of Joseph when his brother was killed.

This may have influenced his decision because shortly afterwards he asked to join the Royal Flying Corpse and to train as a pilot.

There was always a shortage of pilots and his request was soon sanctioned. The quiet and studious young man received his 'wings' and was posted to No 12 Squadron. I do hope he had some exciting times, however his chances of survival were slim, such was the carnage taking place in the skies above the Western Front, let alone at ground level!

Unlike 1939-45, parachutes were not provided for airmen: senior officials believing it would erode the fighting spirit of the pilot. If the aeroplane crashed –fingers crossed for the pilot.

Second Lieutenant Alfred Emmerson was shot-down by a German aircraft on the 3rd April 1917, dying from severe injuries one day later. He is buried at Warlincourt Halte Cemetery near to Arras in France. He was just twenty-five years of age, and his wife was inconsolable. They had spent so little time together as a married couple, and I have been informed that she never remarried.

In less than three years Mr. Jay and Mrs. Annie Emmerson lost two bright stars from their life, and Mary two devoted brothers. Jay continued to manage the colliery at Bagworth in an efficient and business-like fashion until retirement, but their lives and homestead remained in a shadow. His brother,

The solitary grave of Annie Emmerson in the cemetery of Bagworth Parish Church. January 1858-August 1921

Alfred, at Ellistown did all he could to soften the blow, but consolation proved of little value. The foibles of war, within the same family circle one father looses two sons, whereas his brother's sons survive the conflict. Could it all be down to the random toss of a dice? Their stepmother, Annie, never recovered from her distress and died in August 1921. Jay lived on to 1951, having reached ninety-three years.

Northwest Leicestershire lost two of her most outstanding sons; the only consolation was that the name of Emmerson, if possible, was even more respected.

The name of Alfred Emmerson can be read on the Ashby de la Zouch Grammar School Roll of Honour 1914-18.

I cannot find a reason, nor understand the absence of both their names on the Bagworth Parish Church War Memorial. Indeed, and with great sadness, I cannot find their names on any War Memorial. I do hope that measures will be taken to ensure this alarming omission is quickly corrected!

My thanks to Blanche Wyatt, granddaughter of Alfred Emmerson senior.

Jabez Emmerson Snr: 1858-1951. Lost two sons during World War 1.

ROLAND FARMER

Roland Farmer of Tamworth Road, Ashby de la Zouch was the eldest surviving son of Mr. & Mrs. George Farmer when he was killed at the age of thirty years on the 22nd March 1916.

Yet another of the Ashby Grammar School set, he was an excellent all round sportsman playing for the local Hastings Cricket Club, Hastings Tennis Club and the town's Golf Club. He was particularly popular on the cricket field and Aubrey Moore in his book: 'A Son Of The Rectory' writes: *I was playing my last game for the Hastings on Saturday, 1st August 1914, the day before we went to the ill fated camp at Bridlington. We were playing Castle Donington at Ashby. They included three Shields in their team, John was top class, Charlie and Joe both average. We were all great friends. We fielded and*

Castle Donington knocked-up a sizable score. Frank Joyce, our captain said, " Come on in with me and we'll knock-up a hundred for the first wicket!" We made a big score thanks to Frank, a great hitter; I just stonewalled and got four. Roland Farmer, another player and great friend of us all had, like Charlie Shields and myself, recently been commissioned into the Fifth Leicestershire. We walked off the field in golden sunlight; we had a drink and talked about the forthcoming camp and journey next day. Many walked off that field for the last time.'

Before the outbreak of war, Roland had been assistant clerk to the Ashby Board of Guardians and was held in high esteem throughout the neighbourhood. He had been with the Ashby Company of Territorial soldiers for several pre-war

years and he was always described as performing with great zeal and eagerness, and he frequently carried off the honours in prize-shooting competitions.

Following the outbreak of war he was a Lieutenant in 'C' Shepshed Company of the Fifth Leicestershire Battalion. He embarked with the Battalion in late February 1915 and served with them until his first leave soon after Christmas in 1915. By early 1916, Captain Farmer, in command of the Company and with Aubrey Moore as his second in command, had just taken over the Line at Vimy Ridge in France. Aubrey's book describes the conditions: '*The trenches were shallow. The so-called sandbag parapets making the firing positions were only one bag thick, as we knew later to our cost. Sanitation was awful. There was hardly any trench wire to be seen, except German. The enemy soon began to throw everything at us they could find. We were heavily mortared with horrible things about the size of a five-gallon oil drum; they were very noisy and destructive. They were known as minenwerfer and one resulted in the death of Roland. We had lookouts posted and when one came over they would shout "mini-left" or "mini-right"! Roland was an expert dodger, and we feel he must have slipped and fell because a mini landed near to him. He was blown out of the trench and when we found his body he was head down in a water filled shell hole!*'

The Battalion's commanding officer, Colonel C. H. Jones wrote a letter on the same day that Roland died to Mrs Farmer: '*Your son was one of the coolest and bravest men that ever lived. I have seen him on many occasions under severe fire and nothing has ever disturbed him. He never flinched, never hesitated to go and do what he knew was right, without a thought for himself, only for the cause that he was upholding. We are all sorry. We feel his loss.*'

Captain Roland Farmer's name can be read on the Ashby de la Zouch War Memorial.

The cricket ground n'er again witnessed the dazzling all round talents of Roland Farmer.

With thanks to John Williams of Ashby de la Zouch Grammar School.

GEORGE T. GADSBY

George was born in 1890, the son of Mr. & Mrs. G. Gadsby of Ellistown, and as a youngster his parents moved to nearby Hugglescote. He had a brother, Harry, and the family worshipped at St. John The Baptist Church in the village, with both George and Harry being educated at the Church School. Upon leaving school George obtained employment at Ibstock Colliery, and at Coalville in 1912 he enlisted into the Fifth Leicestershire Battalion, service number 1212. Bill Barney enlisted around the same time and I understand they were good friends.

George married in 1913 and the couple lived at 30, Mill Row at Hugglescote. The following June his wife gave birth to a girl who was christened, Hilda.

George was with the Fifth Territorial Battalion at their annual training camp at Bridlington on the day that the Great War started, and upon mobilisation was quickly dispatched to Luton for further training.

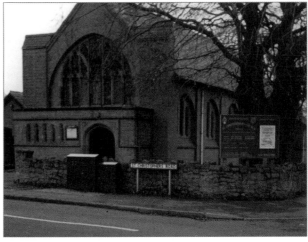

St. Christopher's Church at Ellistown

St. Christopher's Memorial to the men who fell in the Great War. Note such names as W. Barney, G, Gadsby and W. Petitt, one of the Famous Fifty.

With his Battalion he embarked for France in late February 1915, and served in such dangerous sectors as the Messines Ridge and the Ypres Salient in Belgium. His brother, Harry, enlisted at Coalville in late September 1914, service number 3148, into the same Battalion and joined his brother at Ypres, however, before then George had the company of his best friend, George Daft, formerly of Margaret Street, Coalville.

Many an experienced soldier develops a foreboding that he will soon die in battle, and it appears this was the case with Private George Gadsby. He had been aware for a few weeks that his Battalion was going to be involved in a huge battle at a German strongpoint. Three days before the battle, and without awaiting a reply from his wife for an earlier letter, he wrote once again.

Last letter home:

> *10th October 1915.*
> *France.*

My dear wife,

> *I expect you will be a bit surprised at me writing before having a letter from you, but I though it my duty as a husband to write. By the time you get my letter I shall perhaps be in a tight corner. I hope the Lord will spare me and get me through it, as I so much want to see you and Hilda again. I hope that you will pray to God above to spare all of us out here, because we need the prayers of everyone! But if I don't get through it, you will know that I did my duty. Bless Hilda for me. I will write as soon as I can, if only on a postcard. I am in the best of health at the time of writing and hope you two are the same. I received Hilda's photograph but it took me all my time to realise who it was, it being over a year. She has grown a lot and I wish I were at home to see her. Well, dear wife, don't write again until you hear from me again, it may only be a postcard, but then I will look forward to your reply. Well, goodbye for the present. I trust that my prayers will be heard and God will spare me so that I may see you both again.*

> *Your ever-loving husband,*
> *George. xxxx.*

Private George Daft wrote a letter to his best pal's wife to pass on the bad news of his death.

> *16th October 1915.*
> *France.*

Dear Mrs.Gadsby,

> *It is with very deep sympathy for you that I write these few lines. The reason I am writing is because George has been killed and we were such big pals as you know, and his death has grieved me to the heart. I know what a big loss this is to you! All the men and officers of his platoon, who feel his loss keenly, respected him. It was with a fearless heart that he advanced towards the enemy trenches until he was hit by a bullet.*

> *His death was instantaneous and he suffered no pain. I was by his side when he died, and I*

hope this knowledge reassures you. He had a good character and he died doing his duty, I hope this will comfort you in your sorrow. I have been asked to express the deep sympathy of his platoon.

I remain, yours faithfully,

George Daft. (Private, 5th Leics).

Harry Gadsby sent an unusual letter to his sister-in-law.

25th October 1915.
France.
5th Leicestershire.

Dear sister-in-law,

Just a few lines hoping to find you well, as it leaves me in good health, although I am worried about George. I saw it in the Coalville times of October 22nd that he was reported as being killed! I hope you don't worry too much about it, although I know it is hard for you and Hilda! I would sooner it had been me a thousand times than him! When I last saw George he was in a shell hole between the lines, I should have stopped with him only there were several chaps with him, including Daft. A lot of bullets were flying about at the time so I went on and got into a captured trench. I gave him Hilda's photo the day before the battle, so he had it on him when he died. I hope this letter consoles you.

Love, Harry.

(George's death was confirmed in the Coalville Times on the 5th November 1915).

Mrs Gadsby also received a memorial card from Lord Aberconway containing lines of consolation for the widow.

In memory of Private George Gadsby, Fifth Leicestershire Battalion.

A gallant soldier who gave his life for his country in the Great War.

'If I should die, think only this of me:
That there's some corner of a foreign field
That is forever England. There shall be
In that rich earth a richer dust concealed;
A dust whom England bore, shaped, made aware,

Gave, once, her flowers to love, her ways to roam,
A body of England's, breathing English air,
Washed by the rivers, blessed by sons at home.

And think, this heart, all evil shed away,
A pulse in the eternal mind, no less
Gives somewhere back the thoughts by England given;
Her sights and sounds; dreams happy as her day;
And laughter, learnt of friends; and gentleness,
In hearts at peace, under an English heaven.
(The Soldier by Rupert Brooke. 1914).

Private George Gadsby was killed on the first day of the Charge of the Hohenzollern Redoubt.

His name can be found on the Coalville Clock Tower Memorial and on the Memorial Tablet in St. John The Baptist Church, Hugglescote and the same in St. Christopher's Parish Church, Ellistown.

Other local men of the Fifth Battalion killed in the Battle of The Hohenzollern Redoubt: Frederick Bartlam (one of the Famous Fifty) from Osbaston, Charles Betts of Sileby, James Biddles of Loughborough, Albert Brodribb of Moira, George Colver of Appleby Magna, George Fletcher of Ellistown, Lewis Gadd and John Hall of Mountsorrel, Captain R.A. Hastings of Ashby de la Zouch, George Henney of Ashby de la Zouch, John Monk of Loughborough, Ernest Newton of Shepshed, Ernest Pringle of Ashby de la Zouch, Thomas Squires of Loughborough, Francis Tunicliff of Castle Donnington, Albert Watterson of Mountsorrel.

Of the Fourth Leicestershire Battalion: 2nd Lieutenant Joseph Emmerson of Bagworth and Edward Tapp of Shepshed.

REGINALD HENRY ERNEST GLOVER M.M.

Reginald was born on the 27th November 1898 at Sileby, a village about twelve kilometres (eight miles) north of Leicester City centre. He was one of four sons including Edwin, Jack and Joe, born to Mr. & Mrs. William Glover. When he was three years old his parents moved to Hugglescote, with the family worshiping at St. John the Baptist Church and Reginald attending the Church School (along with many other future Great War soldiers). From his school days he fondly remembered the headmaster, Mr 'Johnny' Hubbard and the vicar, Canon Broughton.

Reginald was keen on physical activities and the outdoor life and liked the uniform of the

Reginald Henry Glover during his middle years. He served with the 2/5th Leicestershire Battalion from 1914-18 and was awarded the Military Medal for his bravery.

Hugglescote Church Lads' Brigade (C.L.B.), which he ultimately joined. At the age of thirteen years he left the happy confines of school to work as a miner at Ibstock Colliery. One year later his parents moved the few miles to the village of Bagworth, and Reginald successfully obtained employment at the colliery there (managed by Jabez Emmerson Snr).

Indeed, apart from his military service he continued to work at Bagworth Colliery until retirement. In his memoirs Reginald reflected that he could well remember the Miners' General Strike of 1911. '*All they were asking for was eight working hours a day for eight bob*.' (Bob = old shilling - 5 new pence).

Pre-war he was an outstanding football player and sprinter, and in the summer of 1914 was promised a professional footballing career with Everton Football Club at Liverpool. Reginald saw this as a wonderful opportunity to escape from the dirt and dangers of pit-life. Events of a worldly nature initially postponed and subsequently blighted any such dreams of stardom!

On the 4th August 1914 Reginald was in the company of hundreds of Leicestershire lads at Ripon in Yorkshire, for the Church Lads' Brigade annual camp. Orders were received to immediately return home! On the steam-train journey towards home an officer informed the excited bunch that the army was creating a new regiment, of which only C.L.B. personnel would be enlisted. It was to be known as the King's Royal Rifles (K.R.R.). By the time the train arrived at Coalville, Reginald and nine other local lads had agreed to join the K.R.R. On the Saturday morning they breezily walked to the top of Coalville to enlist. Reginald was only a lad of sixteen: '*a straightforward white lie pulled me through*.' When he jubilantly told his parents of his actions they were furious with worry, and his father ordered him to leave the house, which he did.

For the majority of the early volunteers, life changed little; they had a few train journeys to different barracks but they remained in civilian clothing. After three-four weeks they were called-up and entrained for Loughborough where they were billeted. Other units from all over Leicestershire gradually arrived over the weeks. Collectively they formed a new battalion, the Second Fifth (2/5th) Leicestershire. In November 1914 they welcomed an issue of uniforms, and at long last began to feel like soldiers. Reginald was rather vexed at the time, because he only received 7/6d (37^1/$_2$ new pence) for all the wear and tear to his civilian clothes. In the next month two hundred rifles arrived, only a fifth of the requirement, and so rifles and ammunition manufactured in Japan were distributed as a temporary measure. By late 1914 there was a general shortage of equipment, and new battalions had to wait their turn. It was not until late 1915 to early 1916 that the M.L.E. Mark 111 was issued to the 2/5th Battalion.

Reginald, service number 2540, and his friends were hoping to be part of the King's Royal Rifles, however, they were *more than content to be soldiers in the famed 'Tigers'*. Their battalion was swelled by soldiers from the 1/4th and 1/5th Battalions, who, for a variety of reasons were unwilling to undertake the imperial service obligation. (To fight abroad). These drafts of experienced 'terriers' proved of great assistance in training the raw recruits. In January 1915 they were absorbed into a new Division, the 59th (2nd) North Midland Division.

The 2/5th Battalion was at Loughborough for quite some time receiving training, most of the outdoor preparation in the town's parks, of which there were several, with indoor activities in Granby Street's Drill Hall, home of the 1/5th Battalion.

In late January 1915 three senior officers met at the Crown Hotel at Luton to discuss a telegram from the War Office: *'Are you prepared to receive troops?'* Following the answer it was left to the Civil Police of Luton to receive and arrange for billets for ten thousand soldiers.

The Coalville Times of the 5th February 1915 informed: *'The soldiers have progressed quickly in smartness and efficiency under the command of Lieutenant Colonel E. C. Atkins. He is a Hinckley man and chairman of the local hosiery firm that carries his name.*

Orders were received on the Wednesday to leave the area and the Battalion fell-in in the Market Place, (just like the 1/5th in August 1914) at nine in the morning, and marched to the Midland Station around one hour later. Two special trains took them to a destination unknown.' It also revealed that a few of the 2/5th had been sent to the Fifth (1/5th) Battalion and a few have been selected to guard German prisoners.

In the early days of the war the Battalion was classified as the Fifth Reserve, and the 'destination unknown' was of course, Luton, forming a section of the Third Army, Central Force. During the spring of 1915 men were often transferred to the Fifth (1/5th)

Leicestershire and occasionally vice-versa, as was to prove necessary, mainly to top-up battalion losses on the Western Front.

The 2/5th Battalion, part of the 177th Brigade, was given a few hours notice to entrain for Liverpool and embark for Ireland following trouble that started on the 24th April 1916. It began at the Easter Monday Race Meeting of the Meath Hunt just outside of Dublin, and spread into the city centre. The 178th Brigade of the 59th Division were first to disembark at Kingstown and four battalions of Sherwood Foresters were sent to control the heavy fighting which was labelled, the 'Irish Rebellion.' The troops were ambushed and Major-General A. E. Sandbach, C.B., D.S.O. wrote: *'Five officers and one hundred and fifty other ranks approximately became casualties,'* hence they became 'the Army of Occupation in Ireland.' The 2/5th Battalion was quickly deployed to Ballsbridge, a strong I.R.A.suburb of Dublin, and arrested ringleaders of that organisation. The Battalion was outstanding, and the Easter Uprising was quelled within five days and no casualties incurred. A resident of Ballsbridge, Harry Butler, wrote to Lt. Colonel Atkins congratulating him on the conduct of the Leicestershire Regiment, and that it had won golden opinions from all over the district.

Sir John French, as Commander of Chief of Home Forces made a tour of inspection of military establishments and reviewed the entire Division on the great open area on the Curragh. It was described as a good old-fashioned review and march past, carried out by young soldiers in fine style, and the praise from the veteran Field Marshal was unstinted and well earned.

Reginald continues: *'Our first active service came with the Easter Irish Up-rising in April 1916. We were shipped to Ireland not knowing anything about it, and given orders that we must carry our weapons at all times, and not to walk alone. We were also instructed to fire on unauthorised civilians carrying weapons. Two other English battalions supported us. The shooting in Dublin did not last long, but not without its casualties. Our Company was then sent to Trallee (County Kerry), the others to Fermoy. We had to detain any known leaders of the Movement and anyone behaving in a suspicious*

Private Reginald Glover, rear row and third from the left. He is with soldiers of the 1/5th and 2/5th Leicestershire Battalions at Loughborough in October 1914.

manner. This was very difficult because we found to our cost that even certain women and children could not be trusted. We were about one hundred and sixty strong, and we split into quarters to cover different areas, regrouping at sunset at predestined places.

The time came, early February 1917, when we were shipped to England and entrained for Aldershot where the King inspected us on the 13th February 1917.'

Reginald continued: 'By March 1917 our whole Division was stationed around Mericourt on the Western Front. I have recorded our involvements below.

1) March 17th - April 5th, the German retreat to the Hindenburg Line.

2) September 23 - 25th, Battle of Menin Road Ridge, Ypres.

3) September 27th - 28th, Battle of Polygon Wood, Ypres Salient.

4) November 28th, Battle of Bourlon Wood, Cambrai.

5) November 30th - December 3rd, German Counter Attacks, Cambrai.

6) March 21st-23rd 1918, Battle of St. Quentin.

7) March 24 - 25th, Battle of Bapaume.

8) April 14 - 15th, Battle of Bailleul.

9) First Battle of Kemmel Ridge.

10) August 21st - 22nd, Battle of Albert, Somme.

11) October 2nd - November 11th 1918, The Final Advance.

Altogether our 2/5th Battalion lost over one hundred and fifty officers and other ranks during battles that were waged on the Western Front.'

The Division hadn't been in the frontline long when the Germans retired across the Somme in March 1917. They left behind a scorched-earth policy and difficult times for the pursuing raw troops, having to contend with destroyed roads, railways, bridges, houses, poisoned food and water wells. There were also many fatalities as troops entered booby-trapped dugouts or opened containers, etc! Soon it was ordered that all troops were to live entirely under canvas.

From September 1st the Division went into billets around Winnezeele in Flanders. The troops marched through the ruins of Ypres to relieve the 55th Division after their success opposite Gravenstafel on the opening day, September 20th, of the big battle.

The Battle of Polygon Wood in the Ypres Salient was an experience that stuck deep in Reginald's mind, and only a few days later Colonel Philip Bent won a posthumous Victoria Cross on the same battlefield. On the 29th September New

Zealanders relieved the Division, which had suffered two thousand casualties in the recent ferocious battles. They retired for the night to Poperinghe, it was a brilliant moonlit night and enemy bombers dropped 250 bombs on the town, incredibly there were no casualties.

They retired to the Lens district, which at that time was relatively peaceful, and on November 20th marched during dark hours only (to avoid aircraft reconnaissance) to arrive twelve days later to relieve the Guards within the salient of Bourlon Wood, just to the west of Cambria. On December 1st the enemy launched a heavy bombardment and deluged the area with gas shells, their attack was beaten-off with great success, but not so further south where the enemy captured Gouzeaucourt and Gonnelieu, and placed the immediate frontline in peril. With the salient looking unsteady the troops were ordered to retire with the Germans hot on their tails.

Following a spell at Passchendaele in early 1918, then a quiet frontline stagnating in an environment of craters filled with foul water and bodies from 1917, they moved a little to the south to counter the German Spring Offensive of March 1918. **Shortly before this date the 2/5th Leicestershire Battalion had been disbanded**, with most of their troops being posted to bring the 1/5th and 1/4th Leicestershire Battalions up to full strength. A few men may have stayed with the 59th Division but most were posted to the 46th North Midland Division. I will, nevertheless briefly continue with the service history of the 59th Division.

In the Spring Offensive the enemy had captured Armentieres and were pushing towards Neuve Eglise and Bailleul.

On the 14th April 1918 the 176th and 177th Brigades took-up positions around Locre, only to be swiftly moved to support a position directly in front of Bailleul that was under heavy attack. Initially the two brigades held their frontline (over five kilometres in length), but eventually it crumbled under a sustained bombardment and with successive waves of storm troopers. The excellent Lieutenant Colonel Roffey of 177 Brigade being killed in this battle, and shortly afterwards, thankfully, the enemy attack lost its momentum. On May 6th the Division retired to St. Omer and following a decision by the

supreme authorities to break-up several divisions, 159 became a casualty, all down to the massive wastage of our nation's manpower!

Returning to Reginald, his daughter, Barbara, recalls an incident when her father lay in a morgue amongst a collection of dead bodies to prevent being captured or shot by German troops.

Reginald Glover joined the Fifth Leicestershire Battalion at the Cambrin Right Sector just to the north of Loos. Reginald recalled: '*I stayed with the Leicestershire Regiment until I was badly wounded on the 1st November 1918, when making our third attack of the day. I was picked up by the stretcher-bearers, received first aid and then sent to hospital for an operation. After that I was shipped to Bristol Hospital on November 9th.*' It was a 'Blighty' but what use was that two days before war's end!" He received his wound whilst dragging a wounded officer from the battlefield into the relative safety of a shell-hole, and whilst doing so received a wicked wound to the knee from a piece of shrapnel. This wound was to prevent him from pursuing a career of a professional football player.

Reginald was kept in hospital until late March 1919, and was then sent to Grantham for an Army Discharge. When he arrived home to continue employment at Bagworth Colliery he was still only twenty-one years of age.

At no time did Reginald mention or write in his memoirs that **he was awarded the Military Medal** at Pontruet for outstanding bravery on the field of battle! Many thanks to his son, Philip, for providing this information.

The Military Medal
'*Your gallant conduct in the field on the 24th September 1918 as a company runner, in taking messages through heavy barrages has been reported to me, and I have much pleasure in reading the record of your gallantry*'. Signed: S. G. Cranfurd. *Brigadier General Commanding 18th Infantry Brigade. 11th October 1918.*'

Reginald continued to work at the colliery and after four years, in 1923, he married 'his dark haired beauty' Barbara Butler. Three years later in 1926 the couple were blessed with a son, Reginald. The couple then had to separate for a time during the Miner's

Strike, because they could no longer afford the small rent on their Ellistown cottage.

The years trickled by and Reginald and Barbara eventually had six children Reginald, Cathlyn, Margaret, Harry, Barbara and Philip.

Reginald wrote: '*I liked the camaraderie of the ex-servicemen's clubs and I was a member of The Royal British Legion. We had lads from Bagworth, Thornton, Stanton under Bardon, and Ellistown, and whenever we ran short of cash we arranged carnivals, whist-drives and flower shows, the public never let us down! We always helped our mates, I remember taking a new sewing machine round to one pal who had lost a leg, and this enabled his wife to make things and sell to bring in a bit of money.*

I recall another pal who'd lost part of his leg; he had a small pension but not enough! We took him to Nottingham to meet the medical board. They agreed it wasn't enough, but they wouldn't back date it.'

In the late 1920s he was appointed the workmen's representative for Bagworth Colliery. This gave him a seat on the Miners' Council, and after an area ballot he was appointed a Trustee.

When the Mines were nationalised in 1945, the Trustees were responsible for investing £35,000, and the dividends proved there worth to many miners over lots of years. He joined the Labour Party when Arthur Allen was the local Member of Parliament, and he attended monthly meetings at New Walk in the centre of Leicester.

'*I was elected Chairman of the Bosworth Labour Party the year we selected Woodrow Wyatt to represent Bosworth. As time went on I was elected onto the local Urban Council for the South East Ward. During this spell I was Chairman of two committees, Water and Baths and Plans and Development, and in 1953 Chairman of the Council. I was the first miner to hold such a position and the first to wear its Chain of Office. I must say two important items during my period of office was to provide first class lighting throughout the District. Another was to ensure that five hundred council houses and an old people's home were built on Green Hill, Coalville.*

I worked on the coalface for fifty-two years without an accident or illness and during this time I also attended daily, weekend and evening meetings. Fortnightly I attended discussions at colleges and schools arranged by the Labour Party, and also at home and abroad to such places as Oslo, Brussels and Geneva. I must not forget Labour Party Conferences, the Trades Union Council and Local Government Conferences.*'

The National Coal Board presented him with a certificate for 'Long and Meritorious Service'.

'*On looking back, none of these offices or activities was part of my design. I was usually pushed into them and did my best to improve the lot for the workingman.*

I could never have succeeded in achieving so much without the constant help and support of that dark haired girl I married back in 1923.'

As for Reginald's brothers, Edwin was killed in World War 2, and Joe never married but bought a house at 2, King's Walk, Leicester Forest East and invited his parents to live with him until they passed on.

Reginald was a typical father of his age, believing in discipline being akin to love. He also had a strong work ethic, and believed it important to work hard towards achieving any goals set for him in life! He taught his children to be realistic and to stand up for themselves, and his daughter, Barbara, says that it was the ideal upbringing for life's problems that are sure to come. Continuing, "*I helped my father on his allotment. I felt so proud on Sunday mornings when we walked from his Ellistown allotment with a barrel full of potatoes, cabbage, brussels, gooseberries, and a bunch of roses for mother.*"

Reginald died on 3rd July 1981 at the age of 83 years.

With many thanks to the late Harry Glover, Barbara Elliott and Philip Glover.

I hold a lot of respect for Reginald. He was a tough disciplinarian, but that never harmed his children and they knew he loved them. He devoted a lot of his spare time doing his utmost to improve the lot of the workingman. Like all of the names in this book, it was their innate qualities that held the name of Great Britain in high regard throughout the civilised world.

GEORGE DAVID LAWRENCE GOUGH

He always preferred to be addressed as: Lawrence, and as so I will continue. Born on the 27th March 1892 at Hucknall Tolkard, a village twelve kilometres (eight miles) northwest of Nottingham, his roots were of Leicestershire. His father, George Gough, was a Whitwick man while his mother, Naomi (nee Thompson, nee Blencoe of Husbands Bosworth), a village twenty-two kilometres (thirteen miles) south of Leicester city centre.

George, born in 1842, was a striking and familiar figure. An old soldier he stood at well over six feet and was powerfully built. He joined the West Riding Regiment as a sixteen year old (1859) and served for two years before a transfer to the East Norfolk Regiment. He had many escapades overseas including being nearly shipwrecked off Gibraltar; a 190 miles trek across South African desert regions (before rail) in 1865, and fought under Lord Napier in the 1868 Abyssinian war. Stationed at St. Helena in 1870-1 he brought home relics including a picture of Napoleon's tomb. Becoming ill George was invalided home from the latter post, and finally retired from the Army after twelve meritorious years. In later life he was to recount how the officers used to have their men flogged on the least of pretences. On leaving the military he settled for a while in Nottinghamshire and this is where he met his future wife and stepchildren.

For George the 1886 marriage was his first, however, Naomi's first husband, John Thompson, had died in 1880 and she was left with three children.

Lawrence, in many respects viewed as the youngest of four children, started his education at Beardall Street Infant School on the 13th April 1896. He was a clever lad and it was remarked he had a particularly strong character. In 1902 his elder stepbrother, John, and stepsister, Louisa, decided their future prospects lay in the new world, the United States of America. Louisa in particular became prosperous and occasionally returned to her homeland to shower expensive gifts upon her English family. Soon after their emigration the Gough family, Lawrence being ten and his other stepsister, Margaret, twenty-one years of age moved to Thringstone, a village three kilometres north of Coalville. The family lived on Bauble Yard, Main

Street, with George employed by Ashby Rural Council as a 'Roadman'.

Lawrence continued his education at the village school and progressed so well that the headmaster recommended he sat an entrance examination for the famed Ashby Grammar School. His parents were so pleased that they bought him a suit for him to wear whilst sitting the examination, he passed! He did extremely well at Ashby Grammar, particularly so with music: becoming an accomplished musician capable of composition and orchestration. He was also a vocalist of some merit. Upon leaving school the powerfully built young man was selected for a position within a solicitor's office, and his future appeared to be rosy.

Sgt. Lawrence Gough in 1915. He served with the 1/5th and the 2/5th Leicestershire between 1914-18.

Lawrence was an excellent all-round sportsman and it was only his parents' insistence to keep a 'proper' job that prevented him from becoming a professional with Blackburn Rovers Football Club, and likewise with Derbyshire County Cricket Club.

One can only guess why on Christmas Day, 1911, at the marriage of Lawrence Gough and Lillie

Football Team of the 1/5th Leicestershire Battalion 1916. Fourth row from the front, first left, George Smith. Third row from the front extreme left, Sergeant Walter Butterworth. Same row fourth from the right, Lawrence Gough. Second row on the right, Charles Hatter. The team lost 2-3 in the Brigade Final against the Fourth Leicestershire.

Burton at the Wesleyan Chapel at Thringstone, that his occupation was given as: Coal-miner. Perhaps the collieries paid a higher wage, but relatives and friends expected better from the well-educated nineteen year old! Settling at 190, Talbot Street, Whitwick he was happy at the colliery, and his powerful physique developed more so with physical labour. He also played regularly for local amateur football and cricket teams. Throughout his life he was a devoted and vociferous fan of Leicester City Football and Leicestershire County Cricket Club, spending a lot of time at Filbert Street and the cricket ground.

The couple's first child, Irene, was born on the 10th November 1913.

Perhaps his service career epitomises so many of his fine qualities and also what his son, Bert, describes: *"He was very strong-minded; a man who fiercely defended his opinions and did not suffer fools gladly."*

Lawrence enlisted at Coalville in mid-August 1914 into the 2/5th Leicestershire Battalion, and in the early stages followed an identical pathway to that of Private Reginald Glover.

The Coalville Times of the 19th March 1915 prints Lawrence Gough, together with twenty-five others serving with the King's Forces from St. Andrew's Parish. A further twenty-five were from the ecclesiastical portion of the parish: from outside the area. Whereas the majority were private soldiers, Lawrence was a sergeant, service number 2529 (240615). Indeed the local newspaper on the 5th March 1915 prints that he was promoted due to excellent progress; with his educational background a commission should have been forthcoming. It is known that he was friendly with Wilfred Sykes, who enlisted at the same time, and lived a few doors away and served in the same battalion.

On Friday 26th February 1915 Lawrence rushed home from Epping due to his father's poor health, only to return the following day with George much improved. Sadly, on Sunday 28th the old soldier died of heart failure (aged 72 years), and was buried at St. Andrew's Churchyard on March 3rd. Thirty members of the Whitwick and Thringstone Citizen Corpse were present as a bugler played the 'Last Post' by his grave.

An auntie of Bert's said that Lillie Gough

It was at this house, 190, Talbot Street, Whitwick, that Lawrence Gough and his wife, Lillie, made their first home around 1912. The couple's first child, Irene, was born there and Lawrence relished the physical activity and camaraderie of colliery life, together with football in the winter and cricket in the summer. It was all to change in 1914.

conceived her second born whilst visiting Lawrence during battalion training at Luton. Subsequently, Phyllis was born on the 1st January 1916.

It is known that on the 25th June 1915 Lawrence embarked with a batch of twelve returning casualties and eighty NCOs and men. The War Diary of June 27th states as much and expresses: *'a very welcome addition to our ranks!'* He joined the Battalion during its sojourn within the Ypres Salient, so he certainly had a baptism of fire.

Bert is uncertain of the reasons why his father, on more than one occasion, flipped between the Fifth (1/5th) and the Second-Fifth (2/5th) Battalions, also regarding the amount of stripes on his arms: increasing after bravery and good work, decreasing perhaps after being too outspoken. It must be written that whatever the circumstances, confrontational and questioning men such as Lawrence are an exceptional breed, and an essential requirement during times of warfare!

Apart from the early photograph of Sergeant Gough with the 2/5th Battalion there is a later one with him with the Fifth's (1/5th) Football team at Lucheux in the spring of 1916, so I feel it is likely he took part in the Battle of the Somme at Gommecourt.

For whatever reasons, Lawrence returned to the 2/5th Battalion and was engaged in the Battle of

Passchendaele Ridge, part of 3rd Ypres, which started on the 31st July 1917. The name evokes passionately strong feelings of loss, and rightly so. A dreadfully wet summer, aided by a heavy barrage totally destabilised an already high water margin. The Ridge was captured after sixteen weeks of vicious fighting in the worst possible of quagmires. Allied losses were nearly one third of a million, whilst the Germans suffered one quarter of a million. Many of the injured were never found; they collapsed in the glutinous mass and slid into the foul water-filled shell-craters. As part of this battle, and some seven kilometres (four miles) to the southeast, the British attacked at Polygon Wood. By 1917 the wood was a shell battered collection of stumps and exposed roots: ideal locations for machine-guns and snipers. (It is only four kilometres northeast of Trench 50, where several of the Famous Fifty were killed in 1915.)

On the 26th September 1917 the 2/5th Leicestershire Battalion opened the attack against Polygon Wood. Within their numbers were Sergeant Gough, Corporal Wilfred Sykes and Sergeant George Saddington of Coalville (appears later in this book).

The Sykes' family and the Gough's were related by marriage. On most days Wilfred's mother would ask Laurence's wife if any letters had arrived and vice-versa.

An important part of military discipline is that during an attack the only concern is the objective. If friends or colleagues are wounded by enemy action they must be ignored, irrespective of pleads, the momentum of the attack comes first! Bert has told me that relatives of the Gough and Sykes' families have long and often spoke of Lawrence: *"He carried Wilfred in you know, but he got into terrible trouble for it!"* Bert continues: *"The auntie who told me about the Sykes incident was born in 1902, so she was a teenager during the war and lived at home with her mother and father about three doors from the Sykes family. Even in old age, she spoke with pride of the deed by Lawrence."*

During the attack Wilfred Sykes was seriously wounded, rolling in agony close to the top of a crater. I've explained how Lawrence was independent minded: he would react to his ideals, in this instance it was to attempt to save Wilfred.

Lawrence 'carried his friend in', but Corporal Wilfred Sykes (service number 240594) died shortly afterwards, aged twenty-one years. He is buried at Dochy Farm New British Cemetery, seven kilometres (just over four miles) northeast of Ypres. He was the son of William and Eve Sykes of Co-operative Cottages at Thringstone. In all but military strategy this was an exceptionally brave deed. Shortly afterwards Sergeant L. Gough was summoned by his commanding officer and reduced to the ranks: he never regained his stripes!

The Wood was eventually taken, and Lieutenant Colonel Bent of the 9th Leicestershire won a posthumous Victoria Cross whilst defending an enemy counter attack on the 1st October 1917.

In early 1918 the dreadful losses incurred within the Leicestershire Regiment meant that as part of a reorganisation, the 2/5th Battalion was absorbed into the Fifth Leicestershire, and yet another return of Lawrence to that battalion!

The name of Wilfred Sykes can be read on the Memorial Plaque in St. Andrews Church, Thringstone. Included are the names of two of the Famous Fifty, Isaac Hall and James Bancroft.

After hostilities ceased on the Western Front, Lawrence joined the Royal Fusiliers, service number 129728, and went to Archangel in Russia to fight on behalf of the White Russian Army against the Red Communists. Bert believes that an officer of the Leicestershire Regiment persuaded Lawrence to accompany him with the new battalions (45th and 46th) for the Russian venture. Research shows that within the two battalions were eight Leicestershire Regimental officers. He returned from the deep-frozen wastes in December 1919.

Lawrence and Lillie had a further six children, George David (4th May 1921), Thomas Eric (25th February 1923), Joyce (20th March 1925), John Raymond (13th April 1927), Albert (Bert) William (5th September 1929) and Rita Naomi (30th October 1933).

In the mid-thirties the family moved to Deal, fourteen kilometres (nine miles) to the north of Dover on the Kent coast, with Lawrence working in the local coalmines. Unfortunately, he received a serious injury and had to look for alternative employment. This he found at Kilburn, six kilometres (four miles) northwest of Westminster in central London, employed as a lathe operator. He grieved at Lillie's passing at a relatively young age in

A section showing the inside of the Hohenzollern Redoubt following its capture. It was against this formidable system of dugouts and machine-gun nests that the soldiers of Leicestershire attacked with disastrous consequences.

Ruth and Lawrence Gough enjoying a holiday walk. Circa 1950. His first wife, Lillie died in 1940.

1940. Bert recalls time in London during the bombing Blitz of autumn 1940 into early 1941: "*I was twelve years old and a gang of us used to collect shrapnel—sometimes it was still warm!*"

Lawrence married for the second time in 1946, Ruth Elkin, a German girl of Jewish decent who had fled from Germany just prior to World War 2.

Lawrence was a brave, tough, no nonsense sort of person and he brought-up his children with a degree of discipline. What I find noteworthy is that when he had to choose, he attempted to save the life of his best friend, irrespective of his platoon. Militarily an incorrect decision, but it showed that beneath a bluff exterior beat a heart of warmth and compassion. In only slightly different circumstances, for instance, if he had died sacrificing his life to save a friend he would have been merited with 'no greater love'.

Bert continues: "*If ever I asked father anything about the war, he would close his eyes and shake his head. He took me to the Cenotaph at London when I was about eleven years of age, and it was quite a shock to see this tough ex-coal-miner and thousands of others crying like babies.*" In his later years, Lawrence told his daughter, Rita, that at Polygon

Wood he told Wilfred Sykes to keep his head down because it was 'hotting-up'. He also said that Wilfred was so badly wounded that he just could not leave him lying there!

Again with Bert: "*Years ago my brother, John and I went to visit our grandmother and decided to visit the 'Rose and Crown' for a lunchtime drink. An elderly gentleman in a wheelchair asked us if we were Lawrence Gough's boys. He said he was with him in France and that he was a good bloke to be with, kept us out of trouble, looked after us. He remembered one of Sergeant Gough's men being wounded, and that he shouted "Don't leave me here Goughie"—and your dad went back and got him! He ended up in trouble for this as well.*"

"*As a young man I used to find people praising my father quite embarrassing, as one does. I could recall my sister telling me about a Mrs Moss writing to our father on several occasions regarding her son. He had served with father and wanted to know how he died! Years later when I was in London with my father we were passing William Moss and Sons Depot (London, Loughborough and Liverpool) when my father mentioned that he was with the son in World War 1, but he wouldn't continue the conversation! Years later I checked out the name and it was 2nd Lieutenant Howard James Harding Moss of the Fifth Battalion, and he was killed at the charge of the Hohenzollern Redoubt on the 13th October 1915. The War Diary states that Captain Hastings and 2nd Lieutenant Moss were leading a charge towards the junction of 'Little Willie' and 'N. Face' and were killed near the second enemy line by a combination of bombs and machine-gun fire!*"

Lawrence continued his sporting prowess between the two wars, especially cricket, and the famous benefactor, Charles Booth, always picked him to play against Leicestershire County Cricket Club in their annual game at Gracedieu Manor. He was happy enough working down the mines and loved the camaraderie between the men, maybe that was what attracted him to the job in the first place.

Son Raymond recalls his father taking him to Wembley to watch Leicester City lose to Wolverhampton 3:1. "*I was really surprised that it made my father cry with emotion!*"

Lawrence died in London in 1968, aged

MINISTRY OF DEFENCE CS(RM)2b
Bourne Avenue Hayes Middlesex UB3 1RF

Telephone 0181-573 3831 ext 318

Mr R Robinson
86A Park Lane
Thatcham
Newbury
Berkshire
RG13 3PG

Your reference

Our reference

94/80982/CS(RM)2b/1

Date

22 June 1995

Dear Mr Robinson

In reply to your letter, I apologise for the delay in replying. Our
records show the following particulars of the military service of
16712 Private Joseph ROBINSON - Leicestershire Regiment.

Enlisted into the Leicestershire Regiment short service
  (for the Duration of the War)

Posted to the Depot	12.01.15
Posted to the 3rd Battalion	12.01.15
Posted to the 2nd Battalion	17.01.15
Posted to the Egyptian Expeditionary Force (Persian Gulf)	04.05.15
Posted to the Depot India	10.11.15
Posted to the Depot England	04.07.16
Posted to the 3rd Battalion	01.01.17
Discharged "Ceasing to fulfil Army physical requirements	26.06.17
	26.09.17

Overseas Service: France   04.05.15 to 09.11.15
                Egypt/India 10.11.15 to 31.07.16

Medals issued etc: 1914-15 Star, British War Medal, Victory Medal.

Further information available:

Age on enlistment - 31 years 148 days
Address on enlistment - Baubel Yard, Thringstone, Leicester.
Civilian trade - Collier
Next of kin - Wife, Margaret Ellen ROBINSON (nee THOMPSON)
Married - 23.12.05
Children - Joseph   born 14.09.10
            Roland   born 26.02.12
            Naomi   born 04.05.13
            Walter   born 26.12.15

You are advised that military service documents are of a purely
administrative nature and do not therefore contain detailed
information regarding the exact locations and movements of
individual servicemen or Units.

Information of this nature may be available however from the
"Commanders War Diaries" which are held by the Public Records
Office, Ruskin Avenue, Kew, Richmond, Surrey TW9 4DU. 0181 3925200.

Recycled Paper

The War Record of Private Joseph Robinson, a relative of Lawrence Gough.

seventy-six years. A born leader of men. A free spirit who challenged authority and spoke his mind. If he had been more diplomatic he would have been commissioned: on more than one occasion he was overlooked for awards for bravery. In all respects a very brave and resolute man who throughout life would swim against the current if he felt it necessary! Society needs a quota of clever strong-minded men.

Incidentally, Bert's grandmother, Naomi (nee Blencoe), was related to Sir John and Lady Blencoe of an earlier century. Bert said she was a forceful character, so it is not difficult to see why Lawrence was the man he was.

His stepsister, Margaret, married Thringstone man, Joseph Robinson*, and they lived next door to her mother in the Baubel Yard at Thringstone.

Joseph, aged thirty-one, enlisted into the Leicestershire Regiment on the 12th January 1915, and after spending three months of training with the 3rd Battalion was posted to the 2nd Battalion on the 4th May 1915. Private Robinson was with the Battalion in France for six months and for the same period in the Middle East, before a posting to the Depot in India on the 4th July 1916. He may have been recovering from wounds because he returned to England on the 1st January 1917 and was discharged: '*Ceasing to fulfil Army physical requirements on the 26th September 1917.*

* See service record on earlier page.

Many thanks to Bert Gough for his friendship and information, likewise to Ray Gough.

EDWARD FEWKES-GRIFFIN
AND HAROLD DEAKIN

Edward Fewkes-Griffin with daughter, Arlene in 1947

Edward was born on 10th October 1894 on North Street, Whitwick. He was the first born of five children, his sisters being, Rebecca, Emma, Frances and the youngest, a brother, Arthur. Their father, Charles Fewkes-Griffin was a participant in South Africa during the Boer War, working as a farrier for the British Army.

Upon leaving school Edward was employed as a miner at Whitwick Colliery.

Shortly after the outbreak of the Great War he took the bus to Loughborough, enlisted, and was allocated to the Fourth (1/4th) Battalion of the Leicestershire Regiment, and followed the training programme for recruits at Luton, etc, as described in my earlier book.

During the Battle of Hohenzollern Redoubt on the 13th October 1915, an enemy bullet struck his rifle butt and was deflected into his left arm, causing serious damage to his muscles. After hospitalisation in England the Military Injuries Board decided that he was no longer suitable for frontline duties, sic: '*No longer capable of supporting or aiming a rifle.*'

He was upset to be invalided out of the Battalion, but six or seven months later he travelled to Tamworth and voluntarily enlisted into a Pioneer Company, who were desperately in need of men, so becoming a soldier in the South Staffordshire Regiment.

Edward, still a strong and able man, was detailed to trench-digging and vital carrying duties, such as food, drink and ammunition supplies. In 1916, whilst serving in the Neuve Chapelle Sector he was gassed, and was once again returned to a hospital in England. For two/three months he convalesced at Whitstable, on the Kent coast, where fresh air eased the symptoms and helped the recovery process.

Returning to his unit, Edward, in the summer of 1917, was involved in Third Ypres: the Battle of Paschendaele. During a ferocious spell an officer appealed for anyone who could shoot a gun, and Edward swiftly volunteered. Whilst under cover in a shell-hole he shot two German troopers, and in spite of being shielded by human remains received serious shrapnel wounds to the foot. It proved to be a 'Blighty' wound and terminated the military career of a brave and determined soldier.

Upon returning to northwest Leicestershire he rejoined Whitwick Colliery and subsequently married Frances Cooke (born 5th December 1893), settling down to a happy home life at 40, Broughton Street, Coalville. They had three children, Edward Terence (Terry), born 1924, Norma, who never married (1927-1961) and Gwen (1929-1976) who married Ivan Morris and had two children, Steven and Susan.

Edward died on 8th December 1976, aged 82 years, and he lays at rest in Broom Leys' Cemetery, Coalville.

His son, Terry, was to join the Royal Navy and become a Petty Officer by the age of twenty years during World War 2, and much more can be read of his experiences in a later book.

A wartime friend of Edward's was Leicester born Edwin Barnes, who later moved to Ellistown and opened a shop: a ladies and gents outfitter. He employed a very young Terry Griffin to deliver goods by bicycle to Bagworth and Ibstock on Saturday mornings, and the odd evening. Terry recalls: "*Mr. Barnes was also gassed during the war, and I*

Edward Fewkes-Griffin circa 1968.

remember that he had two bayonets hanging from the living room wall. He used to pay me about three shillings for my deliveries, and I felt quite rich."

Harold Deakin

Another good friend of Edward's was Hugglescote man, Harold Deakin. Born on 24th November 1897 he attended St. John The Baptist Church and Church School, and became a miner on leaving school. He knew many of Coalville's Famous Fifty.

Harold enlisted into the 1/5th Battalion of the Leicestershire Regiment on the 9th June 1913: he was just fifteen years of age, but totally acceptable for the purposes of home defence. Harold and Ellistown's William Barney were young pre-war soldiers together.

When the war commenced, at aged sixteen, he was too young for service overseas and was duly reposted to the 2/5th (Reserve) Leicestershire Battalion. His service number was 1648 and revised in 1916 as 240223. During the war, Harold was in the same unit as Percy Cliff and Reginald Glover.

The 2/5th Battalion, part of the 177th Brigade, 59th North Midland Division, was given a few hours notice to entrain for Liverpool and embark for

Private Harold Deakin: circa 1914.

The future Mrs. Gladys Deakin. 'Dolly.'

Ireland following trouble that started on the 24th April 1916. It began at the Easter Monday Race Meeting of the Meath Hunt just outside of Dublin, and spread into the city centre. The 178th Brigade were first to disembark at Kingstown and four battalions of Sherwood Foresters were sent to control the heavy fighting which was labelled, the 'Irish Rebellion.' The troops were ambushed and Major-General A. E. Sandbach, C.B., D.S.O. wrote that: '*five officers and one hundred and fifty other ranks approximately became casualties,*' hence the Division became an 'Army of Occupation.

Corporal Harold Deakin (centre) with friends in France 1917.

The 2/5th Battalion was quickly deployed to Ballsbridge, a strong I. R.A. suburb of Dublin, and arrested ringleaders of that organisation. The Battalion excelled, and the Easter Uprising was quelled within five days and no casualties were incurred.

Reginald Glover's Company was then sent to Trallee (County Kerry), whilst Harold went to Fermoy. At the New Barracks Camp he received, amongst others, two postcards that congratulated him on his nineteenth birthday. The first was from his parents. '*Dear Harold, Wishing you many happy returns, and please send a piece of cardboard the size of your finger, we can buy you a ring. Love from Mother and Dad xxxx.*'

The second card: '*Wishing you many happy returns. From you sister, Mary. xxxx*'.

The Battalion had to detain any known leaders of the Movement and anyone behaving in a suspicious manner. This was very difficult because even certain women and children could not be trusted.

In early February 1917, they were shipped to England and entrained for Aldershot where the King inspected them on the 13th February 1917." By March 1917 the whole Division was stationed around Mericourt on the Western Front.

Harold saw plenty of fierce action on the Western Front, still with the same Battalion: 59th North Midland Division, and was subsequently promoted to corporal and later sergeant.

(Details of this action can be read in Reginald Glover's essay.)

Post war he returned to mining at Whitwick Colliery, well known as 'Leggy' (because of his rather long legs in proportion to his frame.)

He married Gladys (always called Dolly), a local girl, and had a long and happy married life. Gladys' sister married one of the Choyce brothers (relatives of the author). George and Dan Choyce were owners of 'Mattersons', an engineering firm manufacturing shuttles and looms, etc, anything requiring milling, drilling and centre lathes.

For most of their married life the couple lived at 14, Broom Leys Road, and like so many other folk in the district housed an evacuee during the Second World War.

Harold became a deeply religious man:

Harold Deakin stands second from the right back row at Briton's Camp, St. Albans, Hertfordshire. August 1915.

The reverse of the above postcard of Harold Deakin at Briton's Camp.

2/5th Battalion Leicestershire Regiment: 'Somewhere in England: 1914-15.' Middle row, second from the left: Stanley Butler who died of wounds on 9th Sept 1918. Back row: fourth from left: Harold Deakin.

becoming verger at St. David's Chapel in Broom Leys, and his wife, possessing a splendid voice, was a member of the choir. Harold was a close friend to two other parishioners, Great War veterans and members of the Famous Fifty, namely (Captain) Jabez Emmerson and (Lieutenant) Walter Handford.

The grim reaper eventually took Harold on Christmas Day 1969, aged seventy-two years, with Gladys surviving until February 1984.

Whereas time has washed away many memories of Harold, I was spoilt for choice with photographs.

I am indebted to Terry Griffin for the above information and photographs. Only recently Terry found another old photograph: it is of an old pal of Harold's: Corporal Stanley Butler. Stanley was a Hinckley man who transferred from the 2/5th to the 2/4th Battalion of the Leicestershire Regiment. They kept in touch, with Stanley, service number 241872, sending a card in 1918 to Harold and stating he was a temporary sergeant. The friendship was lost, but not the card, when Stanley died of wounds on 4th September 1918.

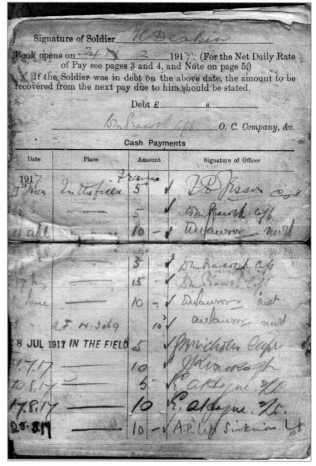

Corporal Harold Deakin's pay book.

REGINALD RAWDON-HASTINGS

Reginald was the elder son of the Hon. Paulyn Rawdon-Hastings and Lady Maud Hastings of the Manor House at Ashby de la Zouch. He was the grandson of Baron Donington and Lady Edith Hastings and nephew of the Earl of Loudoun and the Duke of Norfolk, and heir to the Donington and Loudon estates.

He was born at Old Park, Ashby de la Zouch on the 27th November 1889, and educated at Eton and Christ Church, after which he was private secretary for Sir A. Griffiths Boscawen.

A keen sportsman he often turned out for Ashby de la Zouch cricket team with such friends as Aubrey Moore, the brothers John,

Captain Reginald Rawdon-Hastings was an Ashby de la Zouch man who fought with the Fifth Leicestershire Battalion until he was killed leading a charge at the Battle of the Hohenzollern Redoubt on the 13th October 1915.

Charles and Joseph Shields and Roland Farmer.

Reginald was a pre-war territorial officer and was with the Fifth Leicestershire Battalion at their annual training camp at Bridlington when war was declared.

Born with a powerful physique and imbued with the chivalry and bravery of his great ancestors, he also possessed a natural charm and confidence. Reginald had all the qualities to make an ideal officer to lead his men in the conflict that shortly followed.

It was written that he was quick to see where danger lay and eager to act upon it, often exposing himself to considerable risk, and his attitude won him the esteem and admiration of his fellow officers and

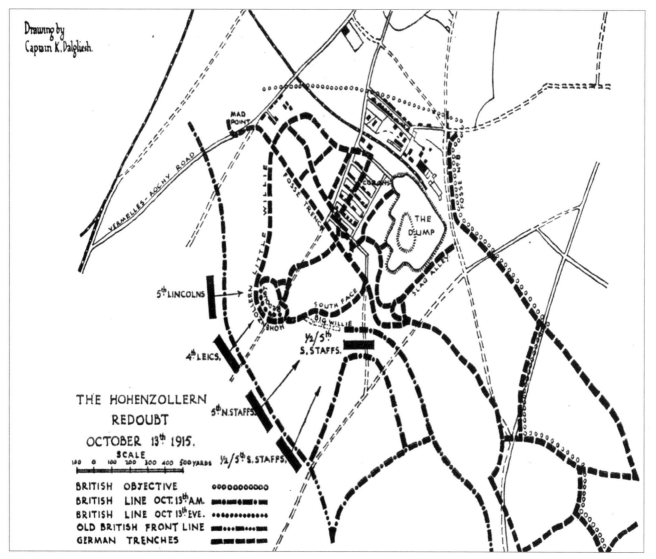

Drawing by Captain K. Dalgliesh.

THE HOHENZOLLERN
REDOUBT
OCTOBER 13th 1915.

SCALE
100 0 100 200 300 400 500 YARDS

BRITISH   OBJECTIVE   ooooooooooo
BRITISH   LINE OCT. 13th A.M. ■■o■■o■■o■o■
BRITISH   LINE OCT 13th EVE.   ••••••••••••••
OLD BRITISH FRONT LINE   ■■•••■■•••■■
GERMAN   TRENCHES   ■■■■■■■■■■■

After the initial attack by the 5th Lincolns, Captain Hastings led his men forward and bayonet charged the left of the Redoubt. They had almost reached the second line of trenches when a hail of machine-gun bullets killed the gallant officer and 2nd Lieutenant Moss.

men. In the military his attitude was necessarily stern and unyielding, but he was also invariably kind and considerate, and self-interest never clouded his judgements.

He landed in France with the Fifth Leicestershire Battalion in February 1915, as second in command of 'A' Company under Major W. S. N. Toller, a Quorndon man. He fought with the Battalion on the Messines Ridge and on the Ypres salient. On the death of his batman, Private Frederick Pringle, on the 1st September 1915, he sent a sympathetic and consoling letter to Mr. & Mrs. Walter Pringle. He wrote of how they used to chat in the dugout about their lives when the war was over. During the artillery bombardment, which killed his batman, he was buried and stunned and was dug out by his men.

The brave Captain, aged twenty-six years, lost his life leading his men at the Charge of the Hohenzollern Redoubt on the 13th October 1915. The War Diary states: *'Captain Hastings of 'A'*

Company decided to attempt a bayonet attack against the German opposition on the left of the Redoubt, and he himself led his men in the attack. Platoon commanders were again the first to fall as they climbed out of their trenches, 2nd Lieutenant Lawton was mortally wounded in the stomach and 2nd Lieutenant Petch badly shot through the arm. However this did not delay the attack, and the Company crossing the German frontline quickened their pace and made for the junctions of 'Little Willie' and 'N. Face.' Once more bombs and machine-guns were too hot for them, and first Captain Hastings, then 2nd Lieutenant Moss were killed near to the German second line.'

2nd Lieutenant Moss was only nineteen years old; he was the son of Mr. & Mrs. Wilfred Moss of the Knoll, Nanpanton, near Loughborough.

The Battalion lost four officers and twenty-two other ranks killed, six officers and one hundred and thirty-two men wounded with thirteen men missing (killed). Another of Captain Hastings's brother officers was badly wounded in the charge, namely Lieutenant W. N. Riley, the Leicestershire C.C.C. and Cambridge University cricketer. One of his legs was so shattered that it had to be amputated, the other was in a mess and he was also wounded in the head. His parents resided at Appleby Magna.

Lance Corporal T. Ault sent a letter home after the gallant charge led by his officer. '*I shall never forget the 13th as long as I live. I shall never forget Captain Hastings's last words to the Fifth Leicestershire and then he got hit. We shall feel his loss very much as he was a grand officer and liked by very many of his men.*'

Most who knew Captain Hastings felt that he died as he had lived; they knew that put to the ultimate test he would give everything for King and country.

A recorded incident reveals the depth and soul of the man. Without his knowledge he was seen by fellow officers bending over the form of a wounded German soldier, supporting his head and giving him a drink of water, and consoling him in his dying agony. It was also observed that a smile of gratitude was on the German's face as he passed away.

Certainly Captain Hastings is fondly remembered in his hometown to this day. He was keenly interested in local affairs and was always to the fore in ensuring that only good fortune came to Ashby de la Zouch, indeed as an epitaph it could be written that his one desire in public life was to do good. He was patron of the living of Ashby de la Zouch and was a sidesman at the Church of St. Helen's. He was deeply devoted to the Church, whose influence upon him was seen in many of his acts. One of the last of these, when home on leave shortly after the death of his brother, was the sending out of two-hundred and fifty Prayer Books to the men of his Company in the frontline. Also, he had recently erected upon the family burial ground in the Chapel at the Castle, a large crucifix of exquisite design, which he obtained when on a visit to Italy. A muffled peal was rung on the bells of the Parish Church on Tuesday, October 19th 1915, and the family flag, bearing the manche, flew at half-mast from the Earl's Tower at the Castle.

Reginald's younger brother, Edward, was born in 1895 and was educated at Eton and was still at Magdalen College, Oxford when the war broke out. He was granted a commission with the regiment that his forefathers had distinguished themselves in, the Black Watch. After serving at the front for eight months, Lieutenant Edward Rawdon-Hastings was admitted to Boulogne Hospital in September 1915 with enteric fever. It was considered so serious that Lady Hastings travelled out to be with him, and she was until he died on the 15th September 1915. It is written that the twenty year old had a pleasing and agreeable manner and was well liked. He also had a high conception of duty, to which he added zeal and energy that was very marked. He is interred in the cemetery at Wimereux, near Boulogne.

A public memorial service was held in the Parish Church, Ashby de la Zouch, on Wednesday, October 27th, at 3.00 pm, in memory of Captain Hastings and Lieutenant Hastings.

An interesting article appeared in the Leicester Mercury (29th May 2006) entitled: '**THIS IS MICHAEL, HE COULD BE OUR KING.**'

Michael Abney-Hastings was travelling from Australia with a film crew to make a documentary about his claim to the throne. Michael's claim stems from recent evidence that King Edward 1V was an illegitimate birth and therefore the royal line should have passed to Edward's brother. In 2003 it emerged, following research by historian, Doctor Michael Jones, that details in Rouen Cathedral proved that the earlier King was illegitimate. He said: "I was looking into the cathedral records of the 100 Years War and found that it stated that Edward was conceived in 1441 to the Duke of York. This was physically and geographically impossible because he was away fighting at Pontois. I couldn't quite believe this at first, something as scandalous and sensational as this, but it did!"

If that had been the case, Michael (14th Earl of Loudoun) would have now been King of Great Britain and her Commonwealth. Michael's family lived in Ashby Castle in the 15th century.

Author's footnote.

It is a sobering point that possibly, it was Reginald Rawdon-Hastings who was the last 'KING' of our nation to be killed in battle.

BERNARD HATTER

Bernard was born in 1895 on North Street, later named Central Road, at Hugglescote. His father, Thomas (Tom) Hatter was born in 1867, and was a master-carpenter who employed several craftsmen in a building and joinery company. Tom had an elder brother, Charles, born in 1862, and one of his sons; also named Charles was one of the Famous Fifty.

Bernard's mother, Sarah Anne (nee Rawlinson), came from a well-respected Wigston family.

She was an excellent speaker and before marriage was a teacher at the Hugglescote Church School. Bernard had a younger sister, Gladys, who was born in 1897, and like her mother became a teacher, this time at the Infant's section of Bridge Road School at Coalville.

Bernard was a choirboy at St. John The Baptist and he also attended their Church School, knowing many of the people whom I have mentioned in my books. He was an outgoing and confident young man with a determined personality. He was par for the course as a patrol-leader with the Coalville Scout Troop, and was friendly with fellow scouts such as Frederick Hart, Charlie Jewsbury, Johnnie Lowe and Allen Ford. Upon leaving school he joined the family

2nd Lieutenant Bernard Hatter, 2nd Leicestershire Battalion, April 1915.

business, and did not disguise his ultimate aim of running his own carpentry concern.

In pre-war days Bernard is mentioned several times in the Coalville Times. They reported that he had excellent musical qualities, and that he sang with the 'Coalville Lyric Quartette'.

It was also reported that he was a fine all-round sportsman, and invariably took-up the challenge as opening batsman for St. John The Baptist Cricket Team.

His adventurous spirit, and love of the outdoors led him to enlisting into the Fifth Leicestershire Territorial Battalion in 1913. He almost certainly enlisted at Ashby de la Zouch, where, as a young man his father was in the Ashby Company of the Leicestershire Rifle Volunteers. In the Battalion at that time were men like Bill Barney, Charlie Jewsbury and George Gadsby. Tall and fit, Bernard made an immediate impact and rapidly received promotion, and at the outbreak of war he was at the annual summer camp at Bridlington.

Not one of the Famous Fifty, however he was educated and grew-up with many of them, and was with them for several months prior to their embarkation. When Sergeant Stone of the Seaforth Highlanders had completed his task, that of providing two months of basic training for the Fifty

Bernard and Gladys Hatter early 1900s.

Bernard Hatter at St. John The Baptist Church, Hugglescote, in the early 1900s.

near to Coalville, he received a presentation. The Coalville Times of October 1914 announced that Sergeant Bernard Hatter, speaking on behalf of the Fifty, thanked the Highlander for his excellent efforts and presented him with a dressing case. The Fifty then entrained for Luton and Bernard helped with their training programme. Whatever and whenever he was asked to do a job, he accomplished it in a very professional manner, and although only nineteen years of age was a natural leader of men. Bernard was no different to all those around him, he was desperately wanting to prove himself on the field of battle. He was convinced that he would accompany the Battalion in the very near future to France. Unfortunately his ability went against him, and he was dreadfully disappointed! Instead the Regiment graded him as an officer cadet. Some soldiers may have been delighted at promotion, but not so Bernard. Whilst on leave in January 1915, he informed his parents that he had been selected for officer training, a course which would take three months. He returned to Luton and bade a fond farewell to his friends (and cousin, Charles) in the Fifth Battalion, and vowed that one day they would all meet up again.

He was duly promoted to 2nd Lieutenant on the 27th April 1915, and posted to the 2nd Leicestershire Battalion (regulars). He was given home leave and then, as was the local custom was invited to ride with the Quorn Hunt on a few occasions. Shortly afterwards he embarked and joined the 2nd Battalion in France. Following a period in the frontlines he was posted to the School of Mortars, to receive instruction on all matters concerning commanding a battery of trench-mortar-guns. Bernard was then detailed to report to the 3rd Leicestershire Battalion in France.

The Battle of Loos has long been a black day in the history of the British Army! Never had it been the intention of British Generals to attack the strong German defences in the Loos Sector of France in 1915. They were forced by political imperative to conduct such an operation at the bequest of the French, who were suffering horrendous casualties at the nearby Battle of Artois!

The Hugglescote home of Tom and Sarah Hatter, they never fully recovered from the loss of their son in 1915.

The omens leading up to the battle were ominous. The British soldiers had marched for days to this sector, and as a result were weary, and never had the opportunity for rest. To the rear the lines of communication were fragmenting, as troops intended to support the first waves of attackers were finding progress difficult in congested communication trenches. On the 25th September 1915, at 5.48 am, a huge roar was heard when one ton of gun cotton in a British mine was detonated! Two minutes later British guns laid a heavy barrage on German trenches, and at 6.00 am the 'poor old infantry' went 'over the top' under the screen of smoke shells. We erroneously or recklessly released some of our gas, and the treacherous breeze betrayed to the extent whereby some of our own troops were gassed! The errant breeze then removed the smoke screen to expose our forward units.

A counter barrage and enemy machine-gun fire produced heavy casualties, yet still some enemy lines were reached and breached, but with dreadful losses, **especially to officers**. The War Diary quotes: *"Cannot record battle with accuracy, owing to the impossibility of observation due to the impenetrable wall of smoke and gas."* 2nd Lieutenant Bernard Hatter lost his life just as his unit reached the German trenches, falling mortally wounded into them. At 4.30 pm orders were given to retire to their own trenches. The Leicestershire battalions fought with great bravery, but too many parts of the enemy's **barbed-wire had not been cut-up by the barrage**, so channelling our troops into firing range of the awaiting enemy machine guns. (In 1915 our artillery was short on heavy-explosive shells, and many of those available had been made by raw-labour and possessed faulty detonators.)

My wife, Beryl and I have visited this battlefield several times. Coincidentally it is a coalmining area, and we find it ironic that many Leicestershire colliers lost their lives in this part of French Flanders.

Bernard's body fell in an area fought over many times, especially during the following five weeks, and sadly he has no known grave. A memorial service was held at St. John The Baptist Church, and the pulpit was draped with black crepe and shrouded with a union jack. Two members of the Church Lads' Brigade, namely Palmer and Mathieson sounded a bugle call, and the organist, Miss Wells played the 'Dead March'. The church was packed to capacity, and his parents, especially his mother never fully recovered from the tragedy!

Bernard was just twenty years of age and his name is etched on Panel 42-44 of the Remembrance Wall at Loos Cemetery, and also on the Coalville Clock Tower Memorial.

The Letter Explaining How He Died
A letter received from Lieutenant A.V. Nicholson of the 62nd Trench Mortar Battery, 1st Corps, 74th Division explained how he died.

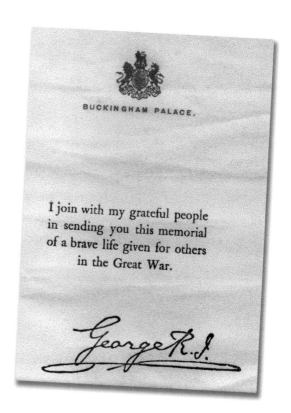

BUCKINGHAM PALACE.

I join with my grateful people in sending you this memorial of a brave life given for others in the Great War.

George R.I.

Sent for 2nd Lieutenant Bernard Hatter.

'I must say how awfully grieved I was when I heard of your son's death. He and I were at the School of Mortars. I have just seen a man who acted as servant to him, and he told me the following: "The attack took place on September 25th. Lieutenant James and Lieutenant Hatter had ordered the advance with our guns. A few minutes later James was shot and Lieutenant Hatter took command. As soon as he realised what had happened he rallied us and told the boys to make the most of it! He had advanced to within a few yards of the parapet when a German musketeer shot him right through the heart. He shouted: "Oh God!" The man said Bernard then fell into the German trench. He did not suffer and there was no time for him to leave a message.

All the men in Bernard's Battery said that he died a noble death, and that they miss him very much. Your son was always full of optimism. All through Battery school, and before the attack he said he should never get shot, and that he would see England again. He died a noble death, and you have my sympathy and condolences. I miss him terribly as he was a good friend of mine. I believe his kit has been sent on. If there is anything I can for you, let me know and I will do it with good will.

I am yours faithfully,
A.V.Nicholson. (Lieut).'

A similar letter was received from the batman in question, Gunner R. Mercer R.G.A.

'*I wish to express my deep regret at the Lieutenant's death and send my condolences. I hope it makes you feel better to know that I covered his body over after the fatal shot, but then I had to take refuge in a shell hole until I was relieved because of the dreadful barrage.*'

Many thanks for the information and photographs supplied by Bernard's nephew, Doctor Michael Pepper MB.BS.MFCM.DPH, and his daughter, Penny.

As the above account states, Bernard's cousin was my grandfather, Charles Hatter. Naturally I am saddened that a relative of mine was killed, but at the same time I feel proud of him. Proud to think that someone of my flesh and blood died in such a honourable fashion whilst fighting for his country. (Author).

The name of Bernard Hatter on the Memorial Wall at Loos Cemetery.

JAMES ROLAND HILL D.C.M. AND **JOHN HENRY SHAW**

A man by the name of Linden Hill married Ann Murfin at Shardlow, a village ten kilometres southeast of Derby city centre. Their son, James Roland Hill was born at Coalville on 14th January 1880, and he always preferred to be called by his second Christian name. He had three sisters, Phoebe, May and Gladys of which Phoebe married a Mr. Wilton from Ashby-de-la-Zouch, May a Mr. Smith from Elsmouth in Yorkshire and with Gladys never marrying. From an early age Roland took a great interest in the military and served for nine years with the Leicestershire Volunteers prior to the 1908 birth of the Territorial Army. Along with Coalville man, Jack Sheffield, whose story is also in this book, he fought in the Boer War of 1899-1902, travelling to South Africa in 1900 and taking part in the Siege of Ladysmith. Soon afterwards he was invalided out after a bad accident requiring surgery (from the same doctor who later operated on King George VI) and suffering from enteric fever.

A religious family, he attended the town's Christ Church School and Bible Class and in 1892, at twelve years of age, started as a part-timer at Stableford's Brick Works near to the Coalville 'Bridges'. He received the princely sum of six old pence per day (just over two new pence). Upon leaving school Roland continued at Stableford's, joined the engineering side as a fitter/mechanic (wagon works), at six shillings a week (thirty new pence.) Apart from the war years he stayed with the firm until 1929.

Roland married Elizabeth Ann Horton, a lady from the town of Smethwick, just west of Birmingham, at Christ Church, Coalville, on 8th April 1901, and the couple set up home at 26, Melbourne Street in the town. Sad to write his mother, Anne, died on 1st November 1901. Elizabeth and Roland had six children; the eldest Jack, was born in 1901 then came Leonard, Frank, Marjorie, Tommy and finally James (Jim) in 1916.

Sergeant Major James Roland Hill in 1914 He was decorated with the D.C.M. for outstanding bravery at the Battle of the Somme on July 1st 1916.

Leicestershire Volunteers at Bradgate Park, 1899. All from Coalville. Left rear: J. Brown, W. Wain and R.J. Hill. Left front: Sgt. E. Hanson, **Jack Sheffield** (featured later), W. Roberts, F. Clay and F. Gough.

After returning from South Africa, Roland often reminisced about his annual summer camps with the Volunteers. His first was at Bradgate Park in 1896, then Woodhouse, Yarmouth, Bradgate 1899, Salisbury, Aldershot and Conway. He had a photograph taken with his pals from Coalville at the second Bradgate camp: the view shows Sergeant E. Hanson, Jack Sheffield, W. Roberts, F. Clay and Roland, then a private. Above all matters musketry was a case of practise until perfect and Roland was an excellent shot, and he passed on this skill in later years. From 1908 Roland automatically continued his military career, service number 6736, with the Fifth (1/5th) Leicestershire Territorial Battalion, and in the early years was based with the Ashby-de-la-Zouch Company, with their headquarters at Loughborough.

His first camp with his new battalion was at Garendon, and in August 1914 Sergeant Major J. R. Hill was with the Terriers at Bridlington, their annual summer camp, when news of the outbreak of war sent them scurrying back to base under order of mobilisation. In my earlier book I wrote about the entraining for Luton and movements from there onwards.

Roland was well respected at Stableford's and by early January 1915 there were no fewer than seventy of his ex-work colleagues who had followed him into the Armed Forces. He played a vital part in training the 'Famous Fifty' and my grandfather, Charles Hatter, said he was taught to be a sniper by his sergeant major.

The Coalville Times of the 25th June 1915 remarked that Sgt. Mjr. Roland Hill was home on leave from June 17th to the 24th. The article said his

Above left: Sergeant Major J.R. Hill drilling troops of the 1/5 Leicestershire Battalion in 1914.

face was still cut and bruised from a German bullet that had shattered his trench periscope whilst observing the enemy frontline. Roland also commented: *'Most of the Coalville and District lads are in my Company and they are getting on well and are in the best of spirits. The food we get is good and plentiful and they are well supplied with tobacco. The weather conditions in the trenches are very good-similar to what you are getting here in England.'*

He was also gassed in the same year, almost certainly at the Hohenzollern Redoubt on 13th October 1915.

Elizabeth Hill with one month old son James in November 1916.

Several of the 'Famous Fifty' mention kind words regarding the Sergeant Major in their letters home. They appreciated he had to maintain discipline and could be tough, but also recognised his experience and kindly attributes.

On the opening day of the Battle of the Somme, the 1st July 1916, the NCO distinguished himself with a typical act of outstanding bravery.

I have discussed this battle in my earlier book, and I mentioned that at 7.30am four waves of our infantry walked across No-Man's-Land under cover of a smokescreen.

The smoke was blown away and many soldiers were lost by a combination of machine-gun fire and shrapnel shells. It was at this time the daring deed was done.

From Battalion Records: *'Captain Ward Jackson and his Company Sergeant Major-J. R. Hill and two platoons (Hepworth and Salmon) went forward with the leading parties to dig their trench from the Sucrerie. In spite of the heavy fire, and losses of the attacking Brigades, they started work and actually marked out their trench.*

But their task was impossible. Captain Ward Jackson, hit in the back and shoulder and very badly wounded, was only saved by Sergeant Major Hill, who pluckily carried him out of the fight, and, seeing that the attack had failed, 2nd Lieutenant Hepworth ordered the party back to our lines.'

For his bravery Roland was awarded the Distinguished Conduct Medal (D.C.M.), second only to the Victoria Cross. In this same action he was wounded and admitted into hospital. In November 1916 the Coalville Times reported that Sgt. Mjr. Roland Hill was hospitalised in the Midlands and suffering from trench fever: shortly afterwards he was honourably discharged as unfit for military service.

Roland received his D.C.M. from General Sir John Maxwell during a public investiture at Leeds Town Hall. (As did Lance-corporal T. W. Brown.)

The Hill family circa 1922. rear left: Jack, Thomas, Marjorie, Leonard and Frank. Front: Roland, Jim and Elizabeth.

Once recuperated he returned to his old job at Stableford's and became quite a celebrity within the town for his actions in the two wars. He was then living at 301, Ashby Road, Coalville, and after war's end remained with the Battalion, assisting in training until 1939: a total of half a century, and he never missed leading the Coalville Armistice Parade. Wearing his bowler hat, seven campaign medals and his cane he cut a familiar and highly respected figure. Without doubt Roland Hill was one of Coalville's finest and bravest soldiers, and also considered the smartest dressed man in town.

For very many years Elizabeth Hill was the cookhouse keeper for Christ Church vicarage, and certainly we know that for James' marriage the vicar waived the fee in appreciation of her loyal services. The Hill family also kept a pig at the bottom of the garden, and once fattened and killed, Elizabeth had it hung up so she could scrub, scrape, salt, cut it, and then left it to hang in muslin to await consumption. The Coalville Times reported on the 20th February 1920 that Roland's son, Jack, had been hurt in an

explosion whilst conducting an experiment. I do not think it was too serious, however, the Hill family were in mourning in May 1927. The Times of the 13th May informed readers that Thomas Albert Hill had been killed in a motorbike accident. It continued that it was not his bike, it was loaned and it was his first journey on it. The accident, a mortal head wound, took place opposite Broom Leys' School on the outskirts of the town.

Local folk will recall Stableford's (Stebe) pond; in reality it was an old clay pit, very deep with a raft in the middle and a high diving stand. Galas were a regular social function there, and regretfully it was also the neighbourhood's suicide spot. The occasion arose when Roland witnessed a suicide; he dived into the pond fully clothed in an unsuccessful attempt at rescue: only to find a man's body. For his bravery he was awarded a certificate from the 'Royal Humane Society'.

Roland was one of the last names on the books when Stableford's Wagon Works went into bankruptcy. Just after leaving the firm after thirty-seven years service, whilst walking in Coalville, he met Mr. L. L. Baldwin, the Coalville Council surveyor, who promptly offered him the position of Bath's

The Hill's home, 301 Ashby Road, Coalville, in 2005.

Attendant at the newly opened Public Baths on Avenue Road.

He gleefully accepted and remained in the job for sixteen years, only leaving on his retirement, 4th December 1945. Mr. F. W. Newbold A.C.I.S., clerk to the council, wrote a fine letter to express the council's appreciation of his loyal services.

The Coalville Times of 4th July 1952 wrote an article whereby Roland said that he deserved his retirement: he had worked for long enough, a good innings and deserving of a good rest! Yet, seven years later he was still "working and enjoying every minute of it."

I am a Genuine Ex-Service Man,
NOT AN IMPOSTER !

It is just a simple story
That I want to tell to you,
Yet in spite of its simplicity,
It is, alas too true.

I'm but a disabled soldier
Who once answered duty's call,
Now forgotten by my Country—
Left to wither and to fall.

When I saw that I was needed
I enlisted full of pride—
They said I was a hero *then*,
But *now* I'm cast aside.

As in the song called "Playthings,"
I am one of England's toys,
Life is but a drama
With its sorrows and its joys.

I have tramped along the highways
I have searched each city through,
But good luck never comes my way,
I can find no work to do.

And this is England's gratitude,
To the men who fought and bled,
Our reward was just a medal
We were left to want for bread.

So now you know my story,
I ask you if you can,
To try and spare a trifle
For a poor ex-service man.

2d. per Packet.

PLEASE NOTE—If you do not purchase this Packet, it will be collected with thanks and civility when called for.

A leaflet distributed to ex-servicemen to authenticate their status. Unscrupulous civilians often masqueraded as having served in the forces.

St. Peter's Memorial, Bardon.

A few months after the earlier comments he was offered the job of Coalville Park attendant: looking after tennis bookings and making sure that children didn't come to any harm. *"I love children, we get on very well together."* The article completed by stating that his wife and he had celebrated their golden wedding the previous year. *"We are as happy now as the day we got married. I have always been a hard worker and my advice to the younger generation is not to be frightened by hard work: it never hurt anyone."*

He took a passionate interest in his native town; indeed, he kept a scrapbook in which he recorded all of the great events in the town's history, with many people consulting him about the district's past.

Roland Hill died at his home in 1958, aged seventy-eight years. He left a widow, four sons and a daughter.

His eldest son Jack spent virtually his entire employment working in various collieries. In those difficult and hard times he'd leave his shift wet through: there were no works-baths, and on bitterly cold days his clothes froze to his body as he walked home! He then had to thaw in front of an open fire before he could remove them. Bathing followed in a zinc tub whilst his mother attempted to dry his clothes in preparation for the next shift.

Leonard joined the Lancashire Fusiliers in the Twenties and spent a considerable period of time serving in India. Having left the service he was mobilised in 1939, but remained in England throughout the war years. After the war he was employed as head gardener at Markfield Sanatorium in northwest Leicestershire. Two boys, Peter and David, graced his marriage.

Marjorie, (1st November 1908-May 2003), married and gave birth to one daughter, Sheila, who married Wilf Shelton. They live happily at Shepshed. The General Post Office employed Frank for most of his working life. He was a very fine local cricketer: a player responsible for developing and serving Broom Ley's Cricket Club during the Thirties, especially, and beyond. The club still maintains a significant stature in the county circuit. Irene is his daughter.

The youngest son, James (Jim), born 5th October 1916, sang for Christ Church choir from the age of ten years and later served in the Second World War. He was also a big driving force behind the town's famed Rugby Club, playing with the well-known Ball brothers on many occasions. During the war Jim played several times for Rugby League side, Castleford. He married local girl, Elsie Amy Cox, who had connections with the old 'Fox and Goose' public house. He has two sons.

My thanks to Jim Hill, a wonderful sprightly man in his nineties who still adores his rugby.

John Henry Shaw

I often visit the lonely grave of Private John Henry Shaw. He lies in a shady and sheltered spot in St. Peter's Cemetery at Bardon, not too far from where schoolboy friend, Isaac Bancroft is buried. John was in the Fifth (1/5th) Battalion of the Leicestershire Regiment and enlisted at Coalville, service number 2813, in late September 1914.

He served with Sergeant Major Roland Hill and pre-war knew most of the Hugglescote contingent of the Famous Fifty.

His parents, Henry and Fanny Elizabeth Shaw, worked Moore's Farm on the Bardon Road.

John was badly wounded in the notorious trench 50, near to Hill 60, on the outskirts of the Ypres in Flanders, where several of the Famous Fifty lost their lives.

He recovered sufficiently to be allowed to return home to convalesce, sadly, complications set in and he died on the 28th April 1916 at York Hospital.

Private Moon of Melbourne Street and Bugler S. Jones of Belvoir Road, both Coalville lads sent a letter of sympathy to his parents:

'*John was well liked by all members of the Company and everyone found him kind and straightforward in every detail. It is hard to take that after fighting and toiling as he had done, to depart after recovering from his wounds, but we realise that he died nobly in the defence of his country. We have had a collection and with the money could you buy a wreath and put it on his grave for us?*'

John, aged just twenty-one was interred on the 2nd May 1916 and his name can be read on the Coalville Clock Tower Memorial and St. Peter's War Memorial.

Rest easy, John.

The grave of Private John Henry Shaw.

JOHN CHARLES HILL

John Charles Hill was born around 1894 at Stoney Stanton, a village fifteen kilometres (ten miles) southwest of the centre of Leicester city.

He enlisted at Stoney Stanton in November 1914 into the Eighth Leicestershire Battalion, received the King's Shilling, and shortly afterwards was forwarded to Wigston Barracks at Glen Parva, near Leicester, for initial training. John Hill's battalion was created together with the Sixth, Seventh and Ninth as purely volunteer, 'Service Battalions' for the duration of the war, to meet the enthusiastic rush of men answering Lord Kitchener's call: '*You're Country Needs You*'. Collectively the four battalions became the 110th Brigade, subsequently of the 37th Division, and an integral part of the New Army.

In the autumn of 1914 service battalions from all over the country converged on the military town of Aldershot in Hampshire, with the Eighth Leicestershire being allotted Bourley Camp on the outskirts of the town. However weather conditions deteriorated so badly with the approach of winter: they were living under canvas, that just before Christmas they had to be moved into a barrack block at Aldershot.

In March of 1915 the Eighth Battalion went to

Folkestone on the Channel coast of Kent, where the men were billeted in residential houses in the Leas and along Sandgate Road in the town. For those not provided for, uniforms and rifles arrived, and serious route marches and tactical manoeuvres took-a-speed to groom the volunteers into frontline troops. The Sixth Battalion followed a similar routine at Liphook, in the centre of eastern Hampshire, the Seventh near to Andover in central Hampshire and the Ninth to Kent: New Romney, twenty-three kilometres (fourteen miles) southwest of Folkestone.

By the end of April 1915 the Brigade came together in the vicinity of Perham Down in the Salisbury Plain of Wiltshire. Here they received final intensive training, such as following compass bearings in countryside at night, signalling and more musketry courses. In addition, individual battalions were also given patches so that men good be readily classified on the battle-front, the Eighth had a green patch, the Sixth had black, the Seventh had red and the Ninth a yellow patch, to be sown on the left hand side of the wearer's collar. It was hoped that by this means battalion identification would be deprived from the enemy in the event of capture. On June 25th King George V inspected and passed the Brigade, a real fillip for the soldiers who now realised that they were considered worthy and competent to wear their uniform.

On the 29th July 1915 the Eighth and sister Battalions embarked from England and arrived at Boulogne or Le Havre in France. In total they amounted to three thousand men, and it is sad to write that nearly half of them were killed in the war, and scores of those who died never had leave, so never saw home shores again.

After a week in the Kemmel Sector of Belgium, seeing frontline trenches for the first time near Locre, and involving marches to Dickiebusch in the Ypres Sector; they entrained to arrive at Doullens, to march through undamaged and beautiful scenery to the village of Mondicourt, not too far from Arras in France. The Brigade manned a stretch of trenches opposite to the ruined village of Monchy-au-Bois, which at that time was in German hands. They spent the winter in this district, a particularly bleak winter and rated as one of the coldest of the century, and the bitterness of the fighting competed with the

Private John Charles Hill of the 8th Leicestershire Battalion.

conditions, with opposing sides suffering high casualties. As consolation, by staying in this area for so long they had the opportunity to name some of the trenches to their liking: High Cross Street, Gallowtree Gate, Humberstone Gate and Narborough Road, etc. On the 24th - 25th December a volley of shells from the Royal Artillery ensured there would be no 1915 Christmas Truce.

Towards the end of March 1916 the Brigade was relieved and marched to rest billets near Sus-St-Leger and Warluzel, where they had a six weeks stay before spending two weeks at Doullens. The two weeks were spent practising bayonet skills, musketry and gas helmet drill in splendidly warm springtime weather.

At the time of the opening day of the Battle of the Somme on the 1st July 1916, the 110th Brigade had returned to its original winter area around Bienvillers-Bailleulmont, however, on the July 6th they marched south to support the faltering attacks on the Somme. For the soldiers of the Brigade it was a gruelling march, and everyone was pleased upon arrival at the village of Hangest, where they rested for the night. The following day, somewhat refreshed they continued their march to a central part of the Somme Sector known as Mametz Wood and Bezentin-le-Petit. The earlier six days of intense battle had left the area looking like a scene from hell. There was shell–scarred churned-up earth, the stench of decomposing corpses in No-Man's-Land and the pungent aroma of lachrymatory gas. The subsequent horrifying battle that raged on the rolling hills in this region of the Somme lies beyond the realms of this book, enough to write that this area of France should remain sacred to the fallen of Leicestershire.

On the 4th October 1916 the Brigade entrained for Bethune, and then marched south to the unglamorous coalmining area of the Loos Sector, with its slagheaps and pithead winding machinery. Here they remained until the 1st January 1917. Then, in extremely cold conditions of deep snow and sharp frost they returned to the familiar area just to the north of Ypres. The infantryman was not called 'the foot-soldier' for no just reason, and with it being even colder than the previous winter they noticed that the Yser Canal was frozen solid, but thoughts were far removed from a 'Swan Lake' theme.

Late February 1917 saw the Brigade entrain to return to Bethune, with a march south to the Loos Sector. Their stay was unexpectedly cut short due to the enemy's retirement in the same month to the Hindenburg Line, so shortening their frontline and concentrating available resources. The 110th Brigade left the trenches for Bethune, where buses transported them south for the Arras Sector.

The Hindenburg Line was supposedly impregnable; it was built in the summer and autumn of 1916 by thousands of prisoners of war, especially Russians, and designed by Germany's finest military engineers.

On the 3rd May 1917, as part of the Battle of Bullecourt, the Leicestershire Brigade attacked the Line at Fontaine Les Croisilles, with casualties expected to be high, and statisticians were not disappointed. The Eighth and Ninth Battalions attacked under a moonless evening, and the enemy barrage matched our own so that No-Man's-Land was a pandemonium, with many men being either casualties or taken prisoner. Somehow they managed to take the village of Cherisy and Fontaine Wood, but then had to retire under the cover provided by the Seventh Battalion.

The War Diary of the Eighth Battalion for the attack on May3rd:

'The battalion was disposed in two waves of two lines each, with a wave of moppers-up behind. From right to left 'A' Company (Lt. F. R. Oliver), 'B' Company (Capt. A. G. Astle), 'C' Company (Major T. L. Warner) formed the line of attack, each company having a two-platoon frontage. 'D' Company (2nd Lt. J. W. Corbett) was drawn up in two lines, sixty yards in the rear. The formation was two waves, each of two lines, ten yards between lines and sixty yards between waves, with 'D' Company as moppers-up.'

Reports stated that large numbers of the enemy attacked from the left and right flanks and used bombs and guns to great effect, a deadly slaughter!

The tanks used in the battle were Mark 11 training tanks pressed into action and they proved highly vulnerable. At sometime during the mayhem in No-Man's-Land, Private John Charles Hill met his death in the service of his country.

John Hill's fiancée was too upset regarding his death and never married.

As mentioned earlier, the Leicestershire poet, Lieutenant Arthur Newberry Choyce of Hugglescote was at Fontaine Les Croiselles with the 9th Leicestershire Battalion. On the morning of the 5th May 1917 he wrote the following whilst resting in a trench.

Destiny

A dead boy lies in the sunlight.
His cold lips say to me
How safe though tiredly trod
The path of Destiny
Still wanders through a troubled night
To God.

The officer-poet is quite clear in his composition. The sights witnessed by frontline soldiers were truly horrendous. The early morning rays of spring sunshine had gently revealed the body of a boy-soldier. He had died during the night, lying alone in No-Man's-Land, and had suffered a painful and protracted death, 'a troubled pathway to God.'

Arthur Newberry Choyce himself was soon to be badly wounded, and it is felt that the repercussions of that wound led to his untimely death in his early forties. When I placed a wooden poppy cross upon Arthur's grave in Hugglescote cemetery on 11th November 2003, I also prayed for John Hill and the boy-soldier. I will continue to do so.

Many thanks to John's nephew, Jack Huddlestone; in the hope John's memory will be preserved. Readers of my first book may recall that Jack is married to Jean (nee Hodgetts).

For detailed information regarding the 110th Brigade I can recommend the book: 'The Tigers' by Mathew Richardson, published in 2000.

WILLIAM OGDEN HODEN

I am always delighted to receive fresh information with which to cast a ray of light upon an apparently forlorn name, etched upon Coalville's Clock Tower memorial; it is similar to finding a much-treasured lost book.

So was the instance in September 2005 when I was contacted by Pauline Hoden, whose husband John is the grandson of the above soldier.

Alfred and Ellen Hoden originated from Ashby Magna, a village fifteen kilometres (ten miles) due south of Leicester, and married at the nearby village of Dunton Bassett. Here they settled with Alfred an accomplished tailor: following his father and several relatives into the cloth-trade. The couple had four sons, Charles (born 1877), Arthur (born 1879), William Ogden (born 16th February 1880 at Leire) and Henry (born 1882), and life was indeed very rosy until tragedy struck in 1890. After a gap of eight years Ellen prepared to give birth to another child and both she and Alfred were dearly hoping for a girl. Their wishes were granted and Charlotte Ann

Private William Ogden Hoden of the 1st Battalion Warwickshire Regiment. Circa 1914.

was born in 1890, alas Ellen died during a difficult birth. The emotions within the family circle were bittersweet, and with William being just ten years of age, life must have been very traumatic for him and the rest of the family circle.

In 1901 William Ogden Hoden's employment was classed as that of a journeyman-baker.

On the 7th August 1905, at the Leicester Register Office, he married Ellen Bartlett, a girl from the village who was two years his junior and already caring for a son, Joseph Henry Adnitt (known as Harry) Bartlett (born 1901) from an earlier relationship.

William and Ellen settled in the village and in 1906 were blessed with the birth of Arthur Frederick and Alfred Edward in 1907. The couple then moved to Page's Hill at Hugglescote, where Lottie May was born on the 30th July 1909 and John (Jack) Charles in 1911. Almost certainly the family moved to the area to allow William to work as a coal miner (a hewer).

My text seemed to flow in a very satisfactory manner until August 1914, when William received a telegram ordering him to report to his old unit, the 1st Royal Warwickshire Battalion. Clearly he had been a regular soldier (service number 9066) at some earlier time. I believe he enlisted at a very early age, certainly he left school at the age of thirteen years, and I think he told a white lie and took the King's shilling in 1894. After a service of seven years he departed, but knew that in the event of a war he would be called-up as a reservist.

The children of William and Ellen Hoden. Rear left: Joseph Henry Adnitt Bartlett. Rear centre: Alfred Edward Hoden. Rear right: Arthur Frederick Hoden Below: Charlotte May and John Charles Hoden. This photograph was taken in the playground (now car park) outside of the Church School at Hugglescote. Circa 1914-15.

Thirty-four year old William had no option but to pack his bags and kiss his wife and children good-bye for the war's duration. A family member recalled that William was seen walking along North Street (now Central Road) towards Coalville with a live cockerel tucked under his arm. A well wisher who knew he was going to war shouted: 'Good luck, Billy!'

Billy's Battalion was part of the British Expeditionary Force (B.E.F.) that embarked for France in August 1914. It consisted of five infantry battalions and one cavalry division and accounted for 100,000 men.

He would have seen action at the Battle of Mons on the 22nd August 1914, when a German Force of 160, 000 men broke through between the British right flank and the French 5th Army. The British dug-in and believed the French would return, unfortunately this was not to be and the B.E.F. was in serious trouble until eventually they managed to retire. It was a rearguard action all the way! The soldiers were footsore and exhausted: '*Men stumbling more like ghosts than living soldiers, unconscious of everything about them, but still moving under the magic impulse of discipline and regimental pride.*' (John Terraine - top military historian).

At Le Cateau, British troops stood and fought the overwhelming German forces and held them for a time. Both sides suffered appalling losses.

William was also involved in the 1st Battle of the Marne: 5-9th September 1914. Three German armies were swinging from Belgium to sweep through France and encircle Paris. Allied troops counter-attacked the enemy flank and stopped them, and finally trenches were dug to form that infamous line of death known as the Western Front.

The Germans attempted another powerful thrust to push the B.E.F. into the sea and this engagement was to be called: 'The 1st Battle of Ypres' (Wipers). It was indeed a fearsome battle with very heavy casualties on both sides, and it raged between October and November 1914. It was during this battle that Private William Ogden Hoden lost his life. Before and following this battle individual battalions of Territorial troops had to embark for Belgium to support the B.E.F., who in four months had lost most of their numbers.

Only individual readers could possibly imagine the emotions of Ellen when she received a telegram from the War Office, notifying her that William had been killed on active service! Somehow she was to look after five children, of which the eldest (Harry) was thirteen and was about to seek employment. Where there is a will, there was a way. Harry immediately found employment and passed his precious earnings to his mother every week. (Harry's son, Martin, confirms this).

The Book of Remembrance at St. Mary's Church, Warwick. Ninth down on the right hand side: Private William Ogden Hoden, died 13th October 1914.

Quite some time after William's death, Ellen married widower, Joseph Handford, the local blacksmith and twenty years her senior. They lived at 4, Central Road (opposite to the Church School) and she gave birth to a daughter, Ivy in 1921, and twins, Olive Mary and Joseph Charles in 1922, the latter dying in infancy. Ellen died at the age of 58 years in 1940, and Joe in 1943 at the age of 78 years.

Regarding William's brothers: Charles, the eldest became a boot-maker and upon marriage moved to nearby Broughton Astley.

Arthur, the second eldest moved initially to Hotel Yard, Ellistown, and after marrying at the age of nineteen, onto Hugglescote. He was employed as a miner by a local colliery; indeed he and his wife, Susan, lived on Central Road near to William, Ellen and family. In the early years they were desperately poor attempting to care for Annie (born 1898), Ethel May (born 1900), Frederick Arthur (born 1902- married Mabel Swain in 1922, died 1984), Ivy (born 1915, died aged one year) and Violet (1915- died aged six months: possibly twins), and Arthur Ogden (died in 1928 aged 18 months).

Arthur died in 1963 (aged 85 years) and Susan in 1950 (aged 69 years), both at 85, Station Road, Hugglescote. Ethel married Arthur (Dennis) Hodgetts, one of the 'Famous Fifty' on the 21st December 1921 at Christ Church, Coalville. The couple lived at 205, Ashby Road, Coalville, where Ethel gave birth to Dorothy. Two stillborn sons followed before Ethel had Jean, and then utter sadness when she died on the 5th March 1932 from complications. Dennis Hodgetts died in accidental circumstances when repairing an electrical cable in 1938. Little is known of Ethel's elder sister, Annie.

The youngest son, Henry became a baker, taking and plying his trade at Bromley-by-Bow near to London.

William's only sister, Charlotte (always known as Lottie) was brought up by her aunt, Jane Hoden in the same village. Jane was a skilled dressmaker and Lottie remained in Dunton Bassett and became self-employed in the same skill. Like so many of her generation she remained unmarried due to the chronic shortage of young men following the war.

The children of William and Ellen: Harry Bartlett, worked as a pharmacy assistant at Restalls Chemist at Ibstock. He dispensed prescriptions and often delivered them on a bike. In 1939 he joined the Royal Army Medical Corps, trained at hospitals in Taunton and Birmingham before embarking for Bone Hospital in North Africa. Late in the war he required a major operation and was medically discharged. He worked as a stores manager at Forest Road Garage, Coalville, for fourteen years and then occupied a similar position at Ford Motors, Coalville, until

The Chapel of the Royal Warwickshire Regiment at St. Mary's Church Warwick.

retirement.

He lived in Ellistown with his wife, Olive, and had three children: Martin and John (who live in Coalville with their families) and Ann (similarly in Barrow on Soar.) Harry died in 1981, aged 80 years.

Arthur Frederick had various jobs throughout his life. Following service in the army during World War, he was a foreman at Owen Brown of Loughborough, and supervised the erection of marquees around the country and even went to do a job in Russia.

A married man, his wife, Lily, gave birth to one daughter, Marian, and had two grandchildren. Unfortunately, his marriage ended in divorce, and by the time of his death in 1993, aged 87 years, he was quite a wealthy man, and living in a bungalow, which he personally built on a parcel of land that he owned at Lount.

Alfred Edward was a miner at Whitwick Colliery. Whilst working 'on the bank' in 1954 he had a dreadful accident when his leg was crushed. He continued working there but was only capable of light duties. He was married to Audrey, but had no children. Later in life he lived in a bungalow on Grange Road, opposite to St. John the Baptist Church at Hugglescote. He died in 1990 at the age of 83 years in a nursing home at Leicester.

John Charles (Jack) worked for twenty-five years for Hugglescote's Frank Whitmore. He delivered papers and magazines for the wholesaler to various retail outlets throughout northwest Leicestershire.

He spent six years during World War 2 fighting in North Africa, Italy and Greece. After the war he and his wife, Emily, had three sons and lived coincidentally on Page's Hill. (A group of terraced cottages now demolished due to subsidence and which were opposite to St. John the Baptist Church, Hugglescote.) Their house was only yards from where his father lived prior to the Great War! Details regarding Jack's war record will be released in book 4: 'Sons and Daughters.' Jack died in 1965. Of their sons, Robert and his wife live at Coalville (two daughters and grandchildren), Brian and his wife live at Swadlincote (daughter), and John and his wife *Pauline, live in Narborough (son and daughter and grandchildren.)

Lottie May was in service until her marriage to Frederick Horsley in 1930. Living at 46, Leicester Road, Loughborough, she undertook a cleaning position until many years of service at Johnson's hosiery factory in the town. In 1932 she gave birth to Frederick William, and followed with John Charles (died 1981), Jean and Freda. Lottie May died in 1983, but the remaining children and families still live in the Loughborough area.

Almost certainly all of the Hoden children from the two generations attended the Church School on the corner of Grange Road and Central Road, Hugglescote.

Private Ogden Hoden, 9066, Royal Warwickshire Regiment was killed on the 13th October 1914 and is remembered at Meteren Military Cemetery. Grave/Memorial Ref: 111.L.884 (buried near this spot). His name can also be found in the Book of Remembrance in the Chapel of The Royal Warwickshire Regiment, St. Mary's Church, Warwick.

I am very grateful to *Pauline for casting a ray of light onto the etched name of William Ogden Hoden. Now he will be remembered. Also thanks to Jean Hodgkinson, Lottie May Hoden's daughter, for supplying two excellent photographs.

PERCY AND WILFRID JARVIS

Thomas Jarvis was born in Wales and as a young man moved to Ellistown, near Coalville in Leicestershire. He obtained employment at Ellistown Colliery, and was the engine-winder there until the age of seventy years, and was highly respected and considered one of the best to hold that position.

In the eighteen-nineties he met Mary Jane Oliver, a Whitwick girl who was working at T. & J. Jones, latterly known as Joseph Burgess and Son in Belvoir Road at Coalville. They married and settled down at 184, Whitehill Road at Ellistown, next door to his mother at 182. At the former house the couple had six children: Percy William in 1893, Ethel (always called Tiddy), Wilfrid Thomas on the 21st June 1896, Maud, Olive, and Gwenfred. Shortly after the latter's birth the family moved next door to 182, and in 1911 Dorothy was born, unfortunately her twin, Nora, was to die at the age of five months through a heart defect.

All of the eldest children attended the nearby Hugglescote Baptist School, with the youngest attending a newly opened school in the village. Percy

and Wilfrid furthered their education at the prestigious Ashby de la Zouch Grammar School, even though the purse strings were tight.

They studied in the company of future soldiers like Jabez, William and Alfred Emmerson, Frederic Scott and Philip Bent.

Private Wilfrid Jarvis, centre back row, training with the 1/4th Leicestershire Battalion at Sawbridgeworth in late 1914.

Percy progressed to Birmingham University, and to Wilfrid's chagrin, despite proving he was as equally intelligent as his elder brother, was told by his father that they couldn't possibly afford to send him to university too! Just before Percy was to sit his Batchelor of Arts illness struck, and so had to pass it via a correspondence course. He then left Leicestershire to teach at Peterborough.

Tiddy, like her two brothers had to walk a way to catch a train for Grammar School, and often she arrived soaked in rainwater. At the age of fifteen years she developed pneumonia and died. Her parents believed that her travels to school were responsible for her death, and, unjustifiably so felt partly responsible! Tiddy is buried at Hugglescote Cemetery.

At the outbreak of the war both sons enlisted into the Forces. In 1914 Percy enlisted at Peterborough into the Northamptonshire Regiment, whilst Wilfrid enlisted at Leicester into the Fourth (1/4th) Leicestershire Battalion.

During basic training Percy's qualifications and leadership qualities were noted, and he was selected as an officer cadet, and, following training at Harrogate was commissioned as a 2nd Lieutenant. He was with the 'Northamptons' throughout most of their major battles on the Western Front, including a

Percy Jarvis at 182 Whitehill Road, Ellistown in 1915.

Lance Corporal Percy Jarvis front centre.

posting to the Salonika Front. On his birthday in November 1917, and at the battle at Cambrai in France, he received gunshot wounds to the leg and was forced to crawl through No-Man's-Land to his own trenches. He was returned for hospitalisation on England's south coast at Weymouth in Dorset. It was here that he was to meet his future wife, Elsie. After

the war they married and settled down locally, having two children, Pauline and Philip. He continued as a teacher and in 1922 became the headmaster at nearby Ravenstone Primary School until 1930. Percy then undertook a similar position at Kirby Muxloe School, a village six kilometres (four miles) due west of the centre of Leicester until his retirement in 1958. Percy died in 1985 at the grand age of ninety-two years, and he lies at rest in Kirby Muxloe Cemetery.

Wilfrid was another great survivor of the war, this time with the Fourth Leicestershire Battalion. He reserved his annoyance when he was instated as a private with them, for in his opinion the only difference between his officer-brother and he was a university degree. It is completely understandable, yet so sad, that for the remainder of their lives the two brothers were constantly at loggerheads. Wilfrid served with distinction at Ypres, the charge at the Hohenzollern Redoubt, the Somme, Lens, Bellenglise and indeed all of the battles described by

Percy Jarvis with his parents, brother and sisters on Spring Hill, Charnwood Forest. 1914. Percy kept this photograph with him throughout the war.

Percy Jarvis in Salonika with the Northamptons.

Private Wilfrid Jarvis on the left in the rear garden of 182, Whitehill Road, Ellistown. September 1914.

Percy Jarvis with sister Dorothy on Spring Hill in 1918.

Edward Chapman earlier in this book.

Following four years of devoted service he left the Colours as a sergeant, highly respected, but in his mind he always felt as though he underachieved.

In the early nineteen-twenties he married a local girl, Dorothy Fowkes, and they had two children, Roger and Gwenfred. Wilfrid was employed in the responsible position of head-clerk at nearby Ibstock Colliery, and they had a happy life together at 48, Central Road at Hugglescote.

Cruelly, after a lifetime of industry Wilfrid died in the year of his retirement in 1961, at the age of sixty-five years. He is now at rest in Hugglescote Cemetery.

Many thanks to Dorothy Dowell (nee Jarvis), sister to Percy and Wilfrid, and still going very strongly at ninety-six years of age. Some readers may recall her husband, William Ernest Dowell, who was always known locally as 'Mank'! They had four children, John Derek, Janet, Jill Dorothy and Philip Ernest. Also thanks to Dorothy's daughter, Jill Harris for her assistance.

Percy Jarvis alongside his future wife at Weymouth in 1918.

CHARLES WILLIAM JEWSBURY

Charles, always known as, Charlie, was born in 1895 at Coalville. His father, Thomas Jewsbury, was an engine driver for the L.and NW. Railways, and the family home was in Bakewell Street in the town. Thomas was a valued and highly respected officer of the Coalville Men's Adult School on Bridge Road. The family worshipped at the London Road Baptist Chapel.

Two of the Famous Fifty, Frederick Hart and Johnny Lowe were great friends of Charlie's; all were scouts in the town's Scout Troop. Frederick was a drummer and Charlie a bugler in the troop's-band, and they adored to parade along High Street amid cheering crowds with Hugglescote's Bernard Hatter as their patrol leader.

Naturally enough, as boys and young men there was little they enjoyed more than sleeping under a canopy of leaves within their nearby haunts at

Charnwood Forest. They lived under canvas: often sleeping under the stars, and cooked over an open log fire, and in the evenings shared stories and jokes under a moonlight glow, and this idyllic lifestyle continued until the summer of 1914.

After leaving school Charlie's first employment was as a telegraph messenger at the Coalville Post Office, where he worked with another young man, Clifford Scott, who was to become one of the famed fifty. Charlie later moved to Stableford's Wagon Works where as a fitter he was able to earn a little extra money, and worked with Roland Hill, a sergeant major in the local territorial battalion.

No doubt influenced by Roland Hill, and with his zest for the outdoor life and a sense of adventure, Charlie, service number 1897, enlisted at Ashby de la Zouch in February 1913 into the Fifth Leicestershire Territorial Battalion. He was just eighteen years of age, and in the summer of 1913 spent a fortnight with the Battalion at the annual training camp at Denton Park, Grantham in Lincolnshire. Following his basic training he was selected to receive tuition on the machine-gun, and proving to be a good shot, became part of the Machine-gun team under and responsible to Lieutenant A.T. Sharpe of 'A' Company, a famed Leicestershire County Cricketer from Whitwick.

In August of 1914 he was at the annual training camp at Bridlington on the North Yorkshire coast, with local territorials such as Bill Barney, George Saddington, Allan Evans and George Gadsby. I have detailed the footsteps of the Fifth Battalion elsewhere, and only pain and sadness were regular companions while on their sojourn through France and Flanders.

Charlie embarked with the Battalion on the 26th February 1915, and proved to be a more than capable soldier until he lost his life on the slopes of Spanbroekmolen (Hill 76), the Messines Ridge of Flanders on the 6th June 1915, aged twenty years.

Lieutenant Sharpe wrote to Thomas Jewsbury.

'*It is with the deepest regret that I have to inform you of the death of your son. He was killed on the 6th June 1915 by a large shell, and suffered no pain, dying almost at once. I feel his loss very much, firstly because he was a very efficient machine-gunner and secondly because he was conscientious and thoroughly trustworthy. He was in charge of one of the guns, and I always found him brave and fearless. He was a great favourite with the men and knowing that he died like a soldier may lesson some of the grief that you feel.*'

Another letter was received from Ashby man, Allan Evans.

'*As his good friend I want to express my sympathy. By his straightforwardness he gained our respect, and he was usually cheery, and his death has cast a gloomy shadow over us. He was washing at the time in a shell hole with two other men of the section. All three tried to take cover, but Charlie was hit, but he didn't suffer. The other two are suffering slightly from shock. Charlie and I agreed that if anything should happen to one of us then the other would visit the parents as soon as they return to England, and this I will do. He has been properly buried, the same night, and we will maintain his grave while we are here.*

A parcel arrived from you and so I opened it and shared it around, as I thought this would be your wish. I will return his letters and belongings in due time. I do hope his brother, Alf, will have better luck.'

The letter was also signed by: Sergeant G. H. Broadhurst, Corporal G. Hutchinson, Corporal R. F. Astle, Lance Corporal Hutchinson, A. Green, George Beale, T. Dennis, E. H. Buswell, H. Smith, L. H. Burditt, E. W. Hyde, R. Harvey, O. Ward, G. Johnstone, E. Wilson, F. Tupp, A. C. Siddons, A. Young, E. Widdowson, John W. Lowe, C. Buswell, J. H. Fuller, John Hill, W. S. Bagshaw, James Ottey, E. Carter, J. P. W. Adams, A. Allen and G. Benskin.

A letter from Private Albert W. Hanson (later sergeant of 50, Bakewell Street), dated the 10th June 1915 accompanied the personal effects. In those effects was a partly written letter from Charlie: '*Sunday, June 6th. This is our fifth day in the trenches and we are expecting four or five days rest. It is a simply a glorious day, and it difficult to imagine that a war can take place on a day such as today! There is some restless beggar whizzing over one or two shells. I should like to go to the London Road Baptist Chapel tonight, just for old times sake. I am sending you one or two German and French bullets. I have got hold of a German bayonet and then lost the thing, it would have looked all right crossed over the* *mantle-piece. I am going to have a swill now in the shell hole, so I will finish tomorrow.'*

Minutes later he was dead.

Two days later Private Frederick Hart was chatting to Private C. Hatter: "*I can't get over the suddenness of Charlie's death, I spoke to him twenty minutes before he died. He was with two of the machine-gun lads; they were having a wash in a shell-hole when a big shell exploded! He stood no chance and died straight away.*" Shortly after this conversation with my grandfather, Frederick, one of the famed fifty was sniped in the chest and died within seconds.

Charlie's brother, Alfred, used to work in the boot-repairing department at the Coalville Co-operative Stores, and in 1915 was serving in the Coldstream Guards. Thankfully he survived the war.

The deaths of Charlie Jewsbury and Frederick Hart, great friends as they were, are recorded in the Coalville Times issue dated June 18th 1915.

Charlie Jewsbury, together with twenty-eight other men, are remembered on a Memorial Tablet in the London Road Baptist Chapel. Unfortunately, the tablet was considered surplus to requirements when the chapel moved to nearby Charnborough Road! Fortunately, all other local churches and chapels do remember their fallen members: 'At the going down of the sun.' The repaired tablet is now on display at Dixie Grammar School, Market Bosworth.

I like to think and believe it could be true that when Charlie and Frederick Hart were together in those frozen, inky-dark trenches on the Western Front in early 1915, that they recalled earlier days 'of stories and jokes under a moonlight glow in Charnwood Forest.'

I am pleased to inform readers that Charlie's name can be read on the Coalville Clock Tower Memorial.

THOMAS KENDRICK

Tom Kendrick, a stone quarry labourer and coalminer, fathered the above-mentioned soldier. He was born in 1863 at Greenhill, Whitwick and married Mary Ann Mugglestone of Hugglescote, three years his junior (a nurse-domestic), on the 3rd June 1884 at St. John the Baptist, Hugglescote. They originally set-up home at Donington-le-Heath and had their first three children there, later moving to Hugglescote.

Thomas was born on the 8th February 1893 at 5, Crescent Road, Hugglescote. He was the fifth of nine children, Martha (born 1885), Mary Jane (1888) Laura (1889), Lillian May called: Lill (1891), Thomas (1893), Harry (late 1893, infant death early '94), Harry (1895), Mabel (1898) and Mary Frances (1909). Tom died at the relatively early age of forty-nine years, leaving Mary Ann to bring up her two youngest children alone.

When Thomas left nearby Bridge Road School at thirteen years, he undertook an engineering apprenticeship at Stableford's Wagon Works at Coalville. He was tall man for the time (six feet in height) and possessed a very athletic build.

In 1914 two of his first cousins, John and Sidney Summers of Hugglescote, volunteered into the Famous Fifty. Sadly both perished in the later stages of the war.

As a qualified engineer he plied his trade during the early years of the war, when skilled men were vital to industries assisting the war effort. On the 16th

Thomas Kendrick and his fiancée, May Walden in 1918

Top left: Able Bodied Thomas Kendrick, Hawke Battalion, Royal Naval Division. Recovering from wounds at a convalescent home in 1918.

February 1916 he was placed on Army Reserve, meanwhile, heavy losses by the Royal Naval Division at the Dardanelles Campaign, etc, meant he was mobilised and posted to them on the 6th July 1917. Thomas travelled down to Blandford in Dorset for training, and officially joined the Fourth Reserve Battalion on the 10th July 1917, and ultimately to Hawke Battalion on the 5th November 1917.

The Royal Naval Division (R.N.D.) was created in 1914, just before the Great War, the brainchild of the Committee of Imperial Defence. They authorised the Admiralty to arrange for a: '*Land Force to be used for the seizure, fortification or protection of any temporary naval bases, which might be required overseas*'. So it was, that some eight thousand naval reservists were sent to Walmer and Betteshanger, (about six kilometres west of Deal in Kent) to construct their own camps, and to establish themselves as eight infantry battalions. They formed two Brigades, which collectively comprised the Royal Naval Division. The majority of the officers were from the Royal Naval Volunteer Reserve (R.N.V.R.), together with a touch of steel, officers

from a Brigade of Guards. Hawke Battalion was officially known as the Second Battalion of the 1st Royal Naval Brigade, and their first commanding officer was, Commander Beadle, R.N., and their first adjutant, Major Fletcher, of the Scots Guards.

A period of tough and intensive training followed at Crystal Palace Depot, which left some men struggling and replacements were drafted in, fitness requirements were very high!

On Saturday the 8th May 1915, the Battalion boarded '*Ascania*' and '*Ivernia*' for the passage to the Mediterranean Sea. On May 27th Hawke Battalion disembarked at Cape Helles, on the Gallipoli Peninsula as part of General Mercer's 1st Naval Brigade. Cape Helles had a coastal plain of about fourteen hundred metres (twelve hundred yards), and then came the abrupt cliff heights. Hawke had a gentle baptism into trench life and warfare with losses being low. As summer progressed so did the amount of flies, and many suffered from gastro-enteritis, and later with jaundice. The War Diary quotes: '*July 12th, captured some trenches from the Turks. Few things more trying than landing in ill-dug and unsanitary trenches in the height of summer, to wrestle for two days and nights with the combined duties of scavenger, navvy, grave-digger, sanitary inspector and not least soldier!' September nights are described as bitterly cold. It continues— December 26th: 'Trenches almost knee deep in water in places, a foot or two of mud in others, some trenches have five feet of water. Turks gave us plenty of shells on Christmas Eve, and over three days we lost seventy men including Rev. Davis.'*

The object of the Campaign was to control the entrance to the Black Sea and to inflict a crushing blow on the Turks.

Strategically the idea was good, unfortunately senior military figures failed to appreciate the practicalities of the location, and the Dardanelles affair was a humiliating failure, despite the heroics of very many soldiers. From April 1915 to January 1916, over one hundred thousand lives were lost on both sides! The entire Allied Force was evacuated during darkness, and a few days later on the 9th January 1916 'Hawke' was safely in Mudros Harbour (Greece). By late May 1916 the Battalion had travelled by train from Marseilles to Doudelainville, a few kilometres from Abbeville, France. Here the men were refitted with rifles, Lewis guns, Stokes Mortars and field kitchens, etc.

On July 17th the R.N.D. occupied trenches in the Vimy Ridge Sector, with Hawke in the area of Souchez, then a relatively quiet spot considering the carnage that took place to French Armies one year before. The Battalion occupied this ruin of a village until the autumn. On October 7th they were posted to the Somme Sector, occupying Forceville, a small town about six kilometres (four miles) from Thiepval Ridge. The German's main pivotal points north of the River Ancre were at Serre, Beaumont Hamel and Beaucourt. The R. N. D. was in front of the village of Hamel, and Hawke advanced along the Ancre Valley on October 19th. Matters came to a head on November 13th when, after a heavy barrage added smoke and fumes to an early morning mist, the first waves of Hawke went 'over the top' and disappeared into the smog. Twenty officers and four hundred and fifteen men went over in four waves at sixty metres intervals. Survivors told of horrendous scenes, pals perforated by machine-gun fire and others hanging

Thomas Kendrick was born at 5, Crescent Road at Hugglescote.

from enemy barbed wire. No officers returned unhurt, and less than twenty men in the same category.

It was established that the majority of the casualties occurred within five minutes of leaving their trenches, enemy machine-guns reaping a harvest of death. The remnants of the Battalion were rested to allow reorganisation and refit with fresh drafts of men.

Hawke Battalion had a very busy 1917, continuing on the Ancre, followed by Gavrelle (Arras), then Passchendaele (Ypres), and finally at Welsh Ridge (Cambrai).

February 3rd saw a refreshed Hawke attack once again in the Ancre Valley. From 11.00 pm they moved forward in two waves, and bitter fighting followed during the night, and the enemy launched a barrage and counter-attacked repeatedly. (There was also ten degrees of frost (F)). It raged on for two days with the Battalion winning a tactical battle, but at a cost of nearly one hundred dead and eighty-seven wounded. Following these losses the Battalion went down with an epidemic of 'fever' and was sidelined for a week. After a spell at Poziere on the muddy Somme, they marched to the green fields behind the Lens-Arras Front, and on April 23rd the R.N.D. attacked and secured Gavrelle in the Arras Sector. The Germans desperately tried to recapture the village but failed in spite of deluging the village with high explosive shells and gas. Hawke spent the following six months in the Gavrell-Oppy sector of Arras, and on September 29th moved to the devastated wilderness of Passchendaele, near Ypres.

On the 10th March 1917 Thomas Kendrick was baptised at St. John The Baptist Church, Hugglescote, and eight months later, 5th November 1917, Able Bodied Seaman Thomas Kendrick, service number R/4837, embarked from Folkestone and arrived at Boulogne on November 11th. There he entrained for Calais, and then proceeded inland to join his unit.

In the summer of 1917 one million British, Canadian and Anzac troops fought in the Battle of Passchendaele (named after the small Flemish village). The name was synonymous with death and mud, and the area was still a quagmire, with thousands of bodies of both sides lying in shell holes filled with mud and foul waste.

The R.N.D made small inroads on the German Lines, but the conditions were primarily the victors, and any attempts to improve communication trenches and transport lines resulted in loss of life from continuous shelling.

The Division entrained on December 8th and travelled south to Bapaume in the Somme.

An officer's letter recounts the soldiers of Hawke marching from Bapaume singing: '*We saw him, we saw him, drinking all the buckshee rum.*' On the December 15th the Battalion moved onto Welsh Ridge, a vital and yet precarious position on the Flesquieres Ridge (Cambrai Sector). It was known that if the position fell, so would four miles of the Hindenburg Line that had earlier been captured. The conditions were desperately wet and cold, with very sharp frosts. On December 30th the Germans launched a fierce barrage, and this was followed by overwhelmingly superior numbers of storm troops. Bravely, Hawke's men went over the top with bayonets drawn and confronted the enemy on the open ground.

The opposing forces clashed, and the tough naval troops drove the numerically stronger elite enemy forces back. Two of Hawke's officers were awarded posthumous Military Crosses for their daring and bravery in leading the charge.

After the attack, a wallet full of enemy documents was found which stated: "*Our troops must expect desperate resistance for we will be attacking the Royal Naval Division.*" How right they were, and certainly they did not expect to be attacked by a lesser force.

The Division earned many compliments for their magnificent achievement! The War Diary's comment regarding the enemy: '*They were in strength and had shown themselves resolute, brave and skilful.*' (Magnanimous in victory).

The 5th January 1918 saw the Battalion relieved from the frontline to a support position on Welsh Ridge. A senior officer, Geoffrey Price wrote on January 7th: '*Frozen water, wet wood, clothes unwashed for ten days, unshaved, sleeping on a sandbag on a frozen floor of mud, steel helmet for a pillow, perpetual shell fire, some men have frost bite others have fever, men exhausted, rations poor, long dark nights, men sleep in open.*'

Hawke went back to the frontline during the night of the 8-9th January 1918, when there was ten degrees of frost (F). Arriving and departing from frontline trenches was always a fearful time, with the German snipers acknowledged as masters in their craft. Just before light, Able Bodied Seaman Thomas Kendrick was severely wounded in the left scapular region of his shoulder, only just above his heart. A thaw had set in, and stretcher-bearers carried Thomas, who was in considerable pain, through trenches that in places were four feet deep with slush, to a first aid post where he was patched-up. A Red Cross van then drove him on a seemingly endless journey, through eighteen miles of despoiled and unpopulated country. On January 11th he was admitted to Rouen Hospital for a few days, and finally invalided to England on January 14th, to arrive at Graylingwell War Hospital at Chichester the following day.

The defence of Welsh Ridge is regarded as the R.N.D.'s most notable achievement of the war, and I am pleased that Thomas received his share of the praise for his outstanding bravery.

Hawke Battalion continued to be in the thick of it. The Germans continued to attack strongly in their spring offensive and on March 12th, at Ribecourt, Hawke lost four officers and one hundred and thirty five men. On the following day, three officers and one hundred and twenty seven men, all gassed. The

R.N.D., now well below strength had to fall back as determined German Forces pushed them westerly. Further massive attacks on March 21st led to the whole Line having to retire, first to High Wood and then to the Thiepval Plateau on the Somme. In May, June and July the Division occupied trenches opposite Hamel and Auchonvillers Ridge. Gradually the enemy attacks slowed down, and during August the R.N.D. attacked and reclaimed land as far as Bapaume. Later in August the Division fought in battles for Arras, with the object of seizing the northern section of the Hindenburg Line. They were victories, but Hawke alone lost several officers and over fifty men killed, together with over three hundred wounded.

As was the case, further drafts topped up the manpower. Right up until the Armistice, Hawke continued to push and secure victories and more than did its share in the Allies' ultimate victory.

Thomas recovered after several months of hospitalisation and convalescence and received furlough (leave) from the 29th June - 8th July 1918. On August 27th he was assessed at the Royal Naval Hospital, Aldershot, where his wound was considered 'Severe' and was discharged the following day (invalided to 17th September 1918), and passed-out with a King's discharge on October 19th.

Thomas's younger brother, Harry, also fought in the Great War as a frontline soldier with the 6th Battalion of the Northumberland Fusiliers. He survived, but suffered for many years as a consequence of being a German prisoner of war.

Thomas returned to his engineering job at Stableford's Wagon Works, and soon married Adelaide Beatrice Walden (born in 1887 at Lutterworth). Adelaide, (always known as May) was the daughter of Charles (a tailor) and Elizabeth Ann Walden. The couple with May's daughter, Ivy (born 1913) resided at 17, Wyggeston Road, Coalville. The marriage was blessed with a son Leslie, 1919-2006, daughter Mabel, 1922-2005 and Percy, 1928.

The Stableford Works went into decline and finally closed in 1924. Thomas, with his war-wound proving a burden to his health, sought employment down the mines, and became a collier at South Leicestershire Colliery at Ellistown.

The locality suffered especially so during the Miner's Strike, and the Depression, with money a scarce commodity, especially for wounded old soldiers! His wife, May, did her utmost to help the family by taking-in washing to earn a few extra shilling a week. Such a job was very hard manual labour at that time. Thomas's son, Leslie (Les), did all he could to earn some money; from the age of twelve he delivered a full paper round before school. Les had passed his examinations for grammar school but his parents couldn't afford to send him, and by the age of fourteen he was Head Boy at Bridge Road School. He had no alternative but to leave and to start work as a labourer at Heather Brickyard. His first week totalled sixty-six hours at 4 1/2d (about two new pence per hour). Les added: *"Father was often not fit enough for work, but if he was he'd come home from the pit and washed in the backyard. He had a small hole where the bullet entered his chest, but at the back was a deep hole with wizened skin pulled and stitched together."* Les was academic and athletic. He was captain of his School's football and cricketing teams, and head choirboy at St. John The Baptist Church, at Hugglescote, but his parents needed and relied on his extra income! He was captured at Singapore in February 1942 during World War 2, and was a Japanese prisoner of war until 1945.

May's health deteriorated and she became wheelchair bound with rheumatoid arthritis, and suffered terrible pain for several years until passing-away on the 2nd January 1943, aged fifty-two. May lies in Hugglescote cemetery, and Les, shortly before his death, bought a new headstone.

Thomas remarried to an Irish nurse, Honor Sundiral in 1944 and moved to 63, Little Glen Road, Blaby. For a few years he worked at a shoe-manufacturing factory in Leicester, until dying on the 14th December 1949, at the age of fifty-six years.

Les married Betty Hatter, daughter of Charles Hatter, one of the Famous Fifty, on the 15th December 1945. He retired at the age of sixty-two, whilst holding a position on the board of directors of Hilton's Footwear Retail Firm at Leicester. He passed away on the 5th January 2006, shortly after their Diamond Wedding Anniversary.

Readers may well have guessed that Thomas Kendrick was my grandfather. My parents told me he saw me a few times when I was in my pram.

Unfortunately the early deaths of both my paternal grandparents meant that I never got to know them, nevertheless, I feel proud of what Thomas (and May) achieved in their lifetimes.

Two other local men served in Hawke Battalion and both came from Donington-le-Heath:

Able Bodied William Lowe, R/5370 of 4, Townsend Lane and Able Bodied David Watts*, B/5372 of 2, Townsend Lane. Additional men in the Royal Naval Division: Able Bodied George Henry Mee, R/5293 of 110, Church Lane, Whitwick, and from the same village.

Thomas Kendrick circa 1940.

Able Bodied Albert Roome, R/5297 of Leicester Road, Able Bodied William Sear, BZ/4088 of 108, Hermitage Road, Able Bodied Herbert Webster*, R/5090 of 138, Church Lane, and Lance Sergeant Alfred John Wilson*, TZ/5575 of 32, Silver Street, Able Bodied Charles Burton, R/1466 of Eggintons Hill, Peggs Green, Able Bodied Horace Hallam, BZ/4771 of Hough Hill, Swannington, Able Bodied J. T. Fortnam of Thringstone*, Able Bodied R. Underwood of Whitwick*, Petty Officer Harry Smith of Ibstock*, Able Bodied John H. Storer of Ibstock*, Able Bodied William Potter of Sinope*, Able Bodied John Heighton of Whitwick *, * Killed in action.

The famous poet, Rupert Brooke, who wrote amongst others: 'The Soldier' - "*If I should die, think only this of me: That there's some corner of a foreign field that is forever England.*" He was a Sub-lieutenant in the Royal Naval Division, and lies buried on the island of Skyros in the Aegean Sea.

Regarding Thomas's siblings. Martha married Charles Edward Weston, who was the son of Samuel (a wheelwright) and Harriet Weston of Hugglescote.

Little is known of Mary, but it is thought she married in 1906.

Laura married George Fleet Boot on the 2nd August 1915. George, a farmer, was the son of Joseph (a miner) and Jane Boot of Coalville. This is the same family circle as Samuel Boot—one of the Famous Fifty.

Lillian (Lill) married William Winkless of Donington-le-Heath, the son of Harry Winkless, a collier.

Harry fought in the Great War and it is believed that he married Ada Ann Donaldson at some time during the Great War. Certainly in 1918 his home address was that of his mother's at 5, Crescent Road, Hugglescote.

Little is known of Mabel, but Mary Frances, the last-born married Herbert H. A. Walne.

It is of interest that my great-grandfather, Tom Kendrick, had a sister, four years older, named, Eliza. She was born in 1862 and married when she was just seventeen years of age. Her husband, Reuben Summers was born in 1854, a railway guard and later a coal miner of Coalville. They lived at 152, Ashburton Road, Hugglescote (now demolished) and two of their children, John and Sidney Summers were of the Famous Fifty. John was killed on the 20th July 1918 and Sidney on the 24th September 1918. They were Thomas Kendrick's first cousins.

Also, when deciding to write a book about the Famous Fifty, I thought my only connection was by my maternal grandfather, Charles Hatter. It now appears that I am also related to Sam Boot (Charles Hatter's second cousin) as well as the above two. Sam was the first of the Fifty to be killed.

WILLIAM THOMAS MACE

William was born during the eighteen-nineties at the village of Todenham in Gloucestershire, about eighteen kilometres (twelve miles) due south of Stratford on Avon.

Not a lot is known of the man, but I was given his photograph by his grandnephew, and he was enthused when I promised that one day his great uncle's name would be remembered in a book! Around this time, about four years ago, he and his wife owned a shop on Belvoir Road at Coalville, which dealt with house-clearances and second hand crafts, books, etc. It is to my sadness that the shop closed down and therefore I cannot quote his name or address.

William was living in the district of Bardon, a hamlet a few kilometres from Coalville at the time of his volunteering to join the army. The main occupation for the majority of the men within the community was at the local quarry, please read about Isaac Bancroft.

William enlisted at Coalville, possibly in late 1914 into the Leicestershire Regiment and was issued the service number 24999. In the early days he was almost certainly intended to be part of one of the Leicestershire Service Battalions, the Sixth, Seventh, Eighth and Ninth as written in detail by Mathew Richardson. I believe he trained with one of the above and was subsequently transferred to the 1st Leicestershire Battalion following a run of appalling casualties. He probably joined the Battalion in the autumn of 1915.

The Battle of the Somme opened on the 1st July 1916, and on that fateful day the British Army lost twenty thousand dead alone, with double that numbered in casualties. The bloody battle was to rage until mid-November of 1916, and further documentation can be read in the Francis Martin section. I mention that one of the strongest German fortifications within the Somme Sector was known as the Quadrilateral, an infamous redoubt that had already claimed thousands of allied lives. On September 15th at 6.20 am the 1st Leicestershire Battalion went over the top to attack this defensive hotbed. They were located in a position facing northeast along the general line of a sunken road running due south from Ginchy. Our soldiers went over in a thick mist at a steady pace, advancing in four waves, and the enemy quickly opened up with heavy machine-gun fire. The advancing troops did not reach their objective, their efforts not being assisted by very thick, strong, thick and wholly undamaged enemy barbed wire. The men of 'A' Company, led by Captain J. Mosse entrenched on a small ridge to assess the situation. In the meantime men of Companies 'B', (Captain H. Pickbourne)'C' (Captain G. Salmon) and 'D' (Captain C. Herbison) had suffered terribly. The enemy then laid-down an almighty barrage, and soon visual signals were impossible with Brigade Headquarters and runners also found it almost impossible to make progress. By nightfall the soldiers of the First had dug themselves into reasonably good cover, and had been supported by reserves. On the following morning nine enemy aeroplanes circled over their trenches to obtain location points and to strafe their lines. The position was held and just after nightfall troops of the 1st West Yorkshire Battalion relieved the Tigers.

Private William Mace in 1915. 1st Battalion Leicestershire Regiment.

The Battalion's losses for the 15th and 16th are described as grievous. Fourteen officers and 410 other ranks were killed or injured and William Mace of Bardon was one of them.

Major General C. Ross, the Commander of the 6th Division sent the following message: *"Great appreciation... splendid fashion... most difficult task ... which can be given to soldiers... was carried out with unflinching gallantry and devotion."*

Like so many in the Great War, William was either cut-down by machine-gun fire or blown to the winds by heavy explosive artillery shells.

William Thomas Mace's name can be read on the Coalville Clock Tower Memorial.

Many thanks to the couple that shared a few private moments with me, and I do hope that they find out that William has not been forgotten.

FRANCIS FREDERICK MARTIN

Francis, more usually known as Frank, was born in 1887 at Coleorton, a village between Coalville and Ashby de la Zouch. His father, Frank Martin, was employed as an engine driver at Ellistown for South Leicestershire Colliery, and together with his wife and three other sons they lived on Club Row at Coalville.

After leaving school Francis worked as a miner for a short time, but decided to seek a more adventurous and outdoor life whilst still young. He travelled into Leicester in the early years of the century, and enlisted as a regular soldier, service number 6613, and committed himself to eight years in the 1st Battalion of the Leicestershire Regiment, spending several years in India. After honouring his stay he opted for civilian life, and obtained a job as a miner at Whitwick Colliery. Shortly afterwards he

Private Francis Martin had been a regular soldier before the Great War, serving in India. On August 5th 1914 he received a telegram ordering him to rejoin his old unit, the 1st Leicestershire Battalion. He was badly wounded close to Armentieres and was hospitalised at Boulogne Hospital and then transported to Sheffield Hospital where he died on the 11th June 1915. He received a full military funeral at Coalville London Road Cemetery.

married his fiancée, and they resided at 35, Victoria Street, Coalville, with his wife giving birth to a boy in 1913. After leaving the Army, Francis, as was normal practice was retained as a reservist, and this retention would have been completed in December 1914. On the 5th August 1914, Francis received a telegram ordering him to report to his former battalion with the Leicestershire Regiment. The regulars and the reservist congregated at a camp on Coldham Common, near to Cambridge, and then travelled the short distance to the village of Grantchester, famed by the poet, Rupert Brooke. Soon afterwards they marched to Royston, and on September 7th entrained for Southampton. The *'Braemar Castle'* shipped them across the Channel to the westerly French port of St. Nazaire. This was a precautionary measure because Boulogne and Le Havre appeared threatened by the German advances. On September 11th the Battalion, as part of the 6th Division, British Expeditionary Force (B.E.F.), entrained for billets in the area of Mortcerf, to the east of Paris. The period of the 13th to 19th September 1914 is documented as the 'March to the Aisne'. The Tigers marched from Mortcerf to the Courcelles district and crossed the Aisne on the evening of September 21st; taking up trenches on the line La Fosse Marguel. It was in this sector that the Battalion suffered its first casualties, albeit light in their first encounter with the German Army.

On the night of October 12th-13th the Battalion left the above district and proceeded by rail to Cassel in Belgium, and then by road to Croix Blanche. On

St. John The Baptist Church Lads' Brigade, Hugglescote. Circa 1915.

the morning of October 20th potent German Forces stormed into the attack, with the 1st Leicestershire Battalion holding a position on the Line, 'Rue du Bois La Houssoie', and thence to 'Porte Egale'. Their frontline received a preliminary heavy barrage, then came ferocious hand-to-hand fighting as the enemy attempted to thrust towards the Channel. The Allies believed that if the enemy succeeded in capturing vital Channel ports then France could succumb. Neither side would surrender any ground, and the resulting stalemate produced a new phenomenon, namely 'trench warfare.' During ten days the 1st Battalion defended resolutely but losses mounted, four officers and forty-seven other ranks killed, and five officers and one hundred and thirty four wounded! In addition there was over one hundred missing men. A total of **two hundred and eighty-seven casualties**.

The Divisional Diary quotes: '*The German artillery was very active during the whole period, 20th to 30th October, whilst our guns were woefully short of ammunition and consequently a greater strain was thrown on our infantry.*'

Gradually the frontline quietened down and November saw a fortnight of continuous frosts, followed by a thaw, to leave the shallow trenches knee-deep in water.

On December 22nd the Battalion was in trenches in the Armentieres, Bois Grenier Sector of Flanders. Francis, a vastly experienced soldier was to witness one of the most moving events in his military career. It occurred on late evening on Christmas Eve, and it was a truly enchanting piece of history. The embattled area had received a sprinkling of snow, a haloed moon lit up the night and a freezing, patchy mist hovering here and there. All was silent.

Sentries observed that the enemy trenches possessed an unusual multi-coloured glow. Presently, the joyful singing of a carol could be heard from the same setting, and steadily it grew in volume: 'Stille nacht, Heilige nacht'. In response 'A' Company sang the lines in English: 'Silent night, Holy night' and followed up with: 'Oh, Come all Ye Faithful' and the Germans listened, cheered and then shouted: "Good, Good." The festive singing warmed the hearts of soldiers who had thoughts of families back home and merrier times. Many warm tears crept down icy-cold cheeks on that emotional night. The mysterious lights observed in the enemy trenches were from Christmas trees that they had recently acquired.

On Christmas morning more snow fell, and all was quiet, none of the normal early morning shelling or sniping. The opposing sides hesitantly lifted their heads over the parapets, and some English speaking Germans called out to the Leicesters to arrange a meeting in No-Man's-Land. History was made, even in the depths of winter and with murderous death commonplace something of good in Man's psyche allowed '**A Christmas Truce**.'

The adversaries climbed from their trenches and strolled into No-Man's-Land, where small treats were exchanged such as cigars, cigarettes and photographs. Various reports claimed that a football game transpired, with both sides claiming victories. There were toasts with rum and wine, hands shaken, addresses exchanged and Saxon-British (Anglo-Saxon) friends made. As the weary sun departed, the sentries once again manned the parapets, yet still all remained quiet. Peace on earth, quite literally a silent night, but for how long? A thaw set in on Boxing Day together with heavy rain, and when senior German and British officers heard of the truce, they angrily ordered an immediate commencement of battle. The opposing soldiers shouted warnings 'to their friends' across the trenches explaining that a barrage was to start, and snipers were dormant. This fraternisation was fairly common in Flanders, but steps were taken for troop-movements to other sectors in an attempt to break ties. British troops were ordered never to fraternise with the enemy again, or leave their posts on pain of the death penalty.

Francis Martin experienced all of the above, and doubtless his mind was filled with thoughts of family and friends at Coalville.

As for the 1st Leicestershire Battalion, they moved regularly from billets at Armentierres to the trenches around the Rue du Bois until April, there was little fighting and the only casualties resulted primarily from shelling. For March 1915 just six men were killed and eleven wounded, and for April two killed and thirty wounded.

Francis was badly wounded in his trench in mid-May when a shell exploded close to him. He was patched-up at a first-aid post and sent by rail to Boulogne Hospital, where after three days he had recovered sufficiently to be transferred to Sheffield Infirmary. The War Diary reports that for the month of May, one officer was killed and twenty-four other ranks wounded.

Frank Martin (senior), his father, had recently died, but his mother made several trips to visit her son at Sheffield. Francis had suffered frightful abdominal wounds and the outlook was bleak, but he endeavoured, however, on the 11th June 1915 he passed on. I am pleased to write that his mother was with him at the time of his death. A train returned his body to Coalville, and the local recruiting officer, Captain Stevenson, made arrangements for the funeral to have military honours. It was the Town's first military funeral of the war and literally thousands turned out to honour him. There were six coaches for the mourners, included were his young widow, his mother and three brothers (in khaki). Six other men in khaki acted as bearers for the coffin, which was draped in a Union Jack. The coffin breastplate read: '***Private Frank Martin, 6613, 1st Leicestershire Battalion***'. Francis lies in London Road Cemetery, Coalville. His brother, John Martin, who was later transferred to the same Battalion was killed on the 16th March 1916, near to Boesinghe in the northern part of the Ypres Salient.

On the 30th May 1915 the Battalion marched from Armentieres through Bailleul and Poperinghe into the Ypres Salient, taking over the Wieltje-Ypres Road-West Roosebeke Road part of the frontline on June 2nd. Casualties rose steeply and they received their first 'taste' of gas, and for a time the Battalion linked-up with their regimental Fifth Battalion at Zillebeke Lake Dug-Outs. By middle August the 1st Battalion was defending the main entrance to Ypres,

Recruiting Rally on North Street (Central Road), Hugglescote. 1914
The Breach Cottages can be just seen—set back on the top left.

namely the ramparts and the ancient Menin Gate, and receiving shells fired from sixteen miles deep into enemy territory. The Battalion Diary: '*The 17 inch Howitzer Gun fired a huge shell that arrived with the sound of a railway train, and when it exploded sent earth and bricks over three hundred feet into the air! The shells came every ten minutes, three falling close to Battalion headquarters and left craters sixty feet across and thirty feet deep.*'

September saw the Battalion in frontline trenches at nearby Wieltje, and October at Potijze. The war in the Salient was one of heavy bombardment by enemy artillery and lethal sniping, and it often continued for days without end!

December produced severe gas attacks with the enemy using both chlorine and phosgene, and following a very rough period the Battalion spent their second Christmas in relative peace in billets. Just before Christmas the Scot, General Sir Douglas Haig, took over from Field-Marshal Sir John French as leader of the British Expeditionary Force.

Militarily, little changed within the Salient for the first three months of 1916. Climatically there was heavy snow and sub-zero temperatures, and this resulted in dreadful conditions for the occupants of the trenches. I have spoken to veterans who waded waist deep in slushy water and of their inability to dry clothing or to keep warm. Several have told me that following sleep (if possible) of leaving their outlines in the frosty ground. It speaks volumes for their fitness and levels of durability.

Throughout this period enemy aircraft were active dropping bombs on rest camps and communication trenches.

The 1st July 1916 was the opening day of the Battle of the Somme, with the Battalion in billets in Volkeringhove and Wormhoudt involved in exercises for an attack at Pilckem Ridge, which was eventually cancelled. The days rumbled-on and following a southerly sojourn, the 14th August saw the Battalion relieve the 2nd Grenadier Guards in front of Beaumont Hamel on the Somme. The Leicestershire troops were primarily involved in the third phase of the Somme, and on September 15th they prepared to attack just to the south of Ginchy. At 6.20 am they went over the top, at a steady pace in four waves with thirty pace intervals, with support companies at three hundred and twenty-five metres (three hundred yards) to the rear. Due to a thick mist and gun smoke, communication proved to be difficult, and the chatter of enemy machine-guns soon caused enormous casualties. They were relieved the following day. In two days of fighting **fourteen officers and four hundred and ten** other ranks had been killed or wounded. Come October 21st the remnant of the Battalion was in billets in Corbie, and three days later entrained to the Bethune-La Bassee Sector, with Christmas Day being spent in huts at La Bourse.

January 1917 had severe frosts and deep snowstorms with the Battalion occupying frontline trenches close to Mazingarbe, five kilometres (three

miles) northwest of Loos. Late February had them posted to trenches at nearby Hulluch, and tolerably continuous fighting extended into May. The 46th North Midland Territorial Division (including the 1/4th and 1/5th Leicestershire Battalions) had an offensive opposite to the Lens area in June, and to absorb some of the German counters the 1st Battalion was given a series of diversionary attacks.

In July the First was posted to the adjacent St.Elie Sector, and later travelled to the Cambrai locality for the start of the Battle of Cambrai on November 20th. At 6.20 am the Battalion formed the first infantry wave behind a cover of tanks, and advanced with a creeping barrage to penetrate the Hindenburg Line at Noyelles.

The Germans launched powerful counter attacks with strong artillery support. Afterwards, Field Marshal Douglas Haig in a despatch dated the 20th February 1918 declared: '*We have captured and retained over 12,000 yards (about ten kilometres) of German Front-Line, from La Vacquerie to Boursies, together with 10-11,000 yards (nine kilometres) of the Hindenburg Line!*' He expressed great credit for the soldiers of the 1st Leicestershire Battalion.

For the 1st Battalion their next test came with the German Spring Offensive of March 1918. The morning of March 22nd dawned on the Somme Sector with a thick fog, abetted by a smoky onslaught and high explosive shells from the German artillery. The enemy's target was the Battalion's trench system on the Vaulx-Morchies Line, and on Vaulx itself. The enemy swarmed forward in massive numbers, wave after wave, but were beaten-off by rapid rifle, machine-gun and Lewis-gun fire. Later in the day, even in the smoggy atmospheres German snipers caused many fatalities and casualties. Concentrated and repeated enemy attacks, aided by exceptionally fierce machine-gun fire pushed-back the men of 'A' Company towards the Crucifix End of their trench, before finally having to evacuate. During this withdrawal many were slaughtered by gunfire, and ironically lots fell in Morchies Cemetery. The Line was held, only just, and it had been close to crisis point, but the Tigers held out.

On March 24th the Battalion was thankfully brought up to strength with an enormous draft of twenty-four officers and six hundred and eighty-eight other ranks.

The 6th Division received appropriate praise, which included a letter from General Sir Julian Byng: *'My appreciation of their splendid conduct, by their devotion and courage they have broken up overwhelming attacks and prevented the enemy gaining his object, namely, a decisive victory.'* The King and the Prime Minister expressed similar opinions.

By the 2nd April 1918 the Battalion had left the area and was billeted at Chateau Camp, Ypres. The German advance was pulsating and April 12th tasted-a-day of bitter fighting in the area of Neuve Eglise, and then in an area between Locre and Dranoutre for what was to become the Battle of the Lys. Typically, after dark on April 14th the Battalion's frontline was heavily bombarded and it reached a climax at 3.00 am. Fierce fighting took place and over the next few days 'C' Company, in particular, suffered heavy casualties. After one week's fighting three officers and twenty-eight ranks were killed and over a hundred wounded. Finally, success, the enemy tide was stemmed, and on April 25th the Battalion marched to St. Omer, and entrained to Rainsford

Camp near Watou.

The 14th September 1918 saw the 6th Division move to the Holnnon Wood area, five kilometres (three miles) west of St.Quentin. Over the following weeks the Division attacked the infamous Quadrilateral Redoubt, and were ably supported by the 2nd Durham Light Infantry. By midnight of September 25th-26th the Sixteenth and Eighteenth Infantry Brigades, assisted by the 1st Leicestershire Battalion captured the 'impregnable' Quadrilateral. The War Diary reads: *'The attack was delivered with great gallantry.'*

On October 4th the Battalion travelled by bus and route march to arrive at Magny-la-Fosse, and settled in trenches round the eastern edge of the village. On the 8th they attacked with a thrust in the direction of Bohain, and all objectives were met despite determined fire from machine-gun posts. The Battalion was in billets at Bohain when shortly after **11.00 am on November 11th 1918, the following message was received:** *"Hostilities ceased at 11.00 hours this morning!"*

From George T. Gadsby to S.W. Palmer on the Coalville Clock Tower Memorial. Many of the names will be familiar to readers of my two W.W.1 books.

The 1st Leicestershire Battalion's losses for the Great War are very similar to the 2nd's with just over one thousand men from each.

Besides the deaths of the two brothers, Francis and John Martin, the following lists of other local men of the 1st Battalion who sacrificed their lives.

Harry Allen of Sileby 21/7/18. 2) Lewis Bailey of Markfield 16/4/18. 3) Ernest Bancroft of Quorn 20/12/15. 4) Barrs Barker of Shepshed 19/9/18. 5) Joe Belcher of Willesley 8/10/18. 6) Frederick Bevins of Newbold Verdon 8/10/18. 7) William Brooks of Ravenstone 27/4/16. 8) Arthur Brownlow of Coalville 21/6/15. 9) Herbert Browton of Loughborough 20/11/17. 10) John Clarke of Loughborough 15/9/16. 11) John Clibbery of Coalville 21/7/15. 12) John Curtis of Swannington 18/9/18. 13) Walter Daft of Quorn 20/9/15. 14) Martin Eames of Coalville 19/10/18. 15) George Firban of Coalville 24/3/17. 16) Ernest Flamson of Heather 24/5/17. 17) William Gale of Shepshed 31/7/16. 18) Benjamin Garfield of Thornton 15/9/16. 19) George German of Ashby 7/7/18. 20) Thomas Gilbert of Mountsorrel 29/11/14. 21) George Grice of Moira 22/3/18. 22) James Hall of Whitwick 15/10/17. 23) William Hallam of Quorn 22/10/14. 24) John Hibbitt of Coalville 15/9/16. 25) Frank Hill of Hugglescote 22/7/18. 26) Andrew Hobson of Whitwick. 27) Frederick Holden of Castle Donnington 23/10/18. 28) George Hubbard of Barrow-on-Soar 15/9/16. 29) John Hunt of Moira 7/4/18. 30) Joseph Johnson of Swannington 16/4/15. 31) Jes Jones of Ellistown 15/9/16. 32) Wilfred Jones of Loughborough 15/9/16. 33) Samuel Kirk of Moira 20/11/17. 34) John Lacey of Shepshed 15/9/16. 35) Joseph Marriott of Shepshed 27/10/15. 36) John Mason of Loughborough 4/2/16. 37) Ronald Mason of Ashby 23/5/17. 38) William Moorhouse of Loughborough 4/7/18. 39) Edwin Morris of Bardon 15/9/16. 40) James Nicholls of Coalville 28/7/16. 41) Edward Orton of Ellistown 23/10/16. 42) Frederick Pepper of Barrow-on-Soar 9/10/15. 43) Arthur Prior of Hugglsecote 25/9/16. 44) Joseph Reed of Thornton 4/12/17. 45) John Rolleston of Ibstock 9/3/17. 46) Rudolf Rossell of Shepshed 15/9/16. 47) Albert Rowbotham of Loughborough 15/9/16. 48) Richard Sharpe of Loughborough 27/4/17. 49) Frederick Smith of Ashby 16/4/18. 50) George smith

The grave of Private Francis Martin in London Road Cemetery, Coalville.

of Groby 6/9/17. 51) William Stanley of Coalville 11/10/18. 52) Silas Stevenson of Quorn 15/9/16. 53) Ernest Stinchcombe of Hugglescote 20/3/17. 54) Frank Sutton of Loughborough 22/4/17. 55) Leonard Thornton of Loughborough 16/5/15. 56) Albert Thorpe of Loughborough 25/10/14. 57) Charles Thorpe of Shepshed 22/10/16. 58) George Tomlinson of Loughborough 27/3/17. 59) Frank Towe of Barrow-on-Soar 4/6/15. 60) Ernest Tugby of Whitwick 7/6/15. 60) John Walker of Hugglescote 9/10/18. 61) Ernest Ward of Quorn 27/10/14. 62) George Ward of Loughborough 29/6/15. 63) Percy Whitlock of Ashby 18/10/16. 64) Arthur Wright of Swannington 4/2/17. 65) Benjamin Wright of Miora 15/9/16.

Special mention for Private J. Weston, a Military Medallist, who was the son of Thomas Weston of Belvoir Road, Coalville. After being badly wounded and in hospital, he gallantly gave a pint of blood to save the life of a complete stranger, an officer in the same ward. Mr Weston survived but was unfit to continue in the Forces. He'd previously worked for Stableford's Wagon Works. He won his medal for single handedly taking an enemy position.

Post-script.

Francis Martin died of wounds on the 11th June 1915. The Coalville Times of the 22nd October 1915 prints a letter sent by his friend to Francis's wife:

Mrs Martin.
35, Victoria Street.
Coalville.
Leicestershire.

Dear Mrs Martin,

*   I am writing to say how much I respected your husband, Francis, who was a great friend of mine in the Battalion. I am so sorry about his death; it was a big shock to all of us as he was so highly respected by officers and men alike! He was always a good worker and I have never seen a cleaner soldier. You know he was always a happy chap, he was a one for singing and he used to cheer us all up. We joined up at the same time, we were in the same section and we were always together.*

Please find enclosed your husband's cap badge that he lost when he was wounded. I wish you and your young son all the best of luck in the great struggle through life.

Yours sincerely, Private Hughes.

The newspaper qualifies the above by mentioning that although she had never met Private Hughes she had sent him a letter expressing her deep gratitude.

I am pleased to write that the kind-hearted soldier survived the war.

The following lines written by John Donne come to mind:

'Any man's death diminishes me, because I am involved in
Mankind and therefore never send to know for whom the bell tolls,
It tolls for thee.'

The names of Francis and John Martin can be read on the Coalville Clock Tower War Memorial, with Francis' name also on the Memorial Tablet within Coalville's Christ Church.

Christ Church, Coalville.

IN MEMORY OF OUR FALLEN IN THE GREAT WAR, 1914-1919.
THEY LOVED NOT THEIR LIVES UNTO DEATH R.I.P.

ADCOCK. S.H.	DAKIN. GEO.	JAMES. MAURICE. E.	TIVEY. FRED.
AMOS. ERNEST.	DALE. ALFRED.	JEWSBURY. CH WM	THORPE. THOMAS.A.
ARGENT. J.W.	DAVIS. FRED.	JOHNSON. ALBERT. CPL	TOOKEY. P.
BAILEY. GEORGE.	DEACON. HAROLD.S.	JOHNSON. ARTHUR.	TWELLS. LAUNCELOT.J.
BAKEWELL. WM T.	DEXTER. F.	KEELING. DICK.	WALKER. JOHN.
BAMFORD. R.G.	DOOLEY. T. LT D.C.M.	KETCHER. H.EDWIN.	WARDLE. JAMES.
BATHO. E.	DRINKWATER. D.	LEECH. W.H.CPL	WARDLE. JOSEPH.
BEASLEY. W.	EALES. J.H.	LINE. SAML	WELLS. ALBERT. W.
BECK. L.G. CPL	EATON. JOS L/C.	MARSH. J. J.C.	WESSON. ALF. SGT
BECK. S.	ESSEX. ALBERT.	MARTIN. ARCHIE.	WESSON. G.H. SGT
BENNETT. JOHN.	FANTOM. WALTER.	MARTIN. F.F.	WHARMBY. HERB.G.
BLACK. THOS	GADBY. G.T.	MARTIN. GEO. CPL	WHITE. HUB. R.L/C.
BODLE. SAML	GEE. ERNEST. WM	MASSEY. FDK	WILKINSON. GEO.
BRADSHAW. A.C. SERGT	HAGGER. ARTHUR.	MAWER. J.H.	WILLIAMSON. JNO. CPL
BROTHERHOOD. ERNEST.	HALL. JAS H.	MOORE. ERNEST.	WOODCOCK. C.C.
BROWN. LEONARD. D.	HALL. JOHN. SGT	MORGAN. ERIC. SGT	WOOLHOUSE. F.W.
BROWN. W.J. CECIL.	HALL. ROLAND.	NICHOLLS. JAS W.	WRIGHT. ARTHUR. L/C
BROWNLOW. AMBROSE.	HANCOCK. VICTOR. W.	PAGE. C.	WRIGHT. J.W.
BROWNLOW. ARTHUR.	HARDY. STENSON.	PICKERING. JOHN. W.	
BROWNLOW. ERNEST.	HART. F.W.	ROBERTS. FORESTER.	SERVERS AT THE ALTAR.
BULLOCK. JOHN.	HAY. ROBERT. LT	SADDINGTON. GEO. SGT	BAUM. HORACE.B.
CHAMBERS. W.	HAYES. H.	SCOTT. CLIFFORD. E.	BROWN. SYDNEY. 2LT
CLIBBERY. JOHN.	HEWARD. ARNOLD.S.	SCOTT. F. CAPT M.C.	PECK. OSWYN. J L/C.
COLLIER. J.W.T.	HICKLING. DAVID.	SHEFFIELD. JOHN. D.CPL	WORTLEY. ARCH A.L/C.
COLVER. JOHN. F.	HILL. FRANK.	SHEFFIELD. JOS	
COPLEY. HARRY.	HOLLICK. J.W.	STACEY. SIMEON.	SAMUEL HOSKING.
COPLEY. JOHN	HOLYOAKE. E. CPL	STAFFORD. F.E.	VICAR
CROFT. HORACE. SERGT	HODGETTS. HENRY.	STANLEY. R.	
CRACKNELL. J.F.	HOGAN. J.W.	STANLEY. RICHD	EDWARD ORTON.
CURTIS. ALB. L/C.	HUNT. EDWARD. HY	STANLEY. WM	THOMAS GOACHER.
			CHURCHWARDENS

THE CHRISTMAS TRUCE OF 1914

With mankind crippled spiritually and behaviourally by the original sin.
With massive armies inflicting pain and death onto their brethren.
As biting frosts and stinging snow glittered 'neath a diamante sky bright.
Men of Flanders-field's sang on the sacred night in praise of the Light.

On the Eve the carol 'Stille Nacht' floated as a vapour from enemy dugouts.
Tommies cheered and sang a festive response to remove any doubts!
Christmas Day exchanges of gifts and brotherly love replaced kill or die!
Photos and addresses aired, a game of football and the score was a tie.

The 'mighty' were tucking into their festive pud when they heard.
"Fraternisation with the enemy!" Treachery was their emotive word.
"Open fire with immediate effect and shell the Bosch with high explosive!"
The guns stayed silent as war diaries declared the results 'inconclusive'.

'Twas a miraculous interlude: a day and a night of joy and peace on earth.
A frosty silent-night 'til khaki and grey sang rejoices for a noble birth.
For near-on four years the bloodshed continued: brother-fought father,
Father fought brother, only for that war to be followed by yet another.

Michael Kendrick
Christmas 2004

AUBREY MOORE. MC
& MENTIONED IN DESPATCHES

Aubrey Moore was born on the 30th August 1893 in the Leicestershire village of Appleby Magna, some eight kilometres (five miles) south of Ashby-de-la Zouch. The Moore family had lived in the village since the beginning of the seventeenth century, when Charles Moore purchased the Lordship of the Manor. Aubrey's uncle, George, owned the estate and his younger brother, Aubrey's father, was the Reverend Charles Moore, rector of Appleby Magna for forty-five years. Aubrey's mother, Charlotte Mabel, was the daughter of the Honourable Augustus Byron, son of the 7th Lord Byron who succeeded the poet, the 6th Lord Byron. Aubrey had one sister, Sylvia Mary, and two brothers, George and Charles (also another brother and sister who died in infancy).

After a spell at Appleby Grammar School, Aubrey was educated at the prestigious and centuries old Ashby de la Zouch Grammar School, and among his friends were Jabez and William Emmerson, Walter Handford and Frederic Scott, all of which figured prominently alongside him during the Great War. Another firm school friend was Philip Bent, a Canadian boarder at the school who received a posthumous Victoria Cross in 1917 whilst serving with the 9th Leicestershire Battalion in France.

Lieutenant Aubrey Moore, 5th Battalion, Leicestershire Regiment in 1914.

In 1913, Captain Harry Hassell, who commanded the Ashby Company of the Fifth Battalion of the Leicestershire Regiment, invited Aubrey to apply for a commission, which after training and various interviews he subsequently achieved in December 1913.

At the outbreak of war Lieutenant Aubrey Moore was made second-in-command, under Captain James Griffiths, of 'D' (Hinckley) Company,

and followed the Battalion through the training processes and onto France and Belgium. It was while the Battalion was in the Messines Sector during May 1915, that Aubrey, a qualified coal-mining engineer, was asked to urgently form a counter-mining section using forty soldiers from the Brigade possessing a colliery background. Twenty men came from the Fifth and twenty from the Fourth Battalion, and they were all miners and all volunteers. The Germans were tunnelling under British trenches, placing explosives and detonating the mine(s) to cause maximum destruction. The forty men of the 'Tunnelling Section' were ordered to dig-out a protective tunnel in front of E1-left and E1- right trenches. This they did and exploded their own camouflet, destroying the enemy shafts and the tunnellers too. Shortly afterwards Lieutenant Moore and Corporal Barney, an Ellistown man, went underground to examine the results of another detonation and the two men very nearly died from inhaling various gases and lack of oxygen!

The 'Tunnelling Section' soon undertook counter-mining for the whole Divisional Front and it performed magnificently. In May 1915 the Royal Engineers were digging about two-three feet a day, whereas the Section was digging ten or more yards (forty feet). Aubrey Moore summed it up. *'It was the difference between skilled and unskilled men.'*

When the Fifth Battalion was posted to the Ypres Salient in June 1915, the area was already riddled with underground tunnels, and mine explosions were only too frequent an occurrence. At 7.00 pm on the 19th July 1915, the Royal Engineer's 175 Tunnelling Company detonated a massive mine under an enemy redoubt at the hamlet of Hooge. It consisted of 4,200 lbs of ammonal, 500 lbs of gunpowder and 200lbs of guncotton. This totalled over two tons of explosive (2,2500 kilograms)! Two plungers triggered the explosion from a point near to Sanctuary Wood. The men of the Fifth, in nearby Trench 50 and close to the infamous Hill 60, nervously waited for an enemy reply. It came on the 23rd July. My first book describes the details regarding loss of life, and also the bravery of Jabez Emmerson, Harry Starbuck (of Appleby Magna, later married Lily Butcher) and Bill Toon for ensuring a repeat did not happen on July 30th. All three were awarded the Distinguished Conduct Medal and a Military Cross was awarded to a certain modest lieutenant.

In early August the Battalion was in reserve in the dugouts at Lake Zillebeke, when a heavy shell exploded uncomfortably close to Aubrey. But for his anticipation it is doubtful whether he would have survived, for he took a massive leap and upon landing broke his anklebone, so enduring a period of recuperation in England until mid-November. During this recovery period he spent a few weeks at Battalion Headquarters, Loughborough, where he helped with recruiting. Aubrey was very fortunate indeed to miss further involvements around Hill 60 in the Salient, and the horrendous Battle of the Hohenzollern Redoubt near to Loos in France. Upon his return to the Battalion he was posted to 'C' Company as second-in-command to his old school-friend, Captain Roland Farmer, an Ashby de la Zouch man.

Aubrey was then informed that the Division was to be posted to the Dardanelles, where Turkish soldiers and the Aegean climate were inflicting heavy casualties upon our troops. They entrained for Marseilles, and after three days and two nights of slow travelling arrived at the southern coast of France. Aubrey remembered the train conditions were awful, and that some men travelled on the train-top, however, one man was killed when he failed to duck at a bridge. Following a very pleasant two-week stay they boarded H.M.T. 'Andania' with some trepidation. After a few days they disembarked, still at Marseilles following Lord Kitchener's decision to retire his soldiers from the Gallipollian Disaster.From the beautiful sunshine of southern France the Battalion was despatched, once again, to the evil bog-lands of the Western Front. Some of the Division had already arrived at Egypt when they received orders to return.

They were next posted to a bleak high-spot called Vimy Ridge, about ten kilometres north of Arras. French troops had earlier lost the summit and so the Germans controlled the large plateau and valley below. It was yet another sector noted for its mining activities. When the Fifth Battalion was not at the frontline, they lived and slept in a shallow cave on the slopes of a valley. The weather was snowy and bitterly cold, and apart from mining a major concern was heavy German barrages, and in particular their use of an inter-trench mortar bomb, made from a five-gallon oil drum, the 'minenwerfer.' Many men went down with pneumonia, trench fever and trench foot, at one time twenty-one men had to crawl on their hands and knees to the First Aid Post after a bitterly cold night.

Lieutenant John Barrett. V.C. a friend of Aubrey Moore.

On the 22nd March 1915 Aubrey lost his old friend, Captain Farmer, a man whom he hugely respected. It was acknowledged he was a very good, extremely brave and hardy officer. The Ashby man was killed by the blast of a minenwerfer, and his body was blown-out of his trench and was found

The marriage of Captain Aubrey Moore MC and May Shields on the 1st September 1917 at Isley Walton Church.

lying facedown in a deep water-filled shell-hole.

Major John Norton Griffiths, a middle-aged ex-Member of Parliament, had been responsible for ensuring that the Allies had the knowledge and experience to engage and combat the serious enemy mining threat. Towards the end of 1915 word spread about Lieutenant Moore's excellent tunnellers, and he was approached and invited to lead and transfer his forty men to a Royal Engineers' Tunnelling Company. In March 1916 Aubrey declined and so did thirty-eight of his men. The two men who agreed to leave shortly returned to the Regiment. Aubrey wrote: '*I would have had rapid promotion but in these conditions a Territorial unit was next to home and like a family. If I transferred I would have been working with strangers.*'

The 1st July 1916, Captain Aubrey Moore, now in command of 'C' Company had ordered an issue of rum for his men, who were waiting in assembly trenches at Gommecourt on the Somme. At 7.30 am he could not hear himself speak because of the terrific allied barrage. Soon after the enemy similarly replied, and a shell exploded on the top of a trench and sent a clump of earth thudding into Aubrey's upper back, severely stunning him. His memory of the following two hours never fully returned, and he recalled regaining consciousness in a shell-hole about one hundred yards in advance.

He noted that the whole area was covered with dead bodies and crawled back to his frontline via a small sap. Aubrey was horrified at the slaughter and confusion caused by the enemy barrage within his own trenches, with "*bodies spread all over the place.*"

The G.O.C. visited the Battalion and Aubrey remembers they were told: "*You have done a great job. We had drawn several German Divisions from the south, having led the enemy to believe that the main battle was in the north of the Somme, our bit of the Front.*"

Shortly afterwards Aubrey went to an Army School at Auxi le Chateau, for a four-week course intended for company commanders who were viewed-upon as future battalion or even brigade heads.

In June of 1917 the Fifth Leicestershire was stationed at Lievin, a suburb of Lens in France, and involved in a series of fierce engagements around Fosse 3. After one particular battle the General sent a message: "*Special praise for Captain Moore and 'C' Company for their work with the bayonet!*" Shortly afterwards Aubrey took a well-deserved and overdue spell of leave in England. During this leave he learned of the tragedy that had hit his beloved Company. On June 21st they were occupying Boot and Brick trenches near to Fosse 3, when they heard the familiar explosions of gas cylinders being fired towards enemy lines. A dreadful error meant that several hundred of them landed amongst 'C' Company. Twenty-four died from phosgene poisoning and sixty-two others had to be admitted to hospital, only a few returning to the frontlines! 'D' Company also had nineteen victims. During his leave Aubrey had an accident, the front-tyre of his motorbike burst and he received a nasty head injury, resulting in concussion and a two-week stay in hospital.

August 16th, the Battalion attacked en-force at 10.58 pm in the sector St. Elie Left. A creeping barrage prepared the way, with one shell falling short and badly wounding Captain Charles Shields of 'D' Company. Aubrey led his Company (all with blackened faces) over the top, and was involved in a good deal of 'mopping-up' and demolition work. The War Diary noted that Corporal Tunks and Private Baker excelled in this work. Captain Charles Shield's wound was serious, with one leg almost severed and the other badly shattered. Aubrey went to visit his future brother-in-law at Chocques Hospital, and heard that during the operation to amputate one leg and to repair the other, his temperature and pulse never altered! The surgeon and nurses were amazed at the power and strength of his physique.

On the 1st September 1917 Captain Moore married May Shields (the daughter of John and Helen Shields, both Scots who had moved south around 1880). John Shields was the owner of Breedon and Cloud Hill Quarries. They married at the village church of Isley Walton, only one hundred yards from the Shield's home. The former is a village nine kilometres (six miles) northeast of Ashby de la Zouch. Early March 1918 saw the Regiment reorganising as a result of heavy casualties, and as a result the 2/5th Leicestershire Battalion was broken-up, the majority of the men joining the Fifth (1/5th) Battalion.

Aubrey at this time was acting second-in-command of the Battalion, which was in trenches in the Gorre and Essars area of the La Bassee Sector. The worst aspects on this frontline were mortaring, general shelling and continuous gas shelling.

Aubrey writes: "*We had a week of it, you can't wear your gas mask all of the time, and we were loosing men at frequent intervals, mostly from inhalation of diluted gas.*"

Aubrey was to inhale too strong a dose: "*I awoke in Boulogne Hospital with a nurse bathing my eyes, I knew nothing of my train journey there. I could not open my eyes for two days, my throat and lungs felt very sore also. I soon realised that this was the end of the war for me, but this I faced with gratitude (having survived), but also with depression. My Company meant so much to me, and there were*

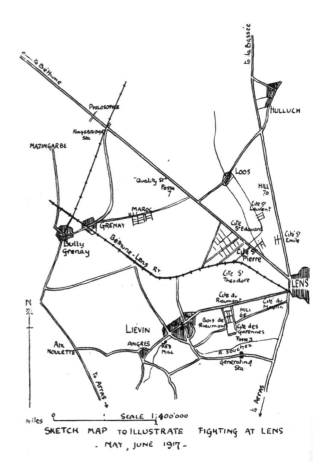

SKETCH MAP TO ILLUSTRATE FIGHTING AT LENS - MAY, JUNE 1917 -

A map of the Lens area where the Fifth Leicestershire Battalion saw so much fighting in May and June 1917.

still about fifty men there from when I initially took over 'C' Company." On the day that Aubrey was gassed so too were another forty-nine men, and they also were admitted to hospital.

"*I was sent to medical boards in Leicester, and they forwarded me to Squires Gate Convalescent Camp in Blackpool. In spite of extra medical attention I was not passed fit, and was not so until six months after the end of the war, that is May 1919.*"

Aubrey held the unusual, if not unique qualification, of working with and having friendships with three holders of the Victoria Cross. I mentioned earlier he was at school with Philip Bent, later Colonel Bent of the 9th Leicestershire who was killed on the 1st October 1917. His housemaster at Ashby Grammar School was Bernard Vann, later Colonel Vann of the 8th Sherwood Foresters who was killed on the 29th September 1918, and finally Lieutenant John Cridlan Barrett who was badly wounded at Pontruet, and with whom he served in the Fifth Leicestershire.

As a result of his tunnelling experiences, when he left the army in 1918 he was suffering from quite serious claustrophobia. Aubrey had to abandon his career as a mining engineer and seek work above

The Old Rectory at Appleby Magna in 1982

ground or in the open air. He joined his brother-in-law, Charlie Shields, in buying a quarry near Much Wenlock. This enterprise was abandoned after a few years, and, in 1925, Aubrey joined the new sugar beet industry at Spalding in the Fens of Lincolnshire, in which he spent the rest of his working life. He rented a large farmhouse in the village of Moulton, near Spalding, where their two children, Rosamond, born in 1919, and Peter, born 16th December 1921 had a very happy upbringing until the outbreak of war in 1939. Aubrey, who was on the Territorial Army Reserves, was recalled to the Leicestershire Regiment at Glen Parva Barracks near Leicester, and the family had to move to Glen Parva.

By the time Peter arrived at Glen Parva his father had been transferred to Sywell Aerodrome, near Wellingborough, Northamptonshire where he was in charge of airfield defence in that area. In 1943 he was demobilised when it became clear that the enemy threat to airfields had gone and that he would be far better employed using his knowledge of sugar production.

As the years trickled-by Aubrey regularly thought of his many friends that had been killed in the conflict. He also spent anxious hours worrying about his son, Major Peter Moore, who during World War 2 served in the Royal Artillery and the Royal Leicestershire Regiment. Peter survived the war and like his father was awarded the Military Cross.

Aubrey and May Moore on a visit to Appleby Magna in 1982.

Aubrey invariably took the salute at Bloxham Remembrance Day parade, a village six kilometres southwest of Banbury.

In 1991 he felt particularly moved and humbled by many memories as he stood by the village war memorial and read: *"They shall not grow old, as we that are left grow old."* It was the seventy-fifth anniversary of the Battle of the Somme.

Aubrey and his wife, May, were regular members of St. Mary's Church congregation at Bloxham, and he was a bell ringer too.

Aubrey's often thought of that gorgeous summer's day when he played his last cricket game for Ashby Hastings. *"It was Saturday, 1st August 1914, and we were playing Castle Donington at Ashby. They included three Shields in their team, John was really top class, and Charlie and Joe both average. We were all great friends. We fielded and Castle Donington knocked-up a sizable score. Frank Joyce, our captain said: " Come on in with me and we'll knock-up a hundred for the first wicket!" We made a big score thanks to Frank, a great hitter. Roland Farmer, another player and great friend of us all had, like Charlie Shields and myself, recently been commissioned into the Fifth Leicestershire. We walked off the field in golden sunlight; we had a drink and talked about the forthcoming camp at Bridlington. Many walked off that field for the last time."*

(Charlie Shields lost a leg as mentioned earlier and John is mentioned later in this book.)

Some forty years ago, my grandfather, Charles Hatter, shared his Great War memories concerning Captain Moore with me. He served under him, and said that not only was the Captain a fine leader of men, but that he was also a gentleman in the very finest sense of the word. He also said that Captain Moore led from the front, and always had the best interests of his men at heart. Finally, he considered Aubrey to be a modest and kindly man, one who could mix easily in whatever social circle he found himself in.

Sadly, Captain Aubrey Moore MC died in 1992.

I am very grateful to Aubrey's son, Major Peter Moore MC for allowing me to extract information from his father's books: 'A Son of the Rectory' and 'From Leicestershire to the Somme.' Peter's absorbing military career will appear in my next book: 'Sons and Daughters'.

THE TUNNELLERS OF 1914-18

Dedicated to Captain Aubrey Moore MC.
Also to the soldiers of his tunnelling party of 1915

Clay-kickers and coal-miners toiling in the world of the troglodyte.
Guns and bombs at the ready when needed for a twentieth-century fight.
Heads-a-thumping and perspiration streaming whilst digging-out runs,
Chopping out clumps of clay and passing it behind to their chums.

Air of fetid grade and flooded passages a vilely prevalent aspect.
Like moles-- soaked in sludge and a roof-collapse a common prospect.
Ear-strained 'listeners' whispered of tappings from an unknown chamber,
And silence pervaded 'cept the rapid beatings of hearts in labour.

Tappings grew and there came a mighty crash followed by a gush of air.
Intruders fought the intruded at a hundred feet depth in sub-earthly layer.
Steel bayonets thrust in dimly lit corridors and bullets found their desire,
Fathers with wives, sons and daughters, lovers killed by masked gunfire!

The battle raged till the plunger fell and set the wires a-tingle with power.
A microsecond flash of orange-light rendered all to a dust-like shower.
Black smoke belched into the heavens and blended with misty clouds,
And for a host of human subterraneans took the value of male-shrouds.

Whatever: Hill 60, Petit Bois or St. Eloi, all in the bowels of the earth.
Those of the tunnelling companies had heroism that matched their worth.
Mining and counter-mining below the battlefields of France and Flanders,
Existing in a twilight world but forever shining in the eyes of admirers.

Michael Kendrick

THOMAS CHARLES PALMER

The young man in the smart uniform of the Leicestershire Regiment looks a determined lad, and no doubt he had to be, what with the shadow of death that hung over earlier generations of his family circle. Joseph Palmer, a Hugglescote coalminer married local girl, Amy, in the year 1862. Between that date and the 3rd March 1875, Joseph was to witness the death of his wife, aged thirty in 1874, and nine children. Of the nine the majority died under the age of three with one, Ann, living to just six years. Three survived, George born 1864, John 1867 and Mary 1872. Pleasingly he was to marry again, Eliza, another local girl and they subsequently had seven more children, to add to the three.

On Thomas' side of the family, his father John E. Palmer, was born in 1861, married Hannah, and among other children they had Thomas Charles Herbert Palmer, just called Tom, who was born in 1894. The family lived at 50, Bridge Road, Coalville and Tom attended Coalville Belvoir Road Wesleyan School, and to name a few his companions: Major Baker, Walter Baker, Ernest Booton, the Bradshaw brothers, Fred Briers, the Usherwood brothers and various relatives.

John Palmer, his father, was an engine driver on the Midland Railway and for a while Tom tried to adapt to life on the railways, but as soon as he was old enough he joined the Regular Army, the 1st Battalion of the Leicestershire Regiment. He enlisted in December 1912, at the age of eighteen and was posted to his battalion at Fermoy in Ireland, within the 16th Brigade, 6th Division. At the outbreak of the war the Battalion moved to Queenstown and then steamed in the 'Heroic', 'Londonderry' and 'Kilkenny' to Holyhead in Anglesey, and entrained for the area around Cambridge for reorganisation. It was at Grantchester that reservists such as Frank Martin joined the Battalion. As part of the British Expeditionary Force they embarked from Southampton on the 8th September 1914 aboard 'Braemar Castle' and disembarked at St. Nazaire.

The Coalville Times sent a reporter to interview Tom, and on the 26th November 1915 printed details of his service: *'The first battle Private Tom Palmer participated in was on the Marne, where the Germans were checked on their rush to Paris and utterly routed. Then his battalion proceeded to the Aisne and were there for three weeks, fighting practically all the time. Subsequently they proceeded to Cassel, over the Belgium border, and afterwards marched to Armentieres. It was in this neighbourhood on the 24th October 1914 that Private Palmer was first wounded. A shell burst near to him and the debris buried him and six comrades, with Tom Palmer receiving a wound in the back. This resulted in him being in hospital at Rouen for a month. Having recovered he went straight back to Armentieres and joined his battalion in the firing*

Private Thomas Charles Palmer in 1913. 1st Leicestershire Battalion.

line. They stayed until November of last year, and remained in that same neighbourhood for the remainder of that bitterly cold winter. In March 1915 he was wounded again when pieces of shell pierced his thigh and heel, in consequence an operation was performed and he was in hospital at Versailles for five weeks. Referring to the latter hospital he spoke in terms of praise for the splendid hospital arrangements, which have been made near to the

Home: 50 Bridge Road, Coalville.

Private Ernest Booton in 1914. 1st Leicestershire Battalion. He suffered frostbite to his toes in the bitter January of 1915. A school friend of Tom Palmer who also served with him on the battlefield.

palaces of the kings of France. They are set among lovely gardens and scenery, which have formed such a great attraction for English visitors to France in happier times. After Versailles Private Palmer then took his place in the firing line, still in the neighbourhood of Armentieres until April when they moved to Ypres. "We have had two doses of gas, but we got over it all right, the respirators we were given proved very effective.'

Answering further questions Private Palmer said, "*Some of the liveliest engagements have been around Hooge. One thrilling incident was when our bombing party attacked the enemy; they were led by Lieutenant Pickbourne, son of the Reverend Pickbourne, pastor of Coalville London Road Baptist Church. They accomplished their mission with only one casualty although they had some narrow escapes.*"

Asked about the condition of the trenches he said: "*There is plenty of rainfall and the parapets fall in, but we keep very cheerful, particularly the Coalville boys. We are faring as well as any of the lads at the frontline, thanks to the kindness of Mrs. L. L. Baldwin and the ladies of the Coalville Comfort Guild. We are well looked after and we have plenty of good food and plenty of warm clothing.*"

Private Palmer's appearance bears this out for he was looking very fit. He emphasised the fact that none were in better spirits than the Coalville boys and as to the position generally they were confident of winning the war. He is an old Wesleyan schoolboy and it was a matter of regret to him that he could not see his old schoolmaster, Mr. Frith, being away in consequences of illness. Another interesting

statement by the soldier was that large numbers of the 'Coalville Times' find their way into the trenches, and that the lads of the district eagerly look forward to them. "Have you had your Times yet, is a remark commonly heard among the Coalville and district boys?" He has brought a few interesting souvenirs home with him, one of them being a pair of coal boxes made from the casings of German shells. He left Coalville to return to the trenches last Tuesday morning.'

Tom was a witness to the Christmas Truce that has previously been mentioned, and also the bitterly cold winter weather, indeed one pal, Ernest Booton was admitted to Le Havre Hospital with frost bitten toes in mid-January 1915. The Coalville Times of the 29th January 1915 printed a pre-Christmas letter: '*We received the Christmas pudding and cake, what an extra? We have plenty of tobacco but could do with some more good solid homemade cakes. I hope everyone has a merry Christmas and happier times in the New Year. Tom Palmer is with me at the front and we had a little tea fight, but I have not seen Horace Briers for a while, he is in another company, I hope he is all right.*'

On the 19th February 1915 Horace Briers, aged twenty, has a letter to his parents printed in the 'Times': '*I wasn't half surprised to see my old mate Booton's photo in the paper, it makes me wish he was in our company, I hope his feet get better soon. I also see Mr. Frith's name mentioned, please remember me to him, I wonder if he remembers me from when I went to his school? I love letters from home; they put*

Private Horace Briers in 1914. 1st Leicestershire Battalion. An old school friend and comrade-in-arms.

new life into me. We were under shellfire the other night, but we all came out all right. I expect Kitchener's Army will be hear soon. When we were at Portsmouth I heard some of them say that they'd like to go to the trenches at once, and they will soon have their chance and I wish them well. I should like to come over to England and see you once more as I've had a good innings since November 8th. I have enough tobacco to last six months.'

Tom was quite a survivor and he continued to battle in the frontline until he saw the arrival of the mechanised 'Tank' on the battlefield. From 1915 the Tank Corpse were seeking personnel with frontline experience to staff their 'Little Willie' and then Mark 1 and 11s. This heavily armoured vehicle could withstand small arms fire, and was designed to assist the movement of infantry across No-Man's-Land. Another vital ingredient was its ability to crush barbed wire in front of enemy trenches, and its ferocious appearance threatened the enemy's resolve with fears of being crushed. These early tanks, especially the 1915 version lumbered forward at eight miles an hour and were unreliable and required four of the crew of eight to steer and control them. The others members fired two adapted 57mm naval guns or three machine guns (male tanks) or five Hotchkiss or Vickers machine-guns (female tanks). The interior of the tank was cramped and filled with fumes from gunfire and the Daimler engine, and some of the deaths when the engine fuel was hit by shellfire replaced any requirement for cremation.

In early 1917 Tom volunteered and following training was given the service number, 308648, and posted to the 18th Tank Corps. I am unsure as to what tasks he was involved with but the tank established itself and played a lead from that time onwards, saving the lives of many soldiers. Tom survived the war and returned to his parent's home at Coalville.

A Mark 1 Tank (male) with six long-barrelled 40-calibre guns and an anti-grenade screen over the top. Sergeant Tom Palmer was a crewmember in a tank similar to this in 1917.

OLIVER H. PRATT

Oliver Pratt was born in the hamlet of Donington-le-Heath, very close to Hugglescote on the 11th January 1894. His parents, Mr. & Mrs. Oliver Pratt moved to 5, Wilkins Lane, (now Fairfield Road) at Hugglescote when he was a toddler. The family worshipped at St. John The Baptist Church with Oliver receiving his education at the Church School. He was also a keen and popular member of the Hugglescote Church Lads' Brigade (C.L.B.) from 1910 right up to the war, and was a good friend of Reginald Glover.

On the 4th August 1914 he was in the company of hundreds of Leicestershire lads at Ripon in Yorkshire, for the C. L. B. annual camp, when they were required to return home. On the steam-train home an officer informed the excited bunch that the

Private Oliver Pratt

army was creating a new regiment, purely for C.L.B. personnel, and would be called the King's Royal Rifles (K.R.R.). By the time the train arrived at Coalville Station, Reginald and nine other local lads had agreed to join them. Oliver spoke to his parents and they pleaded with him to give it a month to see how the conflict developed. He took his parents' advice and on the Monday morning accompanied his father to South Leicestershire Colliery at Ellistown where they were both employed.

As the European situation escalated he again raised the subject and enlist at Coalville on the 5th September 1914 into the Eighth Leicestershire Battalion, service number 13238. In the same battalion was the aforementioned Private John Charles Hill, also Samuel Richards of New Swannington, of whom I write about later.

Private Oliver Pratt was a strongly built young adult, and had accustomed himself extremely well to the demanding life in the trenches, and above all else appreciated the camaraderie that existed with his fellow soldiers, that was why he enjoyed life in the C.L.B. On Boxing Day 1915 **he wrote to his parents**:

'Dear Mother and Father,

I am in excellent health so do not worry about me. We all had a good Christmas Day—what with some pork and veal and some very nice plum pudding and mince pies. The Army has done its very best to make us happy, and we are. I hope you and everyone who knows me has had a very nice Christmas and we will all have a happy new year. We will have returned to the trenches by the time you get this letter but God is good and we must "Fight the Good Fight with all of our Might!" My thoughts were very much with you on Christmas Day, all the day long, but we must make the best of it. I do hope the war will soon be over and that I will soon be home again at Hugglescote. It would be grand if it would end very soon. With my best love, your son, Oliver.'

The Brigade was in the Monchy-au-Bois Sector, to the north of Gommecourt on the Somme, and on December 27th the Battalion returned to the trenches, and they were relatively quiet. Reports said some eerie singing had been heard from the enemy's frontline over the festive period, but no truce was observed. At the same time it was recorded that two of our airmen 'looped the loop' over German trenches, and this brought rounds of cheers from our soldiers. During the hours of darkness we sent out patrols into No-Man's-Land to repair barbed-wire entanglements, and during the day the respective artilleries exchanged a few shells.

On the 28th December the Battalion Chaplain-R. M. Shelton sat in his dugout and **wrote** to Mr. & Mrs. Pratt at Hugglescote; *'I write to tell you that Private Pratt has been rather badly wounded. I trust he will soon get better. He was hit by a shell on the 27th. He will, I expect, be soon in England. May God bless him and restore him to health and strength.'*

Another letter, this time by L. Hamilton, a Church of England Chaplain and dated the 29th December 1915 wrote: *'I am sorry to tell you that your son is in hospital, No4 Casualty Clearing Station, very seriously wounded. He is well looked after and everything possible will be done for him. I am afraid his case is a very, very serious one, as it is a spinal wound. I will let you know his condition again. He is not suffering much pain.'*

On the 3rd January 1916 L. Hamilton **wrote again**: *'I hope my earlier letter prepared you for the sad news that I am about to send you now. Your son passed away on Saturday afternoon, the 1st January. All possible was done to spare him pain, but his wound (spinal) was hopeless from the first. He has been laid to rest in the soldiers cemetery and his grave marked with a cross carrying his name and regiment. I am grieved to have this sad duty to have to carry out and another mother's heart to bring sorrow to, yet proud that your boy was brave in life, and, I believe happy and at peace with Christ.'*

A letter dated the 3rd January 1916 and written by Lieutenant E. S. Allen wrote: *'It is with the deepest regret that I am writing to tell you that your son has died from a wound he received in the trenches a week ago today. As his platoon officer I have known your son for over a year and I feel it all* *the more, as he is the first of my men who has lost his life. There is so little one can say in a case like this. I believe that he suffered very little. A piece of shell hit him in the back and touched his spine. He was very cheerful when he was in the trenches but I am aware this will do little to soften the blow, but I wanted just to assure you of my sympathy and grief at your loss.'*

Captain H. L. Beardsley, a Loughborough man and later Major also addressed his parents: *'On behalf of myself and other officers of 'B' Company, please accept our deepest sympathy in the loss of your boy, who died of wounds received during our tour in the trenches. A piece of shrapnel hit him by the shoulder blade and I fear reached his spine. Private Oliver Pratt was a thoroughly good and conscientious lad and we shall miss him greatly. What few words of comfort I can write I know are small compared to the loss you have sustained, but in the knowledge that he died fighting for his King and Country I hope are of* *some consolation. Yours in sincerity and with kindest sympathy, H. L. Beardsley (Captain).'*

A memorial service was held at Hugglescote Parish Church on the 9th January 1916 by the new curate, the Reverend H. V. Williams, together with an appropriate address. The members of the Church Lads' Brigade attended and with muffled drums accompanied the singing of the hymn, 'Fight the Good Fight'. After the ceremony one of the cadets played 'Last Post' on Oliver's bugle whilst standing on the altar steps.

Mr. & Mrs. Pratt were inconsolable and Mr Pratt had been ill and off work for some time with blood poisoning following an accident in the pit. Oliver was twenty-one years of age.

Private Oliver Pratt is remembered on the Coalville Clock Tower Memorial and also on the Memorial Tablet within St. John The Baptist Church.

SAMUEL RICHARDS

S amuel Richards was born on the 1st January 1892 at Osgathorpe, a village five kilometres (three miles) north of Coalville to Thomas and Harriett (nee Edwards) Richards. His father was a coal-miner and they had six children, one being a daughter. The first son, born on the 7th February 1887 was Frederick, who, following years of mining ran his own fish and chip shop on the Dumps at Whitwick. After Samuel came Rose in 1890, John on the 1st January 1894, a miner turned shopkeeper in later life (he died on the 28th January 1962), and George on the 17th January 1895. The final child, although christened George was always known as Harold, a well-known figure who kept the 'Bull's Head' in the Market Place at Shepshed, later the Crossways Café (and petrol pumps) between Shepshed and Thringstone.

Joyce Stanyard, daughter of John commented that her grandmother said that when Samuel was a young man he was a typical 'Richards'—good looking and inclined to be a bit moody but very witty and amusing.

Samuel was living in New Swannington, a village near to Whitwick, when he enlisted on the 29th August 1914 at Leicester into the Leicestershire Regiment. Ministry of Defence records reveal that he joined the Leicestershire Eighth Battalion on the 29th August 1914, service number 10518. For Battalion details please read Private John Charles Hill.

Samuel, following a typically warm Kentish summer's day boarded the SS *'Golden Eagle'* at Folkestone on the 29th July 1915, and disembarked at Boulogne just before midnight after an uneventful crossing. A small contingent of the Battalion left from Southampton earlier in the day. A wonderful book entitled 'Of Those We Loved', written by Dick Read, in which he served, gives a deep insight into life with the Battalion.

Samuel experienced the autumn and wintry conditions of 1915-16 at Monchy-au-Bois, just to the north of the Somme. Letters from soldiers tell of crisp-white frosts and biting winds that chilled every muscle and joint in the body, of trenches in pitiable conditions with mud levels up to knee-height and more. In January 1916 the cold was so intense that only soldiers who endured sentry watches from midnight until 'stand-to', could ever relate to the dire physical numbness! In the circumstances it was terribly difficult to stay awake: the fact most did so speaks volumes for their attitude and innate qualities. In the early hours of Friday, July 14th 1916, Samuel was with his battalion as it stormed the second-line positions at Bazentin Ridge, between Mametz Wood and Bazentin-le-Petit Wood on the Somme. Accounts of the day write of the devastation of shelling, the rattle of machine-guns and the thud and ricochet of bullets, the red hot poker effect felt when flesh is hit by a bullet, the dead and the dying all around! Dick Read recalled chatting to his pal, Jackie Johnson, as they drank a cup-of-tea just as the light was failing on the battle-churned ground: '*We watched a fatigue party bringing up our rations, dumping piles of bulging sandbags on the ground near to us, and this set us running through the names of our mates we knew already to be killed, wounded or missing. Both of us had lost our best pals, and we sat there with leaden hearts lost in our thoughts. Jackie then broke the silence. "Plenty of rations tonight, Dick!" He nodded at the pile. "Enough for the whole battalion, eh? About six times too many", he added bitterly. "Christ, there'll be hell to pay in Leicester and Loughborough and Coalville and Melton and Uppingham—when they know about this. The Leicester Brigade, eh? Bloody well wiped out!" He trailed off into silence again, immersed in his thoughts.*'

I can vividly remember Martin Batho of North Street, Whitwick, telling me about his great uncle, Lance Corporal Ernest Batho, service number 15926, of the Seventh Battalion being killed on that day. Ernest Batho, a twenty-three year old was previously a miner at South Leicestershire Colliery, Ellistown, and the son of Joseph Batho of Margaret Street, Coalville.

Samuel survived that battle and as the final week of September approached, the Brigade was once again in familiar territory by the edge of Bernafray Wood, just to the south of a shattered Delville Wood and close to Bazentin-le-Petit Wood.

On the night of the 24th September 1916 Samuel's battalion moved to a low ridge, which lay before the enemy held village of Guedecourt. Next day was clear and fine and at 12.35 pm the Seventh and Eighth Battalions attacked the village. Dick Read recalled, '*At zero hour all feelings of nervousness were banished. As though by magic I felt calm and saw that my mates were the same. I pulled back the cocking handle of the gun. We grinned at one another and wished each other the best of luck.*'

The whistles blew and Samuel moved forward at the double, being careful to keep his footing on the badly cratered ground, but it was none to easy carrying a full kit. Suddenly he had to fall to the ground as a German barrage sent clods of earth and human souls up into the heavens. Shortly afterwards his officer, Captain Frank Breacher, stirred them to advance again, only for their position to be hit by enfilade machine-gun fire. The Captain spotted an abandoned bugle on the battlefield and used it to blow the Quorn Hunt: 'Tally-Ho'! This stirred his frustrated men who charged forward again, unfortunately, Captain Breacher was hit by several machine-gun bullets and fell backwards, seriously wounded. Miraculously he recovered and lived for another forty odd years, keeping the bugle as a souvenir. Eventually the German village fell but what expenditure: many casualties and one was Private Samuel Richards, who received bullet wounds to the legs. He was taken across the Channel on the 28th September 1916 and was hospitalised for several months in England. He regained what was regarded as full fitness and was reposted to France, but as was often the case not to his old battalion but to the First Battalion of the Leicestershire Regiment.

This Regular Army Battalion had been in France with the British Expeditionary Force since September 1914, however, few of those early soldiers had survived three years of almost constant warfare. Private Samuel Richards departed home shores on the 17th March 1917 and joined the 1st Leicestershire in the Loos Sector of France. He was invigorated when in April he heard that the United States of America had entered the war against the Imperial German Forces, with a declaration of '*defeating the enemy in the swiftest possible time.*'

During Samuel's second posting in France he

The splendid Cross of Sacrifice in the grounds of Whitwick Parish Church. For the Great War there are listed seventy-nine names that include 'famous fifty' men Charles Cavendish and George Underwood.

Robert Berrington was awarded the Military Medal, as was Arthur Concannon, Thaddeus McCarthy, and Samuel Taylor.

Royal Navy Signaller, George Copson, went down with H.M.S. 'Sparrowhawk' at the 1916 Battle of Jutland and Act-Ord. Seaman Joseph Heggs drowned whilst serving in H.M.S. 'Hampshire' in the same battle, whereas 1st Class Stoker Arthur Griffiths' destroyer sank in the English Channel. The latter two men were close friends and enlisted into the Royal Navy at the same time.

John Ducker of the 9th Leicestershire died in captivity in 1918.

For World War 2 there are thirty-one names of which the same surname appears-Concannon, Freeman, Heggs, and Tookey.

Whitwick Parish Church - John The Baptist

was to spend all of his service between Bethune to the north to the Double Crassier at Loos in the south. His time with the First was **relatively** quiet, but still involved trench-raid parties, shelling and sniping, etc. Billets were at the ruined mining villages of Philosophe or Les Brebis, indeed readers are aware that this is the sector where the Fourth and Fifth Leicestershire Battalions charged the Hohenzollern Redoubt on the 13th October 1915. The whole area had seen the deaths of hundreds of thousands and smelt accordingly, also of gas, 'twas a filthy, cruel and evil place during the war to end all wars.

It was in early June 1917 that Samuel was badly wounded. It is not known how he received his wound, but during this time men were lost to snipers, aerial darts and trench raids. Samuel was stretchered down the line and taken by ambulance to 33rd

Casualty Clearing Station at Bethune. He succumbed to his wounds on the 10th June 1917, and he was twenty-five years of age. Private Samuel Richard's name is remembered with honour and he lies at Grave Ref: V1.F.1 at Bethune Town Cemetery. In 1917 his parents were living at 150, Church Lane, Whitwick. Samuel's mother, Harriet, was a staunch member of the Mother's Union at Whitwick Parish Church and possessed a deep Christian faith. She passed away on the 17th January 1958.

Samuel's name can be read on the Coalville Clock Tower War Memorial and also on the War Memorial in the grounds of St. John The Baptist Parish Church, Whitwick.

Many thanks to Joyce Stanyard, niece of Samuel Richards.

ROLL OF HONOUR AT ST. JOHN THE BAPTIST PARISH CHURCH, WHITWICK

1914-1918		1939-1945
R. Allgood	H. S. Hurst	J. W. Bryan
T. Bailey	E. Jarvis	R. C. Concannon
W. Bakewell	A. C. Johnstone	D. Freeman
C. H. Barker	H. E. Ketcher	J. Gardner
W. Beasley	E. King	A. Garrett
A. Beeson	E. Knight	F. Grice
T. Benson	H. Lakin	C. C. P. Heggs
R. W. Berrington	A. Laundon	J. Hurst Heath
O. Bishop	T. F. McCarthy	H. Jones
W. Boobyear	W. Massey	J. Jones
W. Bradley	B. W. Morley	C. W. Limb
H. Briers	J. J. Morley	J. A. Lovett
E. Brotherhood	A.E. Moreton	S. E. Maddison
L. E. Brotherhood	E. Morris	H. Moore
W. J. G. Brown	J. A. Moult	R. Moore
H. H. Burton	F. F. Myatt	W. Moore
H. S. Burton	C. Myers	J. F.A. Neal
N. Burrell	H. Parish	F. Needham
J. Cairns	W. Z. Parker	J. Newbold
J. A. Carter	W. Parsons	T. H. Oliver
C. Cavendish	W. Partridge	J. Perry
A. Concannon	T. Price	J. Roberts
W. H. Cooke	S. Richards	L. F. Roe
G. H. Copson	E. Roome	L. J. Roe
J. E. D. Ducker	S. W. Taylor	J. W. Skellington
H. Freeman	P. Tookey	S. E. Smith
R. Freeman	E. Tugby	W. Smith
A. Griffiths	C. Turner	F. J. Stanyard
E. Hall	C. W. Underwood	J. H. Tookey
J. A. Hall	F. Underwood	H. B. Wardle
A. Harley	R. Underwood	A. E. Wood
E. A. Hart	E. Walton	
J. B. Haynes	G. Westley	
L. Haywood	B. Whittaker	
J. H. Heggs	L. Whitmore	
G. E. Heighton	A. J. Wilson	
L. Henson	C. Wilson	
A.C. Hobson	A. Warrall	
E. Howe	G. Wright	
	J. H. Wyatt	

GEORGE HERBERT SADDINGTON
AND WILLIAM THOMAS SADDINGTON

Thomas Saddington was born on the 17th July 1862 on Wolvey Road at Hinckley, a market town nineteen kilometres (twelve miles) southwest of Leicester. He spent his formative years with his parents at 'Charnwood Towers', a lodge situated on the Loughborough Road in Charnwood Forest, close to Whitwick in northwest Leicestershire. His father was head-coachman at the Towers, which today remains a private property, and stands within picturesque scenery with splendid views of Mount St Bernard Monastery.

As a relatively young man he took-up the appointment of coachman to the household of Stockton House at Rugby. He held the position for a decade until asking the lady of the house, Emily Linjew, for a reference, which proved to be excellent! He then undertook an improved appointment of groom and coachman to a Dr. Edward Lister L.R.C.P.H., who was a general practitioner and justice of the peace. The doctor lived at Courteney House, Warwick New Road at Leamington Spa, about five kilometres (three miles) east of Warwick.

(It was close to where John Cridlan Barrett was born in 1897, later a 2nd Lieutenant who won the Victoria Cross whilst serving with the Fifth Leicestershire at Pontruet in 1918). It was at this majestic house, or a nearby property that he met his future wife, Louisa Winstone, a domestic servant. She was born on the 17th May 1866 at 'The Armoury', Cirencester and her father was a staff sergeant in the army. The couple married on the 4th July 1888 at nearby Stockton Parish Church and were blessed with seven children, the first four children being born at 16, Gunnery Terrace, New Milverton, near the Spa town, sadly one child dying in infancy. What with the demise of the horse and the increased use of the motor vehicle, Thomas took his family to Coalville in northwest Leicestershire. With many mouths to feed he sought employment as a collier, and obtained such employment thanks to an outstanding reference from Dr. Lister. The children's names were George Herbert, William Thomas, Constance Maud, Florence Beatrice (born 28/2/1899), Robert Winston (born 2/6/1902) and Alex. All of the family

George Saddington on the far right. Sgt Major Walter Hill on far left. Circa summer 1914.

A pre-war photograph of William Saddington taken at Mr Brown's at Blackpool.

worshipped at Christ Church, Coalville and attended the Church's National School.

By the summer of the despoiling year of 1914, the Saddington family was residing at 58, Albert Road in the town. The two eldest brothers, George (born 1892) and William (1893) were already attached to the Leicestershire Regiment. William was employed as an engineer at Stableford's Wagon Works before he enlisted at Coalville in June 1914. This was two months before the conflict, and he did so directly from the National Reserve, having earlier served with the Leicestershire Volunteers. (From the eighteenth century similar amateur-forces existed to defend the homeland against invasion. Firstly they were known as the Militia, then the Yeomanry, and

onto the Volunteers and eventually the Territorials in 1908).

William was initially posted to the 3rd Leicestershire Battalion, and undertook six months of training at a barracks near to Portsmouth. On the 11th December 1914 he was reposted to the 2nd Leicestershire Battalion in France. At the outbreak of the war this regular battalion was serving in India, and arrangements were quickly undertaken to ship it to Marseilles in France by the 12th October. The Battalion's first action was in the La Bassee Sector of northeastern France. William, together with a party of reservists, arrived just after the conflict around Festubert in November, and joined the Battalion's trenches in the same sector. Following bouts of attacking and capturing enemy lines, coping with enemy Maxim guns, artillery barrages and fierce rifle fire, several soldiers of the Battalion were mentioned for their bravery! Amongst them was a certain Private Buckingham. The action smouldered-on until natural elements of heavy rainfall, strong winds and then heavy falls of snow curtailed matters. By January and February of 1915 the whole area was a wilderness of clinging, suffocating mud. On the 10th March 1915 a violent eruption of warfare announced the Battle of Neuve Chapelle.

Following a 7.30 am fierce barrage, the Battalion advanced at 7.45 am towards its objective of a group of houses at point 'D' on the Port Arthur - Neuve Chapelle Road. Every man carried 15 rounds

58 Albert Road, Coalville. It was at this modest homestead that the Saddington family was living before the Great War. Son, George was an accomplished pedal organ player and he spent hours playing for the rest o f the family. On frosty nights, *"Inside the family sat around a roaring fire and sang the ditties of the day to accompany George on the organ."*

Private George Saddington, marked with an X. Playing the joker at training camp with the Fifth Leicestershire Battalion. The soldier on the extreme right of the photograph is Sergeant Major Roland Hill.

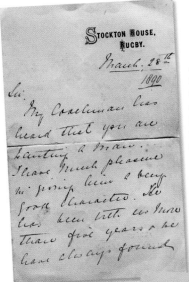

A March 28th 1890 reference for coachman Thomas Saddington from his former employee, Emily Linjew. The letter was good enough for him to secure an improved position at the home of Edward Lister.

After ten years of employment as groom and coachman for Doctor Edward Lister, Thomas asks for a reference letter to seek an alternative position elsewhere.

Leicestershire in the Battle of Neuve Chapelle is full of instances of bravery and brotherly-devotion.

In the course of this battle William was badly wounded. The Coalville Times of the 19th March 1915 shows a photograph of him in a dining suit, and informs readers that his parents had been notified of him being wounded, dangerously so, in action. It also wrote that he was at No2 Stationary Hospital at Boulogne. Shortly before the battle William, who was in 'D' Company, had sent a **letter** to his mother: '*I am having a break; we are at present about five miles from the firing line. I am keeping well, but could you please send me several boxes of matches, as they are very scarce over here. I am also in need of some sticks of shaving soap. We had a concert recently and the comic singer was very good, we all had a hearty laugh. The graveyards over here are a sight worth seeing, they are kept in good order and every grave has a cross with the name of the man on. Love to all, William.*' (The photograph of William must have been taken during a holiday. It was taken by Mr. Brown of Savoy Studios, 9, West Street, Blackpool).

Perhaps Private Buckingham rescued William; certainly he needed rescuing because his left leg was severed during the course of the battle, and what remained of it was later amputated.

Little is known of the remainder of his life. He lived on Park Road in the town for many years, and was the chairman of the local British Legion. Please note the magnificent letter, personally written by Field Marshal Haig, which thanked him for his work, and also for selling Poppies for the British Legion in 1923, 1924, 1925 and 1926: '*The Poppy symbolises the sacrifice of those who laid down their lives, so your kindly help for those gallant survivors who are now in want, typifies that spirit of gratitude and service, which is beyond all praise or earthly reward. Haig. FM. President British Legion.*'

William's disability was improved when he had a false leg fitted, and he married and moved to Leicester at some stage. In the late Thirties, just prior to World War 2 he was landlord of a public house in London, a photograph shows him with his parents. It is sad that no more is known of the remainder of his life.

of ammunition, two sandbags and food rations. It was tough going, the night before had been bitterly cold and snow fell on the lumpy quagmire. However, the Battalion determinedly pushed-back the German troops and captured all that was expected of them. General Haig, Commanding in Chief, sent his heartiest congratulations to all ranks of the First Army for their splendid success. The next day was involved in consolidating the position and the War Diary of March 12th reads: '*The enemy shelled Port Arthur, and at 5.15 am the Germans counter-attacked and they received heavy casualties.*' On March 13th the enemy continued with a heavy barrage and sniper fire, and by the 14th March 1915 all ranks were in need of a rest. In the battle the Battalion lost two officers killed and five wounded. Other ranks amounted to two hundred and fifty dead or wounded. During this battle Private William Buckingham was awarded the Victoria Cross. The Countesthorpe man ventured into No-Man's-Land time and again to rescue and aid wounded men during the heaviest of barrages and machine-gun fire! The story of the 2nd

It was during the Battle of Neuve Chapelle that Ernest Hall of Whitwick was killed. Ernest was the elder brother of Isaac Hall, one of the Famous Fifty. Other local men of the same Battalion who died: Timothy Betteridge of Ashby de la Zouch, Fred Davies of Ibstock, Owen Hallam of Hugglescote, Ernest Moore of Coalville, John Poyser of Ashby de la Zouch, John Twigg of Ibstock, Harry Wareham of Loughborough and John Williamson of Coalville.

George Herbert Saddington was educated at Christ Church National School and pre-war was employed as a collier. His parents owned a pedal organ and he played this extremely well, spending many an hour amusing himself and entertaining the rest of the family.

As a young man he converted to Roman Catholicism and regularly played for Father Degan at St. Saviour's Church.

Recently I strolled past the Saddington's old house on Albert Road and imagined a frosty evening

William Saddington late 1915.

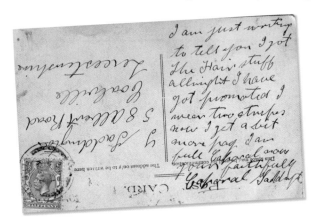

Postcard from 'Corporal' George Saddington on 11th April 1915.

Lance Corporal George Saddington on far right. Circa autumn 1914.

around 1912 with roadside gaslights casting shadows on the cosy terraced cottages.

Inside the family sat round a roaring fire and sang the ditties of the day to accompany George on the organ. Such images mirrored the day, unfortunately, they were soon to be shattered and a golden age of relative innocence was to be lost forever.

George enlisted at Ashby de la Zouch, almost certainly before the war, into the Fifth Leicestershire Battalion. Please note an early photograph showing him squatting alongside Sergeant Major Roland Hill. In the photograph George is playing the clown with his hat twisted at right angles. The group of territorial soldiers are encamped at a weekend or annual training trip. During the Great War, Roland Hill was to distinguish himself with the Battalion and received the Distinguished Conduct Medal for outstanding bravery.

Whilst the Fifth Battalion was at its annual training camp at Bridlington they received orders to return to Loughborough due to the onset of war. Subsequently they entrained for the Luton area and as part of the 46th North Midland Division embarked for France in late February 1915. An outline-history (1914-18) of the Battalion: "A Walk in Their Footprints" can be found in my earlier book.

During his time with the Fifth Battalion George was wounded, and following recovery was reposted to the 2/5th Leicestershire Battalion. Reginald Glover was serving with this unit and was a colleague. The 2/5th formed part of the 59th (2nd) North Midland Division, which in March 1917 was stationed around Mericourt on the Western Front in France. From the autumn of 1914 the town of Ypres had witnessed more than its share of death: the name itself becoming synonymous to a Devil's crucible. An evil place, a salient where mighty guns, asphyxiating gas, flame-throwers and machine-guns reaped a harvest of mother's sons. On the 7th June 1917 at the Messines Ridge on the southern edge of the Salient, following two weeks of bombardment by two thousand guns, nineteen massive mines were detonated deep below ground. Enormous explosions ruptured the ground and killed hundreds of enemy

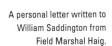

troops with vital enemy strongholds being captured. This was the opening day of 'Third Ypres', which encompassed the highly pernicious Battle of Passchendaele Ridge that started on the 31st July 1917. It had been a dreadfully wet summer and heavy barrages had totally destabilised the already high water margin. The Ridge was finally captured, but

Thomas and Louisa Saddington on holiday. (Circa 1930).
Parents never recover from the loss of a son in battle!

only after sixteen weeks of vicious hostility in the most awful of quagmires. Allied losses were nearly one third of a million, whilst the Germans suffered one quarter of a million. Countless of the injured soldiers were never found; they slid and drowned in the fetid water-filled shell-craters. As part of this battle, and some seven kilometres (four miles) to the southeast the Allies indulged in an offensive at Polygon Wood, starting on the 26th September 1917. The term wood is an inaccuracy, because by this stage in the war it was a battered collection of stumps and exposed tree- roots that made ideal locations for machine-gun nests and sniper posts.

So it was that on September 26th the 2/5th Leicestershire Battalion attacked Polygon Wood. Numerous soldiers floundered in the glutinous mass: shell holes were brimful with polluted water, and decaying bodies of horse and mankind plagued the loathsome land.

Sergeant George Saddington, service number 240289, by the very nature of his position would have led and encouraged his platoon to 'go over the top'. He was seriously wounded and stretcher-bearers carried him back to their frontlines, from where he was taken to a hospital just to the south of Poperinghe, possibly Godewaersvelde. I am not aware of the wounds inflicted but George died in the early hours of the 28th September 1917. He lies buried at Nine Elms British Cemetery, Poperinge, W/Vlaandaren, Belgium. Plot 11.1.

Colonel Philip Bent of the 9th Leicestershire won a posthumous Victoria on the same battlefield on the 1st October 1917.

George's name can be read on Coalville Clock Tower Memorial and on the Memorial Tablet in Christ Church.

His family possess a cherished photograph of George in uniform, and alongside it: '**Greater Love hath no man than he that layeth down his life for his friends**'. So appropriate.

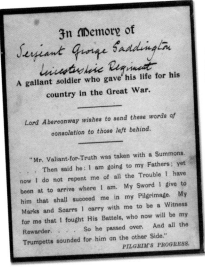

William Saddington as landlord of a public house in London. With him are his parents, Thomas and Louisa. Crica 1938.

Following George's death a friend sent his few possessions home, and amongst them was his damaged and blood-splattered watch.

Other local men of the 2/5th Battalion who died in the battle: James Bird of Coalville, Forester Fowkes of Ravenstone, Reginald Hallam of Shepshed, Francis Harris of Shepshed, John Jacques of Loughborough, Maurice Malyon of Loughborough, Wilfred Mason of Ellistown, John Smith of Mountsorrel, Wilfred Sykes of Thringstone and George Wood of Hugglescote

The brothers' father, Thomas Saddington died in 1945 and his wife, Louisa in 1956. They rest together at Hugglescote Cemetery.

Many thanks to Molly Hunt, daughter of Robert Winston Saddington.

FIVE MORE BROTHERS NAMED SCOTT

In my earlier book about the Famous Fifty I described how Walter Vernon Scott, the Station Master of Coalville East Station, had six sons, four from his first wife, Kate, and two from his second wife, Elizabeth.

The first-born **Walter** V. Scott, 1887-1962, was born in the Station House at Blaby Railway Station. Blaby was then a large village about twenty-five kilometres (fifteen miles) southeast of Coalville. The second eldest brother, Leonard (**Len**) George Scott, was born in 1889, also at Blaby. As a young man he heard of tales of wonderful opportunities available in the New World, and emigrated to the United States of America before the war, and was earning a very good living. At the outbreak of the Great War, Len booked a single ticket and steamed across the Atlantic to the land of his birth. He travelled to Coalville and enlisted into the army, won a promotion to lance corporal and fought throughout until 1918. Len then married his very pretty fiancée, Ethel (nee Cracknell), before returning to the U.S.A. He had an excellent life until his death in 1946, at the age of fifty-seven years.

Frederic (no K) Scott was born in 1893 at Blaby, and in his short life displayed great intelligence and many admirable qualities. After

Clifford Scott. Telegram Messenger.

front row—first right. Clifford Scott. Second row—first on right. Frederic Scott.

leaving the prestigious Ashby de la Zouch Grammar School, where he was a school friend of Philip Bent, later Colonel Bent VC, he sojourned as a trainee teacher at Bridge Road School, and was highly thought of by the headmaster and staff. He then continued with his education at Cambridge University, and a year later in July 1914, was a cadet in the University's Officer Training Corps at Mytchett, five kilometres (three miles) northeast of Aldershot. Shortly after the outbreak of war he was drafted into the Ninth, and later the Sixth Leicestershire Battalion with a commission, that of 2nd lieutenant. In the early winter of 1915, the Battalion was in trenches at Monchy au Bois, just to the north of the Somme, and Frederic and his men were suffering terribly. What with enemy mortars and winter rains that necessitated wading waist deep in foul water, together with bitterly sharp frosts, life was none too easy. Christmas day was none to festive, there was no truce this year, and only the occasional carol could be heard from the enemy Lines. This was the scene when on the 26th December 1915 Lieutenant Frederic Scott was wounded in the eye. The Coalville Times of the 14th January 1916: '*Lieutenant Frederic Scott was superintending support work on the sides of trenches, when an enemy bullet deflected from an entrenching tool into his left eye. An operation was performed at Rouen Hospital before he was moved to a London hospital. It is a nasty wound but it is hoped the sight of his eye will be saved.*'

Frederic recovered and in March rejoined the 9th Battalion. The lieutenant was wounded again, this time whilst leading his men on the 14th July 1916, at the Battle of Bazentin Ridge in the Somme Sector. The wound was a bullet through the arm. This resulted in hospitalisation and home convalescence. The surgeon explained it was crippling, and there

Frederick Scott recovering from injury 1917.

was no requirement for him to continue as a frontline officer. Nevertheless he felt his responsibilities were to his men, and with casualty rates very high he opted to return, and shortly afterwards on October 26th was promoted to captain. A good friend at this time was Ibstock's Lieutenant J. Harratt of the same Battalion, and like Frederic, he was a schoolmaster before the war.

The following spring, Captain Scott, again displayed outstanding bravery and leadership during the Battle of Bullecourt on the 3rd May 1917. He was wounded for a third time, and during convalescence at home received news that was printed in the

Robert Scott – front right as an Army Cadet. Coalville (circa 1914).

Coalville Times of July 27th 1917: '*Captain F. Scott, for conspicuous gallantry during an attack has been awarded the **Military Cross**. Although badly shaken by a bursting shell, he collected thirty men and they dug themselves into a forward position, and held it under heavy fire for a day and a night. He was again wounded but refused attention until he had withdrawn his unit.' The newspaper explained that*

*Frederic was the **first officer in Coalville** to receive such an award.*

Frederic was involved in the Battle of Polygon Wood in October 1917 when his commanding officer and old school friend, Colonel Philip Bent D.S.O., received a posthumous Victoria Cross.

During the Battle of the Aisne on the 27th May 1918, the enemy launched a massive artillery bombardment prior to an infantry attack. There were few survivors in our frontlines, and enemy storm-troops poured through and killed and captured many of our men. It was always believed that Frederic was shot through the head in open battle. He was twenty-

Robert Scott – wireless operator aboard H.M.S. 'Ganges'

Robert Scott's R.N.V.R. Service Certificate

four years of age and has no known grave. **The following information was recently located** in an old copy of the Coalville Times dated the 20th November 1918. It reported that Lieutenant Walter Handford had sent a letter to his wife. Its contents explained that he was captured at the same time as Captain Frederic Scott, and that the latter had been killed **after** being taken prisoner. The same newspaper on the 10th January 1919 announced the welcome return of Walter Handford after his German imprisonment. It also stated that Mr. W. V. Scott, stationmaster of Coalville's N.W. Railway Station, had received a letter from another soldier, who

Coalville East Railway Station. Walter Vernon Scott was the Stationmaster at the above. He had six sons, two of which died World War 1.

Lance Corporal Len Scott and his wife Ethel.

Front centre: First Officer Walter Vernon Scott of Coalville Red Cross Brigade. From left back: H. Mason, T. Wright, N. Bishop, and G. Terry. From left centre: J. Roddis, T. Brewin, and F. Smith. From left front: Hon Surgeon R.W. Jamie, W.V. Scott and J. Brown. Circa 1912.

witnessed the burial of his son while under German guard, **after he'd been shot!** It also stated that his younger brother, Clifford, had been one of the Famous Fifty and had been killed at Ypres in 1915. Mr. W.V. Scott had believed that Frederic had been shot in battle, and the article continued that he had forwarded the letters to the War Office! On the 7th February 1919 Frederic's name had not appeared on any casualty list. No more was heard or said until his name suddenly appeared on a Casualty List dated as captured, the 27th May 1918!

As an enduring mark of respect and gratitude the school where he taught has his name (and others) engraved on a tablet of granite. (Now at Newbridge High School, Coalville).

Clifford Ernest Scott was born in 1895 at Blaby, and as one of the Famous Fifty has been remembered at length in my first book. A credit to the family, he died in the Ypres Salient on the Western Front in the summer of 1915. He was just twenty years of age.

Robert Scott was born on the 22nd June 1900 at Wigston, near Leicester, but spent his early years growing up at the Station House, Coalville East Railway Station. An intelligent boy with light brown hair, blue eyes and a fresh complexion he attended Bridge Road Infant School and Coalville Grammar School, and whilst at the latter was a member of the Army Cadet Corps. Upon leaving school he secured

the position of a Goods Clerk for the L. and N. W. R. Railway, however on the 2nd April 1918, he enlisted, two months before the required age into the Royal Naval Volunteer Reserve. There followed a period of training at the Victory **V1** School, and he passed out with the remarkably high marks of 327/340 for his chosen job as a wireless operator. His character assessment was graded as very good.

Robert was posted to H.M.S. 'Ganges', a 'Q-Boat'. These small freighters had guns concealed in a collapsible deck structure. On being challenged by a U-Boat a 'panic-party' would hastily abandon the freighter leaving a hidden fighting party manning the gun. The U-Boat would be lured into the trap and if all went to plan, sunk! Q-Boats proved to be successful although many were sunk themselves.

Robert also served on minesweepers, and a highly dangerous and responsible duty it was, attempting to locate and remove the highly explosive devices. The war was in its final phase, however, the Germans had planted many mines in the seaways of Europe. In addition enemy submarines were very troublesome and no effort was spared to ensure the safety of the sailors of the Grand Fleet, the Merchant Seaman and passengers thereof. It must be said that the enemy laid their mines indiscriminately, despite the protests of neutral countries. Dealing with sea-mines was perilous, not least the detecting, for some were set very deeply to destroy submarines, whilst

Silk Christmas card from the trenches.

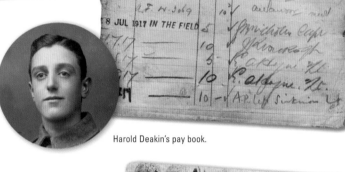

Harold Deakin's pay book.

Maud Haywood:
Future wife of
Percy Cliff.

A 'carte postale'
sent by Jabez
Emmerson.

1917 - 18 Christmas card from the 46th North Midland Division.

Keepsake button
from William
Sharpe's uniform.

Owen Ward's diary and wound certificate stating wounding in battle.

Henry Williams of the 7th Leicestershire Battallion who died in December 1914.

Silk handkerchief memento of the Leicestershire Regiment.

Letters from Henry Walker.

The Attack on the Hohenzollern Redoubt Oct 13th 1915

1:10'000 map issued for the battle — shewing Communication trenches to be used before and during the action.

A original map for the attack on the Hohenzollern Redoubt. (J.D. Hills)

W.W.1 note. (J.D. Hills)

5th Leicestershire Battalion. (J.D. Hills)

MAY YOUR CHRISTMAS BE AS FREE FROM WORRIES AS THE SLAG HEAP IS FROM BOSCHE.

THE 5TH BATTALION, THE LEICESTERSHIRE REGIMENT, CHRISTMAS 1917.

A Happy Christmas 1918 and Prosperous New Year

Selection of books by Arthur Newberry Choyce.

Postcard from George Saddington.

Janet Cartlidge with a framed memorial to her grandfather: Percy Cliff.

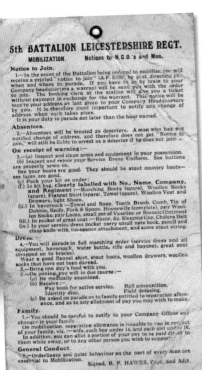

Mobilization certificate, 1914.

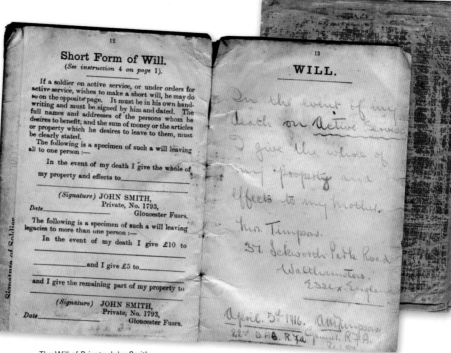

The Will of Private John Smith.

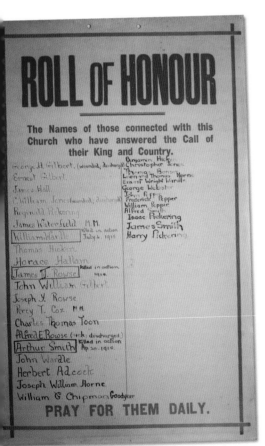

Roll of Honour from St. George's Parish church, Swannington.

Bernard Hatter.

Corporal Mark Cavendish
lays a wreath for the
'Famous Fifty' in 2005.

others sat just below the surface to destroy any oncoming vessel. Robert had a key role in receiving Admiralty instructions, and communication links generally.

A wonderful photograph shows him on-board the *'Ganges'* wearing his headphones on the 15th November 1918. By this date he had lost two brothers to the war.

He was demobilised on 29th March 1919, and returned to his parents' home and his pre-war job. On the 26th December 1923, Robert married twenty-year old Lillian Gwendolyn Underwood (Queenie) and happily settled into family life.

Having progressed to Relief Station Master he was promoted to Station Master for Coalville East when his father retired in 1925. Their first child, Doreen, was born at the station house on the 24th August 1927. A year later, Robert's father (his parents had retired to Southsea) informed him of an excellent job in the offing if he was to move to Southsea. The family did so and he became the landlord of: 'The Eastney Tavern', close to Marine Barracks. Their second child, Anthony was born in there on the 29th January 1931, and the third, Barrie on the 12th July 1933. In 1936 the family moved to Jubilee Road at nearby Portchester, and experienced some of the happiest times of their lives. A few years later, 1939, brought a sad loss to the entire family when Walter Vernon Scott, the head of the family died. He lies in Milton Cemetery, Portsmouth. His second wife, Elizabeth died in 1967. By 1939 Robert was working as an estate agent, then he had a spell at McAlpines and finally employment at the Ordnance Depot, Portsmouth. By early 1940, with the potential of enemy air raids the family wisely returned to Coalville, living with his wife's parents. Their daughter, Anne, was born there on the 22nd July 1941.

After returning, Robert's initial job was with a local munitions factory where he became an inspector. He then worked in the offices of R. J. Kemp & Co, an electrical firm, and he rented a family home in the Market Place, Whitwick. The energetic Robert then joined the Coalville office of Britannic Insurance Co. As a man of many talents he wrote poetry during World War 2 under the pseudonym, 'Blue Orchids'. It was published in a magazine that was printed and sold by the: 'Three Crowns' Public House on behalf of the Whitwick Forces Comfort Fund.

On May 28th 1955, Barrie married June Irene Gee, and I am very grateful for all the information and photographs they have supplied about the Scott Family.

Sadly Queenie died on 13th May 1959, aged only 55 years. In 1963 Robert married a second time to Clarice Goddard, sharing happiness until he died in 1977 at the age of 77 years. Clarice died in 1986.

William Franklin Scott was born in 1905 at Coalville. He married Gladys Chambers, whose brother, William, was the first Coalville man to be killed in the Great War. The unfortunate man was once a regular in the Royal Marines, and just before the war he and a friend decided to walk to Portsmouth to enlist in the Navy. After a few days the friend turned back, so William Chambers continued to walk the two hundred and fifty kilometres (150 miles) on his own. He was killed on the warship, H.M.S. *'Pathfinder.'* In 1927 they and their two children Alma and Roy also moved to Southsea. There later followed the birth of another daughter, Wendy.

William was a professional musician, directing his own orchestra when a friend, the colonel of the

The 'P.H Mask' or Phenate Hexamine Gas Hood was widely used by Allied soldiers in 1915-16.

local territorial battalion, sought his professional services. He joined them and in 1939 they were mobilised for World War 2, William being drafted to the Medical Corps. In 1940 he suffered severe head injuries in an accident and was invalided out of the Corps in the same year. He decided, following medical advice to return to Leicestershire. William, his wife and two daughters set up home at Blaby, about five kilometres south of Leicester City centre. He helped the war effort by working for Power Jet at nearby Whetstone, and also set up a dance band that played at very many venues to help brighten the gloom of the war years throughout the county.

By the summer of 1940 the German Airforce,

William Scott, one of the six sons of Walter Vernon Scott. stationmaster of Coalville East railway Station had a son Roy, who in 1942 entered the Royal Air Force, becoming a fighter pilot and flying Spitfires in both the Middle East and Far East. William carried the photograph shown throughout the war, safe and secure in his wallet.

the Luftwaffe, was turning its bombing offensive against Britain's ports, with specific concentration on the south coast of England. It is well documented how the magnificent 'Few'—the pilots of Fighter Command won the Battle of Britain, however for the citizens of our Isle it was a dangerous time.

Roy decided to stay at Southsea and in 1942 entered the Royal Air Force, becoming a fighter pilot and flying Spitfires in both the Middle East and Far East. William carried the photograph shown throughout the war, safe and secure in his wallet.

In 1947 William and his wife together with the two daughters returned to Southsea, and Roy lives there to this day.

Alma married and emigrated to Australia, Roy remained single and Wendy married a Navy Officer.

William died in 1994 at the age of eighty-nine years and Gladys in 2000.

Many thanks to Barrie and June Scott. Barrie is the son of Robert Scott, half brother to the first four sons, and also to Roy at Southsea for some excellent material used in books one and two. **June Scott**, a delightful cheery lady and full of character also has a fascinating background. Her great uncle was John Albert Gee, '**the little hero**' of the Whitwick Colliery disaster of the 19th April 1898. The folk of Leicestershire know this to be the county's worst mining disaster when thirty colliers died. I was going to type men, however the little hero was only thirteen years of age. John, of Thringstone was the Deputy's Boy, and he had just made his way to the pit bottom when the underground fire broke-out. He reached the surface but was told to go back and warn a group of miners working in a remote area of the danger. Without hesitation he battled to get to the men, alas, they all became trapped and they died, banded-together in each other's arms.

Twenty-seven women were widowed and eighty-four children under the age of thirteen were left fatherless. June's grandfather, Mr. Edward Gee, lived at Barrack Yard, 73, Main Street, Thringstone and was four years older than his brother at the time of John's death. Edward completed fifty-seven years as a miner. In 1965 he recalled, "*I was working on days at No6 pit at Whitwick and my brother should have returned home at 4.00 am, but he didn't arrive. I set out to get to the pit for 6.00 o'clock and on the way I heard about the disaster. John had only been a pit boy for a few weeks. My uncle, James Wright also died in the disaster.*"

Black-edged cards were circulated in memory of the little hero. They told in simple verse that John was a hero worthy of the name and that he bravely heard the call for action. Please note his photograph, poor in quality but rich in character. It was taken the day before he died, and hopefully it will rekindle his memory. I can highly recommend the book: 'Banded Together' by the Whitwick Historical Group.

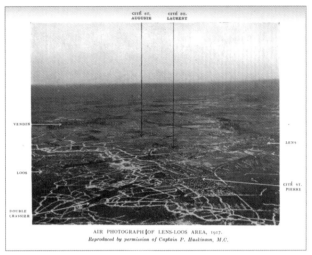

AIR PHOTOGRAPH OF LENS-LOOS AREA, 1917.
Reproduced by permission of Captain P. Huskinson, M.C.

An aerial map of the Lens - Loos battlefield in 1917.
(So often referred to in this book.)

The Scott family are typical of some of the wonderful families that lived in northwest Leicestershire just before the Great War until after World War 2. Within their spirit they possessed (and still do) qualities of great bravery, leadership, resolution and responsibility to their fellow man, especially in times of adversity! **I am pleased that I entitled this book: 'Greater Love'.**

JAMES HERBERT SCOTT

James Herbert Scott or 'Bert' to those who knew him was born at Ibstock on the 27th January 1898. He was only eleven years of age when his father, Harry, died on the 30th May 1909. Harry was a relatively young man and his wife and son were kindly 'taken in' by a relation of the family, Tom Blower, an in-law. Tom was landlord of the Cross Keys Inn at Loughborough and was a famous and popular cyclist of his age. Young Bert was pleased with the arrangement and took an interest in cycling, but found the painful loss of his father difficult to surmount. He attended school in Greenclose Lane in the town, and as the years passed developed into a tall, good-looking and well-balanced young man. He was pleased to have a father figure when his mother married again, to a Reuben Blower, a nephew of Tom's. Their circumstances were similar; unhappily his first wife died and left him with a daughter, Connie. Reuben was a successful businessman, and during his lifetime was leader of the Coalville Town Council on three occasions. He also owned a building and funeral company at nearby Ellistown.

Bert, a determined and focussed young man decided to enlist into the Forces at the age of sixteen, and nothing could deter him. In 1914 he informed the recruitment office that he was eighteen years old, was signed-on as A1. Not the first volunteer to tell a 'white lie' regarding his age! Gunner James Scott (83803) was posted to the 154 Siege Battery of the Royal Garrison Artillery, and was quickly promoted

James Herbert Scott of 154 Siege Battery.

A Sixty pounder of the Royal Garrison Artillery on the Western Front during the Great War.

to Lance Bombardier. After training with the unit at Lydd in Kent, the Battery was issued with four 9.2inch Howitzers, four caterpillar- tracks, thirty-two lorries, one light car and numerous motorcycles. After loading onboard H.M.S. 'Chevington' they steamed from Avonmouth and docked at Boulogne.

In August 1916 the Battery had their first location at Bois de Bouvigny on the Ailette Ridge, near to Bethune in northern France. The huge guns required small-gauge railways (Decauvilles) to carry shells and cartridge packs to the firing position. The Battery also had a forward spotter who reported on the graph location of the first registration shot, and so enabled the surveyor to adjust for greater accuracy. It is quite possible that the athletic Bert spent some time doing this job. In the above instance the spotter was on the heights of the Notre Dame de Lorette, and saw the first shot hit the pithead tower at Fosse 6 near Loos.

September 1916 brought heavy rainfall and conditions became extremely difficult for the gunners, especially handling the heavy and slippery ammunition. The Battery was transferred later that month to the Somme Sector, which had suffered ferocious battles since July 1st. They were sited at Sailly-au-Bois, and gun mounting was dreadfully difficult in a low, flat and muddy field. The conditions for Bert and his pals were equally as bad as soldiers in the frontlines! After three days and nights of slavish labour constructing stable gun-

platforms the men were exhausted. They had to rest and sleep under tarpaulin, and soon several of the gunners became ill, and with two thousand rounds of shells stuck in a muddy cornfield they declared the unit inoperable. The personnel were swiftly moved half a mile to drier ground, and the Howitzers followed at a later date.

November saw the Battery covering Gommecourt in the northern section of the Somme. It was against this fortified village, on July 1st, that the 46th North Midland Division, including many men from Leicestershire, attacked and suffered heavy losses. The Howitzers were deployed in bombarding the enemy trenches at Pigeon Wood and the defences around Serre, Puiseaux and Bucquoy. The work was heavy, smoky and very noisy, but a great threat came from their own shells exploding in the gun-barrels and counter-shelling from the enemy's artillery.

On the 11th November, Beaumont Hamel was shelled incessantly for two days prior to the foggy morning of the thirteenth, when Allied troops swarmed into the attack.

On the day itself the Battery discharged eight hundred rounds, and no Decauvilles were available, all the ammunitions were delivered in trench carts! The gunners took cover regularly as the enemy artillery sought them out; they were habitual with their 'evening lates'!

Christmastide and New Year's Day 1917 were miserable times for Bert and company. The weather was cold and frosty with falls of rain and sleet. They worked on forty-eight hour rotas, working ceaselessly in pushing and dragging carts loaded with shells. Headquarters attempted to help by forwarding a mule called, Lizzie. She was fine if very slow, delivered only ten shells in two-and-a-half hours and then dropped down dead!

Howitzers were not only used to smash buildings and concrete bunkers, they also followed a policy of shelling alternate ends of a trench, so that the incumbents sheltered in the middle section. Five rounds of rapid fire were then concentrated on this central section.

Heavy snow and bitter cold announced the arrival of February 1917. All the gunners served a rota in night observation posts and they described this time as physical torture, and braziers did little to help as the smoke enticed danger from enemy small-arms fire. Bert experienced these appalling hardships, and was accustomed to digging frozen wastes to effect dummy blast-holes to fool enemy observation aircraft. Camouflage and deception were vital aids in the art of survival.

When the Germans withdrew from Miraumont, the most southerly point of the Battery's range, 154 followed by mounting their guns 2-3 kilometres lower at Hebuterne Quarry, visible to the enemy at Serre. They were then ordered to bombard Gommecourt Park.

In March the Battery directed its attention to Bucquoy, with the guns at maximum elevation and concentration! Later a move to Chateau de la Haie where concentration was of another form - a plague of rats. The unit's 'weapon' was a terrier called, 'Punch', and caught eighty rats per day! The knack was to place cordite at the rat-hole whilst Punch waited at another.

The Battery then moved to Anzin St. Aubin, joining many units of the Garrison Artillery, all calibre of guns. General Allenby visited and informed everyone that April 3rd was to be 'V'-Day. He ordered a bombardment of four hundred and fifty rounds to cut a pathway through enemy wire entanglements. On the day a gunner was killed when an enemy shell hit a twelve-inch high pile of fuses. The resultant fire could be seen for miles around. Eleven days later the Battery was posted to St.

Laurent Blangy, to the east of Arras. It was gun-alley with hundreds of different calibre guns firing rounds; unfortunately a counter-barrage resulted in the death of a gunner and the destruction of a cartridge store. The heat from the latter was reported as enormous.

Their next appointment was 'Gas Valley', a valley running at ninety degrees to the Arras-Fampoux road. 154 and three other Siege Batteries plus a brigade of Royal Field Artillery occupied the valley. It was a hot spot, being counter-barraged by heavy shells during the day and by gas shells at night. Everyone found it impossible to continue, and many men were seen staggering around in a blinded and choked condition! Reports quote German shells leaving craters large enough to take a cottage, and every morning four red planes from Baron von Richtofen's Flying Circus machine-gunned the valley. The Battery traded the kettle for the fire when they were posted to Moat Farm in Belgium, three kilometres from the frontline, and covering from Zillebeke in the north (Ypres Salient) to Messines in the south. For two months the Battery suffered extensive casualties from counter shelling,

Doris Moore: later Scott.

alternating heavy explosive and gas shells. The little terrier, Punch, was reduced to atoms when hit by a shell.

On the 6th July 1917 the Battery regrouped and their only protection was a hedge screen.

The Germans swiftly destroyed it, and shortly afterwards a visiting Allied officer by the name of Ffoliot demanded: "*What are you going to do about it?*" The unit adopted this phrase and it helped to relieve stressful times when the enemy rained shells over them! On one day alone thirty gunners were gassed.

Bert battled on; the next mounting was in support of 'Third Ypres', the Battle of Paschendaele. The battle opened on the 31st July with fine drizzle, much of the spotting work now undertaken by aircraft observers. Unfortunately, the guns were not at their best due to heavy wear, and were said to 'perform like trench mortars'. In November, 53 Squadron, who were based at Bailleul did much of the spotting. A dreadful error occurred when one of their planes flew into 154 gun's 'line of fire' and the Battery's spotter, Lieutenant McCullough, was killed along with the pilot. No remains of the men or the aircraft were ever found.

In late December 1917 the guns were targeting areas such as the Ypres Ridge, Stirling Castle, Mountsorrel and Sanctuary Wood. The term for such a bombardment was 'trench punching'.

The German 'Spring Offensive' started in March 1918, and on March 21st the enemy downed a **'terrific barrage with 'B' gun being put of action. The gas was sickening, a dense fog and the earth was sprinkled with chloride of lime.'** It was at this time that Bert was gassed. He was sleeping, the men were so drained they could sleep regardless of noise, when one of his pals threw a boot to warn him of incoming gas. The boot hit him on the head and while concussed inhaled gas. His eyes were swollen and closing and his lungs were foaming. Little could be done for gas cases, but happily after many months he recovered to an extent.

To highlight the bravery and robustness of the Great War generation the following is in the War Diary: '*May 30th, one of our planes struck by shell at 5,000 feet. Part of wing removed, observer climbs out onto stub of wing to correct balance of aircraft. Plane*

The Scott's home: 116 Ashburton Road, Hugglescote.

crashes near to us, observer jumps clear at last moment with pilot extricated from wreckage.Later reported both flying within one month.'

During the Battery's twenty-six months in France and Flanders thirty-one men were killed, one hundred and twenty nine wounded, and less than one-third of the original members survived. They fired 98,000 rounds weighing 12,000 tons. 154 Battery was founded on the 23rd May 1916 and was disbanded on the 1st January 1919.

Bert eventually returned to Ellistown where he assisted in his stepfather's construction and funeral business. Later he met and married a delightful lady, Doris Moore, who herself had a distinguished nursing career in World War 1, serving in Egypt, Palestine, Lebanon, Syria and the Holy Land. One her many patients was a certain **Lawrence of Arabia**, namely Lieutenant T. E. Lawrence after he had been wounded in a skirmish with the Turks. To thank Doris he personally bought her some roses, and later he invited her and the whole team to dinner and entertainment at the famous Shepherd's Hotel at Cairo. Doris recalled that in the centrepiece of the dining table there was an arrangement of red roses, from which red ribbons led to each nurse. Lawrence asked the nurses to gently tug the ribbons, and each ribbon pulled a rose from the arrangement, one for each of them.

When the twenty-year old nurse first arrived in Egypt in 1915 she worked in the fever block of the 17th General Hospital at Alexandria. The hospital coped with two thousand patients at a time with many being under canvas. Doris also remembered: "*It was my first Christmas out there and many of the staff was giving there spare time to making decorations and tying parcels for the patients. On Christmas Day it was very touching seeing the poor boys who were not able to sit up wearing their paper hats.*"

In 1918 she contracted malaria very badly, and throughout her exceptionally long life it occasionally flared up. Doris often served close to the frontline and her grandson, Graham Stocks, said that only towards the end of her life did she reveal how often shells and bullets hit the hospitals she served in.

Post war she trained as a mid-wife at London's Queen Charlotte Hospital under the tutorship of the then Royal Physician.

Bert built the house at 116 Ashburton Road at Hugglescote, and deservedly enjoyed many happy and contented years of family life. Very sadly Bert died in 1963, he was sixty-five years of age, the gas of 1918 finally claiming its victim!

His stepfather Reuben Blower held an army rank during the Great War and was involved in enlistment and appeal tribunals for the Coalville area.

Doris died one month before her ninety-eighth birthday in 1993.

What a magnificent generation.

Many thanks to Graham Stocks, grandson of James Herbert 'Bert' and Doris Scott for sharing such treasured memories with me.

WILLIAM SHARPE

Sergeant William Sharpe, circa: December 1914.

William was born on the 22nd November 1890 at Hugglescote, and was educated at the village Baptist Chapel and School. Later he became a Sunday school teacher at the Wesleyan Chapel, and with close friend, Fred Whitmore, became joint secretary of their football club. Many readers will recall that his relatives were connected with the local post office for many decades; sadly, Lance Corporal F. Whitmore of the Black Watch died of wounds on the 29th May 1915.

Following school, William began employment as a miner at nearby Nailstone Colliery. This necessitated travel through Ellistown to and from work and on one such sojourn he met his future wife, Bertha Ellen Barrs, who was born on the 30th April 1890.

On the 27th March 1909 he married Bertha and on August 6th of the same year their first born, William (always called Bill) Francis Andrew Sharpe, arrived.

Pre-war William became an excellent boxer and trained with close friends, Charles Hatter and Bill Massey, who were to become two of the Famous Fifty.

Approaching the outbreak of the war William

William Sharpe of the 8th Leicestershire Battalion with Bertha and Bill, 1915.

William was friendly with the regimental tailor and arranged for a uniform to be cut for five years old, Bill. 1915.

was living with his wife in the pretty little cottage of 5, The Green, Hugglescote.

He enlisted on the 5th September 1914 into the 8th Leicestershire Battalion, 110th Brigade, at Coalville and entrained for Wigston Barracks at Glen Parva, near Leicester. Personality wise he relished in keeping active, and possessed a natural inclination towards undertaking responsibility, especially for his fellow man. Adapting very quickly to army life, William swiftly made an impression on his officers. He believed in the principles of: 'If a job is worth doing it's worth doing well', maintaining smartness of dress and a disciplined approach towards life.

The original photograph of William Sharpe is somewhat faded and unclear, but there remains a charm in this shot that was kept in a locket around Bertha's neck from 1914-18.

When his battalion moved to a training camp at Bourley, near Aldershot, there followed a rapid series of promotions! On the 5th October 1914 he was made a lance corporal and was popular and respected by all around, especially his squaddies. Exactly one month later he was made a full corporal and on the 5th December a full sergeant. On the 14th February

1915 followed an appointment as acting company sergeant major (CSM); confirmed one month on. In addition he received certificates as a 1st Class musketry instructor and 2nd Class warrant officer.

When the 8th Battalion travelled to Folkestone in March 1915, William was billeted on the Lees and whilst there his wife and child visited him for a short stay; and by the end of April his battalion had moved to Perham Down Camp on the Salisbury Plain.

At 10.00 pm on the 29th July 1915, the Brigade embarked from Folkestone in complete darkness and silence with the 8th Battalion aboard the SS 'Golden Eagle', arriving at Boulogne a few hours later. I have written about the Brigade's campaign on the Western Front (see Philip Bent) and William proved to be a very fine soldier: in spite of being badly gassed on at least two occasions.

The Coalville Times of the 26th November 1915, commented that William had been on leave a week earlier and that he visited his old master, Mr. W. Fellows, who was then teaching at the new Council School on the Ashburton Road. It also stated that whilst in France he had declined an offer to undertake officer training, much to the disappointment of his commanding officer. However later in the war he accepted the position of regimental sergeant major (RSM), maintaining that he preferred to mix freely with his men in the ranks.

William was captured during the German

Spring Offensive, 'Operation Michael', which commenced on the 21st March 1918. He and his men had no alternative but to surrender when completely over-run during grim hand-to-hand street fighting whilst defending the St Emillie-Epehy Sector on the Cambrai front. Thringstone man, James Bancroft, one of the Famous Fifty was serving with the 8th Battalion when he was killed on the same day.

RSM Sharpe was route-marched with many other prisoners to Cottbus POW Camp, which was one hundred kilometres (sixty miles) southeast of Berlin.

William's youngest daughter, Edith said, "*My mother wore a locket around her neck throughout the war, and within was a small photograph of father shortly after he enlisted.*

and his responsibility. To help pass the time they formed a Theatre Group, and Ernie Cope from Leicester played the 'leading lady! (See photograph).

I recall father was disappointed when a German officer took his ' Sam Browne belt', he was so proud of it and he never saw it again.

Mother said that when he returned home after the war he was in a terrible mess, however he was a strong man and gradually improved. Father never completely recovered from the gassing to his lungs, and twice suffered from double pneumonia: the doctor said it was unusual to survive one bout let alone two. The doctor used to send him to a convalescent home at Overstrand, near to Cromer on the Norfolk coast, in the hope the bracing sea air would help his breathing!"

William is sitting behind the 'Leading Lady' at Prisoner of War Camp, Cottbus, 1918.

She had a worrying time because it was quite a while before being notified that he was a prisoner, earlier posted as missing presumed dead; and by that time both of her brothers, who were also in the Leicestershire Regiment, had been killed.

After capture, my father was in charge of his fellow prisoners and did whatever he could, but it was very hard for them, especially the last three or four months. He always said that they were his lads

Following the war William returned to colliery life, this time to Ibstock where he was promoted to a 'deputy', and when the pit was closed down was transferred to Nailstone, where he was subsequently promoted to an 'overman' (just below an under-manager).

During this time the family lived at 281, Battram Road in the hamlet of Battram (house no longer standing).

Edith and Dorothy (Joan) Sharpe, circa 1932, at Battram, near Ellistown.

215, Leicester Road, Ibstock, where Edith and Molly were born in 1927.

In 1919 Dorothy Joan (always called Joan) was born, and Jack in 1923, while Edith was born in 1927: her twin Molly, dying at the age of twelve days.

Edith continues: "*He was always on the go, a prolific reader, sitting various examinations, and was a member of the Colliery Ambulance Team.*

Father ran a 'Boy's Club' at Battram (near Ellistown), it was a gymnasium where he taught lads how to box and to use expanders to improve their muscle power. He taught lads like Simeon Woolley, who was the son of Victor Woolley, one of the Famous Fifty, and Eric Jones of Melbourne Street at Coalville. They both became quite famous boxers. Also, local men who wanted to join the police-force came to him to improve their chest measurements: they had to be a certain size before acceptance into the Force. Father was also a fully-fledged referee and supervised boxing matches in the Granby Halls at Leicester."

Bertha and William Sharpe in their middle years.

During the Second World War William trained the 'Bevin Boys', and he thought very highly of most of them, with one lad in particular remaining in the collieries and reaching a senior position. He was also the senior air warden for Battram and district, and often spoke of the night when German bombers flew overhead on their way to blitz Coventry.

William had a fine singing voice, and thoroughly enjoyed vocalising for various chapel choirs over the years; it also helped strengthen his lungs.

Edith said, "*He was a strict father but we knew that he loved us dearly, doing anything to help people, especially those just reaching adulthood that asked for his valued opinions. Father was a very well liked and respected man, and often spoke kindly of his old friend, Charlie Hatter and his wife, Hetty, who lived on the Central Road of Hugglescote.*"

William Sharpe supervises training sessions at his gymnasium at Battram, circa 1935.

Inevitably the gas and coal dust claimed William's life and he passed away on the 29th June 1965: aged seventy-five, whilst living in a bungalow at Markfield. His beloved wife, Bertha, joined him from the same bungalow on the 16th May 1970, aged eighty years. Both were cremated at Gilroes' Cemetery near Leicester.

The grave of Molly Sharpe in Ibstock Cemetery. She died in 1927 at the age of only 12 days.

Edith's husband, Les, said, "*I remember an occasion when father-in-law met his old wartime friend, Captain Frank Breacher (who had been badly wounded leading the 8th Battalion), they were like kin meeting up again! Also, in 1966 I was visiting a convalescent home at Woodhouse Eaves when a war veteran, Lawrence Birch of Barrow upon Soar, mentioned that he was trained during the war as a boxer. He informed me that he was instructed by a CSM William Sharpe, and mentioned how he respected the man; a small world.*"

Son Bill, their first-born in 1909, worked for several years at the pits, and during World War 2 served with the Auxiliary Fire Service. Later he became self-employed: earning a good living in coal haulage. Bill died on Boxing Day 1989. Jack served in the Royal Air Force as an electrician during World War 2, maintaining aircraft (see photograph) dying on the 7th April 1995.

Regarding Bertha's two brothers who fought in the Great War. Both are recorded as the sons of John and Laura Mary Barrs of Ellistown.

A keepsake button taken from the uniform of William Sharpe that was worn from 1914-18.

Private John William Barrs (service number 40246) of Ellistown enlisted at Coalville and served with the 7th Leicestershire Battalion. Details reveal that he was also an old Hugglescote Baptist schoolboy. He was killed on the 27th September 1916 at Guedecourt: his body was never identified but his name can be read on the Thiepval Memorial on the Somme, along with 73,000 others. He was twenty-four years of age.

Private George Barrs (service number 240713) was born at Ellistown but living with his parents at 7, Richmond Terrace, Ibstock when he enlisted at Coalville into the Fifth (1/5th) Leicestershire Battalion. He died of wounds on the 25th May 1917, received whilst fighting in the Lens Sector of France. George was aged twenty-three years, and is buried in Noeux les Mines Communal Cemetery (D937). He is one of 1285 graves of British soldiers.

The name of Private John W. Barrs, 7th Battalion, Leicestershire Regiment is etched onto the Thiepval memorial on The Somme, France. John is the brother of George, right.

The grave of Private George H. Barrs, 5th Battalion, Leicestershire Regiment at Noeux-les-Mines Communal Cemetery, France. George was the brother of Bertha Sharpe.

Jack Sharpe was born in 1923. During World War 2 he served with the Royal Air Force as an electrician, maintaining aircraft. He died on the 7th April 1995

Both brothers are also remembered on the Coalville Clock Tower War Memorial, and also on the Memorial Tablet within St. Christopher's Church, Ellistown.

I do not know if there is a connection but a George Sharpe, a gunner with the Canadian Howitzer Brigade died of wounds in November 1916. He was the son of Mr & Mrs Thomas Sharpe of High Street, Ibstock.

Many thanks to Edith and Les Roberts for their friendship and information.

GEORGE SMITH

Malcolm Smith, son of the above gentleman, contacted me after I posted a copy of 'Fifty Good Men And True' to his address at Wilmslow, Cheshire. I was so impassioned by the love that he had for his father, and impressed by the research of his wartime service, that, I knew, no matter how late the entry, it had to be included in this book.

George was born on 14th June 1895 at 18, Mill Hill, Loughborough. The lane no longer exists but it led off Mill Street (now Market Street) just before Ashby Square. His parents: Samuel Smith (1865-1931) and Francis (nee Brewin 1865-1931) then moved to 17, Mill Street.

Malcolm recalls: '*I never knew my grandparents but two older sisters told me of their weekly visits to see them, and how they received pennies. In 1991 one sister pointed out their home, (then a shoe shop), and stated that both grandparents had died there.*

In 1895 the town was relatively small; there were two main 'Smith clans' with George's family known as, Brindie Smith: reason unknown. Father's younger brother, Sidney, couldn't offer an explanation either.'

On leaving school George joined the town's Brush Electrical and undertook an apprenticeship as a blacksmith; and around his eighteenth birthday (1913) enlisted into the Fifth (1/5th) Territorial Battalion of the Leicestershire Regiment: service number 1876, later 240303. The (county) Battalion had its headquarters in Loughborough and until a decade ago the old Drill Hall could be seen off Granby Street. On the 2nd August 1914, Private George Smith was with the Battalion at their annual training camp at Bridlington. They received orders for mobilisation, and after a final parade in Loughborough's Town Hall Square entrained for Luton. As detailed in my earlier book, the Battalion disembarked at Le Havre on 27th February 1915, with Private George Smith being part of the first full Territorial Division to land in France. He fought in the early Flanders' battles and witnessed the ferocity of shellfire and the devastation of mines at Ypres; it

Private George Smith

Private George Smith

Jane Smith (nee Snow).

was a long summer: an eventful year!

'*Father was badly wounded whilst still twenty years old. An enemy bullet entered his left arm above the top of his wrist and exited below the elbow: smashing bones on the way. The larger of the two scars was where the bullet exited and it puckered when he moved his fingers. As a boy I curiously asked if it hurt; he replied "a bit", and that was the only time I heard him speak of his war experiences. I lived with that dear man for twenty-eight years and it is my greatest regret that it was not until I retired, when I had the time to study W.W.1 in depth, that I came to understand his character, which I am sure was heavily influenced by the things he saw and had to do as a young man. It is also to my undying shame that his stoicism blinded me to his failing health in the last few years of his life.*'

George was twenty years old on 14th June 1915, and if I had to surmise, I would say that his injury did not occur in a trench, more likely during an attack, possibly at Hohenzollern Redoubt on 13th October 1915.

'*The use of father's arm didn't appear to be seriously affected, but the circulation was, and in cold weather his left hand would be dead-white and stone cold.*'

George was hospitalised near to Southampton, (probably in the suburb of Netley near to Southampton Water), and this was followed by at least one home leave during convalescence.

'*Father laughingly told me of his Loughborough leave when, because his arm was in plaster, was very well treated by hostelries, and as a result he fell down and broke his arm again. A policeman lifted him to his feet, recognised him and carried him home somewhat the worse for wear!*'

After recovering from his wounds he returned to his battalion and served with them until the end of the war: seeing many battles and witnessing countless painful deaths.

Battalion life at the front duly observed 'the old boys', not too many of them survived from the beginning to the end, with fresh recruits, especially, looking to them for guidance,

George and Jane Smith in later life.

confidence and leadership.

There is no doubt that George knew my grandfather, Charles Hatter, a fellow blacksmith: they played together in the battalion's football team, and as personalities they seem to have a lot in common. Without doubt George would have known all of the survivors of Coalville's 'Famous Fifty'.

Attempts were always made to 'disembody' (demobilise) 'old boys' first, however, family men usually took priority and so he had to wait until 22nd March 1919. (Active service: four-and-three-quarter years.)

'It has been written that father's generation was the absolute peak of the British race. Though innocently naïve, they were confident of the justice of their cause and of the superiority of the British way of life: unaware of the criminal incompetence of their leaders.'

*"The time must come
when travellers are seen no more
and only the forest of graves
above the Aisne will remain
to tell the tale of the Island race
whose sons were once lords
of these wood's and fields."*

George returned to his hometown and completed his apprenticeship at Brush Electrical.

'Despite pleas to the directors of that company I have been unable to obtain any related records. I cannot believe that a company of that size and repute did not produce a Roll of Honour, and can only assume that change in company ownership post W.W.2 resulted in such 'unimportant' documentation being lost.'

'I have a photograph of Samuel, my grandfather wearing the uniform of the Leicestershire Regiment. I am led to believe he served with them during the war, spending some time serving on the east coast of England.'

At some stage George went to work at Loughborough's famous: Taylor's Bell-foundry, and was involved in the making of hanging frames for the bells, and in forging the strikers (hammers) which struck them. Taylor's have an international reputation and clientele, and Malcolm is very proud that his father's works remains in many parts of the world, especially the United States of America. I can recall visiting the rebuilt church at Messines in Flanders twenty years ago (a young corporal by the name of Adolf Hitler painted its shell damaged structure), to be informed that Taylor's made the bell in the 1930's.

George made the striker that hourly chimes the 'Little John bell', in the Council Office dome at Nottingham.

Frederick Snow junior in W.W. 2.

In 2001, Malcolm, his wife and one remaining sister, Winnie, toured the Bell Foundry and Winnie was able to point out the anvil at which she, and sister, Edna May, watched father work.

'On 15th November 1919 my parents married at Holy Trinity Church, Loughborough. Father was twenty-four and mother, Jane (nee Snow) was twenty-five.'

Born Jane Collier Mackie, she had earlier been married to Frederick Snow, who followed his father into employment on the estate of the Herrick family at Beaumanor Hall, Old Woodhouse, a hamlet a few miles from Loughborough. His father was employed as a wheelwright.

Frederick Snow enlisted into the 8th (Service) Battalion of the Leicestershire Regiment, Kitchener's New Army: service number 40904. He was killed on the 11th April 1917 near to the village of Croisilles,

The grave of Private Frederick Snow at St. Leger cemetery, France.

France during action against the Hindenburg Line.

Jane Snow was living at 4a, Pleasant Place, Factory Street, Loughborough with their four children: Frederick junior (born 1913), Gladys (born 1914), Ivy (born 1916) and Winnie (born 1917 and conceived during Frederick's last and only leave), when she was advised of her husband's death, a handwritten note:

> '8th Leicestershire Battalion,
> B.E.F., 14th April 1917.
>
> *I regret to inform you of the death of Pte. F. Snow who was killed in action 11.4.17. He was one of my company runners and so is a great loss to me personally. I wish to assure you of the sympathy of officers and myself and men of the Company. He was buried in a British cemetery by the chaplain. Yours Sincerely, J. Mathews. (Captain).'*

(Captain J. B. Mathews. M.C. died instantly when shot by an enemy sniper on 1st October 1917.)

Frederick Snow lies buried at St. Leger cemetery. An old photograph, possibly taken during the war, shows an old wooden cross, however, when visited (post-war) by Jane the standard British military headstone was in place. Malcolm has also visited the grave; as a child he recalls playing with the bronze plaque (my big penny), which every family received following a W.W.1 service death.

'After my mother's death I took the bronze plaque and relevant documentation to Australia where Gladys (my late sister) lived with her family. I thought it proper that future relatives in the Antipodes should possess memorabilia of the brave man.'

Frederick Snow's name appears on the Carillon War Memorial at Loughborough and the Memorial outside of St. Paul's Church, Woodhouse Eaves.

Returning from the war a comrade of Frederick's informed Jane that her husband had been killed by shellfire: an explosion had snapped his neck and he had died instantaneously.

George and Jane initially lived at 7, Wellington Street, Loughborough, and it was there that Edna May, a surviving twin was born in 1920, and George (junior) in 1926. They then moved into a brand new council house at 152, Derby Road, Loughborough, and Malcolm was born on the 1st June 1932. It is a family joke that the blue plaque recording this auspicious event is yet to be pinned onto the front of the house.

'During a period of great civil unrest, the General Strike, father was unable to do his normal job and so took temporary employment digging ditches. I remember mother telling me that it was desperately hard work, especially for father with his bad arm, and he often came home looking near to death.

In late 1932 or early 1933 the family moved to Nottingham. I do not know the reason for the move, he still worked at the Bell Foundry, perhaps mother wanted to be nearer to her eldest daughter who had married and moved to Toton.

We never used the term stepchild within our

A round of drinks for the Smith family. From left: Ivy, Edna, daughter in law: Iris, Jane, George and George Junior. Circa 1948.

family, and George was always and simply called: Dad.

Dad was passionately fond of gardening and maintained allotments on Wilford Lane throughout my boyhood.

From about 1938 he worked at the Royal Ordnance factory on Kingsmeadow Road, Nottingham, and always walked there and back no matter what the weather. He would arrive home after a day of heavy physical work; have his meal, then walk to his allotment (at least a three mile round trip) where he worked until dark. I well remember running alongside his fast stride (even difficult in my teens), so I usually rode alongside him on my bike. Only when I read the Fifth Battalion War Diaries did I realise where father developed this ability to walk at speed over long distances, no matter what the conditions!

On one occasion I recall leaving the allotments with Mum, Dad and brother, George; we talked Dad into having a ride on George (junior's) bike.

The bike was sporty and with dropped handlebars, and Dad fell off onto some grass laughing in his own unique way: his eyes screwed up but with no sound of laughter.

He was extremely proud of his tomatoes and chrysanthemums, and sometimes he would stop off at the Town Arms public house (which stood on the city end of Trent Bridge).

You could see his pride when anyone complimented him on his produce, and often gave bits away; he was a big softy! Dad also enjoyed his beer: but he only ever drank draught bitter.'

George was a gentle man, extremely kind and generous and never made any distinction between his own and the four children he adopted. Wherever they lived the large, framed photograph of Private Frederick Snow took pride of place on the living room wall.

'Despite extensive enquiries I have never been able to trace what happened to this photograph in the 1990s. I do hope it found its way to a descendant in Australia.

Father, like many of his Loughborough contemporaries, used to say 'bugger' every now and again, but would forbid any other expletive. Even my brother, Fred, when he was 37 years old, and a veteran of twenty years, first the Leicestershire Regiment and then with the Paratroopers, let the 'F-word' slip, father immediately turned to him and said: "That will do my lad!"

Malcolm also told me that his father never laid a hand on any of his children, to chastise with a withering glance and a shake of the head. The essence revolves around the noun, respect.

Private Malcolm Smith in 1950.

'I can only remember my father crying on two occasions. First it was when we went to see George junior in the Nottingham Eye Hospital; he was recovering from an operation and his eyes were bandaged. The other time was at the end of my embarkation leave; he had taken me to the Midland Station at Nottingham to see me off. Tears were streaming down his face and it was the only time, as an adult, that he embraced me: although I never doubted his love. We had left mother at home and it wasn't until some time later that I realised he had taken time off work, something I never ever knew him to do before or afterwards.

After my discharge from the army my best friend, Peter Humphreys, and I were great fans of the radio comedy: The Goon Show'. It starred Harry Seacombe, Peter Sellers, Spike Milligan and Michael Bentine. This was before most people had television sets, and the Goons were at their peak. We used to roll about laughing and Dad would just tut-tut and shake his head in amazement, doubtless thinking: what is modern day youth coming to!'

Like many old soldiers, George didn't want to make a fuss about his illness, and failed to tell anyone until it was too late for any corrective measures to be taken. The old soldier faded away at the premature age of sixty-three years on 11th January 1958 at 2, Shepherds Close, Nottingham. I rightly leave the final words to Malcolm.

'*Our Dad, George Smith, was born on 14th June 1895 and was a saint. I loved him dearly and will always cherish his memory. His name is now captured within the pages of this book, and may readers long remember such men: soldiers of a lost generation.*

My dad had two younger brothers: Frederick and William Smith. Frederick was born on 5th October 1910, and served with the Grenadier Guards during World War 2. By trade he was a bricklayer, but for many years was the maintenance manager of Genatosan (Sanatogen) at Loughborough.

William was born on 12th April 1912. I saw a lot of him whilst he was on leave during the last war because he was a bachelor. I was so proud of him: such a very tall man in the Royal Marines, and wore a 'Combined Services' flash on his sleeve. As one of a thousand commandoes and five thousand Canadian troops, he took part on a limited objective raid on the coastal town of Dieppe on 18th/19th August 1942. The raid was a failure apart from the commandoes silencing a German coastal Battery. He was a great character.'

The Canadians lost 3,379 men, the commandoes 247 of their number. Many lessons were learned which ensured the success of the 'D'-Day landing two years on.

The children of George, Frederick and Jane are well remembered by Malcolm:

Frederick (Fred junior) Snow (1913-88) served with the 1st Battalion Leicestershire Regiment in India between 1933-39, and then joined the 2/5th Battalion under the command of Major Guy German. Fred was fortunate to escape the beaches of Dunkirk in June 1940, and later served with the Paratroopers for the remainder of World War 2.

'*I remember walking with Mum in Nottingham and seeing this bedraggled soldier. Mum shouted: "There's Fred!" She dashed into the middle of the road and embraced her son, a recent survivor from the beaches of Dunkirk.*

I also recall coming home from school in 1944

Margaret and Malcolm Smith

to see mother in tears: he had been reported missing-in-action. I swore that I would kill every German I met! Fortunately he survived and retired from the army in the late 1950s.'

Gladys (1914-99). Her husband, John (Jock) Greave, born 1911 at St. Andrews, Scotland, was a regular soldier who served with the Royal Tank Regiment (R.T.R.) throughout W.W.2. When he retired they emigrated to Australia to join their children and grandchildren. Jock, like his wife before him, died in Australia in November 2006, aged 95 years.

Ivy (born 1916). Married Jim Attewell who fought in the North African campaign with the Royal Artillery Regiment.

'*I am in regular touch with their son (my nephew) who lives in Derbyshire.*'

Winifred (Winnie: 1917-2005). Her husband, Arthur Musson, was unfit for military service due to a footballing injury. He spent the war years working in a factory at Lincoln: making tanks. '*A dear brother-in-law who was very interested in motorcycles. Winnie was the last of my siblings, and she died last year. An adopted son with whom I am in regular contact survives her.*'

Edna May (1920-1999). Her husband, John (Jack) Dawes (1916-2000), born at Sneinton, Nottinghamshire, served for four years in the Middle East with the Royal Army Service Corpse. After the war he became a self-employed 'green-grocer' and had a number of businesses around Nottingham.

'I regularly visit their daughter, Jane, who lives in Clifton Village, Nottingham. Her son, John, emigrated to Adelaide in Australia some four years ago. (Edna's twin: Phyllis Rose 1920-1920.) Jack was another dear brother-in-law and it was he and Arthur who were responsible for my lifelong interest in motorcycles.'

George Smith (1926-1996) junior: married Iris Dawes (1925-2001). He served with the Royal Air Force in the latter stages of W. W. 2., and is survived by his twins, George and Christopher.

(Edna's husband, Jack Dawes, was the brother of Iris Dawes, who married George Smith junior. This means that their four children are genetically identical.)

'I am in regular contact with the twins. Christopher is taking good care of his grandfather's photograph and medals (Pip, Squeak and Wilfred): mounted and in a prominent position within his home.

I have one daughter, Sarah Louise: born 24th June 1960. She lives at Staley Bridge, about twenty miles away and has two children: Mark, fifteen years and Shelly Jane, eight years. Mark is scrum half and captain of his school team. Sarah is a very keen horsewoman, has her own horse, and rides with the North Cheshire Drag Hunt. She represents the BICC Company in the northern half of England and Scotland.'

Malcolm started his career in I.T. (data processing) in 1956. Shortly after marriage, to Margaret (nee Bird), in 1960, they moved south; after seven years at London they came to the northwest whereby he joined 'Cussons': the Soap Company to run their computer centre.

Malcolm received a directorship of the firm and in his last few years did a fair amount of travelling in Europe, North America and two/three trips a year to West Africa. He retired sixteen years ago having spent twenty-nine years with Cussons.

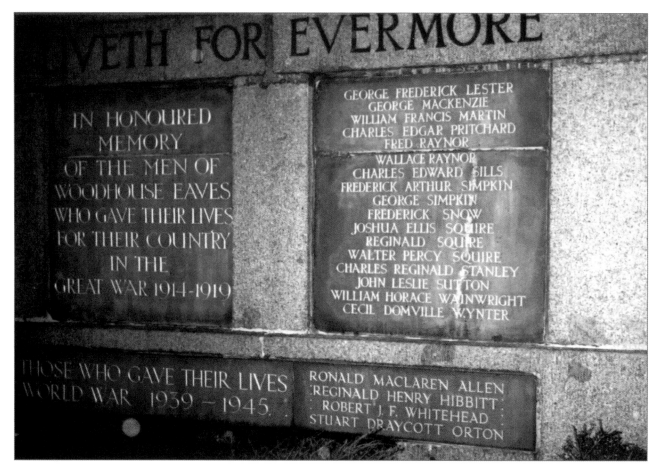

Frederick Snow on St. Paul's Church Memorial, Woodhouse Eaves.

'*Since retiring I have devoted a lot of time to family history, finding it fascinating. Margaret and I do a lot of travelling including seven visits to Australia and New Zealand, where we have many friends. I am also a lifelong motorcycle fan: have two in my garage.*

I usually make two trips a year to Germany to see friends (having revoked my boyhood pledge to kill Germans)'

I believe it is important to remember Jane Smith, wife of Frederick and later, George. She, like most mothers, never fought on any Great War or World War 2 battlefields, but suffered the heartbreak of her husband's violent death. As 'luck' had it Jane's two sisters also lost their husbands during the 1914-18 war. One sister, Emma, married Tom Stephenson. He was born at Newhall and they resided on Albion Street, Woodville, also in Derbyshire. Formally of the Notts and Derbys Regiment (service number 1954), he enlisted at nearby Swadlincote, and was posted to the Lincolnshire Regiment. Sergeant Tom Stephenson M.M. of the 7th Battalion (Service), 51st Brigade, 17th Division, was involved in the Battalion's last battle: 'The Battle of The Sambre' (north of Valenciennes), on the 4th November 1918.

At 19.30 hours on the 3rd November 1918, the 7th Battalion, in absolute darkness set off from Poix and advanced. The following morning a ground mist covered the scene (aided by smoke bombs).

After passing through a wooded area, there was not a lot of opposition, then they had to cross a stretch of open ground and it was inevitable that enemy machine gunners claimed some lives.

Among the six killed was Tom Stephenson, aged twenty-nine years. Three officers and one hundred and five other ranks were wounded. Emma lost her husband, Jane her brother-in-law, just one week before the end of the war. She remarried, to a man by the name of Brabbins.

Jane's other sister was married to James Harold Twells and living at 5, Wood Street, Gresley. He enlisted at Derby into the Royal Garrison Artillery, service number 188780. Gunner James Twells was killed in action whilst serving in Flanders on Saturday 28th September 1918. He lies in Ypres' British Reservoir Cemetery, northwest of Ypres at Vlaanderen: Grave 11 E2. He was killed just six weeks from war's end.

Jane mothered seven children, and please do not forget that of our one million deaths during the two World Wars: every male was a mother's son. Jane was fortunate that she met such a very fine man in George Smith: some were not so lucky and suffered terribly in the 1920/30s, especially. Also, during 1940 her son was rescued from the Dunkirk beaches, as was her youngest brother, Joseph William Collier. (Both in the 2/5th Leicestershire Battalion.) In 1944 she received notification that her eldest son, Frederick, was missing in action: later advised that he was hospital with a severe head wound and loss of memory. A toast to Jane and all the fine women like her.

Malcolm adds the final line to a family where love has played such a key role throughout the generations.

'*My mother died on 13th April 1980. Both my parents were cremated at Wilford Hill Cemetery, Nottingham. A packet of seeds: beautiful flowers: beautiful people recognised by beautiful deeds.*'

JOHN HAROLD STARBUCK M.M.
MENTIONED IN DESPATCHES (2).

Samuel Starbuck was born at East Bridgford, a village seven miles (eleven kilometres) east of the centre of Nottingham in 1870. Whilst in-service in the district he met his future wife, Harriet, who was born in 1860 and similarly employed.

The couple moved to Bardon, a hamlet one mile to the east of Coalville, where Samuel was employed as a shot-firer at Bardon Quarry, and they lived at 24, The Crescent, Bardon.

John, always preferring the name Harold, was born on the 7th October 1894 at nearby Markfield, possibly at the hospital there, and was educated at the

Private John Harold Starbuck of the 2nd Argyll and Sutherland Highlanders.

29th October 1914 when they drove enemy troops from trenches they had earlier captured from the British 19th Brigade south of La Boutillerie.

It was reported that saucy French women in estaminets were eying the kilted warriors as they drank: noting that they wore nothing under their kilts! The military authorities reacted by issuing 'long Johns', the troops responded by cutting them to the thigh. The wonderfully warm kilt was made from eight metres (twenty seven feet) of the finest material: the only problem was that the plentiful French mud dried on the bottom of the kilt and occasioned cuts to the knees. Also, khaki aprons were issued to wear in combat over the tartan design to prevent enemy intelligence from discovering who they were fighting.

Private Harold Starbuck, service number 14571, was part of the fateful attack of the 25th September 1915: the infamous Battle of Loos in French Flanders. He was serving with the 98th Brigade, the 2nd Argyll and Sutherland Highlanders, which also included the 4th Kings, 1/4th Suffolk and 1st Middlesex: part of the 33rd Division. At Loos, Harold's battalion, together with the 1st Middlesex, led a sectional assault with the 1st Scottish Rifles and 2nd Welch Fusiliers in support.

'No-Man's-Land' was pitted with craters, a result of the Tunnellers' war underground and several days of artillery bombardment.

Another feature of the dreadful attack was the unbroken barbed wire; it was reported that in places it was twenty-five feet wide, whilst enemy machine gunners trained their weapons on the uncommon gaps available for advancing troops!

St. Peter's Church School. He also sang for the church choir and one of his Saturday night tasks was to clean and polish the vicar's shoes for Sunday morning service.

Harold was a good all round sportsman: particularly so at football and played for Bardon F.C.

Upon leaving school he sought employment at the Co-Operative Society, and gained invaluable retail experience with several of their outlets.

Harold's son, Desmond, has no idea why his father chose the 'Highland route' to enlist into the Forces in 1914. Harold enlisted into the Princess Louise's Argyll and Sutherland Highlanders, a kilted regiment. It was a union of the old 91st Argyllshire Highlanders and the 93rd Sutherland Highlanders. Regular soldiers of their 1st and 2nd Battalions were the first troops to reach Boulogne as part of the British Expeditionary Force of August 1914; however, Harold required training and was not to join them until the spring of 1915.

The Highlanders were particularly prominent in the 1st Battle of Ypres; especially so on the night of

Notification of bravery award for dates of 23-27 September 1917.

33 DIVISION
BRITISH EXPEDITIONARY FORCE
14571 Pte Harold Starbuck
33 Div Signals attd 98th Inf Bde
Your Commanding Officer and Brigade Commander have informed me that you distinguished yourself in the field on the
I have read their report with much pleasure
Major-General
Commanding 33rd Division

John Harold Starbuck, middle row: 2nd from left, with members of Bardon Football Team. Circa 1925.

The War Diary of the Battalion reads:

'During the night the wire in front of our 'jumping off trenches' was removed and trenches were bridged about 30 to 40 yards in rear of the fire trench. Forty short scaling ladders were in position in each trench. Two companies had two platoons formed up in these 'jumping off' trenches, one standing on the ladders and the other platoon standing by the ladders. The two other platoons of these companies were formed up in the support trenches known as High Street. It was hoped that four waves of troops would emerge almost simultaneously, taking the Germans by surprise.'

Due to the craters the Battalion's frontage was limited to a width of sixty meters, and a slaughter resulted with the Battalion loosing over three hundred casualties.

Co-Operative Grocery managers 1950: John Harold Starbuck sits front row left. Sitting on John's left is Albert Ayris, with brother, Wilfred Ayris, sitting end right. Theo Hart is middle row 2nd in from right.

Harold battled on the Western Front for eighteen months without leave, and after receiving a week's allotment travelled to Calais, only to be recalled following a mighty German offensive.

In early 1916 Sir Douglas Haig singled out the Battalion for special praise, as they were conspicuous for repelling local attacks and delivering aggressive raids in operations around St. Eloi in the Ypres Sector.

The 33rd Division suffered a torrid and bloody summer of 1916, mainly in attacks against High Wood in the Somme Sector. In July 1916 the Wood (Bois des Fourcaux) was behind the German Second Line, in front of Bazentin le Grand and Bazentin le Petit, so familiar to the men of the Leicestershire Service Battalions.

The 2nd Argyll and Sutherland's first attack against High Wood was on the 15th July 1916, resulting in casualties of 117 troops. The 18th August was a particularly bad day, also; they were ordered to capture a section of the Wood, sadly they were unsuccessful as they confronted flame throwers, burning oil drums and pipe pushers, the latter blew a crater in their frontline: 189 casualties.

I recommend reading: 'The Hell They Called High Wood' by Terry Norman ISBN 1-85260-250-3 for a deeper understanding of the lengthy battle.

Harold was awarded the **Military Medal**. Desmond Starbuck:

"It was during a German offensive: they had driven a salient between British and French Forces, and my father, a signaller, laid and maintained a landline long enough for the Allies to communicate and take effective action, so retrieving the situation. Father was not alone; a friend, Private 'Squiffy' Scott, accompanied and assisted him. The two soldiers were recommended to receive Military Medals and the French Croix de Guerre. They subsequently received their British decoration, but when father and Squiffy paraded with others to receive the French award, they had insufficient medals: so were kissed on the cheeks and promised they would be forwarded. Being a quiet man, father never pursued the matter.

Ten years ago I wrote to Colonel Paul Bonnet, a military attaché at the French Embassy. Some two months passed without a reply, and on enquiring received a rather rude letter stating it takes time to find information. In April 1996 the French authorities informed me that World War 1 records for 'foreign' soldiers had not been updated, so could neither confirm nor disprove the matter."

Harold's bravery, he was also '**Mentioned in Despatches**' on two occasions, received an ironical twist whilst on leave and wearing civvies (his uniform had been plunged into the 'hot copper' to remove the filth and lice). A white feather, denoting cowardice for not enlisting into the Forces, was pinned on him by a woman as he walked in Coalville Town!

A snippet of information that I had never heard of: *"My father said he was never too fearful of gas in the early years. He noted that when the rats started sneezing then gas was close by, sufficient time for masks, and he was never wrong. The 1915 scientific method for counteracting the gas was to urinate on a pad and hold it over their mouth and nose."*

Harold survived the dreadful conflict and very many years passed before he would make the odd comment, fortunately recollected by Desmond.

The old soldier returned to the Co-Operative Society and received steady promotions during the inter-war years, never forgetting the bleak Thirties as Great Britain struggled with bankruptcy as a result of the war.

In 1922 he married Coalville girl, Elsie Day (born 25th August 1900), at St. John The Baptist Church, Hugglescote.

Desmond, their only child, was born on the 1st April 1923, laughingly informing me it is April Fools' Day!

For many years the family resided at 41, Burton Road, Hugglescote (later renamed and renumbered as 145, Ashburton Road. Later they had their own house constructed: 190, Ashburton Road, living next door but one to Fred Briers, one of the Famous Fifty.

Harold was happily working at Coalville's Belvoir Road Co-Operative, making plans for retirement, when he suddenly fell ill, dying within four days after contracting Asian influenza. He died two days short of his sixty-third birthday, on the 5th October 1957, and he lies in Hugglescote Cemetery. His dear wife, Elsie passed away on the 11th August 1981, aged eighty years.

My thanks to Desmond Starbuck who asked me to mention that the Germans respectfully called our kilted troops: 'The Ladies From Hell!' Desmond's account of his W.W.2 history will feature in 'Sons and Daughters.'

Soldiers of the 2nd Battalion Argyll and Sutherland Highlanders wearing gas masks. Circa 1915 in trenches.

THE BRITISH EXPEDITIONARY FORCE OF 1914

During May 1914, the Prime Minister, Herbert Asquith, was persuaded by senior military personnel to ignore a report from a sub-committee of Imperial Defence, and to accept a War Office plan to despatch the bulk of a British Expeditionary Force to France if war against Germany commenced. This involved sending the 1st, 2nd, 3rd, 5th and 6th Infantry Divisions at once, while keeping the 4th Division at home. As a result, supply columns and ammunition depots were equipped with mechanical transport as a direct link to railroads. Also, there were special emergency timetables with access to ports and detailed plans prepared whereby specific senior officers would have singular powers relating to embarkation.

The following list shows the strength of the British Army on 1st August 1914:

Regular Army:	247,432.
Army Reservists:	145,347.
Special Reserve:	63,933.
Channel Islands, etc, Militia:	5,613.
Territorial Force:	268,777.
Territorial Reserve:	2,082.
Bermuda & Isle of Man Volunteers:	330.
Total:	**733,514.**

They were organised as such:

Regulars

One Cavalry Division, six Infantry Divisions, and line of communication troops totalling 76 Battalions.

Special Reserve

One Battalion per line regiment as draft finders and trainers, totalling 74 Battalions. Twenty-seven extra Battalions were to relieve Regular Battalions in such locations as Malta and Gibraltar.

Territorials

14 Infantry Divisions, 14 Yeomanry Brigades, coastal defence troops.

Others

National reserve of men over age for military service, Officers Training Corps, Pensioners.

During the early hours of 3rd August 1914 Prime Minister, Asquith, drew out an order for immediate mobilisation: which the Lord Chancellor took to the War Office. Just after 13.00 hours it reached Major-General Wilson who realised it was incomplete: it authorised mobilisation but there was no mention of embarkation. This was partially amended during that evening; it was not until 04.00 on 4th August that mobilisation plans were received at Salisbury at 16.51, and by General Haig at Aldershot twelve minutes later. Only on 6th August was it finally declared that a B.E.F. would embark for the continent.

Reservists possessed an identity certificate to which was attached a railway warrant and a postal order, which endorsed: 'negotiable only on mobilisation'. When the non-commissioned soldier cashed his postal order he went by rail to an appointed depot. Officer reservists possessed written instructions on what to do on the first day of mobilisation. Three days were allowed for mobilisation and twelve days for the movement of combatant units. Transport columns were to move on the thirteenth and fourteenth days.

It was during this same spell that Territorial troops, most of which were attending their annual training camps, were ordered back to their headquarters.

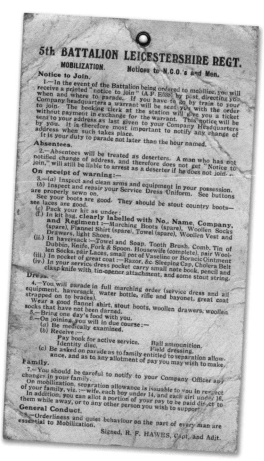

Mobilization certificate, 1914.

British troops arrive at Le Havre in August 1914.

Recruitment poster, 1914.

'*His Majesty the King having been graciously pleased to order by Proclamation that direction be given to the Army Council for Embodying the Territorial Force, all men belonging to the said Force are required to report themselves immediately to their headquarters.*'

Great Britain and Ireland saw 1,800 special trains moving Regulars and Reservists during the busiest five days, and on the busiest day 80 trains (carrying the equivalent of a Division) ran into Southampton Docks, in spite of their being only one double railway line.

Southampton was used for troop embarkation, Avonmouth for motor transport and petrol, Newhaven for stores and supplies; Liverpool for motor transport and frozen meat while Glasgow initially handled a minority.

The average daily number of ships leaving was thirteen, with their destinations being Le Havre and Boulogne.

9th August: stores from Newhaven reach Le Havre.

12th August: fifteen ships carried 587 officers, 16,936 men, 1,166 horses, 417 vehicles, 71 motors and 213 bicycles.

13th August: eighteen ships left Southampton with 664 officers, 19,849 men, 1262 horses, 383 vehicles, 20 motors and 219 bicycles.

22nd August: sixteen ships carried a similar number to the previous day.

By the 26th August: 2,215 officers, 63,599 men, 7,813 horses, 1,486 vehicles, 111 motors, 713 bicycles and 78 pieces of artillery gun had been shipped to France.

Although the original plan was to send five infantry divisions, a revised eight went from and to the following destinations:

1st Infantry Division.
Mobilised at Aldershot, crossed to France between 11-15th August. Concentrated around le Nouvion.

2nd Infantry Division.
Mobilised at Aldershot (Guards at Windsor), crossed to France 11-16th August. Concentrated around Wassigny and Etreux.

3rd Infantry Division.
Stationed in Southern Command with its Heavy Artillery Barracks at Woolwich, units crossed to France 11-16th August, Concentrated around Aulnoye and Avesnes.

4th Infantry Division.
Stationed in Eastern Command at Woolwich, Shorncliffe, Dover and Colchester. Grouped together at Harrow on 18-19th August and crossed on 22nd August. Concentrated around Bohain, Busigny, Le Cateau and Bertry.

5th Infantry Division.
Units spread in Ireland: Belfast, Dublin, Kildare, the Curragh and Londonderry. Crossed to France between 10th-17th August. Concentrated around Landrecies.

6th Infantry Division.
Stationed partly in Ireland and in Northern Command. Grouped at Cambridge and Newmarket.

Crossed on 8th August with first units disembarking at St. Nazaire. Concentrated east of Paris around Coulommiers.

7th Infantry Division.

Formed at Lyndhurst in the New Forest from units based in England and others brought back from Egypt, South Africa, Malta and Gibraltar. Crossed on 5th October and landed at Zeebrugee, moving to Bruges.

8th Infantry Division.

Made up of units returned from overseas postings. Crossed on 5/6th November to Le Havre.

With the above Divisions also went 1st Cavalry Brigade from Aldershot, the 2nd Cavalry Brigade from Tidworth, the 3rd Cavalry Brigade from Ireland (the Curragh, Newbridge and Dublin), and the 4th Cavalry Brigade from Shorncliffe and Canterbury. They formed the Cavalry Division and crossed to France between 15-18th August. They concentrated east and south east of Maubeuge. (During September 1914 it split into the 1st and 2nd Cavalry Divisions.)

Later in the war many of these outdated mounted soldiers became infantry troops.

World War 1 Letter
August - October 1914 with the British Expeditionary Force.

(Found in an old casket by my friend, graphic designer, Martin Bird.)

August

17th - Arrived at Rouen.

20th - Left Rouen for Amiens where we arrived at 5.30 pm. 21st - Left Amiens for Bohain-en-Vermendois via Chevrin de Fer, broke down on road all night. Put right and proceeded via St. Quentin and arrived at Bohain-en-Vermendois in the afternoon.

23rd - Left Bohain-en-Vermendois for Reumont and arrived in the afternoon. First batch of cars left with ammunition for Mons. We proceeded there via le Cateau.

25th - English and French troops retiring, not many French troops on this front.

26th - Left Reumont 2.30 am after alarm call.

Stopped about 8 miles south of Reumont for grub. Had to make a hasty retreat through about 2000 German cavalry coming on the scene. We saw them on the hills about 1500 yards away but they made off in another direction. We were now ordered to St. Quentin. The whole of the column got cut-up here; there were only seven lorries with us, no NCOs only a lieutenant, because owing to our Captain getting an order to return to Reumont with ammunition. The other cars had all returned sound but our seven (the/lying column) were stopped by a staff officer and told to hop it as quick as we could. We took his tip. We stopped at St Quentin for a couple of hours but then had to hop it quick, the German's advance cavalry coming in one end of the town and we going out the other. We were now ordered to Noyon and proceeded via Ham. Pressed hard all the evening and arrived at Noyon about 9.30pm and stayed at a big French barracks. The French soldiers were very good and gave us supper (first grub since breakfast) and hurried out of their beds for us. This was the first time that I had undressed since leaving London.

27th - Our little column, still the seven of us, got orders to proceed to Neuve Chapelle with ammunition for the 3rd Army Corps, whose convoy could not be found.

When we got away from Noyon at about half past ten, we arrived at our destination and we found that all the troops were retiring rapidly, and so we had to turn round and do likewise, We arrived back at Roye, about ten miles back, at about 8 o 'clock at night. We had to wait here for instructions which we got about 9 o 'clock and very nice news it was:

'Get back to Noyon if you can. You have about 25,000 Germans at your rear and each side of you. We had to leave our suppers and sheer off. We were very lucky to get through it because we could see the enemy on each side of us signalling from the hills, but as luck would have it we ran into a heavy ground fog that lasted for about five miles. This was the only thing that saved us! We eventually landed back at Noyon at 3.30 am, not a bad days work! In the morning our lieutenant went to headquarters and was highly complimented on getting the convoy through. Our General also sent us a congratulatory message and a request for the names of all the men on the convoy. Our lieutenant, perhaps you know him is Lieutenant Gunter, Sir William Gunter's son has since been mentioned in despatches over this!

28th - Left Noyon for Montmarcq via Compiegne.

30th - Enemy drove us out of Montmacq and we dashed to Crepy en Valois where we arrived at 1.30am.

31st - Left Crepy en Valois for Nauteuil-le-Haudouin.

September

1st Left Nauteuil-le-Haudouin and proceeded via Dammartin-en-Goele to Claye-Souilly and here we found the remainder of the column.

2nd - Arrived at Villeneuve-le-Comte early morning and left in the afternoon for Guignes. (35km southeast of Paris)

4th - Left Guignes and proceeded via Malune to Pithiviers.

8th - We now start advancing, a change from being driven about. Left Pithiviers (fifty km south of Paris) at 9pm and return to Guignes.

10th - Left Chaumes -en-Brie for Nogent-l'Artaud. There has been heavy fighting all the way through here. "The Germans have ransacked everything, but had left hundreds of men behind, never to return to their own land! Allied losses were only slight.

12th - Captured a German cavalryman in a creepy farmhouse. Altogether about 30 captured in the woods.

16th - Left Nogent I 'Artaudfor Fere-en-Tardenois, about twenty miles from the Aisne. We stopped here until the 3rd October when we travelled via Councy, Rocourst, Grisolles, Neuilly St. Front, Douisguard, and St. Quentin, to Marseuil-sur-Ourcq where we stopped for the night.

October

4th - Left Marseille-en-Beauvaisis for Senlis. Great damage had been done all the way through. Senlis is a fairly large town but the place had been badly shelled. The top end of the town was in a rare mess. This is where the

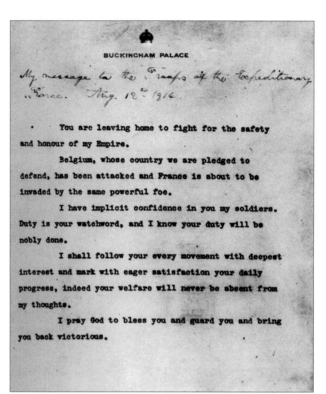

King's message to the British Expeditionary Force.

Germans shot the mayor and about twenty residents, a dastardly act against innocent people.

8th Left Senlis at 4 am and proceeded via Beaumont Persam, La Croise, Ste. Genevieve, Noaille, Warluis, Beauvais, Marseille-en-Beauvaisis and Poix de Picardie to Villerso where we arrived at 11 pm. The distance was about 110 miles. At Beaumont Persam we were only ten miles from Paris. We had to cross the river Oise by a pontoon bridge, the bridge having been blown up by French engineers.

10th - Left Villerso and proceeded to Hesdin via Abbeville.

12th - Joined Fetteso staff.

13th - Left Villerso and proceeded via St. Pol-sur-Ternoise andPernio to Chocques (15km west of La Bassee) to join up with advance section. The park was divided into 3 sections.

16th - Left Chocques and travelled via Bethune to Locon, the battle of the Canals being fought about 3 miles from here.

18th - Left Locon for Chocques to rejoin headquarters,

31st - Still at Chocques.

Sadly, the untimely end to the letter. Happily, part of the old letter survived.

THE TRENCH

Leaving home was wretched: good-bye's always a wrench,
Especially when all we have to return to is a stinking trench.
Standing on duckboards with grimy, bloody water floating by,
Sometimes joke that we must look like pigs standing in a sty.
Get down! It's a whizz-bang: a terrifying little shell.
Shell, ha! Its sandy beach is the yonder shore of hell.
Heavy stuff comes over: rolling explosions in no-man's land.
These are killing fields, the percussion piece of the Devil's band!

Those barbs must be strong: look how they've held dead Fred,
Enemy use him as practice, regularly pump him full of lead.
It's turning cold and a bit snowy; there'll be a frost tonight.
Good job I've got a greatcoat, mind-you the fits a bit tight,
It belonged to a mate from Leeds; a typical Tyke named Seth.
He's no need: called for his mother with his final dying breath.
That fat rat, he doesn't go short of food like we do in this trench.
Bloody rodent is visiting our latrines, that'll add to the stench.

I enjoyed that pipe and the cold is keeping them lice at bay.
Ye, get the odd itch when they're apt to come out and play.
'Dear mum and dad, weather is not too bad, I'm in the pink.'
Don't want to worry them: but I could down a stiff drink.
'I'm thinking of you both. Love you mum, love you dad.'
Will I simply become a memory: a son they once had?
'Remember Jim, my pal from up the lane at number eight?
He got shot in the chest; his folks will have a lot on their plate.'

It's nearly dark; hardly see a thing, its all so flipping still.
I feel hungry, so thirsty and sick, as well as feeling ill.
Wonder if soon I might get wounded: wounded in the head.
Anything so long as I'm not classified, classified as dead!
I'd like to bet that soon I could be leaving this putrid trench.
Hope one day to chat with my mates on a sunny park bench.
I hear singing and there're festive lights above the German line.
Carols and candles, soon we'll be home and all will be fine.

Michael Kendrick.

JOHN DAVENPORT SHEFFIELD

I have traced the family line back to William (the first) and Catherine Sheffield of Ashby de la Zouch. Among other children they had a son, William (the second), who was born in 1842, and in 1847 his parents became landlords of the Railway Hotel at Coalville. It was a dreadful shock when his father died two years later at the age of thirty-seven, however his mother held the post to support her children who were 'taken in' by nearby relatives.

'Jack' Sheffield survived the Boer War of 1899-1902 only to lose his life with the 2nd Battalion of the Leicestershire Regiment in 1915.

When William left school he was apprenticed as a mechanical engineer, working for many years for Thornewill and Wareham Ltd, an engineering firm at Burton on Trent.

By 1861, Emma, William (the second's) younger sister by five years was living with her mother at the Hotel, and by 1881 William was also there together with his wife, Sarah, and children, William (junior) aged six, George Frederick aged four and John Davenport aged one, 'Jack' to his friends and family. Another daughter, Dorothy Catherine, was born in 1882. William, by then aged

thirty-nine years had commenced what was to be many years of public service, firstly being elected to the Whitwick Local Board.

The Railway Hotel was built in 1832 in anticipation of the expected business resulting from the opening of the Leicester and Swannington Railway Line. As the years passed-by the hotel became highly respected, quite the finest around with many travelling dignitaries enjoying good food, the finest ale and a comfortable bed.

William took over the lease when his hard-working mother (aged sixty-eight years, died in 1888). He also maintained the hotel's high reputation, and also furthered his public service commitments. By 1891 he was a Freemason, president of the Licensed Victuallers Association, president of the Coalville Sports and Athletics Club, and churchwarden at Christ Church on the town's London Road. Jack and his siblings were educated at Christ Church National School. Sadly, Jack's elder brother, William (junior) died in 1893.

William also served as a juror at the enquiry regarding the 1898 Whitwick Mining Disaster.

I am pleased to have Jack Sheffield's entry in this book, not least that he fought with the Leicestershire Volunteers in the South African Boer War of 1899-1902. The war was fought between the British and the 'Boers', descendants of Dutch settlers. It was created and inflamed by Boer resentment of British colonial policy, which it was feared would damage or destroy the Transvaal's independence. After the British success, the 1902 Treaty of Vereeniging transferred sovereignty over the Boer Republics of the Orange Free State, and the Transvaal to Great Britain. During the course of this war Jack's leadership and endearing qualities were rewarded by promotion to the rank of corporal. On his return from South Africa, he and other local volunteers like Roland Hill received a great reception in the centre of Coalville. Later they were all invited to a presentation and dinner, given in their honour at the majestic Grand Hotel at Leicester. Pleasing though it was for Jack, it took quite a while to accept that his mother had died in 1900 after a prolonged illness, whilst he fought in South Africa.

Jack was an extremely popular man about town, not only for his South African exploits but also his

The Railway Hotel provided travellers with a booking office, accommodation, and horses for hire to assist in further passage.

A recent photograph taken on Remembrance Day. 'The Railway' looks in particularly good order if somewhat missing the company of a passenger railway service.

sporting capabilities. Football reports of the time describe him as being a 'brilliant footballer', having played for Coalville Swifts and also captaining Coalville Town F.C. He also was an outstanding right-winger for Burton-on Trent F.C. and his 'rare turn of speed made him a terror to opposing defenders.'

Jack was described as possessing a genial disposition, with the adjective, 'popular' being a complete understatement. He was a regular worshipper at Christ Church, always prepared to help anyone, especially the downtrodden and was looked upon as a local hero. I believe it is no exaggeration to describe him as the perfect male role model for any civilised society.

During this time his father was chairman of the Council, and represented them on Ashby de la Zouch District Board of Guardians of the Poor. Jack's elder brother, George Frederick Sheffield was a draughtsman at Stableford's Wagon Works.

At the outbreak of the Great War, Jack immediately enlisted at Coalville, his military experience qualifying him for a posting into the 2nd Leicestershire Battalion (Regulars), service number 12078. He retained his pre-war ranking of corporal

and many of his friends waved him off from Midland Railway Station.

In August 1914 the Battalion was based in India, and it was not until the 12th October 1914 that it disembarked at Marseilles in southern France. Eventually they occupied trenches at Givenchy, some eight kilometres (five miles) due east of Bethune and half that distance west of La Bassee in northern France. Jack joined the Battalion there; it was an area that had already suffered a good deal of artillery bombardment. The relatively shallow trenches were in a very poor state, and the troops, aware of snipers, cautiously set about repairing them. Jack was nevertheless jolted when Captain Tristram was sniped on the very first night there, and a letter home reported as such! They made a few investigative raids on the enemy front, and in return defended several, however, appalling weather conditions resulted in trenches resembling drainage ditches. They constantly had to pump-out waist-deep floodwater as the rainfall streamed through. This tour of battle was connected with the Battle of La Bassee, and the Battalion lost two officers and fourteen non-commissioned officers and men killed, and two officers and seventy-three others ranks wounded.

Following a brief respite the Battalion moved to Gorre, a village on the banks of the La Bassee Canal, and a little later supported the ranks at nearby Festubert following enemy aggression. On the night of the 22nd-23rd November the Germans stormed the frontlines, and by mid-day the situation appeared serious, many parts of our frontline being occupied by enemy troops. At 4.00 pm on November 24th the Battalion counter attacked with Major H. Gordon leading 'B' and 'C' Companies, plus two others from the 107 Pioneers. There followed some bloody hand-to-hand fighting, and in spite of severe enemy bombing the trenches were recaptured, with aid from other units of the Division.

Several 'Tigers' were decorated for their bravery during this action. The Battalion then returned to Gorre and were immediately greeted with enemy shellfire (shrapnel stock).

Shortly after this episode the King inspected the Battalion at Locon. His Majesty graciously commented that his troops looked 'war-torn.' He expressed his keen appreciation of the efforts and fine work rendered by the Battalion during the war, and hoped to see the Regiment again at the earliest opportunity.

Jack was involved in the day-to-day rigours of trench life, which also involved trench raids and being on the receiving end of barrages and Maxim-guns. He did his best to maintain the morale of his section, and was very well liked and admired by all around him.

The Coalville Times of the 26th February 1915 printed letters of appreciation from several troops at the frontline, including from Jack: '*Good Old Coalville! Pleased to receive the parcel safely and to know that you are not behind the other towns in doing your share towards helping the troops here. They were much appreciated especially as they arrived at a time when they were much needed. We have just come out of the trenches for a break.*'

The weather continued to be atrocious, very wet and bitingly cold, and life could only be described as miserable and uncomfortable. Private Ernest Hall, whose younger brother, Isaac, was one of the Famous Fifty, was with Jack when he sent a letter to his wife at 20, Talbot Road, Whitwick, describing the appalling conditions. He tried to reassure her that he was all right, and that the parcel of food from her helped a lot. He relayed his love to his three young children, one a babe-in-arms: "*Thank God the weather is getting a little better now!*"

Late February 1915 saw a gradual build up of troops with Sir John French expressing the opinion: "*Many vital considerations induced me to believe that a vigorous offensive movement by the forces under my command should be planned and carried out at the earliest possible moment.*"

The part of the German Line selected for the British offensive was the village of Neuve Chapelle, six kilometres (four miles) directly north of La Bassee.

On March 9th General Haig informed his troops that they were about to engage the enemy. He told his men that only pluck and determination had helped us against an enemy of superior numbers in both men and guns! He assured his troops that in the forthcoming battle, they had the edge, and that the Flying Corps also had control of the air.

By 5.00 am on the 10th March 1915, several Divisions waited in their trenches, and at 7.30 am the artillery opened and at 8.05 the men of the 2nd Leicestershire went 'over the top'. This was the commencement of the famous Battle of Neuve Chapelle. The Battalion took their objectives and also many prisoners.

The stained glass window dedicated to William Sheffield who was churchwarden at Christ Church from 1891-1911.

The battle raged and insufficient barrage power enabled the enemy to counter-attack. Written works cannot fully describe the horrors of a battlefield, however, Jack would have experienced the cacophony of screaming shells, thunderous explosions and the Maxim-guns spitefully spitting bullets that reaped huge harvests of human life! He would have heard the desperate screams of dying men, wrestled for his very existence in hand-to-hand fighting, and be feverishly aware of the vomit and blood red stained earth that coated the killing ground! No soldier ever forgot the acrid smoke of cordite that stung the back of the throat, that watered the eyes of the living, and complemented the tears of the dying!

Jack survived the battle and indeed letters of the time stated that he was prominently involved. Jack was saddened when he heard that his pal, Ernest Hall, had fallen, leaving a wife and three young children behind!

William Sheffield received several letters from the frontline, all conveyed news that his son had been killed, but he waited until the military officially wrote to him, and on the 2nd April 1915 they confirmed his death. The Coalville Times of the 5th April released the sad news and confirmed that sympathy for the family was even greater because of the ill health of William Sheffield. William died on the 31st August 1915, aged seventy-four years, and six months after retiring from the Urban District Council. He lies in the small cemetery at Christ Church.

One letter from the frontline: *"Jack was always trying to lift our spirits by laughing and*

William (the second) Sheffield 1842-1915, Well liked and highly thought of in Coalville and district. A qualified mechanical engineer, and besides being the landlord of the 'Railway Hotel' devoted a large part of his time to public service. He was president of the Licensed Victuallers Association, president of Coalville Sports and Athletics Club, Churchwarden at Christ Church from 1891-1911 and a Freemason. Following the Whitwick Mining Disaster of 1898 he was a juror at the enquiry.

joking, that was typical of our corporal. We had done very well in the battle and Jack was chatting about how we had captured some enemy trenches and buildings. He said it was a smart bit of work, and just afterwards a sniper shot him straight through the head! He died almost instantly and we buried him nearby. We all miss him terribly."

The name of Jack Sheffield can be read on the Coalville Clock

Left: The grave of Sarah Elizabeth Sheffield, wife of William (the second). Right: The grave of William (the third) Sheffield, eldest son of William and Sarah. Also his brother Jack Davenport Sheffield who was killed at Neuve Chapelle on 13th March 1915 (the date on the headstone wrongly states 10th March).

Tower Memorial and in the Memorial Chapel of Christ Church.

Jack did not know, but two close friends died in the battle, Harry Brown of 17, Forest Road, Hugglescote and John Williamson of Highfields Street, Coalville.

Jack, the 'brilliant footballer', would have been delighted to have seen Coalville Football Club, the Ravens, battle their way to the First Round of the Football Association Cup for the very first time, whilst I was writing this book. A tremendous achievement for the club, supporters and the town!

During The Battle of Neuve Chapelle the Allies lost 190 officers and 2,337 other ranks killed, and with total casualties of 12, 811 officers and other ranks. After early gains a lack of ammunition, amongst other things led to a resumption of the status quo!

Wilfred Owen's poem: 'Dulce et Decorum est (Pro patria mori) would be a fitting ending to the above battle.

SOLDIERS THREE

The day was the 4th August 1914, and the good folk of Swannington, a village three kilometres west of Coalville were basking in typically balmy summer sunshine. The Grove tennis Club was engaged in a match against Shepshed, and near to the grounds of Swannington House, the home of Lady Beaumont, a marquee had been erected for a Conservative and Unionist Garden Fete. Two hundred people were just applauding Alfred Hawley, the prospective Conservative candidate, prior to his opening the fete when news was presented to him - **Great Britain had declared war on Germany**! He quickly abandoned his political speech and instead called upon all present to do their utmost for their country during such a perilous time!

Three young men, all 'old' friends listened carefully and decided to see how events shaped themselves in the coming weeks and after all, they agreed, the British Army would send a Force to support little Belgium. The weeks passed and the situation abroad deteriorated, with enemy troops advancing into France and our troops sustaining heavy losses. There were also newspapers reporting on civilian and baby atrocities, and our government requested men to enlist and help crush Germany's aggressive and expansive exploits.

William Wardle and William Jones were Swannington lads whilst James Blythe came from nearby Coleorton. By late September 1914 the bright and adventurous trio were filled with righteous indignation, and Wardle and Jones enlisted at Coalville, whilst James Blythe at the nearer Ashby de la Zouch. After three-four weeks they were called-up, and entrained for Loughborough where they were billeted. Other units from all over Leicestershire gradually arrived over the weeks. Collectively they formed a new battalion, the Second Fifth (2/5th) Leicestershire or the Fifth Reserve Battalion. The three spent one month training at the market town, however, when some of the Fifth (1/5th) Territorial Battalion soldiers decided, for whatever reasons to opt-out, the 'Soldiers Three,' asking to be kept together, were switched to the Fifth Battalion and continued their training at Sawbridgeworth, and later embarked with them from Southampton to Le Havre in February 1915.

William Wardle, usually called Bill, was born, in Belmont Terrace at Swannington on 1st December 1893, the son of John Wardle, a collier, and his wife, Catherine (nee Moore). He was baptized and with his family worshipped in St. George's Church at Swannington, but when he was just fifteen years of age his mother died, and lies buried in that church cemetery. Bill spent his childhood in Bull Row, and in 1914 was lodging with his sister, Mrs Jinks, in what is now known as 'Bluebell Cottage.' He was the youngest of ten children, and post-war records show that in 1919 a brother Joseph was forty-six, and another, John, was thirty years of age. His sisters were Emily, forty-four, Matilda, forty-two, Caroline,

Private William Wardle in full kit, late 1914 and his grave at Sanctury Wood Cemetery.

Leicestershire-Derbyshire borders. Maria was born in 1871 at nearby Coleorton. He was by occupation a cold ironsmith and in 1901 the family was living on Margaret Street at Coalville, with Charles possibly working at Stableford's Wagon Works.

Shortly after that date they moved to 'Balcony House' on Burton's Lane, Primrose Hill at Swannington. He went to the national school with Bill Wardle, and on numerous occasions they attended Swannington's Wesleyan Methodist Chapel. By all accounts Billy Jones was a lively fellow, full of fun and blessed with a very kind and considerate nature. In March of 1915 whilst in Flanders, Billy, service number 2810, wrote home to his parents explaining how much they looked forward to receiving post: "*You ought to see our chaps jump for joy when the mail comes in. There was a parcel for Jim Blythe. He was not there so I took it for him. There were twelve packets of fags and a tanner and I thought he would go mad. Talk about the relief of Ladysmith! You ask in your letter to let you know what we want. Well, just send me a bit of cake and a bob; also the Coalville Times.*"

A postcard written in Flanders by Lance Corporal William Wardle.

thirty-nine, Mary, thirty-seven and Elizabeth thirty-three. Later Bill attended the Sunday School at Swannington Wesleyan Methodist Chapel. Upon leaving school he followed in the footsteps of his father, and became a miner at South Leicestershire Colliery at Ellistown.

Enlistment records provide a range of details regarding William Wardle. He enlisted on the 30th September 1914, with the service number 2811.He was five feet eight and-a-half inches tall and weighed eleven stone and graded of 'good' physical build. Whilst in military training at Sawbridgeworth the twenty-year-old single soldier met a 'very special girl!'

Charles William Jones liked to be called, Billy. He was born in 1895, the first-born of Mr Charles & Mrs Maria Jones of Worthington, a village five kilometres (three miles) north of Swannington. His siblings were also born there, sister, Florence who was two years younger and brother, Christopher who was four years his junior. Their father was born in 1874 at Castle Gresley, a village six kilometres (four miles) west of Ashby de la Zouch and on the

In a late April 1915 **letter to his father**:

'*I was leaving the trenches one night at about twelve o'clock in a place where the two frontlines are only about thirty yards apart, and the Germans must have spotted it for they lit us up. There were eight of us, and three of us scuttled like rabbits to try and get under cover. The others dropped and lay in the mud till the light (flares) burned out and then ran for it, dodging a volley of lead that they fired at us. The spot is near to the ruins of an old church which has an unexploded shell sticking out of the wall.*'

The Swannington cottage where William Wardle lived with his parents.

Far right: 'Bluebell Cottage' where William Wardle lived with his sister, Mrs Jinks in 1914.

(This would be the night of the 14-15th May when the Battalion dug a new trench inside the Ypres Salient at a spot known as the 'Zillebeke switch'. The ruined church was Zillebeke church - Author.)

James Blythe usually called Jim, was born in 1888 at King's Lynn, Norfolk, one hundred and twenty kilometres (eighty miles) east of Coalville. The place of his birth and his name conjures-up maritime adventures, and I suspect this to be the case.

Jim grew-up on the unfortunately named 'Rotten Row' at nearby Coleorton, a beautiful village with lots of history. Grade 11-listed Coleorton Hall entertained such residents as Wordsworth, Constable, Coleridge, and Sir Walter Scott wrote 'Ivanhoe' whilst staying there. Sadly the military records of William Jones and James Blythe were destroyed during the Blitz of World War 2. Jim's service number is 2809.

Lance Corporal William Wardle wrote many letters from France and Flanders to his family, and especially so to his lady friend, and believed that if he could survive the war their future would be with each other. In one **letter written to his brother**:

Dear Bro, Sue and Nephews,

Just a line or two to let you know I am going on all right, I am pleased to hear that you are all well. I received your letter a week ago but I hadn't the time to answer it as we were going to give the Germans some iron rations (see photograph).

All for now, Love, Bill.

Below is his **last letter home on the 19th June 1915**: *'I am going on all right. We are having some grand weather out here. Billy Jones and Jim Blythe are quite well. I have not much news to tell you except that the Germans want to know if we liked the Lusitania, and when we are going back to London.'* (The passenger ship, Lusitania, a sister ship of the Titanic was reportedly sunk by a German torpedo around that time.)

The Battalion moved to the Ypres Salient in late June 1915 and within a week the young non-commissioned officer was dead. It was their first tour in the 'Salient of Death' in trenches close to Zillebeke and the notorious Hill 60. It was the Battalion's first taste of Trench 50; it would not be their last! Readers of my first book will be aware that several of the Famous Fifty were killed within this trench. In parts the trench was only 90 metres (80 yards) from the enemy frontline, and the shelling and sniping was particularly accurate.

The 4th July 1915 was a Sunday, the enemy was shelling with shrapnel, it was warm and sunny and in any other circumstance it would have been a joy to be alive, when Bill Wardle's life came to a sudden end! He was just twenty-one years of age. A Staffordshire Battalion relieved the Leicestershire soldiers the following day and they marched back to base at Ouderdom and acted as reserve.

A stunned Billy Jones, only an hour after the death of his best pal, propped himself against a dusty trench wall, and whilst still under enemy fire

William Wardle and Billy Jones were regular attendees at The Wesleyan Methodist Chapel at Swannington.

scribbled the following letter to his parents.

> Private William Jones.
> 5th Leicestershire.
> British Expeditionary Force.
> 4th July 1915.

'*My dear mother and father,*

> *I want you to take what I have to tell you as calmly as you can, for I am in great trouble. Poor old William Wardle got killed this morning. He was killed by a bullet that went straight through his hand and heart and the chap who was with him caught him in his arms as he fell dead. Keep it quiet till dad gets home, and then tell him to go down to Jinks's and break the news to the best of his ability. His death was instantaneous and his face looked quite comfortable as the stretcher-bearers carried him down the trench in a waterproof sheet. He now lies on the stretcher, covered over with a blanket about twenty yards from my post. A letter came from his girl at Sawbridgeworth soon after he was killed! Jim Blythe and myself are burying him tonight just behind the firing line and we will bury the letter with him. The Sergeant Major has promised me that all his belongings will be sent home. I can hardly realise yet that the poor chap has gone. When we get out of the trenches I shall miss his company and then I shall begin to realise it! I am sorry it will be a poor funeral for we shall have to bury him under rifle-fire. The grave will be within (Censored) yards of the Germans and they shell round here every day. We shall have to bury him in the middle of the night so we can't be seen.*

> *PS - Trench life is just about the same as when we started it only this time William has proved to be the unlucky one. If any of his relatives wish to know any more of how my old pal met his death I can tell them if they write to me and ask.'*

At a much later date William was reburied alongside a host of his friends who were killed in the Salient. His headstone, clearly visible alongside other members of the Fifth Battalion, lies in a corner of Sanctuary Wood Cemetery. (Plot IV. Row S. Grave 2/4).

I often wonder if his 'special girl' ever received notification of his death. No doubt she often prayed that her Bill would survive the war, and so settle-down to a life together in a world of peace and harmony. If she wasn't informed, no doubt the young lady assumed Bill was yet another cold statistic, one digit in a total of seven hundred and fifty thousand British dead.

> "*Unknowing you may meet*
> *Another stranger, Sweet.*
> *And if he is not quite so old*
> *As the boy you used to know'*
> *And less proud, too, and worthier,*
> *You may not let him go—*
> *(And daisies are truer than passionflowers)*
> *It will be better so.*"

(Extract from: 'Another Stranger' by Roland Leighton, November 1915. He was badly wounded in the stomach by machine-gun bullets and died in December 1915. His fiancée, Vera Brittain, met 'Another Stranger' and married several years later.)

The Sunday after Bill Wardle died, namely the 11th July 1915, the organist in Swannington's Methodist Chapel played the Dead March in honour of Bill, and a silent prayer and tribute was paid to the young man. When Bill's officer wrote to his father he let it be known that if he had survived long enough, then nothing would have hindered him from rising to a good position within the army.

On a happier note, Bill's older brother, John, was a private with the 5th Battalion of the North

Staffordshire and survived the conflict, service number 203765.

Billy Jones battled on and drew strength from the camaraderie that existed within the Battalion. He had seen so many of his Coalville and district friends killed and witnessed other likely lads filling their boots, until such time that the law of averages caught-up with him and he was seriously wounded! Private William Jones's wound almost cost him his life; it was so severe that he was honourably discharged on the 9th June 1916.

He married a local girl and they moved to Nottingham where Billy became landlord of a public house. I am willing to bet that not one day passed without him thinking of his pals that died on the battlefields of France and Flanders, especially a certain Bill Wardle.

Billy's young brother, Christopher was a private in the Grenadier Guards and he too survived.

As the years passed the attrition rates continued to climb from 19,000 per month in 1915 to 75,000 in 1918. Jim Blythe seemingly led a charmed life as the Fifth Battalion's losses closed to nearly a thousand officers and other ranks.

Following the 46th North Midland Division's storming of the St. Quentin Canal at Bellenglise on the 29th September 1918, the Battalion continued to attack enemy positions in French towns, villages and woods. I have written in my first book how Lance-Sergeant Cecil Bradshaw died in France, close to Riquerval Wood. After nearly four years as a frontline soldier, Private James Blythe, service number 240777 lost his life in this same battle! The attack started shortly after midnight on the 11th October and by 5.00am the Battalion was climbing the slopes of the wood. About half way up some ruined cottages and thick scrub hid a force of German machine-gunners, and they opened fire, killing many. In thirty minutes 'D' Company lost ten killed and fourteen wounded. The battle raged all day and at 8.00pm the 5th South Staffordshire Battalion relieved them. Private James Blythe lies buried in a military cemetery near to St. Quentin. He was thirty years of age and his name can be read on the War Memorial in Coleorton Church and likewise at St. George's Church, Swannington.

The names of William Wardle and James Blythe

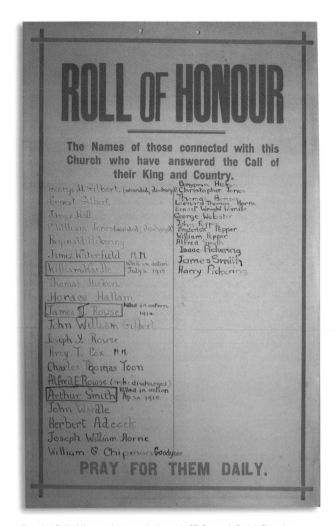

The 1914 Roll of Honour that was displayed in ST. George's Parish Church at Swannington until War's end. With thanks to Lesley Hale.

plus a further twenty-four are on the Memorial plaque in Swannington Church.

An official Peace Day was celebrated on 19th July 1919, and Swannington made sure that children and residents had a good day. A parade of children in comic attire wandered down the Main Street, and there was merriment and smiles on that golden summer's day. Henry Jinks, brother-in-law of William Wardle, was Chairman of the Committee that raised the funds and Dorothy Jones (later Mrs Watson); sister of William Jones won one of the fancy dress prizes.

Private J. Gardner of the Fifth Leicestershire Battalion, son of Mrs. Thurman and the late Mr. David Gardner of Pegg's Green, Swannington was awarded the Military Medal for bravery. He carried vital messages under intense fire whilst on active service in France in May 1917.

Many thanks to Maureen Partridge, whose late husband was the great nephew of William Wardle, for information supplied. Also to Lesley Hale who consented to my use of the title (it could not be bettered) and information on a similar theme.

SILENT WITNESSES OR STONES AND SCARS

Youngsters pay homage at Tyne Cot Cemetery, near Paschendaele on the Ypres Sector. Totalling 11,976 graves of which 8,961 are from Great Britain, 1,368 from Australia, 1,025 from Canada, 520 from New Zealand and 90 South African. Also a Memorial Wall lists 33,707 no-known graves from Great Britain, and 1,179 from New Zealand.

The Great War generation may have faded from view, but Mother Nature preserves her scars as a reminder of the devastation of war: Beaumont Hamel on the Somme. With gratitude to my niece, Laura Gray, for the photographs.

" In the course of my pilgrimage, I have many times asked myself whether there can be more potent advocates of peace upon earth through the years to come, than this massed multitude of silent witnesses to the desolation of war."
King George V, May 1922.

It was during an early visit to this cemetery that the King asked that the Cross of Sacrifice be built upon the German pillbox, as an everlasting monument to the many heroes buried so thickly around its concrete walls.

Cold white headstones? Maybe. Sacred hearts secure memory, Certainly.
Will chalky bones shout for eternity? A tear stained Bible offers immortality.
(Author).

THE GREAT WAR TUNNELLERS

In the autumn of 1914, John Norton Griffiths, the forty-two years old Conservative Member of Parliament for Wednesbury, near Birmingham, was of the opinion that he could contribute to the war effort in a specialised direction. John was a self-created man, and typifying his independent nature ran away from St. Paul's School, Hammersmith at the age of sixteen. While meandering around South Africa and Rhodesia (now Zimbabwe) he developed an entrepreneurial spirit, and engaged himself into the profitable business of railway construction and underground tunnel laying for piping, etc. In December 1914 he suggested that his 'moles': men digging-out tunnels for the Manchester sewers could do a job on the Western Front, where it was known the enemy were well advanced in the aspect of trench mining.

As the months passed Major J. N. Griffiths, a veteran of the Boer War, was asked to pass his, and his moles' experiences onto Tunnelling Companies who were under the auspices of the Royal Engineers. For years the Royal Engineers had been responsible for mine warfare and initially they were none too keen to accept the high spirited and tireless drive of John Norton Griffiths. He arranged for the Army to buy his wife's 1911, two-and-a-half ton chocolate-and-black Rolls Royce for £750, for him to use on his travels up and down the Western Front, it was a frequent and sometimes misunderstood sight! In essence his moles used a method called 'clay kicking' or 'working on the cross'. The diggers sat in their tunnels, their backs supported on a wooden backrest or 'cross' with their feet pointed towards the cutting face. The diggers would use a light spade and gradually remove the clay and then pass it behind to a mate who disposed of it. Teamwork was vital; the job was carried out in tunnels with a diameter no larger than a squatting man, it was very physically demanding, and not one for the claustrophobic. At all times there was the danger of a collapsing roof and natural underground gasses - silent killers.

In early 1915 the enemy had the upper hand, with ten mines being detonated under nearly a kilometre of frontline trenches at Festubert, France. The effect, naturally so, was highly damaging on the morale of troops, it was accepted that they could challenge hand-to-hand fighting, sniping and barrages, but to be silently atomised from below was to 'undermine confidence.'

Accordingly, a good many developments took place over the remaining years of the war, and the different geological features of the ground, a blue clay base around the Ypres area to a chalk base from Festubert to the Somme required different techniques. With the enemy growing in power in a subterranean world it was left to individual Brigades to, where possible, select soldiers with an engineering or coal mining background. I have written that following the experiences of the Fourth and Fifth Leicestershire Battalions at Messines in the spring of 1915, they set-up their own tunnelling party of forty men under Lieutenant Aubrey Moore. They were very fortunate to possess highly skilled surveyors and miners within their ranks, and their efforts involving counter-mining saved many lives. Twice they met the Germans in underground battles and fought with exceptional verve! In early 1916, when the Lieutenant was asked to transfer and lead his men into a tunnelling company, he declined, and all but two did likewise and they returned to their battalion later. Most other units had to await new tunnelling companies, but such men were not readily available, what with coal being an essential mineral in most areas of industry, the Royal Navy and Homeland. John Norton Griffiths encouraged volunteers to come forward, and without the blessing of the colliery proprietors many fine men did so, including those from the coalfields of northwest Leicestershire.

Eventually, under the battle-scarred fields and quagmires of France and Flanders a fierce battle involving twenty thousand men on both sides took place. At its height thirty-two British and Dominion companies were formed.

Vertical shafts, sometimes a hundred feet deep, were dug from frontline trenches, and from these a rabbit warren of horizontal or sloping tunnels were dug-out, or sometimes drilled-out.

At the end of these tunnels, often hundreds of metres in length, were constructed larger chambers or galleries. Into these specifically located chambers were packed massive amounts of explosives, usually ammonal, and detonated under enemy strongholds.

The tunnels were highly dangerous places at

Three ex-colliers who enlisted into 182 Tunnelling Company of the Royal Engineers

All of the men below survived the war - Tom Briggs promised his wife and the parents of Sapper Walker that he'd look after the two lads. He did so and he and another man dug the two out together with nineteen other wounded sappers. A large shell had demolished a house they were sheltering in and which killed eight.

Sapper Tom Briggs of 15, Bagworth Row, Hugglescote. For rescuing twenty-one wounded sappers he was awarded the D.C.M.

Sapper Ernest Briggs who was so proud of his father's bravery.

Sapper Heathcote Walker of Meadow Row, Donington-le-Heath. Received a bad head-wound when a shell hit a house he was sheltering in.

any one time. Even with timber supports it was not possible for an average man to stand upright, and yet in these dark, troglodyte-like, claustrophobic conditions some fierce bayonet and hand-to-hand fighting took place, invariably to the death. Both sides built numerous listening posts adjacent to their tunnels, where men lay for hours attempting to detect sounds or vibrations of enemy workings. If they did so camouflets were planted and detonated so sabotaging the tunnels and the enemy within! On occasions such detonations or underground battles sparked latent methane gas and massive flames shot through the caverns and shafts reducing men to cinders. The officers in support took canaries into the depths to guard against gases, sadly asphyxiating chlorine gas was also used to deadly effect. Everywhere the air quality was rancid, air pumps were old and air vents were limited for obvious reasons. The diggers, always on shifts, came to the surface covered in perspiration and sludge, fatigued, and with thumping headaches caused by the low levels of oxygen in the atmosphere.

Mining featured very strongly from 1915 onwards and some of our detonations were huge. Survivors wrote that the ground shook violently and then the earth convulsed and finally erupted to unleash a mushroom shaped cloud that climbed to hundreds of feet, driven on by vast sheets of flame, orange and crimson in colour. There followed the descent of enormous chunks of earth and boulders together with multitudes of component human parts—still showing traces of uniform. The sound of the explosion was frightening and stunned all who heard it. When the allies exploded nineteen mines on the 7th June 1917 in the Messines Sector it was heard in the Houses of Parliament! Readers may recall the site of one of these, a fortress hillock in this sector that was called Spanbroekmolen. In the spring of 1915 it was used by German snipers to great effect in killing a good many soldiers of the Fifth Leicestershire Battalion. The 171 Tunnelling Company lay a charge of 91,000 lbs of ammonal which, when it erupted left a crater measuring 150 meters from rim to rim. The length of the gallery dug was 520 metres (1,710 feet). Later the crater was purchased by Lord Wakefield and presented to Toc-H as a war memorial. It is now a fifteen-meter (45 feet) deep lake and will be known forever as 'The Pool of Peace'.

If it had not been for the foresight of Major John Norton Griffiths or 'Empire Jack' as he was sometimes known, the enemy would have had complete control of the underground war, in those days equally vital as air superiority! Such odds could well have changed the outcome of the war. Magnificent bravery was shown by all ranks of Allied and German tunnellers and their casualties ran into the tens of thousands each.

Other highly dangerous tasks the tunnellers had to undertake included dealing with booby traps, all aspects of above and underground demolitions and anti-tank mines.

For further reading I would recommend the book called: 'War Underground' by Alexander Barrie.

Proportionately, Coalville and district supplied many colliers to the tunnelling companies and below I have written a digest of a few to represent the many.

Before commencing I must remind readers of the immense contribution towards this subject by some of the earliest tunnellers who eventually returned to frontline soldiering. We must not forget, Lieutenant (later Captain) Aubrey Moore MC, Corporal William Barney, Private Joseph William Cowley, Corporal (later Captain) Jabez Emmerson D.C.M., Sergeant William Emmerson, Private (later Corporal) Cecil Hurley D.C.M., and Private H. Starbuck D.C.M.

Another early tunneller was **Sergeant Edwin James Collier**. His home was 56, Melbourne Street at Coalville. His nephew, Tom Wood, will soon be featured. In 1914 the thirty-eight year old ex-regular soldier rejoined the 2nd Leicestershire Regiment, service number 86523. For a couple of years the father of seven had been a miner at South Leicestershire Colliery, and he felt this vital experience could be put to greater use and joined the 176th Tunnelling Company in 1915.

The Coalville Times of the 11th February 1916 told of how local man, **Sapper Upton**, whilst home on leave, went to the Collier's household and informed the family of Edwin's bravery and a resulting gun-shot wound to his elbow. The next week, in the same paper it reported how Edwin, whilst working a good way under the frontline, heard the Bosche at work. He informed the officer in charge and they planted a counter-mine, detonated it, which exploded the German mine at the same time and so beat them at their own game. The sergeant had twice been recommended for bravery before he was awarded the D.C.M. Soon afterwards he received a commendation for saving three comrades who had been trapped underground by an enemy counter-mine!

Whilst he was recovering at Lincoln Hospital he received the **following letter** from his commanding officer.

'*Dear Sergeant Collier,*

I send you a piece of D.C.M. ribbon, which, as you know I was going to present to you in our Mess before you were wounded. No non commissioned officer or man deserved it as much as you did, and my only regret is that I heard you were wounded last night. You were invaluable to us in every way and you leave a gap I cannot fill! I sincerely hope that your arm will mend all right, although I fear it may be a long time before you can once more display your energy and courage against the Bosche.

Please write to me occasionally so that I may know how you are getting on, and if at any time I can do anything to help you then let me know. It will be the greatest pleasure to help you in anyway! Wishing you all the best of luck. Sincerely, (sadly the Major's name cannot be read).'

Sergeant Collier's bravery was typical of the pitmen who volunteered to join the Tunnelling Companies at their country's time of need. Clearly only a restricted amount were allowed to volunteer because of the vital nature of that reserved occupation, but Edwin represented them wonderfully! He portrayed what most people had always known to be self-evident, miners were the salt of the earth, and possessors of many outstanding qualities, not least of which, is bravery.

Coalville man **Corporal E. H. King**, a former miner of Snibston Colliery, was with the 1st Lincolnshire Battalion when he was posted to the 175th Tunnelling Company. The Coalville Times of the 15th October: '*On the night of the 4th/5th September 1915 at Hooge, near Ypres, Corporal Sapper E. H. King was in a mine with another NCO when the shifts were changing over. The trench entrance was hit by a minenwerfer shell, which killed and injured several men, and also cut the mineshaft! Under fire he carried the wounded to cover* *displaying great gallantry and devotion to duty. Corporal King has been awarded the Distinguished Conduct Medal. He has a wife and two children, and his parents have two other sons, one in the Dardanelles and another in France.'*

The Coalville Clock Tower Memorial displays the names of E. King and W. King.

The Coalville Times of the 22nd October 1915 reports how an enthusiastic crowd waved-off about fifty local colliers who had volunteered to join the Royal Engineer's Tunnelling Companies on the Western Front. Some of these men would have included, firstly, **Sapper R. Robinson** of Thringstone who, like so many, was blown apart by an enemy mine in April of 1916. All too often tunnellers met with tragic deaths in the bowels of the earth.

Another of the fifty, **Sapper T. Griffin** of the 175th Tunnelling Company, one of five sons, wrote home to his parents on the 5th November 1915 to tell them he was fine, whereas the parents of **Sapper D. Knifton** were informed their son was missing. It was not until the 30th August 1918 that they were informed he was a prisoner of war. The Coalville Times of the 21st January 1916 recalls that among the fifty colliers were **Tom Briggs** and his son, **Ernest Briggs**, of 15, Station Street, Hugglescote and **Heathcote Walker** of Donington-le-Heath. All three sappers were posted to the 182nd Tunnelling Company. It was revealed that as the three were resting in a party of forty in a partially demolished house they were hit by a 'Jack Johnson' shell. Many were buried in debris with twenty-one being wounded, and they included Ernest Briggs (136009) and Heathcote Walker. Tom Briggs (119499) was cited for the D.C.M. after he, a Royal Artillery major and two other men rescued the wounded.

Sapper George Miller Chamberlain of Ibstock was a former miner at Nailstone Colliery, and member of the Colliery Rescue Party. He was working on the tunnel face when he heard the enemy working nearby. He engaged them and so stopped them from detonating their charge. Sapper Chamberlain was also awarded the D.C.M.

Sapper Robert Ashby, a good friend of the aforementioned was killed whilst attempting to save the lives of trapped comrades deep underground.

Sapper W. Barrs, also of Ibstock, wrote to Robert Ashby's wife explaining that a mine explosion buried them both, but he managed to escape whereas Robert died a brave man on the 21st December 1915.

Sapper Ernest A. Sparks, an ex-soldier who transferred from the 2nd Leicestershire Battalion sent a letter to the Coalville Times in October 1915. *'I take the pleasure of writing these few words for the Coalville Times. You would be surprised to know how your newspaper brightens our spirits when we read about Coalville and district. I have the papers sent to me every fortnight and I am always eager to look at it, and so are my comrades. I am very pleased to hear of the good recruiting back home, and I am quite sure that if the young men rally to the flag it will bring this terrible war to a speedy end, because we don't want conscription in dear old England. I hope and pray to the Lord that we don't have another winter like the last, because it was so horrible to stand in the trenches, wet through and starved to death. God only knows what we poor devils went through. I might say that I wept through the Battle of Neuve Chapelle on March 10th with the 2nd Battalion, a lot of my Coalville mates went under there. I shall always remember the battle as the longest day I lived. We went into the firing line between five and six in the morning, although it was cold and raining. We had been in the trench about an hour or so when our artillery opened a tremendous rapid fire on the German trenches and played havoc with them for about half an hour, and then the order came to get ready. All of a sudden the order came, "Charge Boys." We were gone like a shot out of a gun. We were like a lot of raving madmen going at the Bosche, and in their first trench we had a tussle with some of them and we soon took them out. There were also three women in that trench; two of them had been killed. About two days after the charge you would have wondered where they came from, there were thousands of them in a counter-attack. I don't think many of them got back to their diggings because they simply walked into our death trap! I would be very pleased if some kind person could send us a football, and also something to keep our feet warm. I have several of my Coalville chums here with me and they recently asked me if I have received a parcel, but I haven't had one since I've been out here.*

I am just going to get ready to go on duty now, so will close. I remain yours, sincerely, Sapper Ernest Sparks. Service Number 11165, 172 Tunnel Company, Royal Engineers, British Expeditionary Force.

P.S. England expects every man to do his duty.'

Before the war Sapper Sparks lived on Margaret Street at Coalville and worked as a miner at Whitwick new pit. Happily he survived the war.

Roll of Honour

Sapper Robert Ashby of Battram was killed on the 21st December 1916.

Sapper Reginald George Bamford was killed on the 12th May 1916. He resided on Waterworks Road at Coalville and left a wife and children.

Sapper Herbert Briers of Whitwick was twenty-five years of age when he was killed on the 7th June 1917. He was a partner in the building firm of Briers and Sons.

Lance Corporal George Miller Chamberlain D.C.M., of the Royal Engineers, an Ibstock man who was killed in January 1917.

Sapper J. W. T. Collier died on the 6th November 1918. The son of Mr & Mrs Collier of Belvoir Street, Coalville.

Private Joseph William Cowley of the Fifth Leicestershire Battalion. A Hugglescote man who served in Captain Aubrey Moore's Tunnelling Party. He worked at South Leicestershire Colliery at Ellistown, and as a blacksmith at Stableford's Wagon Works, Coalville. One of the 'Famous Fifty' he was killed underground at Vimy Ridge on the 8th May 1916, aged twenty years.

Sapper Harold Curtis of Peggs Green, formerly a miner at Coleorton Colliery was killed on the 25th June 1916.

Sapper Isaac Lewis of Ibstock died in June 1917.

Corporal E. Knight of the Royal Engineers died on the 3rd December 1917. He resided on Silver Street at Whitwick, worked at Stableford's Wagon Works at Coalville and was twenty-two years of age.

Sapper R. Robinson of Thringstone died in April 1916. He previously worked at Whitwick Colliery.

Sapper C. H. Walker resided at Donington-le-Heath and was a miner at South Leicestershire Colliery at Ellistown. He died on February 1917.

Many thanks to my friend, Denis Baker, for allowing me to read his copy of 'War Underground' by Alexander Barrie and also for supplying me with information.

MEMOIRS OF AN OLD SOLDIER
BY JAMES MILLER

I know very little about the above gentleman; ex: serviceman, Mr. Brian Simpson of Burbage, sent it to me and asked me to consider it for publication. Brian had to focus deeply on the account because it was so badly faded; sadly the memoir has one page missing.

'I will do my best to give some details leading up to and concerning the Battle of the Somme as I saw it and can remember. It was a long time ago but some things one never forgets when you have been through hell.

I have no gift as a writer, but I will do my best to provide picture and atmosphere of that awful time.

Looking through my old army pay book I see that it was the 10th August 1914 that I joined the Leicestershire Regiment. I was working in Leicestershire at the time in the market town of Lutterworth, and Lord Kitchener had made a call for 100,000 recruits at once. I was looking out of my window when I saw the recruiting sergeant walk past, he had just got off the train, so I walked down to the Town Hall and became the first volunteer from Lutterworth.

Great Britain did not have a large standing army in 1914, what we had was scattered all over the world as we were a great colonial power. Each of England's counties had its own regiment and barracks within. Of Leicestershire's regulars, the 1st Battalion was in Ireland and the 2nd in India. Each county also had two battalions of Territorial Army, all volunteers and formed for home defence, but on mobilisation almost to a man they volunteered for service abroad: so that left us with no reserves hardly at all, hence the call for 100,000 men.

The new battalions began to take shape, mine was the 6th Battalion and by the end of the war the Leicestershire Regiment had expanded to nineteen battalions of which the 6th, 7th, 8th and 9th were service battalions. So great was the enthusiasm that twice the number of men volunteered and barracks were packed out over the country.

As we joined we were formed into Companies and took over barracks vacated by the regulars.

We were trained by old regular army reservists, NCOs, most from foreign service, and they soon licked us into shape. We were stationed at Aldershot for nearly seven months, finishing up with firing practise on the big ranges just outside the town. We passed our firing test by starting at 100 yards and finishing at 1,000 yards and firing fifteen rounds a minute. We could throw a rifle about in rifle drill as well as any Guards' Regiment.

We then went to Salisbury Plain, living under canvas, and finished our field training by such as trench digging, coverage building and sleeping in the open. By June 1915 we were ready for France and we struck camp in June 1915. (I had got married on embarkation leave on the 6th June 1915).

We entrained at Liddington, a small railway station just south of Swindon, and we were locked in until we reached Folkestone. We boarded our ship at midnight, packed in like sardines, not even room to lift our arms, and landed at Boulogne in the early hours, marched up a big hill just outside of town and into an open field until morning. In the morning we had breakfast and then entrained for St. Omer; cattle trucks, forty men in each truck. We nearly suffocated going through the tunnel at Calais. We had our first

payday in a field at a place called Locre, and then we marched to Armentieres. After a week or two we travelled to Kemmel, in the Ypres Sector where we relieved the East Yorkshire Regiment. We were the first 'New Army' men they had seen and they had held this frontline since 1914.

We did not stay there long; it was comparatively quiet with most of the shelling coming from the Germans. Our gunners were rationed because of a shell shortage, which went on for a considerable time and caused the overthrow of our government.

We left the area and moved to Arras where we stayed for twelve months. By the way when I was at Kemmel I had the guard on my rifle shot away by a sniper. My platoon officer came up to me at Stand To and said: "You will not get killed in this war!" (Stand To is when we shaped-up for an hour at daybreak whilst in the trenches.)

When we went just north of the Somme we stayed at a village named Berles-au-Bois, with a twin village called Monchy-au-Bois a few miles to our right. Our 110th Brigade consisted of the 6th, 7th, 8th and 9th Battalions, the 6th and 8th were at Berles and the other two at Monchy, we held about two miles of trenches.

We entered the communication trench in the village orchard and this led to our frontline about half a mile from Berles. We were always within range of the enemy guns even when out of the trenches; we did one week in and then one week out. We remained there throughout the terrible winter of 1915-16. Nearly all through the winter we had to relieve the frontline on top because our communication trench had caved in and was quite impassable. Around about Christmas 1915 I had a second near miss. It was about 4.40pm and my Lewis Gun team had just climbed out of the trench. We were about 250 yards from the enemy when an enemy machine gunner spotted us and we dropped to the ground, none of us was hit. As I got up an enemy sniper targeted me and a bullet went through my hat! We did not have steel helmets at the time and the bullet went through the left side of my hat and only just above my ear. Thankfully the spring arrived and the whole Division, the 21st, was relieved for a few weeks rest (so called).

There was a lot of talk about the big summer

offensive and a lot of activity was going on, mostly at night. Fresh troops were pouring in from England and huge ammunition dumps were appearing everywhere behind our frontline. Our 'rest' turned out to be part of a big trench digging operation.

Our trenches were dug between 100-600 yards from the enemy's frontline. It was decided to reduce the distances where possible in readiness for 'jumping-off' when the offensive started. Our Brigade was allotted the Guillemont sector and we dug our trench at night, it was 250 yards from the enemy. We moved at about dusk (6.00pm or maybe a little later) and given a talk about the need for absolute silence. We took off our equipment and each man was given a pick or shovel before we set out, and we had to be finished so that it could be occupied by daylight. Now in trench warfare there is often great activity at night: patrols from both sides are sent out and wire repairs had to be done. There was intermittent rifle and machine-gun fire and frequent firing of Verey Lights, which floodlit the area and floated in the sky for a minute or two. Talk about a test of nerves! Well we got down to it and felt happy that we were covered by our Lewis Gun teams in case of a sudden German attack. It seemed like a miracle, we were down to four feet before anything happened: several Very Lights shot up and a couple of machine-guns open up together with a lot of rifle fire, but we beat them to it and I bet I could beat a mole for getting underground. After about a quarter of an hour we put our rifles down and carried on digging without another big scare. We finished the trench in time but we got a pasting from our own artillery all the next day and got a lot of casualties.

As we were digging the Royal Engineers were running barbed wire attached to screw in stakes.

I must now give you a few details of the 1915-16 winter. It was very wet and cold and when it didn't rain it snowed. The duckboards, which should be at the bottom of the trench, were floating or buried in mud about thigh deep, and whenever we relieved another battalion it more often than not snowed or poured.

One night we had a terrific snowstorm, we dropped into the trench from over the top and we got very little sleep until we went out again. When we came down off the fire step after sentry duty we were

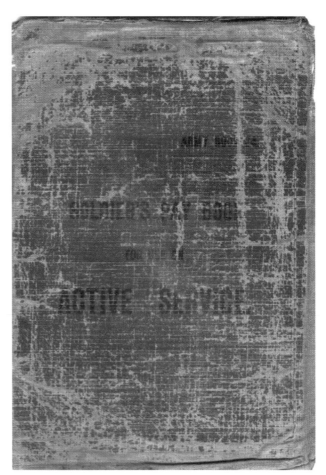

Army Book 44 Soldier's Pay Book. For Use On Active Service
This book belonged to Bombardier Alfred Mortimer Timpson of the R.F.A. (Service number 84457). Several million of the above were issued during the war: and kept for 'safety' in the service men's breast pocket.

called out to shift tons of sandbags that had collapsed. By the time we finished it was time to go back on duty again.

When the week was up we were all in a sorry plight: unwashed, unshaved and lousy. We were not a pretty sight to look at and of course we slept (when we slept) in our cloths. We had a few casualties each tour, perhaps a dozen killed and about that injured.

(A page is missing that describes taking a German trench and what James saw).

.........I believe we were the only ones to go, although the enemy was shelling us. We decided to risk it and nobody stopped us. The first dug out we entered had a long corridor, about twenty yards long with rooms opening off on either side. In this corridor lay six men who had been shot. On the right was an engine room with a large engine (Lister?) with a large flywheel and a dynamo that supplied light to their dugouts. A dead German, evidently the engineer lay spread-eagled across the engine. Just behind the engine was a workbench and on it a large pile of shell driving bands that had been hammered out straight. We grabbed a pocketful each, and I am looking at one now that is sitting on my mantelpiece (the only one left).

We then entered the enemy's Quartermaster's Stores where whole carcasses of meat hung and provisions of all kinds. I got a Prussian Guards Officer's helmet and still have it along with other items.

We then decided to have a look outside and what a sight it was, dead men scattered all over the wood, three of ours at least to every German, it had been a terrific battle for this wood. One of our men was in a kneeling position in the middle of a large branch, his rifle between his legs, we thought he was alive but was dead all right. Another horrible sight was a man, legs blown off and lying near to his trunk, looking like meat in a butcher's shop. A lot of the dead men were Royal West Kent's. I picked up a prayer book that belonged to one of the fallen lads: 'Theodore Kenneth Barlow', it had no address and I still have it. I believe there were at least one hundred dead lying in the wood, and I often wonder what it looks like now. It has been sixty years since I was there, and a new oak tree would be three parts grown now, almost as though nothing had ever happened. The devastation was indescribable: we stayed for about an hour but then it got too hot - the enemy shelling was heavy and we dropped back to our trenches. Not only the wood but all the surrounding countryside was littered with our dead, we stumbled over many of them during the night coming up on the 13th July from Fricourt. Our guides took us to the frontline and we went through a large ravine where our Cavalry was assembled under the shelter of a large bank. On seeing them we wondered how on earth they would get through the tangles of barbed wire. We never saw anything of them again and we were the frontline troops on that terrible morning. We were assembled in Mametz Wood and given a briefing: an attack to take the enemy's frontline positions, then Bazentin-le-Petit Wood and finally the village of Bazentin-le-Petit itself. We were dished out with forty hours of iron rations (bullets) and told to be sparing because they didn't know when could supply us again. A bandolier holding two hundred rounds was slung around us as well as the ammunition in our pouches. I thought it funny when we were also given two handfuls of dried currants to munch on. I ate mine straight away, as I didn't know where to keep them.

Zero hour was at 3.30am on the 14th July, Bastille Day, and we attacked with French Forces over an eight-mile front. The French were on our right and our 7th on the left, and umpteen more took part. I believe that every regiment in the British Army fought on the Somme before the battle ended.

The Germans had two hundred Divisions engaged in the battle, about 750, 000 troops. Our Battalion was extended in a line of about three hundred yards and opposite the enemy covering Bazentin-le-Petit. We were ordered to lie down and fix bayonets and our barrage started at 3.30am. We all knew that it must be one of the biggest barrages in history, we had seen the lines of guns, almost wheel to wheel for miles.

Our Colonel Challenor and the Adjutant, Lieutenant Mason (?), were the only men standing up, and right in front of where I lay. They had their revolvers in their hands (both were to be badly

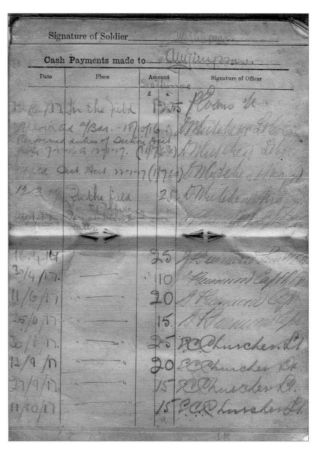

Cash payments made. Earlier in the book it stated that the rate of his pay on the 13th December 1915 was 8 1/2d per day. (Just over 3 new pence).

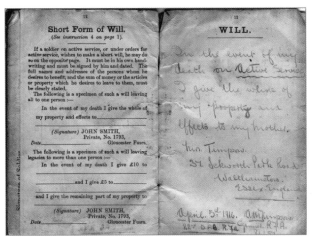

The Last Will. Fortunately the serviceman in question survived the war, but what passed through the minds of teenage soldiers as they filled in the required information.

wounded), and just before Colonel Challenor blew his whistle he turned to me and said: "Pass it down the line that when we advance we make for the left incline." It did not get very far because the barrage came down with an almighty crash, and the enemy trench line looked a line of fire and smoke as it disintegrated. Of course the enemy opened up their barrage seconds after ours started and with the continuous roar of the guns, the rushing shells, the humming shrapnel, the swish of the machine-gun bullets was terrible, but I was lucky and somehow stumbled through it.

We reached the enemy frontline trench and found no resistance; they were either killed or deep in their dugouts. No doubt they surrendered after we passed over them. We reached Bazentin-le-Petit Wood and lay down as ordered until the barrage lifted on the village. We attacked and the machine-gun fire was deadly, it was a case of jumping from one shell hole to another. I was hit at this stage and lay for the biggest part of a day in a shell hole with a broken leg. The village was taken but with a terrible loss of life and every single officer was a casualty. Our Sergeant-Major Clay of 'D' Company took command, and with the aid of a few Lewis Gunners organised some sort of Line and held the enemy until reserves arrived.

I was sent back to England, hospital at Plymouth and made a quick recovery before returning to my unit in February 1917.

Before going any further I will write a few words about the part played by The Royal Flying Corps. It was as though a miracle had happened because before the battle they had obtained complete mastery over the German Air Force. They tackled

them in the air and on the ground; not one enemy plane was allowed to get near to our frontline, and on the 1st July 1916 every single enemy observation balloon was shot down. Now these were the eyes of the enemy and stretched in a double line as far as the eye could see.

Now that covers the first part of the war as far as I am concerned. While in hospital I had a letter from one of my mates telling me that I had been made a full corporal. I had refused another stripe up to now but I had no option since it had been confirmed. Usually one had to wait for months before promotion was confirmed, and the paymaster said he had never heard of it before when Litchfield immediately confirmed it!

I must bring this to a close now as the next: 1917-18 would need a full book to describe it. There was the Battle of Passchendaele Ridge and I went over the top several times including the capture of Polygon Wood in September 1917.'

'These are the memories of James Miller and they were written when he was about 84-85 years of age. He died at the age of 94 years and eleven months.

I am sorry he did not finish writing them. I know that he fought bravely on all battlefields of the Somme during the Great War of 1914-18. I have copied this as he wrote it. **Daughter: M. J. Miller in Ireland.**'

'N.B. Dad was a Lewis Gunner and the Prussian Guard helmet that he brought back can now be seen at the Lutterworth Museum where I hope it will remain for many years.'

Many thanks to Brian Simpson for submitting the above. He re-copied it in September 1999 - only days before the 60th Anniversary of the beginning of World War 2.

The original document consisted of eleven pages. James Miller was indeed another very brave man.

THREE COUNTY CRICKETERS

Over the last century or so northwest Leicestershire has supplied a wealth of sporting talent, particularly in football and cricket. Coalville man, Hughie Adcock was a superb winger for Leicester City and England from 1923-35, and from the same town, Walter Harrison, a top class defender from 1945-50, while Eddie Clamp was a famous star of Wolverhampton Wanderers and England in the Fifties. Ashby de la Zouch Grammar School produced the immaculate David Nish for Leicester City and England from 1965-72, and goal-scoring-winger Rodney Fern for the same Club, 1966-72. Leicester City's finest and fastest right back was Steve Whitworth from Hugglescote, 1968-79, who also represented his country.

In the pages of this book I touched upon two local men who would have played at professional football level but for their sacrifices in World War 1.

On the cricketing scene I will touch upon three of our players who departed the verdant playing fields of England, for the battle-scarred quagmires of France and Flanders.

Lieutenant William Nairn Riley - always called Nairn, was born at Appleby Magna in 1893. He received his early education at the village Boys' School where his father, William Riley, was the headmaster. In addition William played the church organ and was the churchwarden for the Reverend C. T. Moore, father of Aubrey Moore. Nairn was to develop into an outstanding cricketer before the Great War, coming to prominence in 1911 when he made his debut for Leicestershire County Cricket Club, while still a pupil at Atherstone Grammar School. His top score for the club was precisely one hundred. He went on to obtain his cricket blue at Cambridge University, and made a reputation as an elegant and forceful batsman, a useful bowler and brilliant fielder. Besides being a first class cricketer he also won his blue for hockey for Cambridge University and represented England in international matches. After military training he was commissioned and joined the Fifth Leicestershire Battalion in France in late spring 1915, only to be badly wounded in the autumn, possibly at the Hohenzollern Redoubt. One leg, it was said, was so shattered that it had to be amputated and the other leg was badly injured. He also received wounds to the head.

Nairn was a school friend of Aubrey Moore and they remained close throughout their lives. Aubrey remembered with affection their cycle rides to Polesworth to release homing pigeons, and having done so would collect engine names from the expresses on the London and North Western Line, from London Euston to Crewe and beyond. Aubrey wrote that Nairn and his sister, Lilla, who was born in 1892 were both highly intelligent children and adults. Lilla went to France to stay with her brother until he showed improvement; sadly she died at a relatively young age following an unhappy marriage. Nairn survived, his military days over, however he later moved to Sussex and took up a position on their County Cricket Committee. Nairn, in spite of his disability did not lose his flair for sport. He played a good game of golf and was an expert fly fisherman. To this day he is remembered in the village for his generosity in buying a piece of land in Bowley's Lane to be used as a recreational ground. The fateful arms of the war once again extended to him, and he had to have his other leg amputated and died shortly afterwards.

Captain Aubrey Temple Sharp was born in

Captain Aubrey Sharp served with the Fifth Leicestershire Battalion with distinction throughout the Great War. As a batsman with Leicestershire County Cricket team he captained the side for several years and had a top score of 216 runs. The Whitwick man died in 1973 at the age of 85 years of age in tragic circumstances.

1888, his parents, Mr. & Mrs. J. J. Sharp lived in the 'White House' on the Loughborough Road, Whitwick. He was a cricket contemporary of Nairn Riley; indeed, he was a regular player in the Leicestershire County Cricket Club team of 1908. He held his place until 1911 when he missed a considerable part of the season with appendicitis and a subsequent operation.

At the outbreak of the war Aubrey was playing for Leicestershire against Northamptonshire County Cricket Club, and after the war his home county jokingly commented that the war cost them a certain win. Aubrey had batted on the first day, but was immediately mobilised and so

The Leicestershire County Cricket Team of 1913. Left to right standing: J. H. King, W. E. Astill, **G. Geary**, W. Shipman, A. Mounteney (Jnr), A. Skelding, A. Lord and the Earl of Lanesborough (President). Seated: S.C. Packer (Secretary), C. J. B. Wood, **J. Shields (Captain)**, H. M. Bannister and H. Whitehead (N. C. C. C.) Cricket lovers will recall that George Geary was a tremendous fast bowler and fine batsman for his County and England. George scored nearly 12,000 runs with a top score of 122 and captured 1,759 wickets at less than twenty a piece.

missed the second and thereto the County lost by four runs. As a pre-war territorial lieutenant in charge of the Machine-Gun Section, he embarked for France in February 1915 with the Fifth Leicestershire Battalion. He was another good friend of Aubrey Moore, his role was never easy because neither officer nor soldier wanted machine-guns in their vicinity for obvious reasons, they attracted the enemy's artillery like strawberry jam attracts wasps! Having braved the war he resumed his cricketing career and captained his county from 1921 for several years. He did so twice in 1934 when at the age of forty-six, and again during the dark days of World War 2, four times in fact when he was aged fifty-five years. Two years earlier his son, Captain J. A. T. Sharp received the Military Cross for gallant service in the Middle East.

Aubrey Sharp tragically died when a car on Granby Street, Leicester, knocked him down on the 15th February 1973. He distinguished himself on the military and sporting fronts, and at the time of his death was Vice-President of Leicestershire C. C. C. having served the Club on and off the field for sixty-five years. He had a top score of 216 runs.

Lieutenant John Shields was one of the sons of Mr. John Gillies & Mrs. Helen Craig Shield of Isley Walton Magna, a hamlet twelve kilometres (eight miles) northwest of Loughborough. They were of Scottish blood, and had moved to England around 1880. John Gillies was a man of many parts, a farmer on a large scale; he also owned Breedon and Cloud Hill Quarries, and his last work was to start the

Roland Farmer, Aubrey Sharp, Reginald Hastings, Medical Officer, and Aubrey Moore. Luton 1914 with the Fifth Leicestershire Battalion. All four named officers played for Ashby de la Zouch pre-war cricket team.

Donington Park motor racing track at the age of eighty.

John Shields other siblings included Charles, Joseph and sister, May. All three brothers played cricket but it was the wicket-keeping John who secured the attention of the Leicestershire C. C. Club scouts while playing for Ashby Hastings team. He made his debut for the county side in 1906, and although he didn't play for England his quality was such that he was selected to play for the Gentlemen's Eleven at both Lord's and The Oval. At Lord's he executed four stumpings and was complimented on the quality of his keeping. He went on to captain the side from 1911 until the war. During the war he served as an officer with the Royal Field Artillery, happily surviving the conflict. He had a top score of sixty-three runs.

Aubrey Moore married May Shields on the 1st September 1917, and Charles Shields served with the Fifth Leicestershire Battalion until loosing a leg and having the other badly damaged, this happening shortly before the marriage.

Let the sun always shine brightly on cricket pavilions, team bonhomie, stumps and bails, bats and balls. There is so much skill, artistry and elegance within the magnificent game.

I think the opening verse of Henry Newbolt's poem: 'Vitai Lampada,' or 'Torch of Life' conveys many of my thoughts:

There's a breathless hush in the Close tonight-
Ten to make and the match to win-
A bumping pitch and a blinding light,
An hour to play and the last man in.
And it's not for the sake of a ribboned coat,
Or the selfish hope of a season's fame,
But his Captain's hand on his shoulder smote:
'Play up! Play up! And play the game!'

My father was a keen follower of cricket: this was his favourite poem and my sister, Maureen Jarvis, read it at his funeral service in 2006.

GEORGE WALDEN

I am delighted to include a Swannington gentleman who spent an enormous part of his life nursing and looking-after the ill within society. In addition on various occasions, and not just in times of warfare, he jeopardised his own life in an effort to assist or alleviate suffering.

George Arthur Edward Walden was born in 1885, and his desire for travel enabled him to experience the flavour of several continents with their different races, cultures and beliefs, all of which enriched his soul.

At the tender age of fifteen he enlisted into the Northamptonshire Volunteers, and the same year embarked with them to engage the Dutch settlers in the South African Boer War of 1899-1902. Whilst out there he became particularly interested in the various sub-tropical diseases that brought discomfort and death to his fellow soldiers, and hoped that one day he would have the opportunity to learn more about

the subject. During early 1902 he was wounded in the right leg during an enemy ambush and was subsequently shipped home for hospitalisation. George was captivated by the grace and kindness of the nurses who cared for him and instantly decided

Corporal George Walden had a service career of seventeen years, thirteen of which were in the Royal Army Medical Corps. He travelled to China and Singapore where he helped nurse those suffering from highly infectious diseases. George was one of the first men from Coalville and district to land in France in August 1914 with the British Expeditionary Force.

that this was to be his vocation.

In late 1903, fully fit and qualified he volunteered to work abroad with the Royal Army Medical Corpse (R.A.M.C.) and his first posting was to China. At first he nursed patients with highly infectious diseases such as plague, sleeping sickness and smallpox, and eventually undertook three years of assisting at Hong Kong's Pathological and Bacteriological Laboratory. He was absorbed, not just by laboratory methods, medicine and clinical control, but also by the gentle nature of the Chinese culture and their many festivals. His wanderlust returned and George departed in late1906 to arrive in England in January 1907 for a spell of leave. His next posting commenced in November of the same year, and once again George left English shores to arrive at Singapore Military Hospital in Malaysia just before Christmas. Again he adored the different aspects of life and continued to nurse the sick and wounded there until October 1910. Returning to England he married a nurse, Eleanor, and the couple took up the post of caretakers at Ashby Rural District Council's Isolation Hospital, sited at Swannington. Eleanor had been employed by the same Council since 1912, and previously held posts in Lincolnshire: was a fully qualified nurse and paid a uniform allowance of £5 per annum over and above the standard salary. The hospital was in Doctor Jamie's district, he is mentioned later in this book, and the hospital was kept busy with cases of scarlet fever, diphtheria, measles, smallpox, etc.

In the interval between taking up the caretaking position and the war, Eleanor gave birth to a son, Gordon, who in teenage years was noted for his excellent singing voice.

The outbreak of World War 1 brought immediate mobilisation for Private Walden, R.A.M.C., and he was ordered to report for duty, being one of Coalville and district's first men to embark for France. He did so with one of the earliest consignments of the British Expeditionary Force and disembarked on the 17th August 1914. As such he was present at all of the 1914 battles such as Mons, the Aisne and First Ypres. In the later stages of the latter battle he himself had to be admitted to hospital suffering from dysentery. While serving at Ypres he could well have lost his life but for the kindly intervention of fate! He was tending to a seriously wounded soldier in the battlefield when a German sniper aimed and fired to his chest. Unknowingly, George moved a little and the bullet, instead of it hitting flesh hit his silver pocket-watch, penetrating and completely ruining it, however he considered it a cheap price to pay and kept the watch as a memento.

George, quiet and unassuming, never fought in the trenches but was often in them, and on many occasions crawled into No-Man's-Land to administer drugs to the dying and suffering.

He and his erstwhile comrades dragged many a wounded soldier from the battlefield, and in February 1915, during a spell of sick leave, told how barbaric enemy snipers targeted Red Cross volunteers.

George was also quoted in the Coalville Times saying that originally there were eighty men in his Company, but by early 1915 they were down to eleven, although he believed quite a number had been taken prisoner.

He returned to the battlefields but towards the end of the year his enteric health started to decline, possibly due to regular intestinal problems he had suffered during his years in the tropics. In February 1916 a farewell concert was held in the Corporals' Mess of the R.A.M.C. at Aldershot, to commemorate thirteen years of excellent service in the Corps.

At the presentation to Corporal Walden of a case of pipes and a tobacco-pouch, it was said: "*As a soldier his record stands as an example to us all, and as a comrade, he was everything to be desired. Also, we all wish to express our gratitude and appreciation for your services while acting as treasurer of the Club, also our admiration of your conduct as a comrade and as a man.*

The intrinsic value of our presentation is not intended to adequately represent the total cost of your worth. We have the honour of being his comrades in the Corps, and wish to record with feelings is of sincere regard our unalterable good wishes for your future welfare, and trust that the years to come will hold for you, a good store of health, happiness and prosperity."

George returned to his capacity at the Isolation Hospital, but it appears that the Army tried to reinstate him following heavy casualties on the Somme. In the 15th September 1916 Issue of the

Ashby R.D.C. it states that Mr. Walden, caretaker of Swannington Hospital, was only suitable for sedentary tasks within the military and that **they were going to appeal for military exemption for him.** They succeeded.

Records show that on the 1st December 1920 Mr. & Mrs. Walden salary was to be increased to £3 a week as from the 1st July last. Also it mentioned that Mr. Walden: '*Had the liberty to work elsewhere when the hospital was not in use.*'

On the 10th May 1922 a doctor's certificate indicated that George was suffering from a serious infection of the ear, and recommended leave of absence in order that he could benefit from a change of air and rest.

The 19th November 1930 illustrates the tight economy of a bankrupt country. Nurse Matron Walden, medically senior to her husband, made enquiries about superannuation seeing they were appointed eighteen years ago. The Committee contacted the County Finance Department; and she was informed that: '*Only the Nurse Matron would receive an allowance - not the husband!*'

George, a keen gardener was the senior official of the 'Pegg's Green and District Annual Horticultural Show', of which the profits were sent to the Leicester Royal Infirmary. Apparently this was not his only means of raising money for the infirmary, and his charity work also benefited various public and social events around Swannington.

A black day occurred on the 24th September 1932 for Mr. & Mrs. George Walden, when they were given notice of termination of employment as from the 31st October. Under a rationalisation programme drawn up by the new governors, the Leicestershire County Committee, the hospital was closed and the property sold for £425 as a private residence.

The couple eventually found employment at a larger hospital, namely the Markfield Sanatorium, with Eleanor nursing and George becoming the head gardener.

George died suddenly after only two days of illness on the 9th June 1937 at the Lodge House within Markfield Sanatorium. The Coalville Times of the 17th June 1937: '*Many tributes of respect were paid at the funeral, which took place in the Swannington churchyard on the 14th June 1937.*

The service in St. George's Church was conducted by the Reverend A. W. Wray, assisted by the Reverend A. S. Dowling, Rector of Ravenstone. The coffin was draped with the Union Jack and on it were carried the late Mr. Walden's war medals. It was lowered into a grave lined with flowers and evergreens.'

Besides his wife and family at the service were many mourners representing Hospital Committees, Officers, staff and patients of Markfield Hospital, doctors and aldermen and many friends. He was nearly fifty-two years of age.

George Walden was a genuinely good man, a

The Isolation Hospital at Swannington.

sincere and compassionate person who did his utmost to help the suffering of this world. He displayed great bravery, like his comrades, to enter the battlefields without a weapon and having to trust the ethical standards of the enemy to withhold fire. Without his kind a good deal more of the human-race would have died in far less reassuring and painful circumstances.

An interesting letter was sent by a Mrs. B. Shields in the winter of 1995, in which she wrote that her brother, Mr. G. A. Brewin, was choirmaster at St. George's Church: '*Those were the times when we had a full choir and on special occasions enjoyed the glorious voices of Peter Shipley and Gordon Waldren. Gordon lived with his parents at the village hospital.*'

Many thanks to Lesley Hale for information researched and from the Swannington Heritage Trust.

The brave wartime efforts of stretcher bearers and ambulance crews cannot be overestimated, and the following account is comprised from several letters (passed as censured) written by **Private James Brown** of the North Midland Field Ambulance Division during the time of the July 1916 Battle of the Somme:

'*As no doubt you have seen in the newspapers, our artillery has been very active, and our section has, I can assure you, by no means been neglected.*

Strafing has been going on now for several nights, but the past few nights have witnessed the most intense and furious bombardment yet witnessed around here.

Last Monday we left our billets and travelled trenchwards, eventually quartering ourselves in a village just behind the frontline and well within the roar and din of the cannon. From here we made the necessary preparation for the 'Do', which was soon to mature, and with the NCOs and officers wended our way to the various dressing stations, first-aid posts, and other places we were conducting.

On Friday night the artillery was in fine form and souvenirs by the thousands were sent Hunwards. The sight was splendid, the flashes from the guns coupled with the bursting of shrapnel, and more than the usual trench lights making the whole business like a huge firework carnival.

Early next morning our work commenced in earnest, for we made an attack from our quarter, and for nearly two days we were constantly kept at it removing the wounded. Owing to the large amount of rain that had lately fallen, the trenches were in an awful condition, being well thigh deep in mud and water.

Stretcher-bearers were constantly wet legged and it was no uncommon sight to see them wearing sandbags around their loins instead of trousers. Like the Redoubt business we had much work to do, but as already said, every man and officer worked for all they were worth. Not only did we do stretcher bearing from the firing trenches but also several of our men volunteered to go over the top and fetch in the wounded if possible. They did this and their brave and vigilant work was not in vain. The ambulances in the division worked hand-in-hand, as also did the transport sections. The latter did much praiseworthy work what with venturing as far as possible with horses and wagons. They did fine service in conveying slightly wounded and sick cases to casualty clearing stations.

This they were engaged upon for practically speaking thirty-six hours, the only halts being when there was a lull, which was turned to advantage for watering and feeding the animals.

I am sorry to say we had a few casualties: three killed and three wounded. Now those things seem to have quietened down we are a little from the scene of operations and are now conducting hospital work.

The weather is still all sixes and sevens and one never knows when to expect a drenching.

One has often heard or read of episodes regarding the shelling of Red Cross hospitals by the enemy and attached some doubt to the same. However, there can be no questioning the facts that I am about to relate, for they occurred in connection with our unit, and I was present! We took over possession of the hospital a few days ago, and of course there was some shelling every day, but the missiles fell at some distance and caused us little alarm. Yesterday (Thursday) afternoon we had a vastly different experience and one that will live long in the memory of all concerned. We were busily engaged following our various duties when we suddenly perceived the whirl and hissing of Allemande 'souvenirs!' Before we had time to take cover, practically nil, one shell had exploded at the rear of the hospital, with one of our unit being wounded. He was immediately attended to and whilst he was being dressed in the surgery another shell came over and burst to our left. Numerous other shells followed and amongst these was a dud, and a good job too that it was, for it smashed through one of our wards, skidded along the ground and finally buried itself in the ground four feet deep. A fragment of another shell struck one of the patients, who a short time afterwards succumbed to his injuries. Subsequent shells also fell in our area and we suffered two further casualties, both wounded cases and men from our unit.

During the whole shelling our main thoughts were concentrated on the safety of our patients, who numbered between 120-130. These were evacuated to safe quarters with all possible speed, every man regardless of the trying conditions rendering yeomanry service and within a very short period of time all were transferred to a safety zone.

Even after this was successfully accomplished we were still subjected to further shelling, but although these fell around us, happily no further casualties occurred. Nothing in the nature of panic ensued throughout this terrible ordeal, and it speaks volumes for the coolness and bravery of the personnel of this unit. Our commander is Major Turner (in the absence of Lieutenant Colonel West who is ill), and we acted expeditiously and without alarm carrying out the evacuation work. Another piece of smart work was the prompt and orderly way

in which the Transport section released their charges from the frontlines, conveying them to better shelter.

Now whether the shelling was deliberately intended for us or not one cannot say, but if our quarters were spotted by an aeroplane it was easily apparent what we were, large Red Crosses some ten feet or so in diameter were painted on the rooftops of one or two huts whilst a large Red Cross flag was also flying in the grounds.

Many thanks to Brian Simpson of Burbage for providing me with a copy of Private James Brown's letters.

OWEN WARD

Private Owen Ward at Loughborough during August 1914, a soldier in the Fifth Leicestershire Battalion.

Owen was the youngest of fifteen children, born on the 4th February 1896 at Elm Cottage, Wide Street, Hathern. The village is four kilometres (two and a half miles) northwest of Loughborough. He met his future wife, Clarissa Shaw (a twin birth) from nearby Long Whatton, when he was playing in the Hathern Brass Band around 1912. At this time he was working for a woodwork firm and continued to do so until August 1914.

He enlisted at Loughborough into the Fifth Leicestershire Battalion before 1914, served with it and the Machine-Gun Corps during the Great War, and soon afterwards wrote two diaries about his military experiences.

I have slightly abbreviated Owen's first Diary, which he wrote on the 5th February 1919, but all of the relevant details and atmospheric content are intact for readers to absorb. His second diary was written some time later, and is more 'battalion orientated' and some of those facts can be found with my earlier book: 'Fifty Good Men and True'.

Like so many of his companions he was a teenager, just turned nineteen years of age when he first experienced life in the trenches of the Western Front. Owen was a clever and solid individual and mature for his years, and in an age of greater opportunity would have had an outstanding career in

Soldiers of the Fifth Battalion Leicestershire Regiment in France 1916. Corporal Owen Ward far right on front row.

whatever field he ventured into.

During his military career he was involved in most of the major battles between 1914-18, and throughout displayed qualities of resolution and level-headedness time and again.

I believe the reason Owen wrote his first diary so soon after demobilisation was for its cathartic affect; to help him to adjust and face the future with a positive outlook.

A Land fit for Heroes? There was no job available for him at the woodwork firm, so he joined the L. and N.E.R. Railway at Nottingham, and remained with them until retirement.

Also in 1919 he married his fiancée, Clarissa Shaw, at Nottingham and resided at 41, Coppice Road in the city until eventually settling down to family life at nearby Bulwell. The couple had just the one child, a son named after his father.

Owen was a member of the Royal British Legion from its 1921 outset and remained so for all of his life. He founded his own branch at Bulwell, was made the president there and deservedly won all the possible Legion honours going. A truly splendid man, and never happier than when he was tending his garden, doing some fretwork or spending rainy winter days indoors admiring his large stamp collection. He was also a talented artist, and wrote the odd poem, one of which is published in my first book. After a full and varied life Owen passed away on the 5th February 1978, aged eighty-two years. One of Owen's brothers also fought and survived with a Lincolnshire Battalion during the Great War.

Owen (son) joined the Royal Navy in early 1941 and served in the Patrol Service, namely with patrol ships and minesweepers. He was based in Iceland and was on the highly dangerous Russian Convoys. Owen was also aboard H.M.S. 'Adonis' in 1943 when it was attacked and torpedoed in the North Sea by German E-Boats. Only eleven of the thirty-six crewmen survived to fight another day, and thankfully Owen was one! He was also involved in the 'D-Day' invasion of the 6th June 1944.

When Owen junior returned to the printing trade after the war, he followed his father's footsteps and joined the Royal British Legion in 1946. He is now vice-president of the Clifton Branch in Nottinghamshire. The year 2003 saw his **fifty-seventh year distributing poppies for the Appeal**.

Sergeant Owen Ward in 1919. Transferred from Machine-Gun Corps to Fifth Leicestershire and a player in the Regimental Band. Note badge.

Absolutely magnificent! As far as I am concerned, like father like son.

Two splendid men and not untypical of those who have done so much to honour and defend our country. Without their qualities we would not be enjoying the freedom or quality of life that we enjoy today.

More will be written about Owen in the third book of my trilogy.

THE TRENCH DIARY OF PRIVATE/ SERGEANT OWEN WARD

Originally Fifth Leicestershire Battalion then Machine-Gun Corps.
Written in Army Book No 153.
(Field Message Book)

Summary

I joined the Fifth Leicestershire Territorial Battalion on the 16th February 1914.

I travelled to our training camp at Bridlington on the 2nd August 1914.

War was declared between Great Britain and Germany on 4th August 1914.

The Battalion returned to Loughborough and was mobilised on 5th August 1914.

We entrained at Loughborough for posting at Duffield in Derbyshire on 6th August, and on the 10th we entrained for Luton from Derby Station.

Left Luton on the 28th November for Bishops Stortford, and marched all the way.

On the 6th December we left for Sawbridgeworth and on the night of 25th February embarked from Southampton for Le Havre, arriving there on the 26th February 1915.

Went into the trenches for the first time at Armentieres on the 6th March for training purposes, and the 8th went to hold the line at Messines and Kemmel. After holding the line for two months we went to Ypres, Hill 60, St Eloi, Sanctuary Wood, etc. While at the last place the Germans used 'liquid fire' for the first time at Hooge against the King's Royal Rifles.

Left Ypres sector of Belgium in September 1915 and was in reserve for the Battle of Loos, France.

Made the first 'over-the-top' charge on the 13th October and took the Hohenzollern Redoubt, but with heavy losses near Hulluch.

After having a rest for one month we went to the trenches at Lacouture and relieved the Indians. We spent three weeks there before a sudden order came for us to go to Egypt. We were relieved by the Welch Fusiliers and went to Merville where we spent Christmas.

On the 29th December we entrained for Marseilles and had a three-day journey.

Embarked on the 'Andania' on the 6th January 1916 and was promoted to lance corporal. Landed at Alexandria on the 14th January and returned to Marseilles on the 1st February and was promoted to corporal on the 22nd February.

Relived the French at Vimy Ridge in March 1916.

At Gommecourt on the Somme on July 1st 1916.

Transferred to the Machine-Gun Corpse in April 1916 and started training. During May I received my first leave of the war, seven days, and went home!

Returned to Fifth Battalion at the Somme and on 1st July 1916 went 'over the top' at Gommecourt.

Wounded on 5th July and went into hospital at Le Treporte. Left there in early part of September 1916.

Came to England for substitution on 24th September. Joined 197 Company at Belton Park, Grantham, and returned to France on 13th December 1916. Attached to the 9th Division (Scottish) at Arras, France. Took part in the German 'retirement' at the Somme during March and February 1917 and then returned to Arras.

Went with the attack on 9th April and came down to the Somme in July, near to Bapaume at Havrincourt.

Came home on leave in September and returned to Ypres in Belgium. Took part in the Battle of Passchendaele Ridge.

After this we went to La Panne near to Nieuport in November 1917. Promoted to Act/Sergeant and was sent on a course to Camias. I then went to Grantham to qualify for a full rank on December 6th 1917.

6th January 1918 returned to Belgium and was posted to 228 Company, 39th Division, who had just been relieved at Ypres.

Came down on the train from Proven to the Somme at Peronne. Marched to Fins for our billets. Went into the line at Guedecourt in February 1918. Came out to form a Battalion (39th) and while on this the Allied 'retirement' started. (The Germans advance started on March 21st). We went to meet this attack at Nurlew and Tincourt.

Retired on the 22nd March to Peronne. Held the River Somme for three days after which the Germans broke through the Americans on our right, and we retired to Cappy. Next day retired to Provart and then to Domart. Here we held the Germans with French troops that had come up to support us.

Relieved and marched to Amiens. Entrained for Ypres but was cut off at Calonne-sur-la-Lys.

Attached to the 51st Division. Went into the line at Hinges.

Retired next day to Busnes. Went to Flam-en-Artois for billets. (Retirement finished).

After a few days rest went on the line at St Venant. After this we returned to being Army troops as the Division was smashed up! Went to Rombly near Air for training (6 months).

Advance started and we went to Arras with Canadian Division. Advanced to Douai and was then relieved.

Came back to Morcourt and went into the line at Steenwerk, advance continued each day. We went through Armentieres and then onto Lille, Roubaix, and Lannoy and finished up at Leers, which is situated between Lille and Tourcoing near the Belgium frontier on November 1st.

We stayed at Leers until the Armistice was signed on the 11th November 1918. On the night before we were heavily shelled with gas, which did a considerable lot of damage to homes and killed a lot

Corporal Owen Ward, rear left in Machine-Gun Corps. Circa late 1917.

of civilians, but not many soldiers! After this we had a good time giving concerts at different places to amuse the civil population and they in turn were very good to us.

I came home on leave for Christmas and the New Year (the first Christmas I had spent at home since the war started). I returned to France but after only two weeks I was demobilised and came home for good on 24th February 1919.

Additions

***March 6th 1915.** The first time we went into the trenches, it was on the Armentieres front at Le Touquet for 24 hours. It was very quiet but muddy. There were no communication trenches then, and each trench was separate. The trench system had only just started after the allies had got the enemy in check, before then it was open warfare and street fighting in Armentieres. We came out of the trenches at night, and to do this we had to climb out of the back of the trench and run as fast as we could to a place out of range of rifle fire. We then waited there before marching back to the billet, which was a barn on the banks of the river Lys - close to the boundary* line between France and Belgium.

March 7th. The enemy dropped a few shells round about us; in fact one shell came through the thatched roof of our barn and fell with a splash into the river. We went into the trenches at night at Ploegsteert, commonly known as 'Plug-Street'. These trenches were a bit livelier. To get into these trenches was difficult because we had to cross a railway track, and the Germans were firing machine-guns every two or three seconds. We had to run one at a time between each shot and many a lad lost his life there!

After we crossed the track we went in twos or threes down the road until we came to the barriers of sandbags, which was the front-line.

March 8th. Nothing out of the ordinary occurred until close to midnight when we were suddenly ordered out of the line and back to the billets. Upon arriving there we were given a biscuit, a tin of bully beef and a drink and ordered to pack up for marching!

March 9th. We were force-marched until 6 am, many of the men falling out on the roadside exhausted. We halted at a village called Sailly-sur-la-Lys, and informed we were to be reserve for the Battle of Neuve Chapelle, but because of lateness we were not required. In fact 'Sailly' had been taken from the enemy not long before we arrived. We stayed there for two or three days and I went to look at one of our 15" Naval guns firing from a position not far from the village.

We then marched to Locre and Dranoutre where we were billeted in huts.

Easter Sunday. We went to hold the line at Kemmel and Wulverghem in front of Messines.

This was rather a quiet place taking things all round, and those acquainted with this part of the line will remember Frenchman's Farm, Sniper's Post and Neuve Eglise church (which we could see from our trenches), and Lindenhoek.

Jerry came over on a bombing raid one night and drove the 4th Leicestershire out. One man, a corporal stayed, bayoneted, and shot several of the enemy, before the 4th reclaimed the trench!

We used to spend four days and nights in the trench and then the same in reserve.

I visited the small town of Bailleul and also a small hill called Mont Blanc. It is one of five small hills all in a row. Another hill is Mont Caestra on which stands a monastery and convent, and is referred to in history books. (The grand old Duke of York, he had ten thousand men...)!

We hear Jerry has used gas just to the north of Ypres. Also the old Cloth Hall there has been shelled and burnt down.

After being in this area for three months we marched to Reninghelst, where we stayed for one night. We then went to huts situated on the road between Ouderdom and Vlamertinghe, not far from Poperinghe. The first time we went up the line we went to St Eloi for six days and then out to Hill 60 for another six days. We then came out and went to the dugouts in the bank of Zillebeke Lake. By this time the trenches had been linked up with one another and communication trenches had been dug. At this time Jerry used to send his 18inch shells into Ypres, which was clearly visible from our position. We left our Lake-dugouts and marched back to our huts for a six-day break. While there I went out and met some of my old pals who were with the 1st Leicesters.

We returned to the frontline at Ypres by way of the Indian encampment at Kruisstraat, where we waited till dusk. We then travelled along a road

Corporal Owen Ward - second row seated - second from left. 39th Machine Gun Company. (The majority were men from Leicestershire).

leading to Ypres and turned into a cart road and over Bridge 14. Then past the remains of Zillebeke Church and up a track to Maple Copse. We stopped at Sanctuary Wood; this is where Jerry crucified some Canadians. We then moved up the side of the wood into Square Wood, along the track to the burying ground and up the communication trench to that part of the line known as the Horse Shoe or Salient. This part of the line was very hot as Jerry could fire at us from three fronts! One night we blew up a German trench, the first sap going up at 6.50pm. This was just short of the enemy frontline; the second sap went up at 7.00pm. What a sight! It was right under their frontline and the earth went up like a great mushroom. There then followed a bombardment lasting about 30 minutes and then things became quiet and we settled down for the night. At 8.00pm we posted our first night-sentries. After two hours, at 10.00pm, when our sentries were being relieved we felt the first shock. The earth seemed to lift in the air and a dull roar followed.

I was knocked off my feet and flung about five yards into the communication trench at the back of us! The enemy had blown a mine under our trenches!

All I could hear was moaning and groaning from men who were injured or buried. There were cries for help. I started to pull men out but it was dark and I was unable to see. Rifles were sticking out of the earth at different places, men were buried at the other end of them! A good number got out alive but alas many of our comrades were also dead!

Reserves started to arrive to dig our frontline again. The enemy then tried to get into the crater that the exploded mine had created. Our bombers kept them at bay and when daylight came order was restored. The sight around us didn't look very promising, still, the digging carried on but some men were never found! (We made every effort to find them)! The Sappers were tunnelling to try and get into the crater when a surprise met them, another mine had been laid and was ready to be exploded. A corporal took charge and with a lot of risk to himself cut the wire, barricaded the sap and brought out all the explosives thereby saving quite a number of men's lives, including my own. The corporal won a D.C.M for his gallantry. (Corporal Jabez Emmerson, an Ellistown man - author).

This event exposed the weak spot of the Territorial Force, for each company came from one district, and it was the men from Market Harborough who suffered most as a result of this mine. We heard this part of Leicestershire was in mourning. I must say that our future enlistments were split up to ensure this did not happen again to us!

We held this part of the line for four to five months and while here we witnessed the Battle of Hooge, which at that time was just to our left. In this battle Jerry used 'liquid fire ' for the first time. It was used against the King's Royal Rifles.

September. We were relieved from these trenches in September 1915 and went into reserve for the first Battle of Loos.

October 13th 1915. It was on this date that we made the famous charge on the Hohenzollern Redoubt, near to Hullock, France. This was the first time we went 'over the top' and it will live in my memory forever!

We were relieved by a Guards Brigade and came out for a months rest at a place called Hesdigneul. It was here that the King inspected us, along with all the other troops that took part in this big battle. The King was thrown from his horse but did not seem the worst for wear!

We then relieved Indian troops at Lacoutouse, on the La Bassee and Richebourg front. Our trenches were flooded with water above the knees, and we could only take this for one day at a time. After three weeks we were suddenly relieved by the Welch Fusiliers and ordered to travel to Egypt! We travelled to Merville where we spent Christmas.

December 29th. We entrained in cattle trucks at Berguette Station en route for Marseilles - a three-day journey. We were billeted in tents on the Racecourse Borelli Parc.

January 6th 1916. We embarked on the 'Andania' and I was promoted to lance corporal at Alexandria. (January 14th). We had to return to France because of the evacuation from the Dardanelles.

February 22nd I was promoted to full corporal.

The next time we went into the frontline was at Vimy Ridge and we relieved the French. Beforehand we marched to our billets at Villers Cambria, which were barns, to have a rest.

March. We then marched to Carency, up the communication trench to Cabaret Rouge. This was on the Bethune to Arras road and dugouts at the roadside held the reserves. We then walked up another communication trench, which led to Valley-de-la-Morte (Valley of Death). This was a very deep ravine where the French lost 17,000 men in a five-mile advance in September 1915. Lots of bodies were still lying around! We went to the near side, which was lined with dugouts, and then up the steps to the front-line.

A bad spot with mines going up every day and trench mortars and whizz-bangs regularly flying about.

After six days of this we were very pleased to be relieved! Upon our return to the dugouts at Cabaret Rouge, (we were now reserves) we had to bury the rotting bodies of the German and French troops that were lying about, and also make things look a bit more pleasant. This was not a very nice job I can assure you! In some cases we just buried skeletons!

We went back to the frontline for another six days and then came out to the billets, which were right back behind Mont-St-Eloi. The church on that hill could be seen for miles around.

April 1916. We leave the line for training.

May. I come home on leave for the very first time. (7 days).

I return to the Battalion, they were in a small village called Bienvillers, in the region called the Somme. We went into the trenches at Foncquevillers and Hebuterne, opposing an enemy front called Gommecourt.

July 1st 1916. We went 'over the top' at this place as part of the battle of the Somme! We went over at 4.00am following eight days of heavy bombardment. The other parts of the line went over at 6.00am, so we knew we were being sacrificed to draw the enemy towards us, leaving other enemy fronts weaker. The main attack was further south where with the help of 'Tanks' they broke through. This was successful, but what about the lads shot down and slaughtered at Gommecourt? We were exhausted! We remaining men dropped back to our frontline! Our commanding officer was disgusted because we came back. All I can say is that if we had been given a fair chance Jerry would have been driven back, but what chance had we when the barbed wire entanglements were not touched by the bombardment, and there were yards and yards of it to get through! We were supplied with wire cutters, which were attached to our rifles, but this was a very slow process and the enemy was firing at as all the time. It was a wonder that any men got back at all! I was slightly wounded and had to go down to the Casualty Clearing Station to be attended to.

September 1916. I came out of hospital and returned to our unit at Bienvillers.

I was picked out for substitution and returned to England on September 24th.

Now posted to 197 Company at Belton Park at Grantham, Lincolnshire. At this time all Lord Derby's men were there in training for France.

December 13th. Went with 197 Company and the 9th Scottish Division to Arras. We visited the frontline two or three times and then relieved my old company at Bienvillers, on the Somme.

February/March 1917. We went up the trenches (Shell Street) in front of Monchy-au-Bois. We had been in the trenches for two days when Jerry retired. We followed on through Addinfer and several other small villages until we got within rifle fire, and then dug ourselves in.

After being relieved we went back to Arras in front opposite to Blangy.

April 9th. We go 'over the top' at the battle of Arras and advance about ten miles or more to the Chemical Factory at Roeux. We lost a lot of men in this battle, we were held in check by machine-guns, so we waited while they did another bombardment on their lines and then rushed the factory. We didn't want to damage the factory because this is where Jerry was making gas. We took it. We couldn't hold it for long because Jerry started shelling and soon levelled the building! We then attacked again and drove them back to what was called the Greenland Plains. Then we were relieved. I came out for a rest.

July. Back to the Somme again. This time we

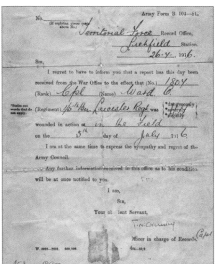

Notification of Corporal Ward being wounded in battle.

marched through Bapaume and onto Havrincourt Wood. This was a quiet place, we made one bombing raid here but little of importance went off.

September. I returned to England on leave. When I returned my unit was at Ypres. We took part in the battle for Paschendaele Ridge. We drove Jerry back a considerable way. This part of the line was always hot and the mud and pillboxes were awful.

I don't think there was any ground that didn't have a shell hole. It was nothing else but murder to go up the line here, you were lucky if you got back all right!

November 1917. After things had quietened down a bit we went to La Panne, on the Belgium

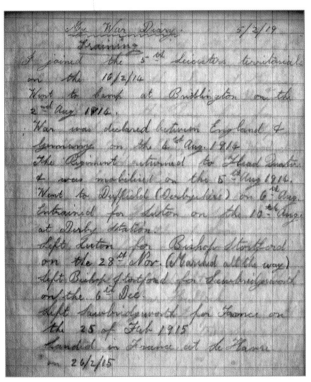

Sergeant Owen Ward's War Diary clearly marked 5/2/19.

coast in the Nieuport Front. It was all sand dunes.

I was promoted to acting-sergeant and was sent on a course of training at Camiess, and from there to Harrowby Camp, Grantham.

December 6th. I qualify for the full rank of sergeant.

January 1918. Back in France as a full sergeant. I was posted to 228 Company, 39th Division, who were at Poperinghe. Entrained at Proven and got off at Peronne and then marched to rest billets at Fins.

February. We soon went up to the trenches at

Gouzeaucourt, which was a quiet place.

March. We came out and formed a battalion. On the 21st the Germans started their big advance. We were hurried up the line to meet the advance and dug trenches at Nurlew and Tincourt. We collected all the bombs and ammunition we could and waited for Jerry. We had no Verey Lights to send up but when Jerry did we knew he was there. The enemy slowly crept towards us and when they were within rifle fire we opened up as hard as we could. It was fairly dark and we felt we were wasting ammunition not to properly pick out a target. The Verey Lights continued to get closer, then we got out of our trench, and each of us threw a bomb and made a dash for our trench. This was all we could do, and still they kept on coming! We had to withdraw to Peronne, which was several miles back. Our Royal Engineers were destroying all they could so nothing of value could fall into their hands. Ammunition dumps and huts were destroyed, even aerodromes! It was getting light as we crossed the River Somme at Peronne, so we dug ourselves in. The river at this point was like a huge 'S', so you could see some of our troops on what appeared to be the other side. We had blown the bridges so Jerry had to stop his advance, but when we saw them we gave them a good reception I can tell you! Our men who were on the other bank had to retire along the flank and Jerry followed, but they could not go any further as our troops had crossed the river further down the letter 'S'! You can tell we were in a very big salient and American troops were on our right. We had no rations and very little ammunition but we stuck it out for two days. Jerry kept trying to get across the river by putting pontoons down at night, but we could hear them distinctly and we put volleys of fire in their direction. We dispersed them every time. One Jerry officer had the cheek to ride up on horseback in broad daylight to the side of the river, but I need hardly say what happened to him. We held them like this for two days but on the second night they managed to break-through the American line. This put us in a serious position because we were in a salient and we could easily have been cut off. We had to retire, and the only place we could get out was at a small village called Cappy. This had a bridge across the estuary running into the Somme. The enemy knew this and he made for this point. How we got there I don't know because it was about 5-6 miles back and we had to run most of the way! It was close; we just crossed the bridge as the Germans entered the other end of the village. We dashed across it and then the Royal Engineers blew it up (they had mined it earlier).

We were now getting near to Amiens, and this was the objective for Jerry's attack. If he took it then we in our line would be split, we would be separated from our French allies. All of us were exhausted, and the only food we had was taken from French households (the civilians had quickly packed up and left). We kept retiring until we got to Provart. Here we rallied a bit! We had a bit of luck because there was a large 'food ration dump'.

We were told to help ourselves before we set it on fire. The only problem was there was no bread and the only substitute we could find was biscuits for our bully beef. I managed to get three or four tins of 'Ideal Milk'. I kept two tins in my haversack. We then retired to Domart. Here we held the enemy until we were relieved by French troops.

A march to Amiens followed by a train to Ypres where Jerry was also trying to break through.

To get there we'd normally pass through Merville, but this had fallen to Jerry, so we had to get out at Calonne-sur-la-Lys. The 51st Division were there so we were directed to assist them at Hinges. We took up a position in the wood over the River Lys and waited but nothing happened. At about 3.00 am the enemy broke through the Portuguese line on our left, so we had to retire, in a rush, to the other side of the river. In the haste we had to leave most of our equipment, so we would not be of much use in stopping the enemy. We retired to Burnes where our transport had stopped. Upon arrival we found out another regiment had relieved us so we travelled to Ham-en-Artois for a rest, which we had well earned. I can tell you the whole line was then relieved by fresh troops and the retirement was checked. After a few days rest we returned to the line as a reserve at St. Venant.

Soon we came out for six months training at Rombley, near to the town of Aire.

The British advance started and we assisted the Canadians at Arras. We advanced to Douai before being relieved and put in reserve at Morcourt. Then we were put in the line at Steenwerk and from here we kept on rapidly advancing through Armentieres and several small villages. We swept on the Lille and Roubaix (shortening our line all the time). Through Lannoy, and to Leers. Here we were cut out so we stayed at this place, which was situated between Lille and Tourcoing near to the Belgium frontier. The Germans had held all of these towns and villages that we liberated since our retirement from Mons in 1914! So you can imagine how the people felt when they saw us. They were very kind to us, and would do anything they could, even polish our boots and buttons! They were compelled to do this for the Germans and even had to sleep on floors while the Germans slept in their beds. There were also a thousand and one other things they did which the people of England didn't realise.

November 1918. We stayed at Leers until the Armistice was signed on the 11th November 1918. The enemy heavily shelled us with gas the night before they signed the Armistice, a lot of damage was done to houses, and a good many civilians were killed.

After the Armistice things were more like the army of pre-war days and nothing of any consequence happened. Leave was started and I came home for Christmas and the New Year. This was the first Christmas at home since before the war started. I returned to Leers but I was only there a fortnight before I returned to England for demobilisation. I can tell you I was very pleased indeed, for I had had enough of the army and everything connected with it. I feel sure anyone else would feel the same who served in the war for over four long years.

My service in the army is as follows.
Started as: Private. O. Ward. Service Number: 1807. 5th Leicestershire Territorial Battalion.
Ended as: Sergeant. O. Ward. Service Number: 22811.
Total Service is 5 years and 16 days.
Sergeant Owen Ward.
5th February 1919.

Many thanks to Owen Ward, son of the above for supplying such absorbing material.

HARRY WATSON

Harry was born in 1898 on North Street in the ancient hamlet of Donington-le-Heath, near to Hugglescote. His father, Benjamin Watson, was born and bred on Wash Lane at Ravenstone, and following his education at the village school became a miner at Ibstock Colliery. Upon marriage the couple moved to North Street where Harry grew up. The family worshipped at St. John The Baptist Church at Hugglescote with Harry receiving education at the Church School (later called the National School).

It is known that Harry, service number 2999, enlisted at Coalville in September 1914 into the 2/5th (Reserve) Leicestershire Battalion. At best he was either sixteen or early seventeen years of age, and his record indicates that he was transferred to the Fifth (1/5th) Battalion shortly before they embarked for France on the 25th February 1915. Harry was wounded by shellfire at Gommecourt on the Somme in July 1916, and had to return to England for hospitalisation. In early February 1917, having passed a medical board to establish his fitness he was reposted to the 2/4th Leicestershire Battalion, 59th Division, with a revised service number 240895. He joined his new battalion at Fovant Camp, about twelve kilometres (eight miles) west of Salisbury in Wiltshire.

On the 24th February 1917 the Division (also containing the 2/5th Leicestershire Battalion: see Reginald Glover) entrained for Southampton and steamed across the Channel to arrive at 2.30 am on the 25th at Le Havre, France. They proceeded to a rest camp and at 9. 20 pm left for Pont du Metz for an eventual destination of Fouencamps. The 2/4th Battalion distinguished itself and fought valiantly throughout 1917, and by the turn of the year Harry was still a mere nineteen years of age!

In the March of 1918 the Germans, having transferred men and equipment from their Russian Campaign, launched a massive offensive, 'Operation Michael', against the Allied Forces on the Western Front. The enemy opened strongly in the Somme Sector of France, and, with specially trained 'storm troopers' acting as a spearhead they advanced with alarming speed to achieve massive territorial gains. Their aggression was also directed against the old battlefield of Neuve Chapelle, attacking towards the Channel between Bethune in the south to Ypres in the north. The combination of battles that followed in this area is classified as the 'Battle of the Lys', named after the canalised river of that name.

As discussed earlier in this book the objective of the German attack was to capture the crucially important Channel ports. It was on Sir Hubert Plummer's head that the burden of responsibility fell: under no circumstances was his Army to fail, his troops had to stand firm! The German commander, Ludendorff, had sixteen divisions at his disposal and his troops were relatively fresh and hungry for continued success. Plummer had only five divisions and a brigade, and they were drained from the earlier Somme battles, and scattered thinly over forty kilometres (twenty-five miles) between La Bassee and the Ypres Canal.

The tempest of battle was unleashed on the 9th April 1918 when the enemy struck-out at the old battlefield of Neuve Chapelle, and in spite of heroics and stubbornness the defenders had to retire a little to the west. Also, Plummer was forced to straighten his frontline at its most northerly point, near to Ypres, under overwhelming attacking strength. By April 12th Merville had fallen, so too Ploegsteert and Kemmel, with Bailleul looking in danger. Armentieres had been evacuated after forty thousand gas-shells rained down on its centre.

So it was, with a spirit of conviction, that on April 14th the 2/4th Battalion was concentrated around Locre, near to the Ravelsberg Ridge on the hills of Belgium Flanders. At 11.00 am they were ordered along the Locre-Dranoutre road as far as Locrehoh Farm. Most of the men were physically drained, having gone several days without sleep and conditions prevented adequate supplies of food and fluids. The German troops poured forward and took up flanking positions, aided by their machine-gunners who roasted the British frontlines.

At 4.00 pm the enemy converged on the Kemmel-Bailleul Front, and with superior infantry numbers and artillery power the situation looked grave, with the 2/4th Battalion in a position by Crucifix Corner. The following day (15th) in what was the Battle of Bailleul, the soldiers of the Battalion made repeated attempts to capture high ground for a garrison box. In their efforts they inflicted substantial losses upon the enemy but were eventually thwarted by enemy machine-gun posts on Ravelsberg Ridge. At noon came an accurate and heavy shrapnel-shell bombardment, and this was followed by another at 2.00 pm. The Brigade was forced to retire as casualties mounted, most falling on the forward slopes of Crucifix Corner. The War Diary commented: '*The assaulting force was fresh, and the enemy artillery was controlled by signal flares, and supported their infantry most skilfully.*'

It was on this day, the 15th April 1918 that 'veteran' soldier, Harry Watson, lost his life.

Harry has no known grave, and I suspect he died during the noon barrage. He was a mere twenty years of age, and his name is engraved on Panel 4 at Ploegsteert Memorial, Belgium. The Memorial is situated about four-five kilometres (three miles) from where he was killed. On that late mid-April evening three German Divisions including the crack Alpine Corps entered and captured the battered town of Bailleul. The following foggy morning German troopers charged and took the shattered remnants of the village of Wytschaete, also the much fought over locality of Spanbroekmolen (Harry served there in the spring of 1915).

Gradually the German advance stuttered to a halt against resolute and valiant troops. Their lines of support and communication became too extended, soldiers tired, casualties rose, and morale plummeted.

A delighted Sir Hubert Plummer spoke: "*Words fail me to express the admiration which I feel for the splendid resistance offered by all ranks of our Army under the most trying of circumstances.*"

Private Harry Watson's death was not in vain, but for men of his calibre the enemy offensive would have succeeded, and the map of Europe could have changed forever.

The 2/4th Battalion lost over two hundred officers and other ranks; with over three hundred wounded during the hostilities. Over half of these figures were sustained during the battles of March and April 1918, and illustrate the perilous situation they found themselves in.

Harry's name can also be read on the Coalville Clock Tower Memorial, and on a Memorial Tablet in St. John The Baptist Church, Hugglescote.

Other local men of the Battalion who lost their lives: Alfred Bowley of Shepshed, Cecil Hunt of Mountsorrel, Albert Mattley of Ibstock, William Poole of Thornton, John Rowe and James Squire of Loughborough, John Squires of Barrow-on-Soar and Ernest Whiting of Loughborough.

Many thanks to Harry's great-nephew, Alwyne Watson for information supplied. Alwyne, a great supporter of the Tiger's Regiment appears on a photograph with details of Edward Chapman.

THOMAS WOOD M.M.

THE MEMOIRS OF A BRAVE AND KIND-HEARTED MAN

Tom was born on the 10th July 1891 at 111, Belvoir Road at Coalville. His parents Mr & Mrs Samuel Wood had seven children including a son, Alfred and daughter, Pattie. His life, like the majority of his generation, was far from easy. Indeed it was demanding, and his pathway and deliverance through the ages started, as it intended to continue, at twelve years of age, when he had to leave school to support the family's income. A decade later followed four years of conflict in the

Great War, and furthermore followed over forty years labouring in unhealthy conditions in the grim bowels of a colliery.

Without doubt Tom was an extremely modest and warm-hearted man, and the following essay was constructed primarily from notes he had written on small pieces of letter-paper. A few years later he decided that such memoirs were of little interest and ripped them in half. Very fortunately they were rescued and are now held together by strips of

Corporal Tom Wood M.M. and his wife, Ivy. 1916.

cellotape, and, together with other belongings of Tom's are treasured by his step-grandson, Robert Newton. In my opinion, Tom, in his own way was a great man, and he symbolised everything that was good and true about a generation all but disappeared, but which must never be forgotten!

Extracts from Tom's memoirs:

'*I was born in a house that was so very near to the old police-station, and I can remember in 1894 walking with my mother to a different house in Vaughan Street. I can recall carrying a small article to our new house, and felt I had contributed to the move.*'

Tom attended the Belvoir Road Methodist Chapel and also the Day School. The highly respected schoolmaster of that age, Mr Frith, was searching for boy-altos to become choristers, and invited the ten-year old Tom to join the choir. The youngster accepted and proudly remained a loyal member until his voice broke. Two years passed before he sang another note, and then to his joy found he could sing soprano, alto and tenor! As we shall read, singing continued to bring him enormous happiness throughout his long life.

From the age of nine he helped-out in the family's fish and chip shop business, 'S. Wood', at 111, Belvoir Road. Around this time he also had a paper-round for the Coalville Times, but he found the deliveries so widespread that it only earned him 4$\frac{1}{2}$d (under 2 new pence) a week.

Tom continues: '*Before I left school a friend and I tried to raise a little extra cash to help our mothers, by carrying railway luggage. After school lessons we walked to Coalville Railway Station and waited for the Burton-on-Trent train to arrive. Once, an old lady took to the platform with lots of parcels, and she was in need of help. We offered, she thanked us gracefully, and we followed her to her house in Park Road. It was now dark and so the lady lit the candles in the hallway and opened her purse, and placed what appeared to be silver into my friend's palm. She again thanked us so much. We departed and cheerfully strolled home to find that the silver was a pearl button. What disappointment!*'

Samuel Wood, Tom's father, was a miner, but with seven children to support, money was always short. At the age of twelve Tom was asked to leave school and go to work for a draper, cleaning boots and looking after the horses for four shillings a week. (20 new pence).

T. BALLARD. T.S.STORER. H. EDMONDS. C.POYTON.
J.JONES. T.C.WOOD. J.THOMPSON.
(5th Leicestershire, High-Tor, Whitwick, Leics., circa 1912)

'*We had some grand times as a family. My parents owned a small float and pony, and they used to decorate this, and the wheels also with paper flowers of all colours. All the family joined in, making a beautiful canopy for the top. The youngest six children sat inside dressed in white, and we walked alongside. Some of the galas were eight and ten miles away, but we always used to win 1st prize.*'

When Tom was seventeen in 1908, he enlisted, almost certainly at Ashby de la Zouch, into the newly formed Fifth Territorial Battalion of the Leicestershire Regiment.

He enjoyed spending regular weekends and annual summer training camps at such places as High-Tor (Whitwick) on two occasions, also at Buxton in Derbyshire and Aberystwyth in Wales. The camps were usually in isolated spots, some distance from the towns. He recalled when encamped at High-Tor he worked from home during the day, and then walked to camp every evening, returning the following morning. Tom was content enough but there was always the nagging worry of insufficient money for the siblings.

Tom writes: '*Whatever the occupation wages were not good in those days, and so, after obtaining employment with Midland Railway I took promotion when it was offered to me, but it meant moving to Skipton in Yorkshire. Upon arrival I found myself some digs, they were good and the lady cooked lovely pasties and mince-tarts, which I took to work with me. There was one problem! On my first week I earned 15 shillings (75 new pence). I had to pay 13 shillings for board, and on top of that I had to pay one shilling and three pence (six new pence), every other week towards our sick-club. I spent my nineteenth birthday there, and received a rise of one shilling, but soon my father sent for me and advised me to return and work down the pit with him. I started at Ibstock Colliery, but it was a long walk from Vaughan Street, and then a mile-long walk underground to the point where I spent my days filling-up coal wagons. They held half a ton each! After the long days work I then walked all the way home. They were long days. My father was the boss, and my three uncles also gave me good tuition and eventually I became a collier, earning nineteen shillings a week (ninety-five new pence). From that time on, apart from the war years my job was down the pit and I retired at 65 years of age from Ellistown Colliery.*'

Following the outbreak of the war, Tom enlisted at Coalville into the Seventh (Service) Leicestershire Battalion, and after a period of training at Aldershot, Andover and Perham Down prepared for embarkation for France. Before leaving he

PATTIE WOOD. TOM WOOD, SAMUEL WOOD, MRS WOOD, ALFRED WOOD.
(Outside the fish and chip shop on Belvoir Road, Coalville. 1913.)

accomplished something very important to him, marrying Ivy Jowett, his fiancée from Kent. Soon afterwards she moved to stay with Tom's parents for the duration of the war; they were then living at 69, Highfield Street, Coalville.

Tom: '*I found myself on the Western Front, in trenches and surrounded with death and disease. It was a severe test for my Christian faith, but it did not desert me and it strengthened me, so enabling me to help others and inspire my future heroism!*

Initially I was kitted out at Glen Parva at Leicester and then entrained to Aldershot, on the Salisbury Plain (Perham Down) before leaving for France in late July 1915. I was in the Seventh Leicestershire Battalion and part of the 110th Brigade that also included the Sixth, Eighth and Ninth battalions of the Regiment. After a period in Belgium with long marches to Kemmel, Dickiebusch and Locre, we eventually arrived at a village named Pommier, not too far from Arras in France. We then marched to the village of Bienvillers, close to the frontline. I was now a lance corporal and had the opportunity of going with my sergeant to take over our billets. The French had occupied them and they were very interested to see us. They all carried wine in their bottles, we had water, and they freely shared some wine with us! Looking around the billets I made a choice for my section. It was in the front room, which was tiled and bare (no beds). The tenants were Monsieur and Mademoiselle Durieu, and they had a daughter, Marie, who was about twenty years old, and had a child. I asked Marie about the dirty floor in the living room. They had their beds downstairs and slept in the room where we had our coffee and they their food! Washing day arrived and after doing the washing, which included some of ours, they tipped over the tub and cleaned the entire downstairs floor! There food was poor and so we gave them a little of our bully beef, jam and biscuits, and some tobacco for father! When we left to go to the frontline trenches they shook us all by the hand, not knowing who would return. They had been very kind to us!'

Tom: *'My sergeant's name was Powdrill, a Wigston man, and our lance sergeant, William Kenderdine of Leicester. Both of these men were good at their jobs. Mr Powdrill was a schoolmaster at Wigston Boy's School. I visited him a few times after the war but he didn't live to see old age. Our frontline on the 6th February 1916 was at Monchy-au-Bois, only fifty yards from the Jerry (Germans), and it was a most uncomfortable spot. It was bitterly cold and the ground was covered in snow. Sergeant Kenderdine felt sure Jerry was cutting the protective barbed wire in front and near to our trenches, so, in darkness he crawled out into No-Man's-Land' to check for himself. The Germans must have heard him for they opened fire and shortly afterwards I heard him calling for help. The Prussians, Jerry's hardest troops, started firing like hell when they heard his calls! I crawled out to him, keeping as low as I could, as Jerry was sweeping the area with machine-gun fire. I found him with a terrible stomach wound; an explosive-bullet had torn it open. I bandaged it the best I could, took my tunic off, and placed it under his head. My sergeant was in so much pain that he begged me to shoot him! I couldn't do that, and the first thing that came into my head was to say that it was not British to do such a thing! In frustration and pain he angrily hit me in the face! Later, another sergeant crawled up to us, I asked him for wire-cutters because Sergeant Kenderdine was lying tangled in a thick bed of barbed wire. We cut him lose and I let him rest his head on my back, and eventually two stretcher-bearers came and gently took him back to our lines. My duty was now finished. Very sadly he died the following evening. An officer and I went out not long after and found his rifle, or what was left of it! He is buried at Humbercamps. I remember an incident when I was detailed for guard duty. Three men and myself marched to a road, which we found was spied upon by a German Observation Balloon. We soon discovered it was not possible to travel*

488. La Guerre 1914-15-16   Bienvilliers-aux-Bois (P.-de-C.)
Visé Paris 488   Les défenses établies par nos poilus.
R. P.

Tom Wood was billeted in building * which was 1,000 yards from 'G' trenches. 1915-16.

along it during daylight hours.'

Tom risked his life to save his sergeant. It is impossible to imagine the fear he must have felt as he crawled in the snow, the night sky lit by enemy flares, and with literally thousands of bullets whistling over his head or splattering the snow ahead of him. Clearly he was prepared to lay down his life for his comrade.

At the end of March 1916, the Brigade was relieved from the frontline sector and rested in the area of Sus-St-Leger and Warluzel, and later on the outskirts of Doullens. During this time the weather was beautiful, as was the surrounding countryside.

Tom: *'We made our headquarters at a farm, the entrance of which was hidden by fruit trees. It was a good warm day and so we settled down, quite happily. Towards lunchtime we thought we would investigate the farm-loft, as there seemed to be a lot of poultry busying themselves around. One of our men came down with nineteen eggs in his hat! I asked the lady farm owner if she would cook us some for a* *treat. The lady cooked us two eggs a piece and then left the rest so we could have a lovely tea.'*

Towards the end of May the Brigade returned once more to the Bienvillers-Bailleulmont Sector, and this is where they remained during the ill-fated opening day (July 1st) Battle of The Somme, about thirty kilometres (twenty miles) to the south. On the 6th July 1916 the Brigade marched south to take part in the fierce fighting at the Somme.

Tom: *'It was a hard march, some men having to fall out, and that was considered serious. We arrived at a village called, Hangest, and we stopped the night at a farm. A lady had kindly put cider into some buckets for us, and we were also given one months pay!'*

The following day the Brigade arrived at its destination, that part of the Somme known as Mametz Wood and Bezentin-le-Petit. What Tom witnessed was a scene from hell. There was battle-scarred, churned up earth, the stench of rotting corpses in No-Man's-Land and the pungent aroma of lachrymatory gas.

Tom: *'I was at Mametz Wood on the Somme and it was there that I was wounded.'*

Tom did not describe the horrors that confronted him, and many Coalville men lost their lives in the battle that raged there, several men coming from Margaret Street. We cannot possibly imagine the horrors of hand-to-hand fighting, heavy shelling and severe machine-gun fire to realise why he decided not to document his deeper thoughts.

Tom's parents received a letter shortly after the 22nd July 1916 stating Tom had a gunshot wound to his side, and that they regret that permission to visit him could not be granted.

Tom: *'I was taken to hospital at Rouen, and then by train to Le Havre, shipped across the Channel to Southampton and finally to Bristol Hospital. They operated and explored the wound near to my hip but missed one piece of shrapnel, and this had to be taken out at Leicester Royal Infirmary twenty-three years later!'*

After leaving Bristol Hospital Tom spent ten days at home, but the severity of the wound meant his war days were over. He was content with the outcome and often said he felt the wound probably saved his life.

Several years after the war, when he had his own home he called it, 'Mametz', for it was in that vicinity that his new life started.

The month of June 1917 was a dreadfully sad one for Tom. His dear Ivy, who was pregnant, suddenly became ill and died five days later on the eighth! The Coalville Times of the 16th June printed the following: *'The funeral took place at Hugglescote Cemetery on the 13th June and was conducted by Rev. T. Cottam, the Wesleyan minister. A short service was held at the house during which the hymn 'Jesu, lover of my soul' was sung. The chief mourners were the husband, his parents, Mr & Mrs Jowett (wife's parents), Mr & Mrs Rose (brother in law and sister), Mr & Mrs Newton, Mrs J. Hall and members of the Coalville Wesleyan Society Class, and others. The coffin was of polished elm and inscribed 'Ivy Melinda Wood, aged 28 years'. The bearers were C. Bradshaw, S. Stacy, L. Fisher, S. Walker, A. Stevenson and C. Brown. A good number of sympathisers were at the graveside and all sang the hymn: 'Safe in the arms of Jesus'. Wreaths were from the husband, his parents, brothers and sisters, Alfred, Nellie, Harry, Alice, Louie, Fred and Sam in France.'*

Tom felt the loss of his dear wife far more than the wound inflicted on the battlefield. Only time and his Christian spirit helped him with his bereavement.

Tom: *'I had to report to Patrington, near Hull for training. I stayed there just the one night but was very fortunate to see my brother, Alfred, who was set to go to France, it was for the last time, he never returned!'*

Alfred Wood had enlisted at Coalville and was in the Eighth Leicestershire Battalion, the same Brigade as Tom. On the 1st October 1917, the 110th Brigade was in the vicinity of Guedecourt on the Somme. Alfred was involved in some reconnoitre work in No-Man's-Land when he was mortally wounded. His name can be read as G. A. Wood on the Coalville Clock Tower Memorial.

Tom continues: *'I left for a training camp at Stafford Barracks and following the course passed as a physical training instructor. I was to hold courses at York, Newcastle and Aldershot. Our unit then moved to Ashford, the Duke of Portland Estate (Clipstone Camp), Kent, on the 11th November 1918,*

Armistice Day. My time as a soldier was coming to an end and in early December I was back at the Ellistown Colliery to complete my apprenticeship. All in all I was a miner for forty-six years.'

It must still have been too heart breaking, for nowhere in his account does he mention his first wife, Ivy, their meeting, their brief life together nor her premature death! Many years later Tom remarried, but in 1935 he was to lose his second wife in tragic circumstances. Two years later he married for the third time to Lily, and they lived at Lily's General Store, a shop at 211, Belvoir Road, and later

Lily and Tom Wood at Ilfracombe 1952

a residence at 85, Highfield Street with his two stepdaughters, Betty and Norma.

Tom served in the Home Guard throughout World War 2, and many times said that he would never allow enemy troops to touch his wife or children, and was overjoyed on V.E. Day.

A few years after the war he was very surprised

to see a friend he never thought he'd see again.

Tom: '*I remember a day in September 1950, when our postman said an Australian had written to Coalville Post Office to enquire whether a Tom Wood still lived in the town. Three weeks later I had a letter from one of my great friends, Arthur Westcott. We were very close and looked after each other in the trenches. I was just returning home from watching Leicester City F.C. play, and when I walked around the corner into my street I noticed a man standing outside my house carrying a small attaché case. We recognised each other straight away. We were both injured on the same day in 1916 and had not been in contact since, it was thirty-four years! We both laughed about the name of my house, 'Mametz'! Arthur was a Dorset man who had left for Australia shortly after the Great War, and he was now a wealthy and successful vineyard owner.'*

Tom loved his football and as a boy and youth played in various leagues, and at all times was a keen supporter of Leicester City F.C. Another love of his life was singing. With three friends, S. Walker, Stanley Allard and M. Eames (who died in war) they sang in the Coalville Wesleyan Quartet, and in 1926 joined the Ebenezer Male Voice Choir. Later Tom was a stalwart member of the Coalville and District Male Voice Choir for many a year.

Tom: '*I sang two solos in a concert with my alto voice, and then sang in soprano. After the concert I called into a fish and chip shop opposite to the Clock Tower on my way home. I stood at the back while two ladies were being served. They didn't know I was there and started talking about the man with the lady's voice! Very complimentary I thought! As they were leaving I bid them a good evening, and they walked away laughing.'*

The kindly natured Tom was always very good-humoured and had many close friends, and because of his limitless energy often threw himself into lots of ventures.

'*My last day at the pit arrived. I have a melodeon, and I took it with me on the last day. I sat and played it for short intervals. My Overman came together with the afternoon under-manager and I played for them. The under-manager sang along to me and afterwards he said he didn't think he would see or hear anything like this ever again down the pit! I finished at 10.30 pm and I was at Llandudno in Wales on holiday by 11.00am the following morning.*

I looked forward to developing my hobbies. I loved all the sport I could find, and was fond of gardening and I liked out-door painting on a very large scale. One of our choir members, Charlie, asked me to join him on his travels. He was a lorry driver, delivering bricks and pipes and we had some lovely trips all around England. On a trip to Bata Shoe Factory near to Tilbury we drove past a cricket ground. On the way back we stopped and watched for an hour. It was at Ilford and Essex C.C.C. was playing a county match. A lovely experience but we didn't get back home to Coalville until 10.45pm! I also visited many churches on my travels, and if I had the chance to play the organ I did. I remember when we stopped at Great Bowden Church, near Market Harborough. I had the organ to myself. I switched on the power and played 'Abide With Me'. The vicar's wife thought it was lovely.'

Tom was an exceptional organist.

Although in his early Seventies, he had for many years yearned to return to France for a personal reunion with his war-memories. He particularly wanted to see Bienvillers village, where the Durieu family had helped them so much in 1915.

Tom: '*Soon after Christmas in 1962 I had a talk with my wife and made arrangements for travel to France. On March 19th I left Dover for Calais, and took the train to Arras.*

I arrived at 'La Modern Hotel' and was fixed up with room number 13. It was very nice and I had dinner. I had a look around the town and bought a few post cards, but I had to trust the shopkeeper, because I was used to the old franc whereby it was now the new franc.

The next day I sat in Arras Cathedral listening to some beautiful music. Later I asked a young lady how I could get to the English Military Cemetery there. She understood I was an old soldier and in her broken English she explained she would take me there! She took my hand as I thanked her by the cemetery gates! I was most moved by her kindness. I passed down the rows; there are 2,583 and also a memorial with the names of 35,942 officers and men who have no known grave! As I was walking back to my hotel I chatted to a green grocer, who was

Betty, Tom and Norma.

*standing outside his shop. I said I was Anglais, pensioner, soldat. He took me into his living room and introduced me to his wife. Out came a bottle of wine and a 'Bon Sontie'! I also had chats with some of the gendarmes. I returned to my hotel and had a delicious piece of beef, but it was **surrounded by watercress**, it was good. Next day I arranged for a taxi to take me to Bienvillers. We travelled the twelve miles along countryside that was still familiar and at last arrived at the village. I knew where this military cemetery was for I had buried some of my friends in there during 1916. I met a Mr Humphries, a grand fellow, and I pointed out some of the boys that I had known. There was the grave of Mr Lovel, Mr Barkby and local man, John Pegg. When I returned to Coalville I visited brothers and sisters of some of the lads buried there, and that pleased them.*

From the cemetery in Bienvillers I went to look at the church, now fully restored, but it was in a poor way back in 1916! I made enquiries in a café as to whether a Marie Durieu still lived in the village. The lady there said she did and was quite well! She took me to this large house and upon entering I met Marie once again after 46 years. I showed her my photograph taken in 1918 and she shouted "Thomas"! Out came the wine and 'Bon Sontie'! We then travelled to Humbercamps so that I could see Sergeant Kenderdine's grave. It was beautifully kept and I stood in silence looking at the date on the headstone, 7th February 1916. Yes, I thought, I was there! I would have liked to stay another day in the village but I knew I had to get back to Arras and prepare for my return home. I travelled to Calais via Vimy Ridge and Lens and what a great experience I had!

Later, from home I wrote to Mr Humphries, who I had met at the cemetery and explained my meeting with Marie Durieu. He told me he had lived in the village since 1921 and had married a French lady, who was a great friend of Marie, and sent me many old photographs of his time there. I explained that I was so disappointed that I could not have spent longer in the village. Before I went to France I had written to the mayor of Bienvillers, asking if there was any place where I could stay. It was only after I arrived back in England that he replied saying that I could stay in the café I had visited. What a pity!

I returned to 'Mametz', my home, a little earlier than my wife expected, and she had gone to bed after a busy day. She insisted on getting-up to see me and it wasn't long before tea was ready, and then we retired to bed. Very early mornings I used to sing a song:

Now I'm in England, in England today.

I'm thanking my God I've come home to stay.

As I sang it that following morning, whilst shaving I realised I was so pleased to be back in England again!"

I believe the gentleman that Tom met in France, Mr Humphries, was working for the War Graves Commission.

Corporal: later Sergeant Kenderdine with his wife.
He died of his wounds despite a valiant effort by Tom Wood to rescue him.

What a life story about a very fine and modest man who possessed wonderful standards based entirely on his firm Christian beliefs. It is so typical of the man that the last line in his memoir states: '*I was honoured by my Country for bravery*'. **It must have been written at a later date**, because the ink was of a different colour.

Tom was decorated for bravery; he was awarded the Military Medal for his efforts in attempting to save the life of his sergeant. **He was the first non-commissioned Coalville soldier** to receive this medal for bravery above the call of duty!

I have already written that Tom had a very demanding life, but I didn't mention that his job down the pits was so very physical and dangerous! **Tom was to write** in a 1971 magazine article: '*My job was that of a 'stone-man', making roads underground through solid stone, often working in deep water. I was not always too happy doing the job, but the companionship of the men around was great! It made up for some of the misery and it helped us all.*'

Tom often said that life began for him at seventy-five years of age. It was at that time in his life that he decided to attempt landscape and seascape painting. He was naturally talented and won a lot of prizes in Midland competitions, and people from as far away as South Africa tried to buy his paintings.

At the age of seventy-nine he wrote that for Christmas just past he had eighteen pensioners around home, he had his painting of: 'The Wise Men Going into the Stable', hanging outside and all lit up. "*We all sat round and sang carols and old songs together.*"

Still people wanted to buy his paintings, but Tom declared that he was a Coalville man and he wanted his paintings to stay in Coalville. He never did sell any, and they eventually passed down to Betty and Norma. He simply said: "*I'm only an amateur!*"

I have studied the quality of his paintings, and realise the quality and ability within the man himself. I find it extraordinary that the life-worn, swollen fingers of Tom could paint with such a degree of fineness and finesse, and with no technical training! I feel sure that Tom, if born at a later age would certainly have been a famous artist. As it is Tom Wood was a very good, caring and brave man, and certainly one of Coalville Town's finest.

Tom Wood passed away in Leicester in 1984.

It has been a privilege to share this life story, and I thank Tom's stepdaughter, Betty Newton of Hugglescote, and her son, Robert, who lovingly and

Coalville and District Male Voice Choir 1961

Back row; from the left: T. Lilley, J. Skellington, **TOM WOOD**, A. Ward, G. Handy, H. Waterfield, R. Anderson, ? Haines, J. Eames, W. Benniston, B. Wilson, P. Bennett, Joe Kirk.
Middle row; from the left: K. Hodges, L. Tyler, Reginald Wardle, G. Lewin, B. Lester, O. Gilberd, E. Sparham, T. Hodges, G. Munday, B. Palmer, P. Collins, G. Willet, B. Cook, G. Wilson, C. Bishop, L. Heath, S. Shaw.
Front row; from the left: Mary Shaw, C. Tyler, L. Anderson, Reverend F. Parker, T. Smith, J. Reid, T. Spare, A. Bevin (Snr).
Tom Wood in the company of friends as a member of the celebrated Coalville Male Voice Choir, many of which were veterans of the Great and Second World War.
Reginald Wardle's wife, Elsie (nee Robinson), was the daughter of Hetty, my grandfather's (Charles Hatter) sister.

proudly cares for Tom's old photographs and war medals. Betty's sister, Norma, married Philip Emmerson, son of the famed Jabez Emmerson of the Famous Fifty.

As a footnote I feel sure that Tom must have been very proud of his uncle, Sergeant Edwin James Collier (86523), who lived at 56, Melbourne Street in Coalville.

Originally a frontline soldier in the 2nd Battalion Royal Leicestershire Regiment, he was transferred to the 176 Tunnelling Company, Royal Engineer's Detachment R.D.C. in 1915.

More can be read of the brave sapper in the Great War Tunnellers section of this book.

Other local men who served with Tom Wood in the Seventh Leicestershire and lost their lives: The brothers James and John Adcock of Stanton-under-Bardon, Albert Barker of Loughborough, John Barrs of Ibstock, Eric Barsby of Loughborough, Ernest Batho of Coalville, John Black of Loughborough, Albert Bowler of Shepshed, George Bradbury of Ashby de la Zouch, Gilman Bramley of Loughborough, Thomas Brown of Thornton, Frederick Burgess of Castle Donington, George Chawner and Cornelius Clayton of Ashby de la Zouch, Mathew Cockerill of Loughborough, Joseph Cross of Kegworth, Albert Darby of Shepshed, George Doughty of Kegworth, Walter Gould of Loughborough, Frank Gray of Ibstock, Harry Greaves of Castle Donington, Walter Hammond of Loughborough, Ernest Harper of Coalville, Frederick Harper of Measham, Joseph Haywood of Markfield, Thomas Hickin of Market Bosworth, Walter Hill of Hugglescote, Joseph Hodgkinson of Whitwick, William Hulin of Loughborough, Horace Hunt of Markfield, William Hutchinson of Kegworth, John Impett of Loughborough, Herbert Ingram of Groby, Wilfred Jarvis of Market Bosworth, Reuben Kent of Measham, Thomas Kinson of Measham, William Leech of Swannington, George Lovett of Mountsorrel, Albert Marlow of Barrow-on-Soar, George Mathews of Loughborough, Frank Moore of

Breedon-on-the-Hill, Arthur Ottey of Ibstock, Thomas Robey of Loughborough, Allen Rossell of Shepshed, Ambrose Samson of Measham, Walter Sharp of Loughborough, Fred and William Shillcross of Kegworth, John Simmons of Loughborough, Amos Smith of Barrow-on-Soar, Arthur Smith of Swannington, Oliver Smith of Loughborough, Percy Smith of Sileby, Frederick Spencer of Long Whatton, Charles Stanford of Whitwick, William Stott of Ashby de la Zouch, Cornelius Summers of Moira, John Taylor of Mountsorrel, George Thornton of Ashby de la Zouch, Robert Timmins of Ibstock, Percy Tookey of Whitwick, John Waldron of Shepshed, Joseph Waring of Sileby, Frederick West of Loughborough, Ernest Wheatley of Twycross, Michael Wileman of Moira, and George Woolley of Kegworth.

Five hundred and one soldiers of the Seventh Leicestershire Battalion died in the Great War.

THE WORTLEY FAMILY
ANOTHER OF COALVILLE'S FINEST

In the early years of the second decade of the twentieth century, Amos Wortley, a portly middle-aged man who was born in 1857 and his beloved wife, Mary Ann (nee Pape), were enjoying a spiritually rich and bountiful life together. They had nurtured and raised seven fit and healthy children, all were God fearing and a credit to society. Martha was born 1880, Elizabeth 1883, Benjamin 1887, Robert 1888, Harry 1891, Harold Amos 1892 and Archie 1899/1900.

By 1914 most of their children had left the family nest, and the middle years of their lives revolved around Christ Church, Coalville. Amos was, and had been for many years, the churchwarden there, and twice every Sunday he put on his best coat and bowler-hat to walk the few hundred yards to his church. Additionally he owned and managed a successful shop that made and repaired shoes. They resided at 20, Hotel Street, within the town and were well liked and respected within the community. In his younger days Amos was a keen sportsman, and in middle age maintained a keen interest in sport by sitting on the committee of Coalville Athletic Club. Over many years Amos, together with fourteen members of that club organised a multitude of fetes, social evenings, football and cricket matches with the objective of raising sufficient funds to **purchase a park for the town**. They achieved their objective and I believe the town should be eternally grateful. It is important that the park be maintained by the local council to the highest standard, a haven for leisurely relaxation in a world of bustle and where our countryside is disappearing under concrete and glass!

The year 1914 not only signified the opening of the Great War, it also abruptly ended nearly forty years of marital bliss when Amos died at early age of fifty-seven years, leaving Mary grief stricken. He lies buried in the small cemetery just to the rear of the church, its location signifying the appreciation and grateful respect for a devout gentleman! Amos had displayed commendable time and effort working on behalf of **Christ's** Church.

Mary, though still grieving became genuinely worried concerning the war and its implications for her two youngest sons, twenty-two year old Harold and fourteen year old Archie.

Harold was employed at Messrs. T. and J. Jones Elastic Web factory on the town's Belvoir Road, later taken over by Joseph Burgess and Sons Ltd. My dear grandmother, Hetty Palmer, was employed there at the same time. Harold also learned to repair shoes in his father's shop and occasionally helped out afterwards. His youngest daughter, Sheila, told me of a tragic and historic event he could recall when as a lad he stood with his father outside the pit gates. It was on the 19th April 1898 and a crowd was waiting for news of the trapped miners at Whitwick Pit. He also said that the family attended the funerals of the bodies recovered!

In 1915 he married local girl, Florrie Read, and

Gunner Harold Amos Wortley of the Royal Artillery in 1915.

shortly afterwards enlisted at Coalville into the Royal Artillery, and much to his mother's relief was able to spend the war years in England. His service number was 134120, and was in the Royal Garrison Artillery in the London Heavy Battery. It is known he spent his early years driving ammunition for the Western Front from London to Folkestone, but later was on anti-aircraft guns in southern England, what with London being bombed by Zeppelins and giant German Gotha bombers, a foretaste of the London Blitz of 1940-1 during World War 2. His home address was given as 97, Melbourne Street, Coalville.

Harold Amos Wortley returned to his wife, Florrie, after the war and they had five children: Eric, Sylvia, Harry, Colin and Sheila the youngest.

The Vicar of Christ Church, Reverend Hoskins, encouraged **Archie**, the youngest son to become a choirboy and also an altar-server, it was a wise choice and he adored singing and the companionship of the church. Upon leaving school he became a Telegram Messenger, and was a friend of Clifford Scott who held a similar position and was one of the Famous Fifty.

Archie liked his uniform, and a photograph

shows him looking very smart, however, he was soon to change it for another of rustic colouring.

It was almost certainly in late 1916 that the under-age Archie enlisted at Coalville into the 2/4th King's Own Yorkshire Light Infantry. Sheila Millington (nee Wortley) tells me: *"My grandmother, Mary, spent two years worrying about him and not knowing where he was. She absolutely dreaded anyone knocking on the door, she always felt it could be a telegram with bad news!"*

As the years passed she became more relaxed and positive, especially since the allied armies had achieved great victories; the end of the war looked in sight. **Less than one week** before the Armistice a knock came on the door. A telegram was delivered (ironically so) and placed in her hand. She politely thanked the boy and settled in a chair at the dining table. Slowly, very slowly Mary opened the official letter - **Private Archie Wortley had been killed, whilst on active duty in France!** Shortly afterwards she instinctively wanted to see her son's grave, and to know how and where he had died, unfortunately no such details were ever given! Mary, grief stricken, sobbed believing that her youngest son was lost to

Churchwarden Amos Wortley at the entrance to Christ Church. Circa 1908.

the family forever! Indeed, Archie was lost to the family for eighty-three years, until in 2001 a friend of the family researched and found that he was killed on the 4th November 1918. Archie's body was recovered and he lies in a small cemetery with just over one hundred comrades. (Grave E9, at Villers-Pol Communal Cemetery. (259,2) France.

I find it so sad to relate that Archie died exactly one week before the end of the Great War.

On that very same Monday morning that eighteen years old Archie was killed, my grandfather, Charles Hatter, was marrying Hetty Palmer at nearby Ebenezer Baptist Chapel. My grandparent's lives were just about to blossom as young Archie's faded and fell in a violent end.

The 2nd/4th King's Own was fighting on the French-Belgium borders, when Sir Douglas Haig decided that one final battle would bring the war to an immediate conclusion. Which it did! The Battle of Valenciennes, sixty kilometres (forty miles) east of Arras, was fought against some eight German Divisions. The attacking forces consisted of British and Canadian troops of the First, Third and Fourth Armies together with various French units. On the

Private Archie Wortley. 2/4th King's Own Yorkshire Light Infantry in 1916. (Aged sixteen years).

night of November 3rd/4th the Germans began to withdraw from the Le Quesnoy-Valenciennes Front. Just before dawn, when the moonless night was at its darkest on Monday 4th November, the Allies opened with a powerful creeping barrage to accompany an infantry thrust. The progress was troublesome and slow because of the swampy countryside - the river Sambre and a multitude of streams had created a clinging and sucking quagmire. The allied troops were pleased en-route to have the remains of the Mormal Forest to offer a degree of shelter and cover from machine-gun and sniper fire. The attack was eventually successful, however, the 2nd/4th's War Diary reported that the Germans fought gallantly and with dogged resistance.

The majority of the Battalion's fatalities during the battle were from machine-gun and some from small arms fire. It transpired that several bullets riddled the eighteen-year-old body of Archie! The fearsome nature of the machine-gun is that it usually results in a very quick death, and we hope this was the case.

The name of Private Archie A. Wortley can be clearly read on the Coalville Clock Tower Memorial. It can also be seen in Christ Church's Book of Communion - 'In memory of H. Baun, S. Brown, O. Peck and A. Wortley, servers of the altar who gave their lives in the 1914-18 War.'

Benjamin, who had been assisting his father in the shop, was twenty-seven years old when his father died, and he continued the business to the same high standard.

Robert, a year younger than his brother above became churchwarden of All Saints Church, a sister church of Christ Church. Following the closure of the earlier church he took over the role that his father performed so magnificently at Christ Church for many years.

Harry was twenty-three years old, married and with children when his father died. He immediately invited his mother to stay with them at 20, Hotel Street. Sadly Mary's sight faded very badly in older age until being registered as blind.

Another fine family that typified the bedrock of early twentieth century society.

Many thanks to Sheila Millington (nee Wortley) for the information and photographs.

THE WILLIAMS BROTHERS

Israel Williams was a farmer, and he and is wife, Frances (nee Rue), moved from Long Eaton, then a village twelve kilometres (eight miles) due west of Derby, to live at Quorndon (Quorn), a village three kilometres southeast of Loughborough. The couple lived in one of the Kirbell Cottages on the Barrow Road and had three daughters and four sons, and the latter four all enlisted into the Forces within the first two months of the 1914-18 War.

Private Henry Williams 7th Leicestershire Regiment

Henry James Williams was born at Ratcliffe-on-Soar, near to Long Eaton, and enlisted at Loughborough during October 1914. He was allocated to the Seventh (Service) Leicestershire Battalion, a part of Kitchener's New Army. In late 1914 the army was ill prepared to equip and accommodate the large amount of recruits who were joining the Colours. Whilst the Battalion was undergoing training at Aldershot, the volunteers were living and sleeping under canvas. The wintry conditions were bitterly cold and many a recruit became infected and suffered with a pneumonia virus, with several dying as a result. Henry contracted the virulent illness and died within a matter of days on the 26th December, 1914. His heart-broken parents travelled down by train to attend the funeral, which was held at the Gun Hill Cemetery, Aldershot, and Henry is buried nearby.

Another brother, **Ben Williams**, enlisted at Loughborough in September 1914 and was allocated into the Northumberland Fusiliers. He received a wound to the ankle in late May 1915, during the tail end of the 2nd Battle of Ypres in Belgium. Ben was hospitalised in England for a time but recovered quickly to return to the frontline. Later in that year he was again wounded, this time to the arm and spent a period in Woolwich Hospital, followed by recuperation at his parent's home at Quorn. He again returned to his unit, who were at that time fighting the Bulgarians in the Salonican Campaign, only to be wounded yet again and taken to hospital at Cairo, Egypt. Returning to his unit once again he was sent home in 1916 suffering from shell shock. Ben was also thoroughly depressed and he brought his entire kit home, and announced that he would not be returning to the battlefields! When his leave was over his parents (unwillingly) had to bully and push him to the local railway station, with sister, Emily, dragging his heavy kit bag all of the way. He recovered, and his fine work at the frontline was appreciated and he returned home for the Christmas of 1917. Two days after the German spring-offensive started on March 21st 1918, Ben was captured and imprisoned in a German prisoner-of-war-camp. Conditions were dire, and food supplies were infrequent and twice he was sent to hospital for breakdowns in health. Ben told his family that he owed his life to a Belgium lady and her daughter who gave him a little food. He finally returned home in 1919, but was never a fit man again and earlier illnesses left him with digestive problems for the remainder of his life.

The third brother, **Frank Williams**, enlisted with Ben at Loughborough into the Northumberland Fusiliers; it is believed the Fusiliers had a recruiting campaign in the county at that time. He was wounded in June 1915 when he was a lance corporal and entered Woolwich Hospital to recover. Frank was a very tall man, six feet four inches, and at some time during his military career was transferred to the Guards, returning home on leave wearing a Busby!

The final brother, **Roland Williams**, joined the Royal Navy in early September 1914 and was trained

Private Ben Williams (marked) of the Northumberland Fusiliers in 1914.

as a Gunner at H.M.S. '*Magnificent*'. He served on H.M.S. '*Hibernia*' and witnessed the evacuation of the Dardanelles in 1915, and kept a diary of events as he saw it. He also served aboard H.M.S. '*Oberon*', which was torpedoed in the Mediterranean Sea but which kept afloat long enough to reach port, also H.M.S. '*Tenedos*'. Whether it was a typical complaint for all gunners in the Great War, but Roland, as a result of his experiences became prematurely deaf. Gnr. Williams also served aboard submarines in the later years of the war, regrettably his memories have not been recorded.

The Gallipoli Campaign is well documented in our history books as one of the bloodiest and most futile battles in our history.

Briefly, the military intention was to ensure the Dardanelles Straits remained open to the Sea of Marmara and hence entry to the Black Sea. By doing so the Allies could supply military equipment to our Russian colleagues, and in turn receive grain and other resources. It was also considered an ideal opportunity to defeat and remove Turkey (one of the Central Alliance) from the war. Originally it was hoped that a naval bombardment of the Straits by battleships would suffice, however, following the loss of several capital ships steps were taken to land a force of British, French, Australian and New Zealand (Anzacs) and Indian troops for late April 1915. The annals of history illustrate that names such as Suvla Bay, Anzac Cove and Cape Helles became synonymous with bravery, death, plagues of flies, dysentery, toweringly high temperatures and severe frosts.

The weather in late November 1915 was dreadful: thunder and lightning, torrential rain and hail, sweeping stores and field kitchens away, drowning mules. Artillery guns sank in treacly-thick mud. Early December brought heavy snow and freezing temperatures making guns and rifles jam, and worst still the troops had only been issued with tropical clothing. When the snow abated, sixteen thousand men had to be forwarded to hospitals suffering from exposure and frostbite. The decision to evacuate was taken by Lord Kitchener on the 7th December 1915; it involved the 'retirement' of one hundred and thirty-four thousand men, fourteen thousand horses and mules and four hundred guns. The troop-evacuation commenced on the third week of the month from Anzac Cove and Suvla Bay. Small landing boats and armoured 'Beetle' craft took the men from the shore to the waiting ships during hours of darkness. Small garrisons were left to man the posts, and fortunately the Turks failed to suspect the withdrawal. The garrisons, together with heavy bombardments from the waiting capital ships repelled any Turkish aggression. Later Cape Helles was evacuated during the early part of January 1916.

Lance Corporal Frank Williams, Northumberland Fusiliers in Woolwich Hospital

Throughout the evacuation men wrapped canvas around their feet to prevent any noise, and not a whisper was heard. The Turks, to their huge embarrassment never suspected a thing!

Roland's diary is primarily concerned with the evacuation.

THE DIARY OF
ROLAND WILLIAMS 1915-1916

A Trip To The Dardanelles
aboard H.M.S. Hibernia.

Seaman Roland Williams on the Hibernia 1916

Four battleships of the King Edward V11 class were ordered to Greece owing to diplomatic relations being brought to a crisis over Allied landings in October 1915 at Salonica. (Ten kilometres south of Germany's ally, Bulgaria). The long and short of it was that the troops that landed there were to cease-fire and to embark at once. Of course to England this seemed impracticable, so the four ships were sent in case of trouble!

Out of the four ships that started only two eventually arrived at our Malta base, the other two having to return to Scapa Flow after being damaged by bad weather. I was aboard H.M.S. 'Hibernia', with Admiral Freemantle on board, and the other ship, H.M.S. 'Zealandia', arrived after a very nasty voyage. On the way the admiral told the ship's company that they were out to make a name for the British Navy and themselves. Everyman agreed, and we knew this would not be a pleasure trip.

The situation at the Dardanelles in December changed all of our plans, and we had to steam there to cover the evacuation.

The Bombardment.

We pounded the enemy with our heavy guns, especially to Cape Helles, Achi Baba, and Hill 606. On the Asiatic side are the City of Troy and the plains of Troy, with stretches of ground between the hills.

One stretch held a gun, which we called 'Asiastic Ann', but we couldn't position it to return fire.

The Evacuation.

The following conversation was overheard of an army officer telling his men to be prepared for anything, and I can swear that it is totally true: "Well men, I want to have a few words on what we are doing. I want to be perfectly candid; there is no point in filling you with false hopes. First of all you will have to fight to get out of this hole (Cape Helles), fight for the inches that you retire upon! I very much

doubt whether a navy even three times as strong as ours will get us off here. We rely entirely on our lads in blue whether the Turks know or don't! Maybe it will be every man for himself, but mind how you board the boats. They are not ours but the Navy's!

The evacuation started in December and was carried out at night; some of the evacuees went to Salonica. The weather is very cold.

January 1st 1916. *Hibernia raised steam and stood by to go to sea, as usual to continue bombarding the enemy, but we eventually had to cry-off for the day. About mid-day the wind rose to a gale, so we had to up-anchor and steam round to Alicki Bay, which is the other side of land jutting out from Imbros Island. (Base rest camp for the pongoes). Another day's agony over.*

January 2nd. *Got-up anchor at 12.30 pm and steamed across to the peninsular. Our heavy guns opened fire and continued with the bombardment until 4.30 pm. We then proceeded to our anchorage at Alicki Bay, arriving at 5.00 pm.*

January 3rd. *Proceeded to sea in the full moon at 10.30 pm and arrived at the entrance to the Dardanelles. We dropped our buoy and carried out a very good bombardment according to information received from the Army Signallers. What a picture, the flash of the guns, the explosions and the moon above. I wont forget this in a hurry.*

January 4th. Started the day coaling the ship with 750 tonnes, finishing at 2.30 am. Proceeded to sea and went round to the other side of Alicki Bay. Relief diving parties told us to clear a hauser from a tug's screw, eventually clearing it at daybreak. Our companion ship, H.M.S. 'Russell', spent the day bombarding the Turks and arrived back at 5.00 pm. Weather sprang-up very rough and loppy, so we had to drop a second anchor or we would have ended up ashore. A watch was kept on the anchors all night as the storm's power increased. A coaling party of twenty-five hands went to coal-up a transport ship, but they couldn't get back because the sea was too rough! A trawler was driven ashore by the storm during the night. (A North Sea fishing trawler used for minesweeping).

January 5th. All ships raised steam and proceeded to Alicki Bay, arriving about 11.00 am. We sent out all boats and received a small amount of stores. Weather is now fairly decent.

January 6th. Proceeded to sea about 10.00 am. Bombarded Kum Kale and adjacent forts with our 12-inch, 9.2's and 6-inch shells, and did extensive damage to concealed batteries. We knew their positions because they were located for us by our airmen. These brave pilots take off from airboats that are boats with flat tops.

They also signalled the results of our guns damage by wireless. Ceased at 4.30 pm and returned to Kephalo for 5.15 pm.

January 7th. Having a standoff today. The Hibernia's hydraulic salvage party landed in order to salve what vessels they could and to blow-up the rest.

At 1.15 pm the ammunition ship came alongside, we took aboard 500 shrapnel shells as well as 12-inch, 9.2's and 6-inch. Finished loading about 11.00 pm.

January 8th. All ships proceeded to sea at about 10.30 am in execution of orders planned by Admiral Browning. A general heavy assault by all ships commenced at noon on Achi Baba, fairly successful, and we returned to base harbour at 4.30 pm. Got under-way again at 9.30 pm to provide cover for our troops during their evacuation from Cape Helles. No trouble at all from sleepy Turks, and it went on until the early hours! Sir Ian Hamilton congratulated us all on being successful, having only one casualty, he being knocked-out by the concussion of a shell bursting!

A large dugout was constructed by our troops under cover of our guns, and provisions were left in case any stragglers or escaped prisoners managed to return to our lines.

January 9th. We returned to harbour about 5.30 am after being extremely successful in bluffing the Turks during our darkness evacuation.

An armed boat (a Beetle) belonging to us was sent to the dugout and retrieved six of our men. On the way back to us they had some miraculous escapes from Turkish machine-gun fire and shells, etc.

Commander Sneyd (Royal Navy) joined the ship and for once in a while we received some mail.

January 10th. Our usual salvage gang went ashore to get a few wrecks out of the way. (Demolition).

January 11th. Same parties landed to shift the billets. A man belonging to H.M.S. 'Russell' was killed when an armoured hatch fell onto his head. H.M.S. 'Laforey' arrived carrying the bodies of two of our brave airmen who were killed in an engagement at one thousand feet!

January 12th. We coaled-up a transport-vessel all night. We stood by our usual routine during the day and later prepared to take on coal ourselves.

January 14th. Weather too rough and so we have to stow-away our coaling gear.

January 15th. Salvage team landed to demolish another boat that had gone ashore. A quiet day, nothing doing.

January 16th. Usual routines. Shifted billets. Steamed round to Alicki Bay at 4.00 pm.

January 17th. Enemy aircraft raided us. H.M.S. 'Zealandia' was hit by bombs with two or three men being killed. In the afternoon proceeded to sea. We had to have a shot or two at the town of Gallipoli, in line with the Narrows. We got hit three times, one shell going completely through our funnel without exploding. The Monitor ship 'Abercrombie' assisted us. Arrived back at Kephalo about 5.00 pm. We had another enemy air raid but we drove them off with gunfire!

January 18th. We got underway at 8.00 am and arrived at Alicki Bay for 9.30 am. Prepared to take onboard coal now sea calmer.

January 19th. A party went ashore to place a large beacon on one of the surrounding hills. Zealandia meantime bombarded the peninsular with heavy shells.

January 20th. Our Salvage team went ashore and managed to get the steamer 'Jersey' off the beach.

January 21st. Got underway and steamed to Kephalo, arriving at 7.00 am.

January 22nd. Admiral Freemantle left us and took all of his belongings to Russel. Rumour is we are about to leave for England.

January 23rd. Rumour is true. We left Alicki Bay at 4.00 pm and headed for Mudros Bay. We took aboard 890 tonnes of coal and left Mudros Bay at 11.30 pm with a destination of Gibraltar. Received another batch of mail and also some spuds, the first for a long time.

January 24th. Cleaned outer paintwork. The weather is fairly good and we undertook a series of evolutions.

January 25th. Passed Malta about 9.00 am. Seamen told-off for small steaming parties, a full complement of stokers was not available.

January 26th. Left Gibraltar for England - home and beauty. We had to zigzag all over the ocean because of the enemy submarine threat.

January 27th. Still at sea. Wet through to the skin from heavy seas. Very cheerful weather later in day.

January 28th. Weather is fairly calm so we took advantage and carried out target practice.

Gun-layer and acting Gh 11 firing 12 rounds of 12 pounders. Men qualifying for seaman-gun fired 9 rounds with 3 pounders, which the ship's company didn't go much on! (Didn't enjoy).

January 29th. Arrived back at Gibraltar, but not going to England as thought. Disappointed. Took more coal aboard, 1210 tonnes and finished at 6.00 pm. Captain told us that he couldn't tell us where we were going, but we would not object if we knew. Gave bravery medals to six petty officers.

January 30th. Given two hours leave on the Gibraltar Rock, but all the pubs were shut, so it was not up to much. Very serene. We are all a bit down!

January 31st. Zealandia arrived and took on 1500 tonnes of coal, and we fetched another batch of mail from her. We also took aboard some stores. Later given another two hours leave, which was a bit better. I continued to serve in the Royal navy until the end of the war in 1918.

The Allies lost over fifty thousand lives, with twice that amount suffering from wounds and debilitating illnesses. Turkish figures are unknown, but are believed to be equivalent in terms of combat deaths. The town of Bury lost sixteen hundred men from three battalions during the campaign. The Lancashire town is the regimental home of the Lancashire Fusiliers, who won Six V.C.s 'Before Breakfast' at Gallipoli!

Many thanks to Quorn's Jessie Long, niece of the above four brothers.

FRANCIS AND WILLIAM WILLIAMSON

Terry Williamson lives and works close to the centre of Coalville. For many a year Terry subjected himself to a recurring theme, namely, how to obtain details regarding the death of his great-uncle Francis, during the Great War. On a recent trip to the National Archives at Kew, he found only disappointment due to so many military records being burnt in the 1940-1 Blitz on London. Only recently has information been found and scripted regarding his great-uncle, and that of his grandfather, William, who served in the Royal Navy during the same war.

Terry's great-grandfather, Joseph Edward Williamson and his great-grandmother, Ellen Margaret (nee Mann) lived at Leicester and had ten children, tragically only the following survived into adulthood: William, Francis, Catherine, Margaret, Emily and John.

Seventeen year old Private Francis Williamson seated on the right—2nd Leicestershire Battalion. Circa summer 1914.

Francis Edward Williamson, invariably called **Frank**, was born on the 16th April 1897 at 6, Ernest Cottages on Willow Street, Leicester. Shortly afterwards the family moved to 7, Wood Hill, still at Leicester, and it was at that address that he and his siblings grew-up. Upon leaving school he worked in a shoe-manufacturing factory, and subsequently applied whilst underage to join the Leicestershire Regiment. Twice his father prevented him from enlisting, however on the third occasion he decided to let his son follow his dream. He enlisted at Leicester into the 2nd Battalion, with the service number 9867, and almost immediately the Great War started.

In August 1914 the 2nd Battalion was quartered at Delhi and Ranikhet, India. Within a few days a telegram ordered them to mobilise and return to Europe. On the 15th September 1914, sections sailed from Karachi on the '*Devanha*' and the following day the remainder on the '*Elephanta*'. The 12th October 1914 saw the Battalion disembark at Marseilles, southern France, and reorganised in Le Valentine Camp. They were part of the Garhwal Brigade, under Major-General H.D.U. Keary, C.B. D.S.O. With them were the 2nd Battalion of the 3rd Ghurkha Rifles, together with the 1st and 2nd Battalions of the 39th Garhwal Rifles.

The soldiers of the 1st and 2nd Battalions of the Leicestershire Regiment were professionals (regulars), and as soon as the war started, **reservists** at home: fit ex-regulars under a certain age and within a period of leaving the Colours, were ordered to report to their mother battalions. As the battalion's numbers fell in battle they were topped-up by volunteers following a period of intensive training, or trained soldiers from other units following recovery from wounds.

Frank Williamson was posted to 'A' Company of the 2nd Battalion. He, together with a group of reservists, including William Saddington, Ernest Hall, Jack Sheffield and Harry Brown joined the Battalion in France shortly after its arrival from India.

Towards the end of October the Garhwal Brigade, as part of the Indian Army Corps, was engaged on the Western Front, in trenches near to La Bassee. The area had taken a pounding from German explosive shells and badly damaged trenches were alongside bogs and ditches. They fought in the Battle of that name, and later at nearby Festubert a few weeks later, where they received high acclaim for their efforts. January and February in 1915 were relatively quiet on this Front.

Brigadier-General C.G. Blackader D.S.O

commanded the Brigade, and he became a famous figure enjoying much success until dying of rabies (from a dog bite).

The 2nd Battalion Leicestershire's War Diary for 10th March 1915 quotes: *'All in position by 5 am. At 7.30 am the artillery bombardment commenced. At 8.05 am 'B' and 'C' Companies advanced, each company having two platoons in the front line closely supported by the two other platoons in the second line.'* This was the opening for the massive Battle of Neuve Chapelle that has been written about earlier in the book.

March 1915 saw a general reorganisation, and the Garhwal Brigade became a combination of the 2nd Leicestershire, 3rd London Regiment, The Garhal Rifles, 2nd Battalion of 3rd Ghurkhas, and the 2nd Battalion of the 8th Ghurkhas.

The summer continued to see the 2nd Leicestershire fighting around the La Bassee Sector, until they travelled some six kilometres (four miles) south. Here, together with many other units, they suffered very heavy casualties on the opening day of the Battle of Loos, the 25th September 1915. The Battalion's casualty list was twenty officers and four hundred and thirty other ranks either killed, wounded, missing or gassed. This battle is described in the essay regarding Bernard Hatter. During October a topping-up of nineteen officers and four hundred and ninety six other ranks offset some of the losses!

Ellen and Joseph Williamson. Circa late 1920s.

On November 3rd the Brigade was relieved from the trenches, marched to Thiennes and on November 7th they entrained for Marseilles. On the 10th they sailed aboard *'Clan MacGillivray'* and S.S. *'Oranda'* to arrive at Alexandria on the North African coast on November 16th. They then entrained for the Suez, continued to the River Tigris and upstream to Basra in Mesopotamia (present day Iraq) for the 6th December 1915, arriving one year into the Mesopotamian Campaign against the Turks. Seven days later they were at Ali Gharbi and positioned on a defensive perimeter.

Xmas card sent from Mesopotamia by Frank Williamson to his family at 7, Wood Hill.

At some time after his arrival in Mesopotamia **Frank Williamson sent a Christmas card home** (see photograph) and he wrote: *'I have been round Baghdad but I do not think much of the place, very dirty. Of course our people are beginning to make it look better but it will be a long time before they make it properly. It is not safe to walk about here without a bayonet and fortunately none of the Arabs seem to like that bit of steel!'*

The 2nd Leicestershire was now part of the 28th Infantry Brigade, which contained the 51st and 53rd Sikhs and the 56th Rifles. Major-General Aylmer was in command, and he issued the following Order of the Day: *"We have to relieve our brother soldiers at Kut-al-Amar, who for a month have most gallantly repulsed every hostile assault, such a task must appeal very deeply to us all - every man must do his utmost!"* Following this order on the 4th January 1916, the Brigade fought in the Battle of Shaikh Saad. The advance against the Turks began on January 5th with the Battalion taking the central role, and witnessed enemy cavalry lying dead on the banks of the Tigris. They moved forward into a line of Companies in fours at fifty pace intervals behind the 56th Rifles. The attack was met by heavy rifle and machine-gun fire, with enemy cavalrymen occasionally outflanking the Brigade, so they welcomed nightfall but not the rainfall. On January 7th with a splendid assault, the Brigade stormed the Turkish trenches. The 2nd Leicestershire came across many Turkish dead and eighty prisoners were taken, whilst they had sixteen officers and three hundred and three other ranks killed or wounded.

The conditions were dreadful, with too few doctors, nurses and little accommodation for the wounded. Some wounded had to be left day and night on the ground, with insufficient clothing, food and treatment! One officer wrote: *'It rained heavily and was freezing cold and the mud was awful, the sufferings of the wounded was horrible.'*

At 4.00 pm on January 13th another attack was started against a newish position taken up by the Turks, close to the Suwaikiya Marsh and the Tigris River. The Turks had eleven thousand troops there, and under cover of a barrage the 2nd Leicestershire and the 56th Rifles attacked the Wadi. The attack was *'pushed forward with speed and determination;'* however, fierce machine-gun crossfire meant that they had to retire under cover of darkness. The Battalion lost four officers wounded and one hundred and ninety seven other ranks killed or wounded.

The Turks fell back to an even stronger position known as the Umm-el-Hanna Defile. Attacks were made but heavy rain stopped the battle.

For two months the Brigade's patience and resolve was tested whilst it remained stationary as continuous rain made the Tigris flood much of the

The only battlefield photograph of Francis Williamson in 1917, on the left. It is of poor quality but it justifies its entry by showing the swellings below his eyes and the sunken cheeks

surrounding area. The worrying concern was would the garrison at Kut hold out?

The central point in the Turkish defences between the Tigris and the Shatt-el-Hai was a stronghold known as the Dujaila Redoubt. The Brigade eventually attacked this on March 8th. The War Diary reads: *'Battalion moved forward in two lines of platoon columns. Owing to heavy casualties were compelled to entrench four hundred yards from enemy position.'* A further attack enabled them to entrench two hundred yards from the enemy. Turkish shellfire then made the situation untenable and the action had to be curtailed.

On 3rd April 1916 another draft of two hundred and ninety six non-commissioned officers arrived from England to top-up the Battalion's strength.

Francis Williamson with the 2nd Leicestershire Battalion in Mesopotamia 1916. Second row from the back, 4th from the right.

The War Diary for April 5th and 6th, *'Heavy bombardment on enemy's frontline trenches. Enemy retired to Fallahiya, about two miles. This was attacked and carried and the enemy retired to Sannaiyat. Ordered to carry out night march and to attack at dawn. Compelled to halt through very heavy casualties, so entrenched.'*

An eyewitness wrote: *'Eleven hundred in the 28th Brigade alone fell in the first few minutes, as they attacked strong fortifications across an open plain. A Staff Officer handed me his glasses and asked why a line of khaki, about five hundred yards from the Turkish Line, had not dug themselves in. I replied they're dead.'* The Battalion lost one officer and forty-five dead and nine officers and two hundred and seventy six wounded or missing.

On April 21st orders were issued to attack the Sannaiyat position. The attack commenced on the 22nd and the 28th Brigade advanced in support in four lines, three hundred yards behind the leading waves and each line at three hundred yard intervals. The going was very heavy with thick mud, and floods had seriously narrowed the attacking front. Some of the attackers were up to their knees in mud and water, and when the Turks counter-attacked our troops were forced to retire. General Lake wrote: *'The same troops had attacked time and again to assault strong positions held by a determined enemy. They did all that man could do to overcome, not only the enemy, but also exceptional climatic and physical obstacles, and with rations being insufficient for exertions undergone.'*

Corporal Francis Edward Williamson lost his life during that attack. It cannot be verified but the family have always understood that Frank was killed when a bullet hit him in the mouth.

Whatever happened to the twenty year old his body was never found; no doubt it sank with many others into the cratered quagmire of a battlefield!

On April 29th, after a siege of five months, the British flag at Kut was hauled down and the garrison surrendered and passed into hideous captivity. So near and yet so far away!

The summer months arrived and as the temperatures soared to between 110-120 degrees F (40C), so did the sickness and disease. One Battalion officer quoted: *'We have five effective officers and*

150-200 men. The men's backs are black, covered in flies, and you have to fight to bring food to your mouth!' The battles raged to Kut-al-Amara and losses continued to be heavy. Early January 1918 saw the Battalion in Egypt and Palestine and advancing up the coast, marching into Beirut on the 9th October 1918, and onto Tripoli.

On November 7th the following gracious message was published, General Sir Edmund Allenby had received it from His Majesty the King - *'I wish to express My admiration for the spirit and endurance of the troops under your command, who,*

Ellen Williamson (left) with daughter, Emily outside 7, Wood Hill, Leicester. Circa 1914.

7, Wood Hill, Leicester in 2004. The iron railings were stripped away to help the war effort in 1940.

The medals awarded to Corporal Francis Williamson in 1921. Signed for by his father, Joseph.

Stoker Bill Williamson standing on the right. Circa 1920.

regardless of fatigue and hardships, have so pressed the retreating Turkish as to overcome all resistance. Their efforts have been deservedly rewarded by the complete surrender of the Turkish Forces. This is a glorious and memorable achievement, and on behalf of your grateful fellow countrymen I thank you and all ranks of the Egyptian Expeditionary Force.' Corporal Francis Edward Williamson is remembered with honour on the Basra Memorial in Iraq.

A mystery surrounds Frank some eighty-seven years after his death. On the 16th March 1918 a silk card '1918 Souvenir de France' was received by his family. The writing on the back appears to have been rubbed-out and only the date and the signature can be read with ease. The letter is signed, 'Frank'. No one knows of another Frank, no one can confirm his signature and his niece, Theresa Noonan, wonders if he survived his injury in Mesopotamia and was transferred to the Labour Corps in France. This Corps consisted of men who had been wounded but had been withdrawn from frontline duties until such time they were A1. The Corps was 400,000 strong by November 1918. Unless a photograph appears showing Frank in France in 1918 the mystery will remain unsolved.

Terry's grandfather, **William Joseph Williamson**, 'Bill', was born on the 10th August 1892. He too worked in a shoe-manufacturing factory until he enlisted into the Royal Navy on the 10th December 1909, service number K 5358. His first posting was aboard H.M.S. *'Renown'*. There followed service aboard *'Victoria'*, *'Illustrious'* and when the Great War started he was a 1st Class Stoker/ Acting Leading Stoker with a good conduct badge aboard H.M.S. *'Achilles'*. As the war progressed he was also aboard *'Victory'*, *'Terrible'* and *'Attentive'* (*Nubian*), where he was a Leading Stoker. Whilst on the *'Woolwich'* (*Tristram*) as a Stoker- Petty Officer he received a second good conduct badge. He finished the war on the *'Columbine'* and was awarded 1914,15,16,17,18 Chevrons together with the 1914-18 Star, Victory Medal and British War Medal.

On the 7th June 1919 he married his fiancée, Christina, (nee Harvey) who was employed as a skiver of leather sections in a shoe-manufacturing factory. On the 13th September 1920 she gave birth to twins - Laurence Joseph and Patricia. Later came a daughter, Leticia and a son, Brian. Leticia died in 2003.

John (Jack) Williamson wearing the uniform made by Bill's friend. With his sister, Winifred. Circa 1913.

William retired from the Navy in October 1931 with a pension, a third good conduct badge and a Long Service/Good Conduct Medal. A Lieutenant Commander at Portsmouth Barracks rated his character as: *'Uniformly Very Good'*, *and his general efficiency in carrying-out duties as:* *'Superior'*. The family settled down at 79, Queen's Road at Loughborough in northwest Leicestershire, where William took employment as a postman. In 1934 he obtained an engineering apprenticeship for his son, Laurence, at Herbert Morris, nationally known crane manufacturers of Loughborough. In September 1938, with war clouds gathering William returned to the Navy and during World War 2 served on such ships as *'Dublin'*, *'Weymouth'*, *'Victory'*, *'Centurion'* (*Lades*), *'Harebell'* (*Doon*), *'Columbine'* (*Campbell*), *'Hearber'* (*P.C.74*), *'Courageous'*, *'Frobisher'*, *'Atlantic Guide'* and *'Dundee Castle'*. His family handed down information that during his naval service he was torpedoed, and was in a boat or life raft for two weeks prior to rescue, the stricken ship probably being *'Foxglove'*.

Bill was released from the Navy on the 17th August 1945 with a magnificent service record, especially so when considering that not many people served for their country in both world wars.

An interesting story concerns the youngest brother, John, 'Jack'. Before the Great War, when Bill was aboard *'Achilles*' he asked the ship's tailor if he could make a uniform for his young brother, Jack. The photograph shows 'Able Seaman' Jack Williamson with his sister, Winifred sitting besides him.

Terry's great-grandparents, Joseph (who may have served in the Boer War) and Ellen had to cope with a good deal of sadness and worry during their lives. I mentioned the early deaths of their children, and Winifred was one of them. She died at the age of thirteen years and four months, having completely outgrown her strength. Painfully thin she was six feet three inches tall when she passed away.

The 2nd Leicestershire Battalion dead for the Great War was over one thousand officers and other ranks. Together with Francis Williamson these other local men sacrificed their lives.

1) Samuel Adcock of Coalville 6/4/16. 2) Charles Bailey of Loughborough 6/4/16. 3) Charles Barrett of Loughborough 9/3/16. 4) Timothy Betteridge 13/3/15. 5) William Bird of Coleorton 25/9/15. 6) William Blood of Loughborough 3/10/16. 7) William Bowley of Loughborough

25/9/15. 8) William Bradford of Heather 26/6/16. 9) Alec Brooks of Loughborough 7/1/16. 10) Harry Brown of Hugglescote 13/3/15. 11) William Burnham of Mount Sorrel 26/1/18. 12) John Callier of Ashby 23/4/17.13) Frederick Cooper of Loughborough 14/5/15. 14) Arthur Cunningham of Loughborough 7/1/17. 15) Albert Curtis of Swannington 13/1/16. 16) Fred Davies of Coalville 13/3/15. 17) Herbert Elkin of Hugglescote 25/9/15. 18) Tom Finney of Barlestone 25/9/15. 19) Thomas Foulds of Woodhouse Eaves 9/3/17. 20) George Grain of Newbold Verdon 6/4/16. 21) Charles Gaze of

Bill Williamson on H.M.S. Nubian. Circa summer 1916.

Loughborough 18/8/16. 22) Albert Green of Shepshed 19/9/18. 23) Ernest Hall of Whitwick 13/3/15. 24) Frederick Hall of Loughborough 29/5/18. 25) Owen Hallam of Hugglescote 13/3/15.26) Sten Hardy of Coalville 13/1/16. 27) John Hill of Loughborough 13/1/16. 28) Albert Horrobin of Coalville 8/9/15. 29) Edward Hunt of Whitwick 7/1/16. 30) William Kaberry of Ashby 11/7/16. 31) Rudolph Kirby of Shepshed 17/3/15. 32) Francis Landon of Loughborough 7/1/16. 33) George Lynn of Loughborough 27/4/17. 34) Harry Martin of Bagworth 15/5/15. 35) Charles Mee of Loughborough 14/3/15. 36) Horace Middleton of Sileby 17/3/17. 37) Benjamin Morley of Whitwick 23/4/17. 38) Ernest Morris of Whitwick 30/5/18. 39) Albert Peak of Loughborough 25/9/15. 40) John Poyser of Ashby 13/3/15. 41) Samuel Robbins of Quorn 25/9/15. 42) Thomas Sharpe of Loughborough 15/5/15. 43) John Sharpe of Ibstock 28/8/17. 44) Thomas Sharpe of Loughborough 15/5/15. 45) Gerald Simpkin of Loughborough 26/8/15. 46)

Horace Slater of Loughborough 15/5/15. 47) Albert Stanford of Loughborough 25/9/15. 48) Joseph Taylor of Ellistown 25/9/15. 49) Joe Tebbatt of Hugglescote 25/9/15. 50) Albert Unwin of Ibstock 6/5/16. 51) Percy Walster of Ashby 6/4/16. 52) Louis Walters of Mount Sorrell 22/2/17. 53) Bernard Waring of Loughborough 11/3/17. 54) Edward Watson of Loughborough 25/9/15. 55) Percy Watson of Breedon 25/9/15. 56) John Wells of Mount Sorrell 6/4/16. 57) Frederick West of Loughborough 9/4/16. 58) William West of Sileby 6/4/16. 59) Walter Whise of Loughborough 14/3/17. 60) Bernard Whittaker of Whitwick 25/9/15. 61) Arthur Whittington of Sileby 15/5/15. 62) Ambrose Wileman of Ashby 10/3/15. 63) George Wilkinson of Coalville 13/1/16. 64) Frederick Wilson of Shepshed 28/9/16. 65) Frederick Wilton of Ashby 2/8/15. 66) Harry Whootton of Loughborough 8/3/16.

Bill Williamson served as a stoker aboard H. M. S. 'Achilles' from 12/11/1910 to 9/12/1914. The stoker's job, being below sea level, was particular dangerous when enemy submarines were around. The chances of surviving a torpedo attack were very slim.

Bill Williamson served aboard H.M.S. 'Illustrious' from 11/5/10 to 11/11/1910.

What inspired me to write this book was the undying love existing within family members for their departed relatives to be remembered. It is most noticeably so for men who fought in the Great War. I quote the following from a letter from William's grandson, Terry: *'I have an image of my grandfather as a distinguished looking, clean shaven, white-haired old gentleman in a double-breasted jacket with navy style brass buttons. His eyes were blue and they twinkled as he smiled! The last time I saw him he was in bed at Leicester Hospital. We looked into each other's eyes and gave an impromptu smile, nothing was said, we understood everything immediately; it was like looking into your own soul.'*

William died on the 4th March 1979, aged eighty-six years. His wife, Christina, sadly dying on the 21st December 1967. They rest together in the same grave.

Many thanks to Theresa Noonan, daughter of Emily Williamson of whom the above two gentlemen were uncles, and also to Terry, son of Laurence, more than proud of the findings.

ALFRED WYKES

Alfred Wykes was born in 1875 at the village of Mountsorrel, ten kilometres (six-seven miles) north of the centre of Leicester. By 1912 he was a married man with two children and was managing Messrs. Luke Turner and Company, manufacturers of elastic webbing at Leicester. He was residing with his wife, Sarah Ann, son, Lance and daughter, Dorothy, at their beloved home 'Avondale' in nearby Rothley. Alfred was a devout Christian and was busily involved with the National Council's 'Interchange Movement', which saw many German folk staying at 'Avondale' and the making of several firm friendships.

In August 1914, Alfred and family were

enjoying a holiday at Mablethorpe, on the North Sea coastline, when news broke of Great Britain's declaration of war against Germany! A few weeks later, Alfred was participating in a football match at Woodhouse Eaves in the Charnwood Forest, when Major R. E. Martin approached and asked them to join the Colours. He himself was second-in-command in the Fifth Leicestershire Battalion. Although Alfred was in his late thirties and with German friends, he was becoming increasingly annoyed to read of enemy war atrocities, and asked anyone who wished to enlist to meet at Rothley Liberal Club. Major Martin was there, and after both men made stirring speeches, one hundred and twenty men volunteered. Alfred arranged further meetings and was responsible for many others enlisting into various battalions of the Leicestershire Regiment.

On the 23rd September 1914 he joined the 2/4th Leicestershire Battalion, and by October had been drafted into the 4th (1/4th) Battalion. Alfred kept a war diary of his time in the military, and he vividly described embarkation from Southampton on the 2nd March 1915. '*Our ship was the Golden Eagle, and we left port under cover of darkness. A destroyer escorted us, clearly visible against the sky. As we left Portsmouth behind searchlights blazed across the Channel, sweeping across the waves for possible intruders. A natural quiet came over everybody, as we realised that for some it would be their last view of England.*' Alfred continued, writing that after disembarkation at Le Havre they had a twenty-four hour journey in straw lined cattle trucks, with the only light being supplied by a lantern. He finds 'barn life' to be cold, draughty and damp, and on his first night could not sleep, so at the break of dawn he shaved and bathed in a shallow ditch. He describes the thunderous sound of the British barrage prior to the Battle of Neuve Chapelle, and writes to his son about the German artillery firing at our aeroplanes in the blue sky, leaving white puffs of smoke upon exploding. After a tiring twenty-four kilometres (fifteen miles) march, they had to wait for two hours in a muddy field: '*Captain Faire and the rest of us could not get any wetter. The mud was up to our knees, often half way up our thighs and the heavy downpour took it up to our waists. At the firing trenches we had to crawl in deep mud, one hand holding our rifle, the other, rations. For two days in the trenches there was not a dry spot to sit or lie. It was cold, wet and none of us slept.*'

In a letter to his wife: '*Dear Sarah, I'm sitting in a trench alongside my pal, Ernest Swain. I feel safe from bullets but not from shells. Please send me some soap, boracic ointment, fine emery cloth and a bit of butter. We are short of bread and it took me one hour to nibble my way through a very hard biscuit. I have just been looking at your photograph and thinking of you all and our dear old home, with all my love, Alfred.*'

March 1915.

'*We are all thirsty, wet through and caked in mud! The Germans keep up a persistent fire all night with bullets whistling all around. I returned one hundred bullets in the direction of the enemy. I saw a friend get killed by a shell, a truly horrible sight! I had no*

Alfred Wykes with wife, Sarah, and Dorothy and Lance in 1914.

Alfred Wykes in his later years.

option but to collect some dirty yellow fluid off the trench floor and boil it to make a cup of tea.'

A letter on the 20th March 1915 found Alfred taking a break from the frontline. He wrote of sunnier days, birds pairing and singing, hedges and trees in bud, and warmer nights enabling better sleep. He continues that he is now more used to barn life, but objects to rats trying to eat his food and running over him as he tries to sleep. The following day he sent a letter to his son, Lance. **Alfred wrote on the same theme** and then depicts a scene whereby he and several friends are sitting in an orchard reading and writing. '*Up above an amazing sight, several of our aeroplanes are buzzing about and the Germans are trying to shell them, but they always seem to get away!*'

This particular letter was to seed and germinate within the mind of the teenage Lance, to the benefit of his country during both World Wars!

The Battalion War Diary for March 10th reported the strictness of discipline required. '*It was at Strazeele that Field Punishment No1 was first used for a member of the battalion. The offender was tied to a wagon wheel in front of his comrades. Everyone hated it but it makes all ranks realise that war was a very different proposition to training at home.*'

April 1915.
A wonderful **letter** sent to his wife on Good Friday, 2nd April 1915, fully explains his outlook to the war, his family and his comrades.

'*I can only say once more that I shall take care of myself for your sake. But if duty demands it, I know it will be your desire that I should keep my face to the foe, shoulder to shoulder with my comrades, regardless of the consequences. I hope that the supreme sacrifice will not be necessary and that the happiness of our life may be continued to its natural end.*'

In another **letter** he states that their Rothley garden must be looking very pretty now that April had arrived. '*Here the birds are singing and building nests. The celandine, anemones and dog-violets are evident and the trees are covering themselves with a new green beauty. When I can I find a quiet spot, light up my pipe and think of you all at home.*'

His **Diary** continues:
'*Even miles behind the frontline you can't escape gruesome sights. Big German guns smash the hinterland and you see animals of various descriptions lying around, partly decomposed cows, dogs, mules and the rest. Generally speaking nightly trips to our firing line are full of incidents. Often in pitch darkness we attempt to cross over disused trenches and ditches on a single plank, a real test of equilibrium, especially when bullets are flying about!*

We are near to Messines, a hilly part of Belgium; our trenches are only eighty yards apart. In No-Man's-Land lots of bodies of English and French soldiers lie from an earlier battle. It is strange that most have died on their hands and knees, as though they were all killed instantaneously whilst crawling to the enemy lines! That is all that is left of men made in the image of God!'

Another extract from his Diary:

April 15th - '*It is the middle of April and heavy rain has rendered the conditions to an appalling state. Night parties carrying rations to the firing trenches took nine hours to cover two miles. It is heartbreaking to wade through trenches with filthy water up to our knees. We sleep underground like moles, we have no room to turn over and sleep is not possible. Shells exploding, bullets whistling and the dreadful smell of decomposing bodies is everywhere.*

We all want to go home but 'the wish is father to the thought'. We are all so very tired, and we all have nightmares. Last night I dreamt that I had fallen on my back in the mud and my kit was dragging me under and I was suffocating. I will live with this dream forever.'

April 16th - 'A shell fell ten yards from where three friends and I were working, fortunately it didn't go off! Last night it was a particularly dark evening and I could have been shot for what occurred. There was a 'stand to'; because our officers felt the Germans could make a surprise night attack.

As we stood there the men on either side of me fell asleep on their feet, they were totally exhausted. I kept guard for them, they were only young lads and they looked like puppies nodding in a breeze. No one found out.'

April 18th - 'We are in trench called E1 Left, also called Hell's Kitchen (Spanbroekmolen on the Messines Ridge). The trench consists of an isolated sandbag barricade together with the bodies of British and French 'remains'. Our trench is about 15 yards long and the German trench is only 30 yards away and looks down onto us. The Germans allow their sanitation to run down to us so we have to cover everything with chloride of lime.'

Flying Officer Lance Wykes in 1918.

In a **letter** of the day to his wife he says he's prepared for any hardships and discomforts so long as his life is spared to return home once again to his loved ones. 'I am not afraid to die because of our Christian faith. I am doing my bit for God and humanity, and surely as a consequence the years that still remain to us shall be full of complete happiness.'

The Battalion War Diary describes E1 Left. 'It consists of an isolated sandbag barricade built on dead bodies of both French and British, which has been partially smothered in filth and chloride of lime. No one gets much sleep or food during duty as once the Germans note any sign of cooking they snipe at the sandbags, so that dirt flies into tea and into food, and to put your head over the parapet in the daytime meant instant death with brains flying in all directions.'

The trench system at Spanbroekmolen was also described in my first book, and many a Leicestershire man was either wounded or lost his life in the shallow trenches. Alfred describes in detail what it was like to be wounded in the frontline.

April 22nd - 'I have been sniped in the fleshy part of my hip. My friends lowered me to the floor of the trench and covered me with their greatcoats. I could not stop myself from trembling violently. It was three hours before stretcher-bearers collected me.

I was just about to re-read one of my dear wife's letters, it was 5.00 pm but the bearers wouldn't move me until darkness, it was just too dangerous. I was taken to a First Aid Post where a doctor dressed my wound. I waited for twenty-four hours before being taken to Boulogne, across the Channel to Dover and onto the Woodford and Wanstead Military Hospital.'

On the 13th May 1915, **Lieutenant J. F. Johnson wrote** to him in hospital. It was a very warm letter, expressing his best wishes and congratulating him on his performances on the field of battle. It cheered Alfred a good deal, and later was very upset when he heard that the kindly lieutenant had been killed at the Charge of the Hohenzollern Redoubt on the 13th October 1915. In the same battle fellow officers, Captain L. Corah, Captain R.A. Faire, Lieutenant Whittingham, and 2nd Lieutenants R.C. Harvey and G.E.F. Russell perished.

Alfred eventually returned to his old home, 'the dearest place on earth', and renewed his life of love and contentment for family and friends. He was never to regain his earlier fitness and took no further part in the war, but his military experiences were a revelation to him and they completely altered his outlook towards his fellow men. He wrote the following paragraph and I find its content to be exceptionally stirring and moving, and may provide an insight for many readers, as it was for me.

'To the casual observer the man in the trench is indifferent to the call of the Highest, and has no time for the spirit of God. He drinks, swears, gambles, and can be uncouth. In the depth of his being however, there is potential for good, and he will give glimpses of Christ-like characteristics. These men have shown that they are prepared to make the supreme sacrifice for what they believe to be true and righteous. May I state that my fear of the army was a worry that it could hinder my spiritual development? I could not imagine fellowship and communion to be the highest possible on the battlefield!

I was mistaken, and never have I had deeper spiritual experiences than on the battlefields of Flanders.

During the lonely watches of the night, the rattling of the rifles were forgotten and only the greater silence of God spoke!'

It is unusual to say the least, of the impact warfare can have upon the psyche of an individual, indeed a generation, and to understand its roll-on affect to a family waiting at home. From the two World War's a total of one million British families were never to see their loved one's return!

Alfred lived for a further thirty-two years after being wounded, mostly very happy ones in his *"dearest place on earth"*. His ever-loving wife, Sarah Ann, died in 1956.

The letters sent by his father from Flanders captivated young Lance. He was particularly impressed by reading of the skill and daring of British pilots as they battled against enemy shelling, and of the dogfights against enemy aeroplanes. During his boyhood and teenage years Lance liked nothing better than constructing his own model wooden aircraft. He would throw them into the air and assess their stability in flight. He read of the exploits of ace flyers like Albert Ball, Mick Mannock and James McCudden. When he came of age in 1918 he joined the Royal Flying Corps, soon the Royal Air Force, and qualified as a Flying Officer. Lance rapidly clocked-up over three hundred flying hours over the Western Front. In his Sopwith Camel he was engaged in some fearsome dogfights with German aircraft. He also had over fifty hours flying in **darkness** over the Western Front, and this was a rarity for the time and not intended for the faint-hearted.

Lance or A.L. as he became known developed into a very successful businessman between the World Wars, but the highlight of his fame was to occur during the 1940s in the Second World War, and this will be explored in my next book.

Many thanks to my neighbour, Margot Brookman, the daughter of Lance Wykes, for the loan of her father's diary and photographs.

THE LAST ROLL CALL FROM THE GREAT WAR

Lance Corporal Arthur Ballard of the 2nd Leicestershire Battalion.

Lance Corporal Arthur Ballard was a regular soldier in the 2nd Leicestershire Battalion when on the 10th June 1915 he wrote a letter, 'From Somewhere in France' to his brother. His brother resided at 53, Long Row, Ashby Road at Coalville. *'I am progressing as well as can be expected and the weather is really lovely now. It is now sunny France and we are not up to our waists in water as it has been for many months. You say that I must have had a wonderful constitution to stick it out. Well, you know, God is good and we must put our trust in Him. I believe I am the only Coalville man left who has been in all the engagements and come through without a scratch, thank God for it. As you know I served six years in India before I landed in France on October 10th. Our first experience of fire was when we were relieving* the Worcestershire's who had had a rather rough time of it in the trenches. The Germans opened a heavy fire on our part of the trench or ditch as it was then, but by the time daylight came we had got things into shipshape order. Then the 'Jack Johnson's' started to come over and we had to duck-under. The first man to fall at about 8.00 am was the captain commanding my company, so our first experience of the trenches was not to our liking. We were then in our trenches for twenty-four days and then came out for a short rest, but the Battalion was called out again to retake some trenches that the Germans had captured and we lost a good many men. That was on the night of November 29th. We handed over the trenches to the Ghurkhas, but as we were marching back to our billets the Allemandes let us have a lot of shrapnel. We had to do some ducking and scattering and we lost a few more men. After that we had a few days rest except we had to do digging patrols at night. Digging trenches in front of the Germans with bullets flying around is no joke. On December 19th we made a charge and took the German trenches and also some German Maxim Guns, I read that these were paraded in Leicester. That was a night I shall never forget as we lay for two hours in the rain waiting for the order to advance. We were all shaking, it was either from the cold or from excitement. I pulled through and we took the trench and thank goodness with not many losses. The trenches are bad with knee deep water at the moment but we will survive.'

Arthur went on to thank relatives and friends for tarts and other treats for Christmas, and similarly writes about other battles he negotiated. Happily, he survived the war but lost a good many of his friends in the process.

Private George Henry Barrs, service number 240713, was born at Ellistown and was the son of Mr. & Mrs. John Barrs of Ibstock. He enlisted at Coalville into the Fifth Leicestershire Battalion and fought with them until he was badly wounded at Spanbroekmolen, on the Messines Ridge, just to the south of Ypres, Belgium. He died from his wounds on the 25th May 1915. George is remembered on the Coalville Clock Tower Memorial and the Memorial Plaque within St. Christopher's Parish Church, Ellistown.

Private William Beasley, the son of Mr. & Mrs. Beasley of the Hermitage Hotel, Whitwick and **Private Joseph Hart** of Coalville were both serving in the 1st Leicestershire Battalion when they wrote to the Coalville Times of December 3rd 1915. '*We are both in the best of health and we are so sorry to see in the newspaper the amount of Coalville boys getting killed, but we are doing our best to avenge their deaths and we will do so before we finish. We have just come out of the trenches after a very strenuous fourteen days, and we reckon it is a well deserved rest. We have been fighting where the last big attack at Hooge was. We think the Germans know it is quite impossible to advance around these parts but we keep on giving it to them thick and heavy. We should like you to contradict the rumour that William Beasley is dead. As you can see I am well alive and mean to be for I have not done with those devils on the other side yet. My friend, and me Joseph Hart have had more than one narrow escape, but they have not caught us yet and we hope to give them plenty more in the future. It is the second time out for my chum and me. We have both been in the second battalion and now we are with the first battalion.*

I am sending this letter with a chum of mine from Coalville together with another of the boys coming on furlough. I don't suppose it will be long before we get a break too. I am sorry to tell you that Mick Reed, one of my chums from Coalville, was accidentally shot. I suppose you know him, his brother, Joe, has been with me, but he is now tunnelling. We hope the remainder of the Coalville Boys will answer their county's call and come and help us avenge the deaths of their friends, for the quicker they come the sooner the end will be in sight, and it looks far from sight at the moment. We both wish the people of Coalville a merry Christmas, Yours sincerely, Private W. Beasley, 16531, 'B' Company, 1st Leicestershire and Private J. Hart, 10650, 'A' Company, same regiment.'

William Beasley started in the 2nd Battalion but in the summer of 1915 was invalided home with rheumatic fever, and following recovery was posted to the 1st Battalion. The story that Private Beasley was killed originated from a man's statement saying he read it in a letter from a soldier serving at the front. His parents were greatly distressed upon hearing the news, but were equally elated when they received a letter disproving the rumour.

Sadly, there was no disproving his death when he was killed in action whilst fighting for the same battalion on the 15th September 1916, near to Martinpuich on the Somme. He served under Captain H. Pickbourne, a local man.

Private George Arthur Beale was born in Coalville in 1893 and attended the Coalville Wesleyan School on Belvoir Road. He was a pre-war soldier with the Fifth Leicestershire Battalion, service number 1995-240351, and employed as a miner at South Leicestershire Colliery, Ellistown. A married man living at 70, Melbourne Street, Coalville, he mobilised with his battalion whilst at their annual camp at Bridlington, and served bravely until meeting his death on the 9th June 1917 whilst clearing enemy trenches 'Boot and Brick' on the summit of a slag heap near to Lens, France. The Battalion's chaplain, Reverend C. B. Buck wrote a letter to his wife explaining that he died doing his duty, and that he had a full Christian burial in a nice little cemetery just behind the lines. His name is etched on the Coalville Clock Tower War Memorial.

Corporal Lance George Beck had enlisted at Ashby de la Zouch into the 1st Leicestershire Battalion, and at some stage in his early life served with them as a regular soldier. He was born in 1889, the son of Mr.& Mrs. James Henry Beck, an engine driver on the Midland Railway. His formative years were spent at 71,

Corporal Lance George Beck of the 1st Leicestershire Battalion. Killed in action in on the 21st December 1915.

Park Road at Coalville and the family worshipped at nearby Christ Church, with Lance being educated at the Church School. He worked for a while in Coalville, became a soldier, and later moved to Leicester where he obtained employment in the machine-room of the Leicester Mercury, and following marriage resided with his wife on

Parliament Street, Leicester. Lance received a telegram on the 5th August 1914 to mobilise and merrily met up with old chums from Coalville before they embarked for France. He was another soldier who experienced the amazing 'Christmas Truce'. In February 1915 he sent a letter to the Coalville Times: '*I was pleased to receive the parcel of comforts, which I can assure you was greatly appreciated. Please give my best wishes and thanks to all Coalville friends. We are all in the best of spirits (a bit damp) but still smiling.*'

From the early summer of 1915 the Battalion was serving in the Ypres Salient, being familiar with the territory around Hooge and Sanctuary Wood, and throughout this posting the main danger was from heavy shelling and lachrymatory gas. Whilst in the Salient Lance heard that his father had died.

During an early winter's heavy barrage, that lasted a few days, it was estimated that the German gunners had fired four hundred thousand shells onto the Divisional Front, including gas shells. At one time Battalion Headquarters at St. Jean was bombarded with unceasing fury, and movement was impossible.

Between the 18th and 21st December the Battalion lost nine men, seven later died of gas damage to the lungs, nineteen men were wounded, eighty-eight were suffering from gas and five were missing believed dead.

The War Diary for December reads: '*The stretcher bearers worked strenuously with the wounded and tried to evacuate them from the trenches, but the road was so fiercely shelled that it was impossible to carry them out, and later those who attempted to do so were found dead on the road, having been caught in the terrible barrage put down by the enemy.*'

Corporal Lance G. Beck, as a human being never departed the Ypres Sector, dying on the 21st December 1915, and I surmise he was killed by shellfire, for it does not mention that he died from wounds received.

His sister, Mrs Curtis, who lived at 71, Park Road said that Lance had a most congenial disposition, and had a great sense of humour. His sister also said that she had received a letter from Lance's wife whereby she said she had received her husband's watch and knife, and also a letter from his chums saying how sad they were and that they would send other belongings to her as soon as they could.

Corporal L. G. Beck's name can be read on the Coalville Clock Tower Memorial and also on the Memorial in Christ Church.

Private Arthur Brownlow was an ex-regular

soldier of the 1st Leicestershire Battalion, and like a group of other local men received a telegram on the 5th August 1914 ordering him to rejoin his unit. Among his many comrades was local man, Francis Martin. They embarked with the Battalion in September 1914 as part of

Private Arthur Brownlow of the 1st Leicestershire Battalion. Killed in action: 21st June 1915.

the British Expeditionary Force and fought at the first Battle of the Aisne 14-20th September 1914. They witnessed the remarkable Christmas Truce, fought in the Battle of Neuve Chapelle on 12th - 15th March 1915 and also the Battle of Festubert 9th - 15th May the same year.

In early January 1915 he wrote to his wife at 83, Margaret Street, Coalville, to thank her for sending the mince pies and also to thank the people of the town for sending comforts.

'*It is very cold in the trenches and the comforts will help to keep me warm. I hope you had a merry Christmas. Mine was not too good but never mind we will all have a better one, hopefully next year! Tom Granger and Sten Hardy are with me and a lot of other Coalville boys so we are all right. Will write again. Your loving husband, Arthur.*'

{Private Stenson Hardy, of Tebbett's Yard, Hotel Street, was later transferred to the 2nd Leicestershire Battalion. He had served in India until February 1914, became a reservist and only married nine weeks before being mobilised at the outbreak of the war. He was badly wounded in France by a bullet to the jaw requiring hospitalisation and home leave, during which time his child was born. Stenson recovered sufficiently to embark with the Battalion for Mesopotamia, only to be killed in action at Shaikh Saad on the 13th January 1916. He was twenty-eight years of age and his name can be read on the Coalville Clock Tower Memorial.}

Arthur Brownlow sent a further letter to his wife and young daughter dated the 18th April 1915. He again thanked his wife and the town's folk for various comforts, and stated that the weather was getting warmer, and to thank her father for sending some of his favourite twist-tobacco for his pipe. He wrote that he thinks of his wife and his little daughter at home: '*Bless her; I can't wait to get home and see her again, give her a big kiss. We are in the trenches again and Tom Grainger has told me to remember him to all his friends at Coalville.*'

Arthur Brownlow, service number 6058, died on the 21st June 1915 near to Sanctuary Wood, in the Ypres Salient of Flanders. At the outbreak of the war he was a coal-miner at South Leicestershire Colliery, Ellistown. Living in the same street, and working at the same colliery was **Ernest Brownlow**, younger brother of the above, service number 4178, thirty-one years old and supporting a wife and five children.

He was serving with the Fifth Leicestershire Battalion at Vimy Ridge in France, when the enemy detonated a mine under their trenches. One hundred yards of frontline was damaged and among those troops buried was Ernest. He was quickly extricated but was clearly suffering from severe injuries and died of wounds on the 26th March 1916. He had only been at the front for three weeks. Before the war he was well known in football circles under the nickname, 'Brudge'.

Ambrose Brownlow, the twenty-three year old son of Arthur also worked at South Colliery. The private soldier was killed on the 17th July 1916, service number 10568, whilst serving with the 6th Leicestershire Battalion at the Battle of Bazentin le Petit on the Somme.

All of the Brownlow family lived on Margaret Street and all three have their names on the Coalville Clock Tower Memorial.

Private John H. Bullen, the son of Mr.& Mrs. Mathew Bullen of Highfields Street, Coalville was fighting for the Leicestershire Regiment when he was badly wounded in both legs in August 1917. The gallant soldier was awarded the **Military Medal** for his bravery and whilst at Northfield Hospital, Birmingham was taken to Birmingham University where Major General C. R. R. McGregor presented him with his medal. John's wounds were so bad that his legs had to be amputated. His wife was the daughter of Mr. J. Curtis, formerly manager of the Coalville Workingmen's Club in Margaret Street, Coalville. On the 8th November 1918 it was reported that he was living with his parents, Mr. & Mrs. Mathew Bullen of Eaton Villa, Highfield Street, Coalville awaiting entry into hospital for the fitment of artificial legs.

Sergeant William Cave

Sergeant William Cave, service number 240055, lived just two doors from William Barney of 8, Cumberland Road, Ellistown, who is mentioned in detail earlier in this book. Following William Barney's death. *''I am writing to let you know that William was killed on Wednesday night, June 30th at quarter past nine. Alfred Burton was with him, and just before he was shot he was asking how everyone was getting on back home. He did not suffer much and he died thirty minutes later. His last words were to thank those who had bandaged his wound. The following night they asked me to bury him because he was my mate, and I said I would and did! He was buried in full uniform and we covered him with a blanket so that no dirt could touch his face. Forty of us stood over his grave and prayed for him. I made a cross and put it over his grave and as long as I'm in the area I will care for it. We all miss him but just remember that he died for King and country.'*

William enlisted at Coalville in late August 1914 into the Fifth Leicestershire Battalion and quickly won successive promotions due to his mental ability and bravery in leadership. Sergeant William Cave fought with the Battalion until he was killed in action on the 28th December 1917 at Cambrin Right Sector, just to the north of Loos in France. The War Diary states: *'Whenever work was possible, even at night it was sometimes too light we worked at two new trenches, 'Cardiff' and 'Currin' connecting Bart's Alley with Saville Tunnel. When completed they had to be wired and we suffered at the hands of a German sniper. Sergeant W. E. Cave, a very fine NCO of 'A' Company was killed with a wiring party and one or two more had narrow escapes.'*

Sergeant William Cave is remembered on the Coalville Clock Tower Memorial and the Memorial with St. Christopher's Church, Ellistown.

Private Frederick Chamberlain

Private Frederick Chamberlain lived with his parents, Mr. & Mrs. Thomas Chamberlain at 59, North Street (later 184, Central Road, one of the Breach Cottages, re: Arthur Newberry Choyce) at Hugglescote. He grew up with Bill Cowley, one of the famous fifty; indeed they lived next door. The family attended Hugglescote's Baptist Church with Frederick attending St. John The Baptist Church School. Pre-war he was a miner at Ibstock Colliery and he enlisted in early September 1914 into the 9th Leicestershire Battalion, service number 14552.

Frederick was killed on the 24th May 1916 in the trenches in the Bienvillers-Bailleulmont Sector of France. 2nd Lieutenant H. F. King wrote to his parents. *'It is with the deepest regret that I have to inform you that your son was killed this morning by a shell that fell and which dropped among his section, killing him instantly. Please accept my entire sympathy in your great loss. Your son was one of the very best men in my platoon, a willing boy, a perfect soldier and a good comrade esteemed by all in the*

Company. He is to be buried in a little cemetery set aside by our Battalion in a little village behind the trenches. Your grief, I know, will be difficult to comfort, but it is the knowledge that your son has made the great sacrifice for his country, that will help you in your trouble. I will ensure that your son's belongings will be sent to you as soon as possible.'

Private Frederick Chamberlain was twenty years of age. His name can be read on the Coalville Clock Tower Memorial and on the St. John The Baptist Church Memorial. Bill Cowley was killed whilst serving with the Fifth Leicestershire on the 8th May 1916.

Private Ben Clibberly, youngest son of Mr. & Mrs. John Clibberly of Park Road, Coalville, wrote to his parents to explain the 'Christmas Truce' of 1914. Ben was scout bugler with the Coalville Troop of Boy Scouts before enlisting at Coalville into the 1st Leicestershire Battalion. *'It was rather funny talking to the men we had before been trying to kill, and it was also nice to get out of the trenches during daylight hours to stretch our legs. We had been in the trenches for a fortnight leading up to Christmas and the enemy had been pretty busy all the time. When we went over to them we took plenty of cigarettes, which we exchanged for pipe tobacco and cigars. They seemed to be quite good chaps, so different from what you would think they were. We had bully beef and biscuits for dinner. We stayed in the trenches for twenty-two days, and I can tell you it was pretty bad because for a lot of the time we were up to our knees with water. But still it is no use troubling about small things like that.'* His father was an engine driver with L.& M. Railways and was pleased that his son recovered from a bad wound to survive the war.

Private Alfred Clifford, service number 16638, was born in 1897 at Coleorton, the son of Mr. & Mrs. James Clifford who worked at Desford Colliery. Alfred enlisted at Coalville in December 1914 into the 1st Leicestershire Battalion. His father had moved address to Ashby Road, Coalville when he had a letter form Private Chandler informing him that his son had been killed by a piece of shell on the 10th September 1915 at Ypres, Belgium. Alfred had a married sister, Mrs. J. Smith living on Owen Street, Coalville. Alfred has his name etched on the Coalville Clock Tower Memorial.

A particularly sad story concerns the Copley brothers of Margaret Street, Coalville. **Private Harry Copley** was born in 1893 and at the age of eighteen enlisted at Coalville into the 1st Leicestershire Battalion, service number 8312. As a regular soldier he experienced several years of service in India, during which time he coincidentally met his brother, John, who was a private in the 2nd Leicestershire Battalion. Harry was reposted to the 2nd Leicestershire just prior to the war and fought alongside John until his brother was stricken with a recurrence of malaria. Harry was posted as missing at Festubert, France on the 15th May 1915 - later reported killed in the battle.

Private John Copley was born in 1894 and

Private John Copley

when he was eighteen enlisted at Coalville into the 2nd Leicestershire Battalion, service number 8312. He had served for four years in India, suffering for a time with a bad attack of malaria. The illness returned whilst he was fighting in the frontline in France in April 1915, but he recovered sufficiently to embark with the Battalion in late 1915 to Mesopotamia. He wrote a letter home on the 12th December 1915 when he stated: *'We are going to give the Turks a packet.'* That was his last letter home and John perished in the horrendous battle of Shaikh Saad on the 7th January 1916.

Both brothers died at the age of twenty-three years, and their names can be read on the Coalville Clock Tower Memorial. William Copley, the remaining brother, was a miner and resided at 101, Margaret Street, Coalville.

Gunner William James Cracknell had the distinction of being the very first man in Coalville and district to volunteer for the Forces. He lived with his parents on Bakewell Street, Coalville. Whilst serving with the R.F.A. in France in April 1915 he wrote a letter to his parents. *'I received your letter and parcel all right and thanks very much. You* *should have seen the wild dance by my pals when I opened the parcel; we always share what we have.*

Please thank everybody concerned, and please inform Mr. Roughton that I wish to be remembered to him and that I will write to him soon. You ask about our guns out here, well you can take it from me that our lads outclass the Germans. I have seen some of their 'Jack Johnsons', but we have some little lumps of mischief but I can't tell you the size. It is touching to see our 'Jocks' coming out of their trenches to scrape their kilts, top coats and washing their knees. They don't half look mucky but it takes more than that to dishearten our lads. You ought to see us in the dugouts. We have a mouth organ and an old melodeon and the 'Jocks' have bagpipes and we all have a right singsong. There'll be plenty of work over here for the plumbers when this lot is all over. You can't believe all you read in the papers about the Huns, as it is far worse than that. Please remember me to George Conibear. I don't suppose you see many of my pals as most will have enlisted, but if they haven't been rejected then they are no longer pals of mine anymore.

I went the other day and saw Leslie Cope and his younger brother, Douglas. I also saw a Coalville lad called, Snell. I went and asked him for Leslie, as I knew the Leicesters were only three miles from me. I had about two hours with them, they were pleased to see me, and I them. They are in the pink and as happy as sand boys, and they wish to be remembered to friends. I hope Mrs. Baldwin received a letter of thanks for her nice useful present that she sent to me before Christmas. I am getting quite a dab hand at washing. I washed my shirt today and so did one of the lads and we hung them on a bush to dry. A 'Jack Johnson' came near and blew his shirt to bits. He did swear and I couldn't help but laugh. I would pity that German gunner if he had got hold of him! The job out here may last a long time yet. What with their gas bombs and shooting liquid fire, but it is of no avail to them. They can't leather our boys and our leaders know what they are about and how to carry things out. They are a fine lot of toffs, real good chaps so don't worry about me, and I am in good company and in the best of health. Best love to all and my kind regards to Captain Stevenson at the recruiting centre, I hope he is busy.'

James Frederick Cracknell, Williams's younger brother, who was working at Coventry before the war, having learnt the grocery business at Hunter's Ltd of Coalville, was killed in action on the 2nd April 1916 whilst serving with the R.F.A. His name can be read on the Coalville Clock Tower Memorial. Gunner William Cracknell, the first of the many survived the conflict.

Private Sidney Dodds was born in 1896 at

Private Sidney Dodds

Coalville and lived with his parents at 9, Berrisford Street, Coalville. He was another of Mr. T. Frith's old boys from the Wesleyan School on Belvoir Road, Coalville and was employed in the pattern office of Messrs. Wootton Brothers, an engineering concern in the town. Sidney was an early enlister at Coalville, late August 1914, and was allocated to the 3rd/5th Leicestershire Battalion, service number 2537. After being in various camps throughout England he was posted to France in July 1916, and soon afterwards was transferred to the Royal Sussex Regiment. He was initially posted as missing with this regiment and later was confirmed as being killed in action on the 21st October 1916.

Before the war the bright lad was a regular attendee at Coalville Men's Adult School and with Clifford Scott, one of the famous fifty, was a popular member of the Y.M.C.A. His father was the chauffer to Dr. R. W. Jamie, who later had two sons as officers in the war.

Private Sidney Dodds is remembered on the Coalville Clock Tower War Memorial and the Wesleyan Methodist Church School Memorial on Belvoir Road, Coalville.

Private William Ducksbury, service number

Private William Ducksbury

11950, was born in 1894 and lived with his parents on Highfield Street, Coalville. He was educated at the Wesleyan School on Belvoir Road, Coalville and was employed as a miner at South Leicestershire Colliery, Ellistown. He was killed fighting for the 8th Leicestershire Battalion on the 15th July 1916 at Bazentin le Petit on the Somme, France.

William is remembered on the Coalville Clock Tower memorial and the Wesleyan Chapel Memorial.

Private Albert Essex, service number 240940, lived with his parents, Mr. & Mrs. Albert Essex of 28, James Street, Coalville. His father was a miner at Snibston Colliery, and the seventeen year old was also a miner at Ellistown Colliery before he enlisted in his home town into the 6th Leicestershire Battalion, part of Kitchener's New Army. He was killed, aged twenty years, near to Polygon Wood in the Ypres Salient of Belgium, when a shell burst just a few feet away from him on Sunday evening, the 7th October 1917. Private Albert Essex is remembered on the Coalville Clock Tower Memorial and the Wesleyan Methodist Church School Memorial on Belvoir Road, Coalville. He was a good friend of Sidney Dodds.

Private Albert Essex

Lance Corporal Christopher Fairbrother, service number 13236, was born in 1894 at Ravenstone, and lived with his parents, Mr. & Mrs. C. W. Fairbrother on the Main Street of the village and attended the local Parish Church and school. A miner at nearby Ibstock Colliery he enlisted at Coalville into the 8th Leicestershire Battalion and was killed on the 13th July 1916 near Bazentin le Petit on the Somme, France. Christopher's name is remembered on the Parish Church Memorial.

Lance Corporal Charles Fairbrother

Lance Corporal Joseph Aramathea Hall, service number 16075, was born in 1893 and lived with his wife and child at 11, Brooks Lane at Whitwick. He was the son of Mr. & Mrs. Arthur Hall of Silver Street, Whitwick, and worked with his father at the local colliery. Joseph enlisted in November 1914 at Coalville into the 9th Leicestershire Battalion, and fought with them until he was fatally wounded on the 9th December 1915 at Monchy au Bois, just to the north of the Somme, France. His name is remembered on the Memorial in the grounds of St. John The Baptist Parish Church, Whitwick. Private Walter Gould, service number 12857, of the same battalion wrote to Joseph's wife. '*I regret to write these few lines in regard of your husband's death. All of his comrades feel his loss very much and he was popular with all the men in his platoon. We all send our sympathy at your sad loss. I am sending you the photographs that were with him when he died, they are of you and your child, and I should like to ask if you could send me one of Joseph to keep in his remembrance, as we have been great chums ever since we joined the Army. He has been buried in a cemetery in a village nearby and we will look after it for as long as possible.*'

Private James Haywood, service number 13179, a miner from Ellistown Colliery, was a single man of thirty-two years when he was killed fighting with the 8th Leicestershire Battalion on the 22nd January 1916. His parents, who lived on Brook Terrace at Donington-le-Heath, received a letter from Private Jason Wallace informing them of his death. '*I am sorry to tell you that I have lost my best pal, but I expect you have heard all about it by now. I should have written before but we've had a busy time in the trenches. I wanted to have a last look at him but I was not allowed to do so. It took a lot of steam out of me because I was speaking to him not long before, and you don't know how I miss him.*

Private James Haywood

We had got like two brothers since we had been out here, and he was one of the best pals anybody could have, and there was not a better soldier in all of France than Jim. The enemy keep on picking us out, and I've had some narrow shaves, but have been very lucky up to now. At the rate that are going there will be none of the old hands left who came out here with us.

I can't go into details about his death in this letter, but with luck I should have some home leave soon and then I will tell you all about it. But one thing I can write is that he was doing his duty and that I have lost my best pal. Hoping you are well under the circumstances. I remain your old friend, Private Jason Wallace, 23178, 'B' Company, 8th Leicestershire.'

Private Haywood's officer, Captain T. E. Breacher, also wrote a letter. '*Please accept my sympathy regarding the death of your son who was killed by a German rifle grenade. Private Haywood was a battalion grenadier and has been under my command since the 1st September 1915. He was always a conscientious worker and nothing I set him to do was too much trouble. At the end of a hard day's work when volunteers were called to work to operate the machines that throw our grenades to the German trenches, he was always amongst the first of the men to come forward.'*

Lieutenant E. S. Allen wrote to say that there was no better soldier in his platoon, and he was the best grenadier we had.

Private James Haywood was killed during the bitterly cold January of 1916 at Monchy au Bois, just to the north of the Somme Sector. His name can be read on the Coalville Clock Tower Memorial.

Private Alfred Heathcote, service number 2110, was living at Bagworth when he travelled to Loughborough to enlist into the Fifth Leicestershire Battalion. He was with the Battalion when he was badly wounded in the head by sniper fire at Spanbroekmolen on the Messines Ridge, just south of Ypres. He was swiftly taken to No 8 Casualty Clearing Station but later died. The sister-in-charge wrote on the 26th April 1915 to Alfred's sister. Miss Heathcote at Bagworth. '*I am sorry to tell you that your brother, Private A. Heathcote of the 5th Leicestershire died of his wounds on the 23rd April 1915. He was severely wounded in the head. He was well cared for and looked after but there was never much hope for him. He did not suffer much pain. Yours sincerely, M. S. Mewfests. (Sister-in-Charge.)'*

Alfred is remembered on the Memorial in the grounds of Bagworth Parish Church.

Able Seaman Bert Hodkinson wrote to the Coalville Times, his letter being published on the

Able Seaman Bert Hodkinson served on board H.M.S. 'Princess Royal' during the 1915 Battle of Dogger Bank

29th January 1915 declaring his participation in the naval Battle of Dogger Bank on the 24th January 1915. He also wrote that he was present at the earlier Battle of Heligoland, in which his ship was slightly damaged. He expressed that at Christmas his thoughts were very much of home, and that he missed homely comforts, but he was just one of many who felt that way. He repeated that there really is 'no place like home' even though he had recently been in the sunshine of the West Indies. Bert was an old Wesleyan schoolboy and he lived with his parents on Vaughan Street, Coalville. His father worked on the local railways.

The Battle of Heligoland Bight on the 28th August 1914 was a severe blow to German naval moral. The Bight is a stretch of water between Heligoland and the German mainland that was frequently used by the German fleet for exercises. A British force of two light cruisers, thirty-three destroyers and eight submarines sailed into the Bight and surprised the enemy vessels there. After the initial shock superior German numbers tried to cut-

The German battle cruiser 'Blucher' took part in the Battle of Dogger Bank on January 24th 1915. With a maximum speed of 25.3 knots it was found wanting for speed in the chase across the North Sea. She had twelve 8.2" guns.

off the British from their return route but were met by battle cruiser squadrons of the Grand Fleet under Admiral Beatty. The German forces lost three light cruisers and a destroyer.

Private John Edwin Hibbitt, service number 11475, was born in 1895 on Shaw Lane at Coalville,

Private John Hibbitt

but his family later moved to 1, Castle Yard at Hugglescote. He enlisted at Coalville into the 1st Leicestershire Battalion on the 7th August 1914, making him one of the earliest volunteers in the district.

He was a tall man for the time standing at five feet and ten inches, strongly built and smart and always clean-shaven. He joined his battalion with 2nd Lieutenant J. Wright and twenty-nine other men at Armentieres on the 6th March 1915, after six months of training. He fought through the dreadful barrages within the Ypres Salient and survived until the Battalion attacked a strong enemy fortification, which the Allies called the Quadrilateral, near to Guillemont and Martinpuich on the Somme. The attack was launched at 4.30 am on the 15th September 1916 and during its course John was killed in action. He had earlier been posted as missing, however, following enquiries made by a Mrs. Wykes of Hugglescote, she received a letter on behalf of the Earl of Lucan who enclosed a copy of a report from a Corporal Carroll, who was in hospital in Ireland. The corporal wrote. '*I knew Private Hibbitt; he was in my Company but not my platoon. He was killed on the 15th September just in front of Guillemont. I didn't see him fall but I saw his dead body. He was no doubt buried where he fell, as a burial party went out two days after the action to bury our dead.*'

Before the war John had been a coal miner at Ellistown Colliery where his father was employed as a watchman. The name of Private John Hibbitt can be read on the Coalville Clock Tower Memorial.

Private Walter Irons, service number 3155, was born in 1895 at the hamlet of Bardon and lived with his parents, Mr. & Mrs. W. Irons on Shaw Lane. Before the war he was a miner at South Leicestershire Colliery at Ellistown.

He enlisted around late September at Coalville into the Fifth Leicestershire Battalion, and served with them until he was badly wounded near to Ypres, subsequently dying in the 28th September 1915, aged twenty years. Walter is remembered on the Coalville Clock Tower Memorial.

Gunner Austin Morris was a turret gunner aboard the Admiral Beatty's flagship, H.M.S. '*Lion*', when he also fought in the naval battle of Dogger Bank in the North Sea.

Gunner Austin Morris was on board Admiral Beatty's flagship H.M.S. 'Lion' in the Battle of Dogger Bank.

The son of Mr.& Mrs. William Morris of Belvoir Road, Coalville, he worshipped at Ebenezer Chapel on the Ashby Road and also was a member of the Bible Class there. Among his many friends were Walter Gray, John Williamson, Ernest Knifton and Archie Glover.

In February 1915 he wrote to the Coalville Times and qualified what Bert Hodkinson had to write, adding explaining that a German Squadron was chased and the enemy armoured cruiser, '*Blucher*', was sunk. He added: '*We heard the Germans were somewhere off the Newcastle coast. The North Sea was like a millpond and as soon as they saw us the enemy got away as fast as they could. We opened fire at about fifteen miles and we never got closer than twelve miles.*' He mentions that the '*Blucher*' was one of Germany's capital ships and that his Squadron included the battle cruisers, H.M.S. '*Lion*'; Admiral Beatty's flagship, also '*Tiger*', '*Indomitable*' and '*Princess Royal*' and '*New*

H.M.S. 'Tiger' was the flagship of the squadron and Austin Morris manned one of the guns.

H.M.S. 'Indomitable' could steam at 26 knots and had eight 12" guns.

Zeeland, together with a guard of light cruisers and destroyers.'

The Battle of Dogger Bank was fought on the 24th January 1915 when Admiral David Beatty's Squadron sighted and gave a high-speed chase to a German Fleet; it lasted for five hours and swept from west to east across the North Sea.

In December of 1914 a similar sized enemy fleet had treated the largest navy in the world with impunity, when it stealthily left German waters and steamed alongside England's eastern coast. The fleet shelled the mainland, including famous resorts such as Scarborough and Great Yarmouth and inflicted hundreds of casualties. Such was the furore afterwards that promises stressed that there would be no repetition of the incident. During the battle the first British guns opened fire at 7.25 am as they targeted a force of four large cruisers, '*Derfflinger*', *Seydlitz*, *Moltke* and *Blucher*, six light cruisers, and several destroyers steaming a course to the northwest.

They immediately reversed their course and with Beatty's lighter craft forging at twenty-eight knots they soon closed the gap, and at 9.09 am shells from H.M.S. '*Lion*' made contact with the '*Blucher*', and slowed her down. Shortly afterwards H.M.S. '*Tiger*' achieved hits. Sir David Beatty said: '*About 9.45 am 'Blucher' showed signs of having suffered severely from gunfire, and 'Moltke' and 'Seydlitz' were also on fire.*'

The enemy desperately sent in their destroyers

The German battle cruiser 'Moltke' could steam at 28.4 knots and had ten 11"guns

with torpedo attacks to protect the heavy battle-cruisers, but they were beaten off and Beatty said: '*I ordered 'Indomitable' to make an end of 'Blucher' whilst we chased the remaining force but we turned back upon meeting enemy submarines.*'

Blucher went down with all her men aboard, as did the '*Kolberg*'. A Zeppelin dropping bombs and a seaplane drove off British boats that were attempting to save the enemy crews.

The chase ended about seventy miles from Heligoland. No such naval attacks were attempted on mainland Great Britain again.

Both sailors survived the Great War.

The end of the 'Blucher'. It was sunk with the aid of the guns of H.M.S. 'Tiger' and 'Indomitable'.Gunner Austin Morris and Able Bodied Seaman Bert Hodkinson witnessed the sinking.

Private Samuel Moore

Private Samuel William Moore of 31, Margaret Street, Coalville was serving with the Fourth (1/4) Leicestershire Battalion, service number 235058, when he avenged a German's treachery. He wrote the following letter on the 24th October 1915 to his parents, Mr.& Mrs. Joe Moore of the same address. '*Was glad to hear you are all well as this letter leaves me in the pink. I am going to tell you how we went on our recent charge (Hohenzollern Redoubt). It was six o'clock when we went to our trenches and it was not long before our artillery started and it was on for two and a half hours. It was awful; the ground seemed to be fair shaking.*

Jack and I were in the trench together and we felt a bit nervous so we asked the officer if we could have a little rum. He gave us some and we felt all right after that. As time went on we could hardly see the German trenches because of all the smoke and it made us feel sorry for the poor beggars under those bursting shells. Then the officer came along and told us to get ready to go over and make sure we had some bombs ready. Then over we went and soon the Germans were running like hell with our chaps after them, I followed up just behind with my bombs. It was a sight I can tell you to see all of your pals fall; it fair made my blood boil. I felt mad and started bombing them like hell. Dead were lying all around in heaps. An enemy bomb dropped between Jack and me but I threw about half a dozen back. When I got back to our fire trench two Germans were there and I finished them off. Then I saw eight Germans coming with two of our chaps so I shouted, " Who are you?" and they said they were Fifth Leicesters bringing in prisoners. The Germans were shouting, "Mercy English". I felt sorry for one of them who had been hit by a shell and lifted him over into our trench. I then went out bombing again and saw sights bad enough to turn you over, and my blood rose again and I was up for it. In one dug out about four feet underground I saw four Germans and tossed a bomb into them. In another I saw four bald headed German soldiers and did the same and we held the enemy trench until we were relieved. A bit later I saw a Leicester man helping a German who was partly buried. As soon as the German got out he picked up his gun and shot the lad. I rushed at the German with my bayonet but could not catch him and so I pulled the trigger and shot him dead. When I was in our trench an officer came up and said that some of our chaps were dying because we could not get to them and the telephone was broken. I volunteered to go and see where the wire was broken. As soon as I got over their artillery started again I fell and dropped the wire, but I was able to get back and report and they put a wire across. I should have got the D.C.M. but the officer who saw me do it got killed. I don't want to be in another mess like that. We are in a barn now resting for a few days. We get frozen at night and I think it will not be long before we get snow, it really is so cold at nights. God help us if we are to be here for another winter. I'd sooner be at Margaret Street. Please send me some more mittens. Your loving son, Samuel.'

Private Samuel Moore had to suffer many more cold nights, even worse so, but he survived the entire war and fought to the last day. Without doubt a tough and determined young man, he was so typical of the local young men.

A dreadful accident led to the death of **Private James William Nicholls**, service number 7988, of the 1st Leicestershire Battalion. The Captain of the Battalion wrote to his parents, Mr. & Mrs. Reuben Nicholls of Ashby Road, Coalville on the 28th July 1916 to explain what happened. *I am sorry to have to inform you that your son, Private James Nicholls was killed this afternoon. He was in the trench cleaning bombs when one suddenly exploded, killing two other men and also wounding several others. It may be of some consolation to you to know that your son was killed instantly. He was a good soldier and always did his job conscientiously and he will be deeply missed. The Battalion Chaplain also wrote to offer consolation to the parents.*

Private James Nicholls was thirty years old and at one time was a regular soldier and served in India with the Battalion. As a reservist he was mobilised at the outbreak of war, at the time being employed as a miner at South Leicestershire Colliery. James was a well-known local footballer and played for Coalville Town Football Club. He was a good friend of Jack Sheffield, who was killed in 1915. James' father worked for many years at Snibston Colliery. His name is remembered on the Coalville Clock Tower memorial.

Corporal Ernest Pringle, service number 2004, was born in 1888 at Ashby de la Zouch, the eldest son of Mr. & Mrs. Walter Pringle. Pre-war he was a very good and well-known local footballer and also an established territorial soldier in the local company of the Fifth Leicestershire Battalion. He was at Bridlington with the Battalion at the outbreak of war and served as Sergeant Gore's right hand-man in 'A' Company until his death at the Battle of the Hohenzollern Redoubt on the 13th October 1915. His sergeant wrote to his parents and explained that Ernest was always willing and cheerful and never looked on the black side of things. He stressed that Ernest was killed instantly whilst going over the top, and a place is vacant that will be hard to fill. He died a hero's death for King and Country.

Private Frederick Wilmot Pringle, service number 1144, was the younger brother of Ernest above. He followed the same pathway as his elder brother, but was three years his junior. He again was in the Fifth Leicestershire Battalion that landed in France in February 1915. Frederick, aged twenty-four was killed during a heavy enemy bombardment on Trench 50, near to Hill 60 in the Ypres Salient on the 1st September 1915. The War Diary reads: '*The bombardment took place at 10.45 am and finished at mid-day. The Germans concentrated all of their efforts on 50. They started with salvoes of whizz-bangs and finished with heavy shoot, 8" and 5.9" and shrapnel. They had the most fortunate good fortune in hitting our dugouts, causing many casualties. 'A' Company was particularly badly hit with Private C. E. Scott (one of the first fifty) and Private F. W. Pringle, the two officer's batmen being killed.*'

It was also reported that Sergeant Gore helped with the shovel to try and aid the victims. Sadly, Company Sergeant Major William Gore was killed on the 8th June 1917 when a shell exploded alongside him just before the attack on 'Boot' and 'Brick' trenches near to Lens, France. Captain Hastings who was also buried by the bombardment wrote a letter to his parents. '*He was a universal favourite with everyone, all the Battalion through. We often had talks in the dug-out about what we would do after the war when we all returned to civilian life, it is beginning to look as though a good many of us may not make it. I hope it may be some consolation to all of you that your son, a soldier's son, died a soldier's death, fighting the battle for his country. I pray that he may obtain eternal rest.*'

The brothers are remembered on the War Memorial at Ashby de la Zouch.

Private John Randall, service number 4507, was born in 1896 at Ashby de la Zouch, the son of Mr. & Mrs. Charles Randall of North Street in the town.

He enlisted at Ashby on the 24th June 1915 into the Fifth Leicestershire Battalion and served with them until his death on the 1st day of the Battle of the Somme, the 1st July 1916. He was killed at Gommecourt and is buried at nearby Foncquevillers' Cemetery. 2nd Lieutenant W. Salmon wrote to his parents. '*He was a really good man, always bright and cheerful, and remember sometimes our work is both hard and dangerous, but he never grumbled. He will be sadly missed but please remember that he died fighting for his country and that he was properly buried by an Army Chaplain.*'

The name of the nineteen year old is remembered on the War Memorial at Ashby de la Zouch.

Private Samuel Charles Smith, service number 240054, was born in 1894 and a single man living with his parents, Mr. & Mrs. Thomas Smith of 17, Melbourne Street, Coalville. His father was a moulder at Messrs. Wootton Brothers Iron Works and Samuel, following schooling at Mr. Frith's Coalville Wesleyan School, was employed at South Leicestershire Colliery, Ellistown. Samuel was killed fighting for the 8th Leicestershire Battalion on the 1st October 1917 at Polygon Wood, Ypres. The Battalion chaplain wrote to his parents and explained that he was killed whilst facing a heavy German counter attack. He continued that their son was a good soldier and unflinchingly made the ultimate sacrifice. His name is remembered on the Coalville Clock Tower Memorial and the Wesleyan School Memorial. Thomas Smith had another son in the Forces, Leslie, who had twice been wounded, but had returned to the frontline.

Private Ernest Stinchcombe, service number 32428, was part of a large family circle that lived at Hugglescote and attended St. John The Baptist Church and the Church School. Ernest lived with his parents at St. John's Terrace, near to the Parish Church, and enlisted at Coalville in September of 1916 when he was eighteen years of age, into the 1st Leicestershire Battalion. He was killed in action with that battalion on the 30th March 1917 at Hulluch in the Loos Sector of France. His father was a quarryman at Messrs. Ellis and Everard at Bardon Hill, whilst Ernest was a van-driver for the Coalville Co-Operative Society. Private Ernest Stinchcombe is remembered on the Coalville Clock Tower Memorial and on St. John The Baptist Church Memorial.

Private Ernest Stinchcombe

Relatives in the Forces included Trooper William Stinchcombe, 5869 in the 3rd Guards Machine Gun Corps, Private Francis Stinchcombe,

39657 in the 7th South Staffordshire Battalion and Private George Stinchcombe, 122379 in 'B' Company of the 62nd Machine-gun Corpse. All three brothers lived at 22, Ashburton Road, Hugglescote. Other relatives included Private Albert Stinchcombe, 24090 of the Fifth Leicestershire, Private George Stinchcombe, 3418 of the 1st Life Guards and Gunner Charles Stinchcombe, 270412 of the 8th Reserve Brigade of the R. F. A. who all lived at 4, Fairfield Road, Hugglescote. All the other members of the family circle survived the war.

Private W. Summers of the 1st Leicestershire

Private William Summers

Battalion lived with his parents at 158, Ashby Road, Coalville before becoming a regular soldier. He wrote home in May 1915 to say that he had many letters from family and friends, and that he wouldn't be able to reply to them all but he was very grateful to them. '*We have had the usual trench warfare for months now and what with hail, rain, snow and gales it is getting monotonous, but at present we are getting some pleasant sunshine, and that is making things pick up with nice fresh grass, trees with plenty of foliage. No doubt you have heard of the Germans latest form of warfare, viz, asphyxiating gas, and I should think it has shocked the whole of the civilised world, or at least I hope it has! A thing like this should draw the sympathy of the world on the side of our Allies who are giving-up everything they possess to crush the common foe, German militarism. There is no doubt that the Germans intended to crush and now that they find they cannot they make use of this criminal invention. I hope we shall soon be able to return the compliment.*

Some people might think this is bad sportsmanship, but it is impossible to cope with it otherwise. Why should Germany as one of the biggest subscribers to the Hague Convention, be allowed to break every law in it and get off scot-free? It would never be the wish of our mothers, fathers, brothers, sisters, wives and sweethearts that we should take things of this description lying down.'

Private Summers had another brother, Thomas, serving with the 2nd North Staffs Battalion. Both brothers survived the conflict.

Private Jesse Weston distinguished himself twice during the war. Whilst serving with the 1st Leicestershire Battalion at Ypres on the 24th September 1915, he was awarded the **Military Medal** for attacking an enemy post single-handed and brilliantly securing the position. Whilst recovering in hospital from wounds received during his attack he gallantly donated a pint of his blood to save the life of an officer who was a complete stranger to him. After several months in hospital Jesse returned to his parents house on Belvoir Road to recover. The brave soldier was demobilised and subsequently returned to work at Stableford's Wagon Works at Coalville. He was twenty-three years of age.

Lance Corporal Frederick Whitmore of the

Lance Corporal Frederick Whitmore

Black Watch died of wounds on May 29th 1915, shortly after having his right leg amputated. For many years, his relatives were connected with Hugglescote Post Office.

Gunner Norton Williams of the Royal Garrison Artillery, service number 62329, worked at the Co-Operative Society in the clothing department before he enlisted in November 1915. He could well have known Gunner James Herbert Scott of the Garrison Artillery.

Private Albert Williams

Norton's father, Tom, was a winding engine driver at a local colliery, and the family lived on the Crescent Road at Hugglescote. His elder brother, Albert, was a former Coventry policeman who served with the Royal Warwickshire Regiment at the Dardanelles. The Coventry Corporation allowed all serving policeman eight shillings (forty new pence) a week and kept their positions open for their return. Both brothers survived the war.

Private Frank William Woolhouse was only twenty years of age when he died on the 13th

October 1915 whilst charging at the Battle of the Hohenzollern Redoubt. He served in 'B' Company of the Fifth Leicestershire Battalion and his mother; Mrs. Warren (who had remarried following the death of her husband) of 79, Albert Street, Coalville received a letter from two of his comrades.

The letter signed by **Private Leslie Cross of Hugglescote, and Private Herbert Cato** of 77, Albert Road, Coalville, informed her that he was killed in a bayonet charge while attacking enemy trenches.

Frank, service number 3440, had worked at Whitwick Colliery before enlisting in late 1914, and had also been an excellent forward with Coalville Swifts Football Club. Mrs. Warren said that the last time she heard from Frank was a letter dated the 9th October 1915, in which he thanked her for a parcel, letter and photograph. The dear mother had lost her former husband, Edward Woolhouse, in a pit accident at Whitwick Colliery in 1907.

Her husband, Private Thomas Warren was an ex-regular soldier and with the 2nd Leicestershire Battalion when he was wounded at the Battle of Neuve Chappell in March 1915, and it was reported that he was just behind Corporal Jack Sheffield when the gallant NCO was killed.

Thomas' son, Walter Warren, was with the Norfolk Regiment and was convalescing from a bad wound, and was later posted to the 3rd Leicestershire Battalion. Another son, Thomas Warren was a Royal Marine with H.M.S. '*Hannibal*' and another in the R.F.A. All were young miners at Whitwick Colliery. Private Leslie Cross survived until six weeks from the end of the war being killed at the Battle of Pontruet on the 24th September 1918.

Privates, William Woolhouse, Frank Woolhouse and Leslie Cross are remembered on the Coalville Clock Tower Memorial.

Private Thomas William Willett of the 2nd Leicestershire Battalion sent a letter home to his parents at Ivy Dene Cottage on Highfields, Coalville in June 1915. '*We have just come out of the trenches for a rest and we need it following recent battles. I am feeling much better now after a hot bath, a swim and a clean change of clothing.*

I am pleased to get the 'Coalville Times' when we are in the trenches, and we were in them for six Sundays altogether, although it is often difficult to remember what the day is. Whitsuntide made no difference to the fighting; it carried on just the same. We are giving the Germans 'sock' now and I don't think it will last much longer, I hope not anyway. I have had quite enough of this life and I earnestly hope we will soon be back home for a well-earned rest. I have seen something of this war and thank God I am still alive. I lost two of my pals, and they were by my side and I really have been very lucky not to be hit. I am sending you some poetry written by my mate. He's a good friend to me and I think it is worth printing in the Times. It refers to the same battle that Jack Sheffield and Harry Brown were killed. Lance Corporal Bertram Turner of Peckleton has written the verse.'*

The battle was a fierce one,
And we've many a tale to tell
Of the glorious victory we achieved
In the fight at Neuve Chapelle.

The gallant second Leicesters
Right bravely faced the Huns,
Though comrades were falling
Before their Maxim guns.

Bravely our heroes made the charge'
And hundreds of them fell,
When they reached the German trenches
Which are called the streets of hell.

The Huns came up in thousands,
To frustrate our attack,
But our gallant lads in khaki
Saw that they didn't get back.

Old England ought to be proud
Of all her soldier sons;
Especially our artillery
For the way they manned the guns.

We've seen some funny sights out here,
Since we came across the foam,
And we've many a tale to tell them
When we reach dear old home.

The verses I've made up here,
Are just a simple rhyme,
Of how things go on at the front
Which pals will prove in time.

Corporal Bertram George Turner (11499) and Private Thomas William Willett (15864) were alongside each other when they were killed near to La Bassee on the 25th September 1915. Battalion casualties that day were described as 'very heavy'.

Private Hedley William Wykes, service number 10240, was the only son of Mr. & Mrs. C. L. Wykes of Market Street, Ashby de la Zouch. Mrs Wykes had died before Hedley enlisted in his hometown on the 16th August 1914 into the 6th Leicestershire Battalion. He was badly wounded on the attack against Guedecourt in the Somme on the 26th September and died at Rouen Hospital on the 5th October 1916. He regularly wrote home to his father explaining how he felt about losing so many of his comrades. On one occasion an officer complimented him for his gallantry in rescuing a wounded comrade.

He was buried with military honours at St. Sever Cemetery, Rouen. Hedley's name can be read on the War Memorial at Ashby de la Zouch.

Private George Yates was the youngest of five sons of Mr. & Mrs. George Yates who lived on Church Lane, Ravenstone. He was educated at Ravenstone Church of England School and was a chorister at the local Parish Church, whereby it was often remarked what a very fine singing voice he possessed. George followed his father's footsteps and took up employment as a miner at Ibstock Colliery. He was only seventeen years of age when he enlisted at Coalville in November 1914 and was posted to the 2nd/5th Leicestershire Battalion, service number 240577. He saw service in Ireland during the Easter uprising of 1916, and had been fighting on the Western Front for seven weeks before being killed. Lieutenant J. W. Jamie, son of a local doctor, wrote to his parents to explain how he died near to Bouvincourt, France, on the 16th April 1917 during the German's tactical withdrawal to the Hindenburg Line.

'It is my painful duty to inform you that your son, Private George Yates has died of wounds he received in action on April 16th. Pte. Yates had been doing splendid work in the night attack, which was in progress, and at the time of being wounded was lying close to me and waiting orders. The shell, which severely wounded him, killed his friend, Private Jack Knifton, also of Ravenstone. Your son was a quiet and conscientious soldier and always willing to do someone a good turn and was very popular. He will be very much missed. He suffered little pain as he passed away on the way up to the dressing station.

He has been buried a few miles from the frontline and his grave will be well looked after. Please accept my sympathy and if there is anything I can do then please write and let me know.'

His parents received a beautiful letter from the deceased's old headmaster, Mr. L. G. Burge.

Mr. & Mrs. Yates had two other sons fighting abroad, one in the Leicestershire Yeomanry and one in the Coldstream Guards. Both soldiers survived, although the later was wounded at the First Battle of the Aisne.

Lieutenant J. W. Jamie also wrote to the parents of **Private Jack Knifton**, service number 240602, who was the son of Mr. & Mrs.Charles Knifton of Coronation Cottages on the Coalville Road at Ravenstone. *The Battalion was making a night attack on a village and I was only a few feet away from him when a shell burst and killed him instantly, suffering no pain. His personal effects will be sent on to you. He lies in a grave a few miles from the frontline and it will be well cared for. Always cool in the face of danger he will be much missed by all.'*

The Battalion Chaplain, Reverend J. D. Thomas also wrote and stated that Jack has been buried alongside several of his comrades in the Brigade Cemetery. Jack, along with his two other brothers had been a member of Ebenezer Baptist Bible Class at Coalville. Indeed one of his brothers, Ernest Knifton, was a well-known musician. A few months before the war he joined Wootton Brothers Iron Works, but from leaving school he was employed as a miner at Coleorton Colliery, his father was a miner at Snibston Colliery.

Jack, service number 240602, enlisted at Coalville in August 1914 into the Fifth Reserve (2nd/5th) Leicestershire Battalion and was twenty-one years of age.

Two young men, who grew-up together, went to school together, eventually died together on the Somme battlefield. Privates George Yates and Jack Knifton are remembered on the Ravenstone Parish Church memorial, with Jack's name also on the Ebenezer Baptist Chapel Memorial, Coalville.

Archie Glover, Ernest Knifton, Austin Morris, William Goacher and Walter Gray. Ebenezer Chapel Bible Class 1911.

GREATER LOVE

Our scenic spot was quiet apart from the chattering birds and a breeze,
Which seemed to whisper and sigh as it ventured through the trees.

Bazentin Le Petit.

Michael Kendrick

JUST OLD FRIENDS

They are just boys.
Boys on a village green after a day at school,
Boys chasing girls and acting the fool.
Playing on a park-bench with tin soldier toys.

They are just comrades.
Comrades in trenches during times of war,
Comrades dreaming of knocking on home's door.
Foreign fields where bayonets clash in raids.

They are just pals.
Pals who fought side-by-side on a battlefield,
Pals marry old loves to raise a multiple yield.
Resting on a park-bench with their gals.

They are just old mates.
Mates working together in yonder mills,
Mates helping each other during life's ills.
On an older bench as gals pass heaven's gates.

They are just old friends.
Friends of a lifetime of over sixty odd years,
Friends with shared memories and quotas of tears.
Aged park-bench offers support, never bookends.

They were known as just old friends.
Friends that departed together on a rickety park-bench,
Friends for whom parting was too great a wrench.
They were just old friends.

Michael Kendrick.

HENRY WALKER

Readers of 'Fifty Good Men and True' will be familiar with the name of Henry Walker. Always referred to as Harry, he was indeed one of the Famous Fifty, and I am very pleased and grateful to Mary Mulholland, his niece, for providing so much additional information.

Harry's father, George Walker, was born on the 10th May 1866 at Thrussington, a village eleven kilometres (seven miles) southeast of Loughborough. At the age of fourteen George was a fit and strong agricultural labourer. His mother, Emily (nee Johnson) was born on the 14th July 1871 at Ravenstone, and the couple married at Ravenstone Church on the 19th April 1892.

Harry was born on 26th August 1895 at Ravenstone. He was one of seven children; Ada (born 31st March 1893), Fanny (11th January 1898), Frederick (1st July 1900), Herbert (6th November 1903), Emily (8th September 1905) and Arthur (born the 18th January 1910.)

The Walker family lived in various cottage homes around Snibston (then Snibstone) and Ravenstone, with Harry leaving Snibston School at the age of thirteen years on the 21st September 1908. By nature he was a bouncy individual: full of youthful vitality and confidence, always willing to attempt something new! Possessing a fine voice he was a chorister at the local church where he was also a Sunday school scholar, and among his many friends were George Andrews, Arthur Congrave and William Kendrick. Upon leaving school he commenced employment for South Leicestershire Colliery at Ellistown.

By 1914 his father was working for the Coalville Urban District Council on the Kelham Bridge sewerage farm, and the family lived on Main Street (possibly number 10), Ravenstone.

Eighteen years old Harry, service number 2479, enlisted at Coalville in the first week of the war, joining the Usherwood brothers in Sergeant Major Roland Hill's 'A' Company of the Fifth Leicestershire Battalion. One of his first letters despatched from Belgium was to his cousin:

Private Henry Walker in October 1914 at the age of 19 years.

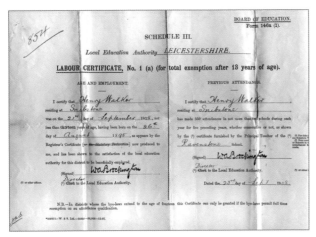

Henry Walker was born on the 26th August 1895 at Ravenstone. The above Labour Certificate shows that he left school at the age of 13 years on the 21st September 1908.

2479 A Company.
5th Leicestershire.
Expeditionary Force.

Dear Cousin,

Received your parcel yesterday with thanks. I got it as soon as I got out of the trenches so I could not tell you when it came. I had seven letters when I got yours so you must excuse me for not answering it straightaway. Should be glad of a cake from any of you any time which come

Henry's letter to a cousin in 1915. Above are pages 1 and 4, below are 2 and 3.

quite as cheap and more welcomed, but toffee went down well not having any since I left England. When I showed the chaps the handkerchief they all wanted to write to you. I expect we shall have some fun with it when we get back in the trenches, holding it up for the Germans to fire at. They don't half get mad; they are only about sixty yards off us. I should think they fired thousands of bullets and only lamed about one of us. I think the French live on dirt, for they are the dirtiest lot I've ever seen, and all the while trying to cut you. You would be surprised to see what luck some chaps have. Some with a bit chipped out of the face and legs and don't know to it until they wash themselves. Wish the weather would clear up as we are up to the ankles in water. There's not half some laughing when we get hold of the papers, as they can't half put it in. One chap had a narrow escape as a shell dropped and buried him. Its not what harm they do you, it's the row they make when they are coming, but we are getting used to them now, and laugh at them. Am expecting to hear a wedding amongst some of you soon so make haste. With best love.

From your affectionate cousin,

Henry Walker.

Please note that the copy of this letter shows that Captain The Hon. Rawdon Hastings of Ashby de la Zouch has censored it.

I would deduce that Harry wrote the above letter in early April 1915 at Spanbroekmolen, on the Messines Ridge in Belgium.

Later, an undated letter was sent to his mother, and guessing I would say that it was late June 1915

and from Trench 35 at Zillebeke near Ypres.

2479 A Company.
No: 2 Platoon.
5th Leicestershire.
Expeditionary Force.

Dear Mother,

Received your letter while I was in the trenches. We are out now, but we are going in again soon. I expect there will be some enlisting in Coalville now.

Has Arthur enlisted yet?* We had an exciting time on Sunday, one of our airmen fetched a German aeroplane down. You should have heard the Germans when our chaps cheered him, they shelled us for about an hour, which did no damage. We have been in our eyeholes this last two days, been grand weather and we've been getting a trench out in the daytime and sleeping at night, which is a bit unusual really. You don't want to believe anything they say about the hill sixty, which has been exchanging hands several times, but in our hands at present. We had an exciting night the other week, some Germans took a trench by surprise or a bit of one from some other regiment. We took one of our platoons across and we soon bombed them clear. We got a gold watch off one (prisoner) and the trench back. What do you reckon of (England's last hopes?)

I must close now.

With love from Harry.

*Arthur Perkins, a relative.

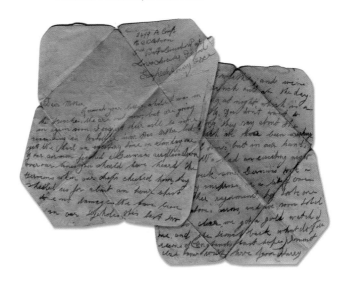

Both sides of a letter sent by Henry Walker to his mother in 1915

Harry sent another correspondence to his cousin in Ravenstone the day before he died. It was written from Trench 50:

Following Henry's death Arthur Congrave and William Kendrick wrote to his parents. Written from 'The Trenches' pages 1 and 4 are above and 2 and 3 below.

> 2479 A Company.
> No 2 Platoon.
> 5th Leicestershire.
> Expeditionary Force.
>
> Dear Cousin,
>
>   I received your welcome letter. We have not done a lot this last fortnight but they will soon have something in store for us. This is our second day in these trenches and we are getting on fine but we do get shelled a lot. Two of us went out on our hands and knees to see what we could find and ran into a German trench, we did scuttle! One chap let his horse run away the day before we came here, so he came with us and got killed the next day. We have just had a fresh lot to reinforce us. Girls who write letters out here have caused many a chap to get killed! They write asking for this and that and the chaps go out to try and get them and many a one never comes back. We are about a thousand yards from the Germans now, because we took this trench off them and they had to fall back into a wood.
>
> Have to close now, best love,
>
> Henry.

Some twenty-four hours later the letter writer lost his mortal life.

It was around 2.30 pm on the 2nd July 1915 that Harry narrowly avoided death in the treacherous Trench 50, near to Hill 60 in the lethal Ypres Salient. A whizz-bang exploded close by and only the zigzag nature of the trench saved his life, it was a severe shock nevertheless! The Germans were able to keep these batteries only 220 metres (180 yards) behind their frontline, and they pinpointed some area of the Battalion frontline to be hit every three hours. Because the batteries were so close the men heard the 'bang' before the 'whizz', so there was little opportunity of escaping them. A few hours later nineteen-year-old Harry did not have a second chance, paying the ultimate price with his life!

It was a bright and sunny morning and as always, even in that perilous area, the birds were in chorus, when the sudden crack of a firing rifle silenced them.

Harry was on guard duty and upon hearing a noise in No-Man's-Land raised his head for a quick peep over the parapet. The enemy may have 'staged' the event and a sniper's bullet passed through his head! His mortal remains slumped to the bottom of the trench. Friends rushed to help him but it was clearly evident that he had died within seconds. Many a veteran has told me that sniper activity was very prevalent within the Salient.

The next day Arthur Congrave and William Kendrick combined their thoughts for the letter below. Recent evidence suggests that it was addressed to the rector of Ravenstone Church, the Reverend S. Dowling, and not George Walker as first thought. Also, Private Congrave had posted a letter to his father a day earlier, viz the 2nd July 1915, stating Harry has been killed. He also said that he would inform Rev. S. Dowling and ask him to convey his sympathy and that of William Kendrick's to Mrs Walker.

> Arthur Congrave No 2595.
> July 3rd 1915.
> The Trenches.
>
> Dear Sir,
>
>   I received your letter dated June 19th and at last I have the chance of writing a few more lines to you. Well, since I wrote to you last I have had a short illness, but I am pleased to say I am quite well again and am in the trenches. All this week

we have had a very warm time of it. Shrapnel is flying over all the time, but while they are sending shrapnel they are not sending any rifle bullets over, so we have a chance to get in the bottom of the trench out of the way. Sir, you said in your letter that you were looking forward to the time when we shall all be back in the village, but I am very sorry to have to tell you that Pte. Harry Walker got killed at 6.00 o'clock on Friday morning. He was on Sentry in the next trench to the one that I am in, and he got up to shoot, but he hardly got his head above the top of the trench when a bullet struck him in the head. He died almost immediately thus suffering no pain whatever. He was buried in the Battalion graveyard last night. Both I and the other Ravenstone lads feel his loss very much, we shall to try to avenge his death somehow or another. He died one of the noblest deaths a man could ever wish to die. He was also well respected by all his comrades. I am writing on behalf of my friend Pte. William Kendrick who lives in Wash Lane. He is not a very good letter writer so he asked me to write on his behalf. And we ask you kindly to convey to Mrs. Walker our heartfelt sympathy on this sad occasion. Well Sir, I hope all are keeping well at Ravenstone as it leaves all here as one can expect. But I can tell you we have to rough it here and I shall be glad when it is all over, but I think it will be a long time yet. I saw in the Coalville Times a while ago that J. Broadhurst was a prisoner of war in Germany and that news had been received from him. I was very pleased to hear he was alright as it makes one think a great deal when anything happens to one of your old pals. Sir, I think I will close now. From Yours Sincerely,
No: 2545 Pte. A. Congrave.
No: 2436 Pte. Wm. Kendrick.

Arthur and William were writing from Trench 50: 'The Trenches', and I find it very moving to think that I have trod this very ground. Please read: 'The Ghosts of Trench 50' in my earlier book.

On the 8th July 1915 Company Sergeant Major Roland Hill, a Coalville man, forwarded a letter to Mrs. Emily Walker:

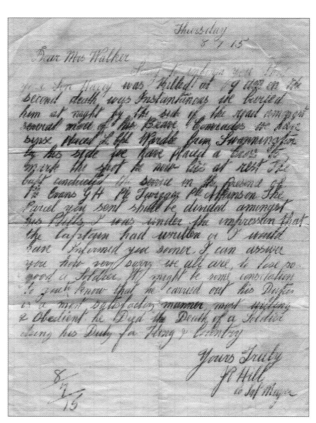

Company Sergeant Major J. Hill sent a letter explaining his sorrow regarding Henry's death. The writer, a Coalville man, trained and offered support to the 'Famous Fifty' from their earliest days. He cared deeply about their welfare and felt their individual and collective deaths acutely.

C.S.M. R. Hill.
5th Leics.
8/7/15.

Dear Mrs. Walker,

Sorry to inform you that your son Harry was killed at 19 on the Second July. Death was instantaneous. We buried him at night by the side of the road amongst several men of his Battalion Comrades. We have since placed Lance Corporal William Wardle from Swannington by his side. We have placed a cross to mark the spot he now lays at rest.

The Captain (P. Rawdon Hastings) conducted the service in the presence of Private Evans (G.HQ), Private Twigger and Private Atkinson. The parcel you sent shall be divided amongst his pals. I was under the impression that the Captain had written or I would have informed you sooner. I can assure you how very sorry we all are to loose such a very good soldier. It might be of some consolation to just know that he carried out his duties in a most satisfactory manner. He was most willing and obedient and he Died the Death of a Soldier doing his Duty for King and Country.
Yours Truly,
J. R. Hill.Co. Sgt. Major.

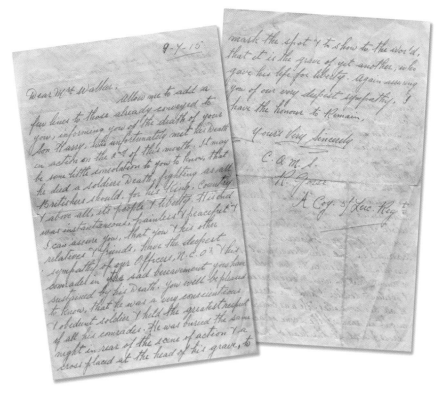

Left: Company Quarter Master Sergeant Major R. Gorse was a Loughborough man who had served for many years with the Fifth Leicestershire. Above: A letter that he wrote to Mrs Walker on the 9th July 1915 to express his sorrow regarding the death of Henry. R.Q.M.S. R. Gorse survived the war and in 1919 was one of The Cadre and Equipment Guard.

Captain The Hon. Rawdon Hastings (of Ashby De la Zouch) was killed at the Battle of Hohenzollern Redoubt on the 13th October1915. Private Lewis Evans was killed in active service on the 21st June 1918.

The day after Roland Hill's letter came further notification from Company Quarter Master Sergeant Major R. Gorse:

9-7-15.

Dear Mrs Walker,

Allow me to add a few lines to those already conveyed to you, informing you of the death of your son, Harry, who unfortunately met his death in action on the 2nd of this month. It may be some little consolation to you to know, that he died a soldier's death, fighting, as all Britishers should, for his King and Country, and above all, its people and liberty. His end was instantaneous, painless and peaceful and I can assure you and his other relatives and friends, have the deepest sympathy of our Officers, N. C. Os. and his comrades

In the sad bereavement you have sustained by his Death. You will be pleased to know, that he was a very conscientious and obedient soldier and held the greatest of all his comrades. He was buried the same night in rear of the scene of *action and a cross placed at the head of his grave, to mark the spot and to show to the world, that it is the grave of yet another, who gave his life for liberty. Again assuring you of our very deepest sympathy, I have the honour to remain,*

Yours Very Sincerely,

C.Q.M.S. R. Gorse. A Coy 5th Battalion, Leicestershire Regiment.

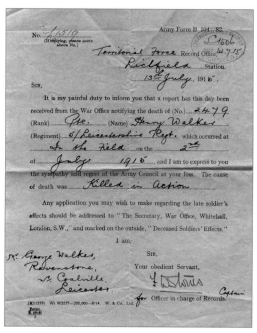

On the 13th July 1915 the Record Office at Lichfield wrote to Mr. George Walker informing him that his son had been killed on the field of battle on the 2nd July 1915.

I believe that Harry's parents were first notified of his death when Thomas Congrave received a letter from his son on the **5th July**. Note from the above letter that Roland Hill says he would have written sooner (8th July).

On the 13th July 1915 The Territorial Records Office at Lichfield sent a letter to Mr.George Walker confirming his son's death 'in the field of battle.' Three days later The Secretary of the War Office forwarded a 'Casualties Form Letter D' in response to Mr. Walker's enquiry on the **5th July**. It reported that H. Walker had now been reported as a casualty 'was killed in action on the 2nd July 1915.'

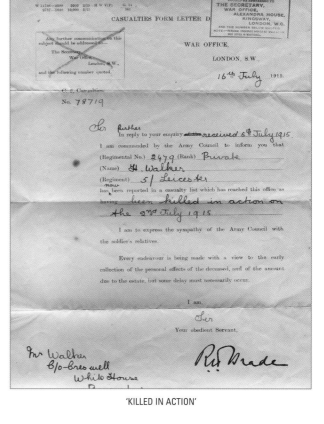

'KILLED IN ACTION'

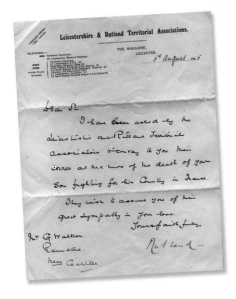

On the 3rd August 1915 Leicestershire and Rutland Territorial Association wrote to George Walker expressing their sorrow at the death of his son. July 1915.

The Leicestershire and Rutland Territorial Association on the 5th August 1915 posted a letter expressing great sympathy to Mr. G. Walker.

The Territorial Records Office at Lichfield then informed Mr. Walker on the 6th August that his son had been buried at Sanctuary Wood near Ypres.

The same Office wrote to Mrs. Walker on the 8th December 1915: *'Under separate cover I beg to forward personal effects of the late No 2479 Private H. Walker, 1/5th Battalion, Leicestershire Regiment.'*

Clearly, the Reverend

A.S. Dowling of Ravenstone Rectory does his best to offer comfort to the Walker family, and following his enquiry receives a letter of the 6th June 1922 from the Imperial War Graves Commission. The letter advises against a visit to where Harry's remains are because the area had been devastated throughout the war years, etc. A letter from the same source and dated the 14th June 1930 informs the Reverend that several bodies had recently been found and that Private Walker now lies beneath a headstone in

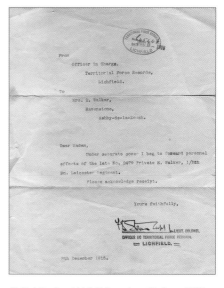
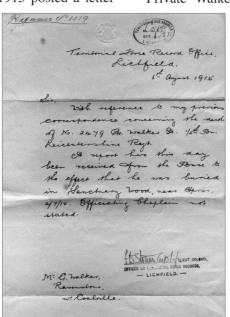

Right: letter from Lichfield Records on 6th August 1915 stating that Henry is buried at Sanctuary Wood. Far right: a request on the 8th December 1915 to return personal effects.

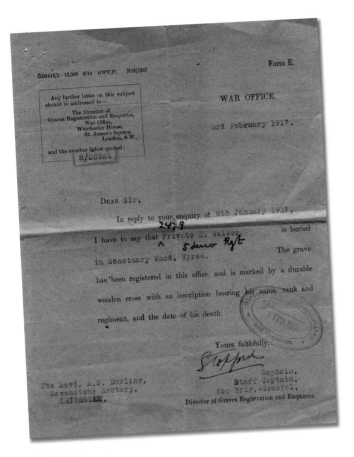

The War Office confirms on the 3rd February 1917 that Henry Walker is buried at Sanctuary Wood, Ypres.

extremely impressed to see a magnificent photograph of the eighteen-year-old Harry in uniform. Within the glass frame was his 'dog tag', a memento of his last seconds on earth. All soldiers wore two dog tags around their necks. If they were killed then one remained with the body while one was returned to the battalion to confirm the owner's death. Often tags were destroyed with their owners by a violent explosion or by entombing (such was the case with tunnellers).

Private Harry Walker's name can be read on the War Memorial in Ravenstone Churchyard.

Life could not and never was the same for the Walker family, though naturally time helped to soothe emotional wounds.

George Walker died on the 2nd December 1951 whilst still residing at Ravenstone; he was 85 years old. He had been living with his daughter, Emily, since the death of his wife on Christmas Eve, 1946, aged 75 years and after 54 years of marriage.

Regarding the siblings; Fanny died aged 92

Left: A letter from the Imperial War Graves Commission on the 6th June 1922 states it would be unwise to visit Sanctuary Wood Cemetery because of war damage. Optimistically it states that bodies are being recovered all the time and are being reburied.

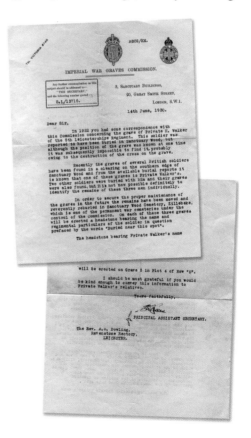

Another letter from the Imperial War Graves Commission on the 14th June 1930 informs the Walker family that several bodies had been found in a clearing on the southern edge of Sanctuary Wood. One of those bodies was of Henry, and the letter continues that he has been reburied at Sanctuary Wood Military Cemetery. The letter finalises by commenting that Henry will have a permanent headstone on Grave 5 on Plot 4 on Row S.

Sanctuary Wood Cemetery. The headstone can be found on Grave 5, Plot 4, and Row S.

Sadly, it is no longer possible to determine whether any of Harry's relatives were fortunate enough to visit his grave. I have done so, and the C.W.G.C. maintain his and all other graves in an immaculate condition. (Www.cwgc.org.uk.)

Whilst visiting Mary Mulholland I was

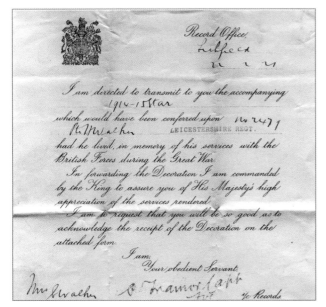

The Records Office at Lichfield enclosed the 1914-1915 Star in a package sent to Henry's father on the 22nd February 1921. It notified him that his son would have received the medal had he lived, in memory of his services with the British Forces during the Great War.

away at Leicester on the 10th November 1987, aged 74 years.

Thank you Mary for such an absorbing account that revolves around the sadness of her uncle's death in Flanders' Fields.

Mary, and his other living niece, Janet Sanders (daughter of Fanny) plan to visit his grave in the near future.

It is quite a coincidence that Mary was born at 152, Ashburton Road at Hugglescote. Readers of my first book will realise that the brothers John and Sidney Summers were born in an earlier house that stood on that site. The brothers were first cousins of my grandfather, Thomas Kendrick.

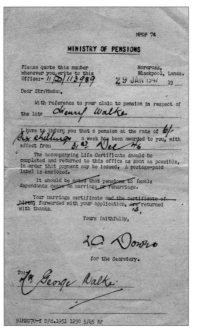

Henry left school at the age of 13 years, then becoming employed as a miner at South Leicestershire Colliery, Ellistown. For his efforts over the period 1908-1914, the Ministry of Pensions informed his father on the 31st December 1946 that he could claim six shillings a week on his behalf. This sum is thirty new pence and equates to somewhere in the region of £8 by today's standards.

years at Loughborough following many years of marriage to Sanford Pratt at 37, Albert Promenade, Loughborough.

Frederick Walker married a Florence Green whilst Ada Walker married Jesse Bowley and had a childless marriage until her death at Snibston on the 2nd April 1958, aged 65 years.

Herbert Walker married a Gwendoline Green and Emily Walker never married and passed away on the 23rd October 1983, aged 78 years. Mary Mulholland's father was the youngest sibling, Arthur. He married Marjorie Hickman on the 5th August 1939 and they settled at Ravenstone. Marjorie was born at Coalville on the 15th March 1913 and passed

HERBERT GLADSTONE WHARMBY

I had almost completed this book when the above surname kept on cropping-up, rarely hearing of the name during the fifty odd years of my life.

Whilst visiting my beloved mother, who suffers from Alzheimer's, in a local Care-Home I met a dear old lady, Mary Hunt (nee Wharmby), who mentioned that she had lost a cousin in the Great War. Soon afterwards I met Raymond Cross, son of Ernest Cross, who is well recalled earlier in this book, only

to find that his wife, Kathleen, was Mary's sister. Whilst being shown other photographs, Kathleen pulled out a photograph of her cousin, namely: Herbert Gladstone Wharmby.

I then recalled that his name appears on the Coalville Clock Tower Memorial, and at last the penny dropped! I turned to my earlier book, 'Fifty Good Men And True', on page 106, to spot the same name on Memorial Tablets that once graced the

Herbert Gladstone Wharmby of Bakewell street, Coalville, originally enlisted into the Leicestershire Regiment. During 1916, and whilst fighting with the 24th Battalion of the London Regiment, he was killed close to the Butte de Warlincourt on the Somme. Not only can his name be seen on the Coalville Clock Tower, but also on a Memorial Tablet within Market Bosworth Dixie Grammar School.

London Road Baptist Chapel at Coalville. Readers may recall the sadness when I found that they had been discarded when the Chapel had moved to nearby Charnborough Road.

The melancholy continues because very little is known about the gentleman. He was the son of Mr. Herbert Wharmby of Bakewell Street, Coalville; the elder brother of Kathleen and Mary's father. Although they were cousins the age gap strung a generation, indeed the future soldier was born in 1887. His father had remarried and so he had several stepsisters.

He must have been a clever lad, because after leaving the Chapel School he undertook a few jobs, until being appointed to the prestigious position of clerk at Ibstock Colliery.

In 1914 he almost certainly enlisted fairly early, and in the 'Coalville Roll of Honour' it states that he served with the Leicestershire Regiment (service number 6474). Possibly he was wounded, whatever, he was later reposted to the 24th Battalion of the London Regiment, 47th London Division.

Undoubtedly, Herbert fought with his unit in the dreadful Somme battle that resulted in the capture of High Wood on the 15th September 1916. The Division then moved to the nearby Martinpuich Sector, and attacked the ruins of Eaucourt L'Abbaye on October 1st. They followed up six days later with an attack upon the infamous: 'Butte de Warlincourt', about three kilometres northwest of Martinpuich and one northwest of Le Sars.

The Butte de Warlincourt is an ancient Roman burial mound, a natural vantage point that overlooks miles of the surrounding area. The Germans tunnelled into the mound, installed deep dugouts, and peppered the location with machine-gun posts. Alongside other reasons the Butte needed to be captured, because it was directing enemy fire over allied positions, and the ensuing fighting was described as very fierce.

The attack was not a success and the War Diary reads: '*The full force of the enemy artillery and machine-gun fire, cleverly sighted in depth, so as to bring a withering fire cross-fire to bear along the western slopes leading to the Butte and the high ground to the south of it. From across the valley the enemy had a magnificent observation of the ground leading to our objective, and made full use of it, not a man turned back, and some got right up under the Butte, but were never seen again.*'

Herbert Wharmby was killed on Sunday, 8th October 1916. He was just one of 296 officers and 7, 475 of the Division killed on the Somme..

The battle for the old mound continued until the 18th November 1916, whence heavy snows halted this particular stage of the Somme battle.

Private Herbert Gladstone Wharmby is

remembered at ref: V11 H31, at Warlincourt British Cemetery.

Finishing on a high note, I was contacted by Philip Hamson, a teacher at The Dixie Grammar School at Market Bosworth. He asked if it was possible for the Dixie to adopt the Memorial Tablets from the aforementioned Baptist Chapel.

On the 8th November 2005 during a Remembrance Ceremony, the Reverend G. Willett (newly appointed at Charnborough Road Baptist Chapel), the School Staff, a full school assembly and myself witnessed the arrival of the Tablets into their new home.

I could not have been happier; neither could the several hundred students and staff within the ancient splendour of the famous Grammar School.

The name of Herbert Gladstone Wharmby can be read on the Coalville Clock Tower Memorial and on Tablets within Dixie Grammar School, Market Bosworth.

A copy of this book will accompany my earlier book within the school's library.

During World War 2, a nephew of the above soldier, Corporal Arthur Wharmby of the 1st Leicestershire Battalion, was captured by Japanese

Corporal Arthur Wharmby, service number 4859967, the nephew of Herbert Wharmby. Arthur, of the 1st Battalion of the Leicestershire Regiment, was captured in Malaysia by the Japanese invaders in February 1942. He died on the 22nd December 1943 whilst labouring on the Burma/Siam: 'Railway of Death.' He was twenty-fours years of age, and is remembered with honour in Chungkai War Cemetery.

troops on the Malaysian peninsula. He toiled as a labourer on the notorious 'Railway of Death' until dying at the age of twenty-four years on the 22nd December 1943. He lies at peace in Chungkai War Cemetery.

His name is remembered on the Coalville Clock Tower Memorial.

With thanks to Kathleen and Mary Cross, and never forgetting the warmth of spirit of all at D.G.S.

JABEZ EMMERSON
AND A FEW ADDITIONS TO THE FAMILY

Jabez Emmerson was, of course, a member of Coalville's Famous Fifty, the son of Alfred Barratt Emmerson: a member of the Whitwick Colliery Rescue team in 1898.

Note the photograph taken in the summer of 1911 at Ellistown shows the five siblings, William, Jabez, young George, Maggie and Helen. No talk of a world war during that balmy summer.

In 1915 Jabez sent a beautiful silk card to one of his sisters; on the reverse he wrote: '*Have received your delightful letter and parcel. Letter follows. Love Jabez. xx.*'

He had two sisters: Maggie, born on the 5th March 1886 and Helen (Nellie) born on the 20th January 1891. He also had two brothers: William,

born December 1888 and Ernest (George) in January 1898.

Jabez Emmerson (far right) with William (second left rear) with sisters Maggie, Helen (Nellie), brother, George, and parents. Summer 1911.

A photograph of Jabez Emmerson—centre rear—with Walter Handford sitting in front of him. 1915 France. Other soldiers are from left clockwise: Boam, Beardmore, Hallam and Neal.

Jabez left the Leicestershire Regiment in 1919 as a full captain and decorated with the Distinguished Conduct Medal (D.C.M.).

Post-war Jabez was a very senior member of 'TOC-H', the society set up during the Great War by the Reverend 'Tubby' Clayton to offer assistance to servicemen, notably for the disabled, it is still in evidence to this day. In 1928, the Prince of Wales, later King Edward V111 who abdicated the throne, invited 'TOC-H' to the Church House, Westminster, for the lighting of a new Lamps of Remembrance. Jabez can be seen standing with his lamp on the far left of the picture.

A recently found 'carte postale' sent by Jabez Emmerson from France to one of his sisters in 1915. A note on the back simply says: 'Have Received your delightful letter and parcel. Letter to follow. Love Jabez xx.'

Jabez had two children with his first wife, Bertha (who died from a brain haemorrhage in 1947), namely Philip and Jean. The latter became a nurse at Leicester Royal Infirmary, married a doctor and moved to Scotland.

Jabez later married a friend of his daughters, also a nurse, named Constance Aldwinkle, and they had just one child, Stuart.

Stuart inherited many of the Emmerson qualities, was educated at university and received a doctorate. He later married and had children with a delightful African lady, have children; they live happily in northwest Leicestershire.

A picture entitled: 'The Prince and 'TOC-H'.' Rev. 'Tubby Clayton', founder of the movement that assisted soldiers of the Great War is kneeling by the Prince of Wales: the future King Edward V111. Jabez Emmerson is standing on the rear left. Church House, Westminster. 1928.

Jay Emmerson

Jay Emmerson was the uncle of Jabez Emmerson as mentioned earlier. His Christian name was in fact Jabez but fortunately his name was corrupted as a young man: thus removing any confusion. He is mentioned earlier in the book against his sons' names: Joe and Alf, both of which were killed in action. Jay and his wife had two other siblings, William and Mary.

William moved to Liverpool in early 1914 and when war was declared he promptly enlisted into a Liverpool Scottish Battalion, indeed, he was taken as a prisoner of war and sent to labour in salt mines. Often below ground, it was his charge to take care of the horses that helped to convey salt from the mines. He often spoke of the complications involved

Jay Emmerson's children: William, Joe, Mary and Alf.

Leicester, and lived until the age of ninety-five. Their son, John, was a captain in the 10th Battalion of the Black Watch during World War 2.

My thanks, once again, to Blanche Wyatt, granddaughter of Alfred Barratt Emmerson and Norma Emmerson, Jabez's daughter-in-law. Sadly John has died.

Mary Herbert and her father Jay Emmerson, 1950.

because the horses had been so badly treated by the German authorities. After the war he returned to Liverpool, and lived on Somerset Road in the suburb of West Derby, later moving to Green Lane, Chilwell. The Liver Works employed him as a manager.

Mary married Walter Herbert of the highly respected Herbert family of Parkhill House,

2nd Lieutenant John Herbert of the Black Watch.

WILLIAM AND JOSEPH MASSEY

Readers of my first book will recall the name of William (Bill) Massey, one of the Famous Fifty, and of his younger brother, Joseph. Sadly, Bill was killed in the infamous Trench 50, but pleasingly additional information has come forward.

Left: George Harry Bennett and Bill Massey at Loughborough in 1914.

Around the turn of the century the Massey family lived at 33, Main Street at Hugglescote, and attended St. John The Baptist Church: with Bill and Joseph receiving education at the Church School.

Their father, Richard Massey, developed: 'Botanic Brewery' on the Forest Road, the building still exists, and the firm bottled mineral water. Bill left school in January 1909, Joseph on the 12th November 1910: confirmed on his 'Labour Certificate', with both working for the families expanding business concern.

Bill's military experiences have already been chronicled, however, below can be read the last letter that he sent to his parents, dated the 8th August 1915. He was to die at 4.00 am the following day, August 9th.

Dear Mother and father,

Just a few lines in answer to your welcome letter, which I got yesterday. I was pleased to hear from you and that you are all well as I am at present. It is rather rough weather here just now, plenty of rain and mud about. As I write this I am in my dugout with a pair of sandbags piled over my shoes and trousers, and they have got about half an inch of caked mud on them, which keeps me very warm and comfortable. We don't bother about dirt here. We are happy enough and keep smiling. We expect to be relieved tomorrow night if all is quiet, and I hope it is. We are going in dugouts about three miles away for six days in reserve for anything that might come, and then we go back to the trenches again for six days when we shall have done our share as we shall have had 22 days of it. I received the Coalville Times. You must not have any hopes of me being able to get leave, as I expect it will be a good while yet. I suppose you have got a letter by this time saying that Charlie Hatter (another Hugglescote soldier) was wounded. I have not heard from him yet. We are in the same trench that was blown up the other week and we can't help but think about it! I expect we shall be having some lively times here, but we shall be prepared for them

With best love to all, Bill.

On the 16th August 1915, a Mrs. Wright of Linby Hall, Swannington, visited Richard and Sarah Massey to inform them that she had received a letter from her son. He too was serving in the trenches, and wrote that Bill had been killed. The letter revealed that Bill was killed just after a charge, and on returning to his trench put his head up to view the enemy only to be immediately sniped.

Richard and Sarah were absolutely stunned, inconsolable, and even the following day the military authorities had not confirmed his death. Regrettably, they were soon to hear.

Mrs Wright's son, Arthur, was killed on the 4th February 1917.

Bill's parents had a Bereavement Card that provides his details together with the following verse:

Not death - but just a parting of the waves -
Divides us from a hero slain,
A patriot sleeps, but with the morning rays,
Fond hearts awake and meet again.

Joseph Massey in 1915.

Joseph enlisted at Coalville on the 19th December 1915. He was posted to the 2/5th Leicestershire Regiment: classed as grade: 'A' and mobilised on the 5th September 1916; serving in Scotland, Ireland, Wales, France, Belgium, Italy, Greece and finally Turkey.

The 2/5th Battalion, part of the 177th Brigade, had its first taste of military duty in Ireland. Riots on the 24th April 1916, at the Easter Monday Race Meeting of the Meath Hunt, just outside of Dublin, spread into the city centre. A little later, whilst stationed at Trallee (County Kerry) he and a friend, Edward Flack, were in the party sent to arrest the Irish conspirator, Sir Robert Casement, who arrived on a German ship. Other details of: 'The Irish Rebellion', as it was labelled, can be found in the essay concerning Reginald Glover.

During his service Joseph was wounded several times; certainly his frame carried a good deal of shrapnel for the remainder of his life. He had a nasty scar on his right forearm: caused by the penetration of a German bayonet and was gassed on several occasions. Following intervals of hospitalisation in England he was reposted to different units, and in August 1917 was a frontline soldier with the 3rd Battalion of the King's Own Royal Lancashire Regiment.

Readers are aware that Bill was a very good pre-war boxer; well it appears such qualities ran in the family, and Joseph won much acclaim as an Army champion. He worked alongside his father developing and maintaining the business until his father died on the 15th November 1933.

Towards the end of his life Joseph became somewhat bent-over. A doctor prescribed tablets for arthritis of the upper spine; it was only after his death, on the 1st January 1979, aged eighty years, that a piece of World War 1 shrapnel was found! Over a period of fifty years it had passed from his right shoulder to one of his neck vertebrae.

My thanks for the additional information to a relative of the brothers.

I republish the photograph of George Harry Bennett alongside Bill Massey for two reasons. Firstly, my sadness at the passing of George's daughter, Florence Storer in 2006: a very dear and intelligent lady, and secondly for the friendship of Andrew Massey. My grandfather, Charles Hatter and Bill were great friends, and over ninety years after

the death of Bill, I find it very moving that Andrew and I are firm friends.

A communication trench leading to Trench 49 and 50: near to Hill 60, Ypres. Men of the 5th Leicestershire Battalion frequently used this trench during the summer of 1915. Bill Massey would have known this trench. (Photo: Richard Lane).

THE HOHENZOLLERN REDOUBT

I wrote an essay in my earlier book regarding the above, however, extra material has recently become available. Firstly, I thank Richard Lane for providing me with a copy of a letter sent by Lieutenant Colonel R. E. Martin, commanding officer of the Fourth Battalion of the Leicestershire Battalion, to Major J. Potter, who, until shortly before the battle was second-in-command of the Battalion.

Letter from Lieutenant Colonel R. E. Martin, Commanding Officer: 1/4th Leicestershire Battalion to Major J. Potter at Divisional Headquarters.

Duchess of Westminster Hospital
Le Touquet
France.
October 30th 1915.

My dear Potter,

I am very glad indeed to see that you are in harness again, even though in a position so uncongenial as an office. But I am perfectly certain that you were right to take it, Territorial Force Regiments notwithstanding. The more people in authority that you can get to know and put into a proper frame of mind by doing good work, the better chance there is of getting where you want to be. And goodness knows you are wanted badly enough with the Regiment. You had evidently not heard, when I wrote, about our show on the 13th, and what it produced in the way of casualties with the Battalion. The Division was turned on to take the Hohenzollern Redoubt and Fosse 8, which adjoined it on the southeast. Our Brigade assaulted the Redoubt and the Staffords the Colliery and spoil heap to the right.

The 5th Lincolns and we did the actual assault, side by side in 4 lines, all 4 companies of each battalion abreast: four rows of four.

There was a big artillery preparation for two hours with gas and smoke. We assaulted at 2.00pm and wish you could have seen them go. There was nothing wrong with them, I can tell you. And it wasn't any blooming picnic either. The machine-gun and rifle fire was very heavy: I

suppose the Hun must have sent their machine-guns into deep dug-outs while our guns were firing and brought them up when they lifted. Every officer was killed or wounded (counting young Cox who was blown up and had to go back.) and between 2/3rds and 3/4qtrs of the men. The 5th Lincolns had one officer left and their rank and file casualties were as heavy. The 4th Lincolns came out in support with the remains of the Monmouths, who had been attached to the Division as a sort of pioneer battalion; there job was to clean out dug-outs and consolidate. The 5th Battalion were in reserve but sent up between 2 and 3 Companies before the show was over, leaving Langdale and Hastings killed, and young Moss. The 8th Sherwoods, who were in further reserve, were also sent in later on, in the early hours of the 14th.

As a result of it all, the Redoubt was taken, and some communication trenches on the flanks, and retained against some pretty heavy bombing counter attacks. So we have been fortunate in not having to be used up to take a position afterwards, as has happened to some troops.

Toller is commanding officer for the time, with Jarvis and Price (whom the extending people were made to dislodge) and a subaltern from the 5th! (***1/5th Battalion**.)
The Brigade went up with 75 combatant officers and came out with 10: so there aren't many to go around.
I wonder whether it would be worth your while to

The Hohenzollern Redoubt was honeycombed with machine-gun posts. (Circa: late 1918.)

*write to T. F. 3 (**Territorial Force**), after talking to your general and say that you understand the*

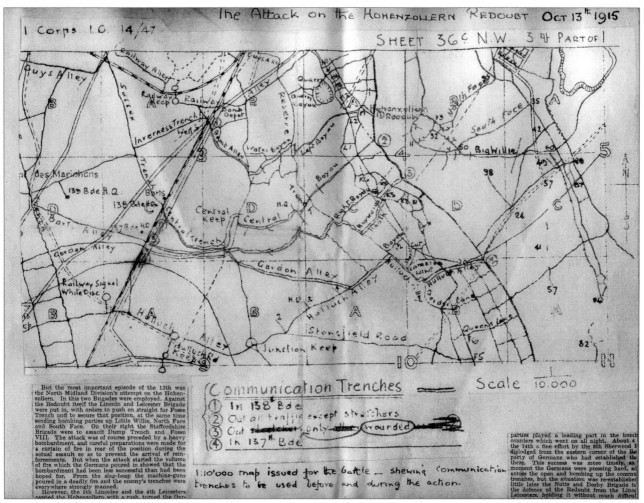

The Attack on the Hohenzollern Redoubt Oct 13th 1915

Copy of an original map as issued to an officer of the 5th Leicestershire Battalion in 1915.

Battalion has lost heavily in officers and ask that your application to return may be considered. Put in, if you like, that you would rather go as a company commander than not at all. Ask, if you like, that my opinion may be sought.

Tetley (**Major F.E. Tetley of the 4th Lincolns assumed position of second-in-command on 1st December 1915**) went home sick before he transferred to us, so although posted he has never joined. We hear that he is better and championing to be sent out. Whether they will give him command in front of someone else I don't know.

I got hit by a bullet through my left leg on our parapet, so got no distance at all, which was pretty sickening. My femur is cracked for 3 or 4 inches up from the knee, and certainly down into the joint. It is doing very well now and I have good hopes that there wont be any complications, though until 3 weeks or so are past, one cannot be quite sure that the danger of septic infection is over. I suspect I shall be here for another fortnight or so and then move to some hospital in

town. It will be a longish job, I think, knees always are: I don't suppose I will be sound before next summer. It is a distracting prospect, but it might have been so very much worse and so am really very thankful.

Our casualties were these: Killed: Faire, Whittingham, Green, Forsell, Harvey, Emmerson, Russell, Scholes, Mogridge, O'Callaghan, Walters, Blunt (died afterwards.) Wounded: Newill, Dyer-Bennett, Johnson, Riley. (**Johnson died of wounds 30/10/15.**)

Missing: Corah, Barker. (**Both killed.**) I much fear that Corah is killed. Barker is reported wounded. Sendall was wounded, Robinson believed killed, and I think 3 company commanders besides others.

To every body of troops comes their day, sooner or later. Let us be thankful that when ours came the men went forward with a good heart and did a fair share of what they were asked to do. I don't think they could have done much more, taking all things into account.

I feel as if my world had fallen to pieces around

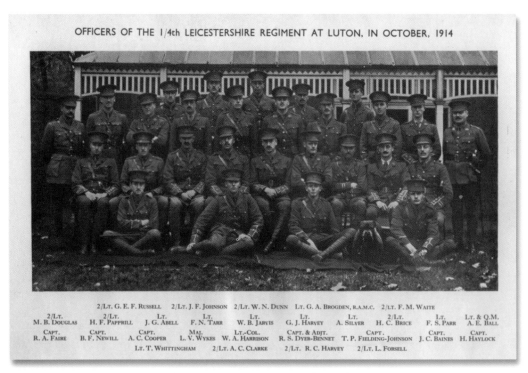

OFFICERS OF THE 1/4th LEICESTERSHIRE REGIMENT AT LUTON, IN OCTOBER, 1914

2/Lt. G. E. F. Russell   2/Lt. J. F. Johnson   2/Lt. W. N. Dunn   Lt. G. A. Brogden, R.A.M.C.   2/Lt. F. M. Waite

2/Lt.   2/Lt.   Lt.   Lt.   Lt.   Lt.   Lt.   2/Lt.   Lt.   Lt. & Q.M.
M. B. Douglas   H. F. Papprill   J. G. Abell   F. N. Tarr   W. B. Jarvis   G. J. Harvey   A. Silver   H. C. Brice   F. S. Parr   A. E. Ball

Capt.   Capt.   Capt.   Maj.   Lt.-Col.   Capt. & Adjt.   Capt.   Capt.   Capt.
R. A. Faire   B. F. Newill   A. C. Cooper   L. V. Wykes   W. A. Harrison   R. S. Dyer-Bennet   T. P. Fielding-Johnson   J. C. Baines   H. Haylock

Lt. T. Whittingham   2/Lt. A. C. Clarke   2/Lt. R. C. Harvey   2/Lt. L. Forsell

(Footprints of the 1/4th Leicestershire Battalion.)

me, even here away from the battalion, but it is what we are all out for, and the main thing is to be able to feel that the battalion, as we knew it, has not gone out for nothing. Let me know how you get on.

Yours sincerely,
R.E. Martin.

*In bold italics inserted by author, so is the following:

Those killed were: Captain Reginald Alfred Faire, Lieutenant Thomas Whittingham, Lieutenant Richard Scott Green, Lieutenant Alan Richard Forsell, Lieutenant Richard Clive Harvey, 2nd Lieutenant Joseph Emmerson, 2nd Lieutenant Guy Edward Frank Russell, 2nd Lieutenant Wilfred Paul Scholes, 2nd Lieutenant Basil Fullelove West Mogridge, 2nd Lieutenant Thomas Francis O'Callaghan, 2nd Lieutenant Frederick William Walters, 2nd Lieutenant Francis Clifford Blunt, Lieutenant John Frederick Johnson, Captain Leslie Corah, 2nd Lieutenant John Edward Barker.

I am truly delighted that 'The 'Hohenzollern Redoubt' has finally received its magnificent memorial to the fallen of the 46th North Midland Division (1915). An old friend, Richard Lane, who served as an officer with the Tigers, has been a prime worker in ensuring a brilliant and satisfactory conclusion to the disastrous events of 13th October

of that year.

We cannot possibly imagine such a scene, or the affect on the mentality of the survivors.

My grandfather, Charles Hatter, took part, and I

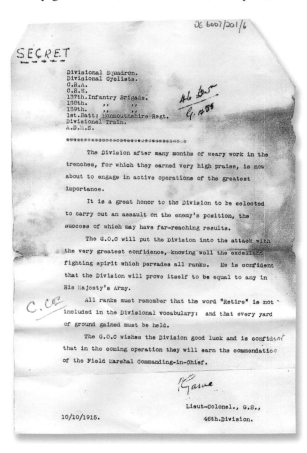

A letter dated 10th October 1915 from a Staff Officer at Div. H. Q. informing the various sections of the 46th North Midland Division, that on the 13th October 1915 they have been selected (even honoured) to assault an important enemy position.

shall always remember his words:

'In early afternoon we scrambled up the trench ladders and bayonet charged the enemy redoubt, but dead men from the 4th Battalion were everywhere, and little wonder with the machine-gun fire and shells.'

Most of the 3, 763 casualties of the day were a result of the honeycombed machine gun nests positioned high in the massive slagheap, with many of the dead remaining on the battlefield until the end of the war; such was the stubbornness and strength of

'Captain Hastings of 'A' Company decided to attempt a bayonet attack against the German opposition on the left of the Redoubt, and he himself led his men in the attack. Platoon commanders were again the first to fall as they climbed out of their trenches, 2nd Lieutenant Lawton was mortally wounded in the stomach and 2nd Lieutenant Petch badly shot through the arm. However this did not delay the attack, and the Company crossing the German frontline quickened their pace and made for the junctions of 'Little Willie' and 'N. Face.' Once

THE KILLING FIELDS OF FLANDERS

These men have shown that they are prepared to make the supreme sacrifice for what they believe to be true and righteous.

the German Redoubt. Lieutenant Joseph Emmerson of Bagworth, son of Jay Emmerson, the colliery manager, was last seen leading his men of the Fourth Battalion on a bayonet-charge to a second-line trench. His body was never found and his name is remembered with honour on the Loos Memorial. He was the cousin of Jabez Emmerson, one of the town's Famous Fifty.

The War Diary of the 5th Leicestershire reads:

more bombs and machine-guns were too hot for them, and first Captain Hastings, then 2nd Lieutenant Moss were killed near to the German second line. Captain Hastings was an Ashby-de-la-Zouch man.

A total of 74 officers and 1,234 other ranks, a total of 1,308 were killed in action or died of wounds. Of the dead infantry only 91 men have identified graves in fourteen different cemeteries. Such was the horror of the battlefield that 93 per cent of the dead have no known grave. Of the 2,368 non-fatal infantry casualties, most were wounded but a few were taken prisoner. The Artillery, Engineers and other divisional units suffered 87 casualties.

4th Leicestershire Battalion had 211 dead and 262 wounded. Total: 473.

5th Leicestershire Battalion had 42 dead and 187 wounded. Total: 229.

4th Lincolnshire Battalion had 169 dead and 228 wounded. Total: 397.

5th Lincolnshire Battalion had 188 dead and 295 wounded. Total: 483.

5th South Staffordshire had 103 men dead and 216 wounded. Total: 319.

6th South Staffordshire had 122 dead and 285 wounded. Total: 407.

5th North Staffordshire had 232 dead and 273 wounded. Total: 505.

6th North Staffordshire had 98 dead and 217 wounded. Total: 315.

5th Notts and Derby had 8 dead and 41 wounded. Total: 49.

6th Notts and Derby had 12 dead and 48 wounded. Total: 60.

7th Notts and Derby had 44 dead and 107 wounded. Total: 151.

8th Notts and Derby had 48 dead and 122 wounded. Total: 170.

1st Monmouthshire had 31 dead and 129 wounded. Total: 160.

A few years ago Richard spotted that part of the old French-Flanders battlefield was being used as a waste-tip. He started a campaign, and with the support of local newspapers contacted the French government; they intervened and the tipping was stopped. Most French locals were unaware of the site's significance and are now proud of the historical

LIEUTENANT-COLONEL R. E. MARTIN, C.M.G., T.D., D.L.

area, peace has been restored. Richard says: "*On the morning of the unveiling, the old battlefield was shrouded with mist; gradually the sun burnt it off to reveal the monument. It was also very moving when a troop of soldiers in Great War uniforms marched to us singing: 'Here we are, here we are, here we are again!' The Leicestershire Battalions sang this as they approached the Redoubt in 1915. The troop also sang: 'Keep The Home Fires Burning', another favourite of that time.*"

The well-known military author, Martin Middlebrook, gave the Address, and the blowing of the same trench whistle used to start the 1915 Battle was used to signal the Last Post. Tim Jones, Her Majesty's Consul-General unveiled the Memorial.

THE FIFTH LEICESTERSHIRE BATTALION
1914-18

A map belonging to an officer of the Fifth Battalion. Below left--- the rimmed crater in Trench 50 that killed many of the Battalion.
During the summer of 1915 six of the Famous Fifty died in that trench, including Bill Massey.
(Photo: Richard Lane)

Officers of the Fifth Leicestershire Battalion: Luton 1914.
(Left to right) 4th Row: Lt. Warley, Capt. Jackson, Lt. Hills, Lt. Marsh, Lt. Knighton, Lt. Barrowcliff.
3rd Row: Lt. Farmer, Capt. Sharpe, Capt. Hastings, Capt. Holmes, Lt. Moore, Lt. Langdale, Lt. Fielden, Lt. Lawton, Lt. Vincent, Capt. Beasley.
2nd Row: Capt. Jeffries, Capt. Bland, Major Shea, Major Martin, Lt. Col. Jones, Capt. Broomfield, Maj. Toller, Capt. Coward, Capt. Griffith.
Front Row: Lt. Allen, Lt. Burnett, Lt. Pullinger, Lt. Woolaston.

The Fifth Battalion had been active on the Western Front since the early spring of 1915, and had lost a lot of very fine Leicestershire men in battles at Ypres, Hohenzollern, Somme and Vimy Ridge.

On 6th June of 1917 they moved to Lievin, a coalmining district and a suburb of Lens in France. By the evening of the 8th they were in readiness for a zero hour attack at 20.30.

The enemy, who were dug-in on the top of a huge thirty feet high slagheap, Fosse 3, received a typical introduction, an artillery barrage of heavy-explosive and shrapnel shells. One early shell detonated the enemy's ammunition dump, and as a result massive fires lit up the Devil's own battlefield. Troops of 'C' Company could be seen swarming up the slag heap towards the German held 'Boot' and 'Brick' trenches on the summit of the slag heap. My grandfather, Pte Charles Hatter, was one of those men: "*I was aware of silhouettes fighting in a red glow and with lots of hand-to-hand stuff.*" A good deal of bayonet work took place, and many dugouts were bombed. A young

Officers of the Fifth Leicestershire Battalion: 1917.
(Left to right) 4th Row from left: Chapman, Trimble, Campbell.
3rd Row: Warley, Marriott, Allen, Dawes, Petch, Ramsden, Morgan.
2nd Row: Shields, Griffiths, Trimble, Wollaston, Burnett.
Front Row: Vezine, Watherstone, Brooke, Buck.
(Photo: Richard Lane).

Post Cards bought by 1/5th Officer in 1915.

officer by the name of 2nd Lieutenant Banwell did exceptionally well, showing a lot of dash, he killed at least eight of the enemy by rifle or bayonet.

The attack on the left flank, 'B' Company, was doomed to failure. Led by Captain Wynne their number had hardly left their line when enemy machine-gun fire swept their ranks. Among those to

Captain Wynne and Lieutenant Farrer: killed on 8th June 1917

fall were Captain Wynne and Lieutenant Farrer. For some time Battalion Headquarters knew nothing of the disaster, and it was only when Lance Corporal Victor Woolley (one of the Famous Fifty) came back to report, that Colonel Trimble (the commanding officer) heard the news. He immediately ordered 'D' Company to fill the gap and so protect the left flank of Captain Aubrey Moore's 'C' Company, which would have been seriously exposed. Success was achieved, and 'C' Company cleared the summit and consolidated 'Boot' and 'Brick' while their forward numbers acted as a protective screen. Soon their position became precarious as enemy artillery

Post Cards bought by Officer of 1/5th in 1915.

pounded them from opposing flanks, and this was followed by a powerful counterattack which forced them to retreat: to oppose them would have resulted in unnecessary deaths.

On the night of the 9th June the Divisional General congratulated them on their brave efforts with Captain Moore receiving special praise. The bullet-ridden bodies of Captain Edward Wynne and Lieutenant Richard Farrer were taken to nearby Bully Grenay and placed under a single wooden cross. 'R.I.P. Here Lie Two Gallant Gentleman. Captain Wynne & Lieutenant Farrer. Killed In Action.'

A few days later a Lincolnshire Battalion re-took 'Boot' and 'Brick' trenches. At dusk on the

21st a message was received that a special brigade of Royal Engineers was to carry out a gas bombardment on mine buildings that were part of Fosse 3. Once again, 'C' Company was occupying the above trenches, and they heard the familiar explosion as the projectors went off: but to their horror many of the gas bombs landed amongst them. The trenches were full of deadly phosgene! Twenty-four died quickly, whilst another sixty-two were taken to hospital.

The error by the Engineers was labelled as; 'deaths by friendly fire'. Such is warfare, and a few more casualties were added to the lost generation.

So young: G. S. Smith of Kirkby House, Barkby.

A form of 'B' Company, Fifth Leicestershire itemising the clothing issued to Private C. Palmer in 1924. Little change from 1914.

CAPTAIN J. D. HILLS M.C. AND BAR.
CROIX DE GUERRE
AUTHOR OF THE FIFTH LEICESTERSHIRE

I am indeed grateful for Captain Hills' excellent account of the activities of the 1/5th Leicestershire Battalion during the Great War, which was published by Loughborough's Echo Press in 1919. The majority of the narrative was based on the Battalion War Diary, but the Captain in his introduction explained how various members of the battalion assisted him.

2nd Lieutenant Hills was in 'D' Company when the Fifth Battalion disembarked at Le Havre in

February 1915, however, such was his academic ability that he was quickly selected to the post of 138th Brigade Intelligence Officer. As such he was one of the party of eleven officers to accompany the commanding officer of the 46th North Midland Division, Major General E. J. Montague Stuart Wortley, to assess the feasibility of a Divisional embarkation for Mesopotamia or similar. They sailed from Marseilles aboard H.M.T. *'Megantic'* (of the White Star Line) and after nine hours on the Suez Canal and four days in camp at Sidi Gaba, near Alexandria, they returned to France on 4th February 1916. Clearly the mission was considered unsatisfactory and the Division left the French Port and returned to the Western front: Vimy Ridge.

Thanks to Richard Lane and the family of J. D. Hills I am also able to print the following post-war letters, photographs and earlier postcards.

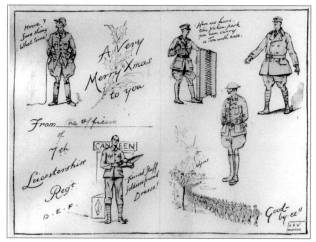

7th Leicestershire Battalion.

Mr. Chas Tailby
Snae Fell
Burfield Avenue
Loughborough
Leicestershire.

Dear Sir,

After reading your book on the Fifth Leicestershire about the war, I congratulate you, but I wish to point out to you that you made a mistake on page 63, which says: 'T. Whitbread, of 'A' Company scraped away the earth with his hands.' It should have read C. Tailby. It was not Whitbread. There were several of us in a dugout, Whitbread, Neal and several more including C.

Tailby, that's me! All at once Cassel came running by, bleeding and shouting that there were more buried round there—-pointing round the corner. I ran round to find most of the trench all filled up with earth through the shelling. The first thing I saw was Pringle's two legs sticking out of the earth. It was loose and I got him out, but he was dead. Then I started scraping away again and I got to Scott, who was alive. Then Sergeant Gore came up and said, "They are dead aren't they? Come on, it's too hot here." I says, "Scott is still alive, and while there's life there's hope." So Sergeant Gore and me carried Scott to the First Aid dugout, walking most of the way on level ground because the trench was full up.

Yours sincerely,

Chas Tailby

5th Leicestershire Battalion for 1917/18. Drawn by 2nd Lt. Shilton.

Author: In 'Fifty Good Men And True': as part of my Clifford Scott essay, I give credit to Private T. Whitbread for trying to save his life. Clifford Scott and Fred Pringle both died on the day in question: 1st

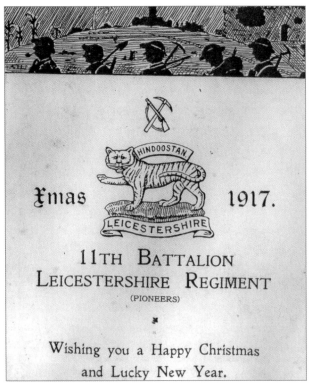

11th Leicestershire Battalion.

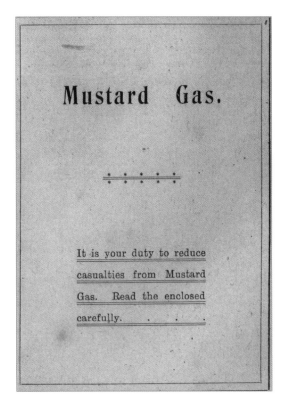

Circa 1915.

September 1915. Private Arthur Whitbread of Loughborough was killed in action on 28th July 1917 in the St. Elie Left section (near Hohenzollern.)

All credit to Private Charles Tailby, an extremely brave man who risked his own life in the attempt to save others. The letter is not dated, but I would take it to be in the 1920's.

> *James Coles*
> *11 Gutteridge Street*
> *Coalville*
> *Leicester*
> > *LE6 2BG.*

Mr. Hills.

> *Dear Sir,*
> > *I am writing this 'Lest We Forget'. It is fifty years since the attack on Pontruet, a long time, much has happened and we are getting old.*

You will wonder what this is all about; well I'm the man who years ago had red hair, M.M., etc, and I thought you would not mind me writing to you. I hope you and all yours are in the best of health, as for myself I never felt better. I hope I have not done wrong writing to you; I got your address from 'Who's Who!' I nearly wrote last anniversary but I thought I would wait until the fifty years were up. I don't suppose you ever heard how that chap, Hooke, went on. I expect he would die. If I had my way, which I haven't, I'm married; I would have one room with pictures of Sunken Roads, bringing up rations, etc, hanging up on the walls. My wife has just said that you will think me queer. I'm O.K., but old fashioned no doubt. I have been retired about seven years now, but about four years ago I got myself a part time job. I think that if you sit back too much you get to feel older. Again, hoping I have not intruded.

> *I remain yours,*
> *Respectfully,*
> *James Coles.*

Doullens — my billet.

Captain Hills billet as they travelled to Vimy Ridge.

James Coles was a military medallist, almost certainly won at the Battle of Pontruet, of which the 50th anniversary would have been 24th September 1968. He may have been a runner for the Battalion, taking or locating information and ensuring it reached the officer in command. In Captain

Mont St Eloi
(now in ruins)

Hill's book, page 293: *'The only post known to 'A' Company was Corporal Barber's at the Cemetery. 'C' Company were supposed to be somewhere at the* other end, *but no one quite knew where. However with Corporal Barber was a 'C' Company soldier, Coles, who undertook to find his own way back to his Company. Our idea was to form a line through the village at once, and, when ammunition arrived, push the line through to the far side. Coles found 'C' Company, but so hot was the sniping from Forgan's (enemy trench), that any idea of moving men in that direction had to be abandoned, at any rate until darkness. Coles, himself was unable to return, so the exact position of 'C' Company was never known at Headquarters.'*

Ablain St Nazarre Church (ruined

Private Albert Edward Hooke of Anstey, service number 202527, was badly wounded during the Battle and died on the following day (25th September 1918.) It was at Pontruet that Lieutenant J.C. Barrett received a Victoria Cross whilst leading a head-on attack on Forgan's Trench. He was seriously wounded, but without doubt his brave action saved many lives.

Souchez (nothing left)

COALVILLE OLD BOYS' MEMORIAL

The Coalville Times of the 2nd April 1920 wrote about the Roll of Honour and a Memorial Tablet containing the names of fifty-one Old Boys of the Belvoir Road Council School, Coalville. The Tablet was unveiled on Saturday March 27th in the presence of a good number of old boys, parents and friends.

Mr. J. W. Taylor, one of the former scholars occupied the chair and in the opening proceedings said: *'I must say how pleased I am to see such good company present, and no doubt feel proud to place something on record of our respect and appreciation to the old boys who gave their lives in the Great War for King and Country. You all know that Mr. Frith, the headmaster, has been at this school for nearly thirty years, during which period a large number of scholars have passed through this school. It is he who thought something should be done. With that in mind a meeting was called through the Press, old scholars and decided to carry out the following programme. 1. A tablet to be erected for the Old Boys. 2. To obtain a Roll of Honour placing the names of old boys who served in H.M. Forces. 3. That a 'Welcome Home' be given to all old boys.'*

THIS TABLET
IS ERECTED TO
THE GLORY OF GOD
AND TO PERPETUATE THE MEMORY, AND
REVERE THE NAMES OF THOSE
WHO FELL IN THE GREAT WAR, 1914-1919.

ALB.T CECIL BRADSHAW	WILFRID HORACE JONES
GEORGE ARTHUR BEALE	JESSE JONES
ERNEST BATHO	WALTER LEWIS
SIDNEY FRANK DODDS	HARRY LEWIS
ALBERT ESSEX	SAM.L CALLADINE SMITH
MARTIN EAMES	JOHN WILL.M SETCHELL
FRED.K WILFRID HART	THO.S HANDLEY USHERWOOD
JAMES HORACE HALL	GEORGE ALFRED WOOD
JOHN HALL	THOMAS WILLOTT WILD
ARTHUR EDW.D JOHNSON	ALBERT WILLIS WELLS

THEIR NAMES SHALL LIVE FOR EVER,
AND THEIR GLORY SHALL NEVER FADE AWAY.

The Belvoir Road Methodist Tablet now safely resides alongside the one on the left.

The inscription reads as follows:

'Belvoir Road Council School (late Wesleyan). For Honour, Truth and Right. To the glory of God, and in memory of the 'Old Boys' who bravely fought and nobly fell in the Great War 1914-1919. This Tablet is erected by past and present Scholars.

T. Frith. Headmaster.

The following names are inscribed:

E. Batho, G. A. Beale, F. P. Benistone, J. C. Bradshaw, J. G. Bennett, W. A. Berrisford, E. S. Boot, A. C. Bradshaw, T. H. Brookes, L. D. Brown, H. T. Cliff, P. W. Cliff, J. Clibbery, J. W. T. Collier, J. F. Colver, J. A. Crookes, S. F. Dodds, D. W. Drinkwater, W. Ducksbury, M. Eames, L. A. P. Finch, H. Geary, W. Gray, J. Hall, V. W. Hancox, E. Harper, J. W. Harper, D. Hickling, W. Hill, J. B. Holmes, E. Holyoak, A. Johnson, A. F. Johnson, J. Jones, H. Lewis, W. Lewis, J. Manders, T. Marriott, S. Mac Lachlan, J. Moon, L. M. Newman, J. W. Setchell, S. C. Smith, S. Stacy, J. W. Tugby, A. W. Wells, T. W. Wild, J. T. Williamson, G. A. Wood, H. Wright,, W. Wright and W. Fantom.

SACRED
TO
THE MEMORY OF SCHOLARS
WHO FELL IN THE GREAT WAR
1914-1918.

J. GEORGE BENNETT.	JULY 15.T 1915.
JOHN CLIBBERY.	JULY 20.T 1915.
ALFRED DALE.	SEP. 15.T 1916.
SIDNEY F. DODDS.	OCT. 21.T 1916.
D. W. DRINKWATER.	JUNE 13.T 1918.
JOSEPH EATON.	DEC. 24.T 1917.
J. HORACE HALL.	OCT. 15.T 1917.
JOHN W. HARPER.	JUNE 7.T 1917.
ERNEST HARPER.	OCT. 10.T 1917.
HORACE HAYES.	MAY 26.T 1917.
E. VICTOR KELHAM.	MAR. 27.T 1918.
SIMEON STACEY.	OCT. 19.T 1918.
JOHN T. WILLIAMSON.	MAR. 10.T 1915.
ARTHUR WRIGHT.	FEB. 4.T 1917.

Marlborough Methodist Church was the spiritual home for the above men.

The Reverend F. Pickbouren of London Road Baptist preached a sermon, and this was followed by a short address by Mr. Frith, who then unveiled the handsome brass tablet mounted on oak.

The schoolchildren sang the school song: 'Belvoir Roadians' and several hymns.

PILGRIMAGE TO THE BATTLEFIELDS

As the years passed after the Great War, quite naturally, there started a campaign for families who had lost loved ones, to visit the appropriate battlefields and where possible to see the relevant graves. The following was published in the Coalville Times 0n the 2nd March 1928, although clearly it was a general circular throughout Great Britain.

British Legion Organises Grand Tour

Ex-Service men and women will be glad to hear that they will shortly get a magnificent opportunity of visiting the battlefields, and the dignified and well kept cemeteries of the late war; at a very small cost. They will be able, in the company of old comrades in arms to revive the memory of those trying days, and to have a three day's holiday in France and Belgium at a cost which is much cheaper than if the trip was made independently. The British Legion in conjunction with The British Empire Service League is organising a Grand Pilgrimage to the British War zone, to take place between the 5th and the 9th August 1928. It is expected that 10,000 ex-Service men and women will take part in this popular and interesting tour, which promises to be a great success. The dates have been well chosen, as the 4th August 1914 marked the entry of Britain into the war, and the 8th August 1918 was the start of the great offensive which culminated in the collapse of the German Armies, and the defeat of Might by Right; thus August 8th must always remain fixed in the minds of us all, and no more fitting date than the tenth anniversary could have been selected for a tour to these famous battlefields. The British Legion has opened its doors wide and extended eligibility to join the pilgrimage, not only to its own members (including the Women's section) and to those of the British Empire Services League, but also to all ex-Service men and women, and to wives and bereaved relatives of ex-Service men. The total cost will only be £4-5shillings, which includes all fares from England, accommodation and meals during the four days. Special trains and boats will be waiting to convey the pilgrims every day, and all the latter will have to do is take their seats in the trains, after that the Legion organisers will do everything for them. Ten years of peace have largely eradicated the ravages of war. Trenches, craters and gun positions have been filled in; villages and towns rebuilt, and crops and foliage conceal what was once a see of mud, where the combatants were in a death-struggle. Yet their still remains a few places where the scars of the great conflict can be seen in their entirety, and the organisers of this pilgrimage that have rightly decided that it is in such places that the pilgrims wish to see, and not the reconstructed towns and villages. Perhaps a 'sine qua non' of the places to be visited is a good commanding view of the surrounding countryside. The places chosen for this tour are Vimy Ridge and the district of Beaumont Hamel, both of which fulfil the necessary conditions. Ypres, The Immortal Salient will also be visited. Is there anyone who took part in the war in France and Belgium who will ever forget the name of Ypres, or as it was more commonly nick named 'Wipers?' At Vimy the Canadian Government has bought a two-mile strip of land running along the famous Ridge, and there are British and German trenches in their original sites. Old German trench mortars have been re-erected in concrete emplacements and the underground tunnels are ravaged by rust and time. Barbed wire still protects the antagonists 'home' of trenches, while the German sniper posts remain untouched, with a warning board: 'Danger-Sniper's Nest' in the British area. The Beaumont Hamel area also contains the Newfoundland, Highland, and Argyll and Sutherland Highlander's Memorials, whilst on the Thiepval Ridge stands the magnificent Ulster Memorial, from the top of which a magnificent view of the Somme battlefield can be obtained. Although the pilgrims will proceed to these places in parties, they will be allowed to wander round individually at will, and to visit any particular spot they desire.

There are very many cemeteries in all of these neighbourhoods which are all well worth a visit just to see how beautiful and inspiring they are. The party organisers will also arrange for special visits to suit the pilgrim's wishes, which will be undertaken by motorcar. Besides paying visits to Vimy Ridge and Beaumont Hamel the pilgrims will proceed to Ypres on August 8th to take part in a solemn commemoration service and a grand 'march past.' Here, Earl Haig was to have taken the salute and his much lamented death will cause great grief to all who would have paid homage to their old comrade in arms and ex-Commander in Chief. Lady Haig is coming and bringing her son in order that his wishes should be fulfilled as nearly as possible. In each town visited the 'Anciens Combattants,' the corresponding organisation to the British Legion, will co-operate with the pilgrims in a short ceremony before the local war memorial. Legion wreaths will be laid at the feet of these memorials as a token of sympathy and homage to those of our brave allies who shed their blood in the name of justice. They are kindly arranging to co-operate in the work accommodating the pilgrims either separately or in groups, in private houses where bed, English breakfast and suppers will be supplied. The Legion organisers will make special arrangements for the mid-day meal so that pilgrims will not waste their valuable time by returning to their lodgings. Should hotel accommodation be preferred to private house, an extra charge of £1 will be made. For those living in the provinces, special reduced fares to London –or to port of embarkation, will be available upon production at the railway booking office of special vouchers, which will be issued with the tickets.

Unless anyone wishes to prolong the tour beyond four scheduled days (in which case the Legion will make special arrangements), passports will not be required, and this will save the pilgrims much worry and loss of time. All those who

contemplate taking part in this great pilgrimage must complete the registration form, obtainable from all branches of the Legion and forward it to the Headquarters of the British Legion, 26 Eccleston Square, London. SW1, together with a deposit of 5 shillings. The balance of £4 (which may be paid in one lump sum or by instalments) must be paid by the 1st June 1928. There is no doubt that the Pilgrimage will be a great success. The tour is comprehensive, the cost is small, and all arrangements will be made by the Legion. A person well versed in the historical associations of the battlefield, who will explain all matters of interest, will conduct each party. For the East Midlands, the party being organised, write to Mr. Hedley C. Hancock, 33 South Street, Long Eaton, and Nr Nottingham. This area covers Northants, Rutland, Notts, Leics, Lincs, and Derbys.

There followed a table that provided addresses for other parties throughout the country.

I do not know the response; certainly some of Coalville and district's wealthier citizens would have taken the tour, but for the majority of the town folk, even the prospect of taking unpaid time off work raised problems. Certainly my family circle could not have afforded £5 per person, although I know they would have liked to pay homage to loved-ones in corners of a foreign land.

SERGEANT MAJOR CHARLES STONE

In my earlier book: 'Fifty Good Men and True,' I mention on page 7 that a Sergeant Stone of the Seaforth Highlanders, helped to militarily instruct the Famous Fifty prior to their joining the 5th Battalion of the Leicestershire Regiment at Luton.

It appears that Sergeant Charles Stone married Annis Beck at 'The Mance,' Inverness, near the Moray Firth of Scotland, in March 1899.

He completed his service with the Seaforth Highlanders and left Scotland to take up the position of gymnasium instructor at Charles Booth's (of Grace Dieu Manor) Thringstone Institute. It was

opened in 1907 by Mr. Charles Booth ((junior), and Charles took over from Major Turnbull, who only occupied the post for a few months.

Charles Stone started his new career on the 3rd February 1908, and one of his duties was to be a 'Drill Class Instructor' for the immediate area including the local schools.

A School of Arms was opened in 1908/9 and a new rifle range building was opened on the 15th April 1910. Outdoor 'Butts' were also constructed on land that is now sites Whitwick's Hermitage Leisure Centre on Silver Street.

The local newspaper (26th April 1912) reported that Charles Stone of Whitwick had divorced his wife on the grounds of her misconduct.

Sergeant Stone was re-enlisted to his unit at the outbreak of war in August 1914, service number 3 / 7962. Internet 372/19 states that he received W.W.1 service medals. It appears he was given consent to train and improve the physical condition of the Fifty prior to rejoining the Highlanders.

By November 1915 he is listed as Sergeant Major Stone. It is known that he manned a Lewis Gun during the attack on Fosse 3, Lievin, near Lens on 7th / 8th June 1917, with the 5th Leicestershire also being present.

Sergeant Major Charles Stone survived the war but did not return to northwest Leicestershire: sadly no more is known of the old soldier.

JAKE ADKIN

Who Typified The Early 1914 Volunteers More Than Jake Adkin? Jake Adkin is sitting in the front centre of the photograph. His arm is resting on his knee and he is immediately to our left of the soldier with a bandaged eye.

Not a lot is known of Jake Adkin, he may have been a teenage pre-war territorial soldier, but I felt I had to include his photographs on the basis that his youthful, innocent facial expression seems to capture the buoyancy and enthusiasm of the 1914 volunteer. 'A bit of adventure on the continent and after all it will be all over by Christmas, wont it?'

The top photograph shows him with members of the Fifth Leicestershire Territorial Battalion at Sawbridgeworth in late 1914. The other scene has him with a group of comrades, almost certainly Coalville and district lads, at training camp around the same period, he appears to be living under canvas at the time.

Jake was an Ellistown man, and would certainly have known George Gadsby, William Barney, Walter Pettit and the Emmerson family. After surviving the war he returned to his village and spent the majority of his working life as a collier, mainly working at the South Leicestershire Colliery. I am also led to believe that he resided for majority of his married life on Whitehill Road, the main road running through the village, and that he and his wife had four children. They were Joyce, who married a Reverend Carter; Shirley, who married a Ballard; Leonard, who became a Flight Lieutenant in World War 2 and later emigrated to Australia, and finally Maurice, who never married and like his father was a miner.

Wherever his descendents are I wish them well and hope they possess his apparent optimism.

Jake Adkin is on the rear left: late 1914.

A WALK IN GRANDFATHER'S FOOTSTEPS

Coalville man, David Cavendish, together with his sister, Kay, and her husband, Roy Elston, travelled to France and Flanders in the sunny, leafy autumn of 2005. Undoubtedly, the three were twenty-first century pilgrims, not to Canterbury, but a pilgrimage to honour the Fallen of the Great War, with particularly homage to Private Charles Cavendish. The soldier was one of the town's Famous Fifty, and whilst serving with the 1/5th and 1/4th Battalions of the Leicestershire Regiment endured four years of conflict on the Western Front.

The conception of the tour was a few years old, and anticipation and emotion heightened until the threesome climbed into their 'Campavan' to begin, what was to prove, an unforgettable and deeply spiritual experience.

Private Charles Cavendish, Fifth Leicestershire Battalion, 1914.

Before the First World War Charles Cavendish worked as a miner at South Leicestershire Colliery, Ellistown, and lived with his wife, Jane, and five children at 84, Ashburton Road, Hugglescote. Joseph was one of his children, and the aforementioned David and Kay are his siblings.

In late August 1914, Charles enlisted into the 1/5th Leicestershire Battalion, and departed from Coalville in late October 1914, to arrive at Le Havre, France in February 1915. I confirm with pride that Charles was one of those early volunteers: one of the

first ex-civilians who set the benchmark for the five million enlistees/1916-18 conscripts.

Bathed in bright sunshine the Pilgrims followed the Way to Dover, and took the ferry to Calais: their first steps on French soil. One destination was Ypres (Wipers) in northern Belgium. The town was completely destroyed during the war, being completely rebuilt using German reparations. To a person unaware of this fact, they would never guess: it has been replicated perfectly. It is a magnificent Flemish market town, an architectural jewel. A few easterly miles outside of town they visited Sanctuary Wood, and soon were literally 'walking in their grandfather's footsteps!' Those deeply channelled scars: trenches, continue to convey messages, especially so at sunset, and when crimson leaves flutter to ground. Incumbent, among others, within those trenches of 1915 were Coalville lads; their names can be read on the Coalville Clock Tower Memorial. Nearby is Hill 62 with a museum that is worth far more than a petite muse, having stunning impact. Also, and so close by, the infamous Hill 60 that was under-mined so often that its core must consist of dead men's bones!

Private Charles Cavendish was wounded at one of the above locations with the 5th Battalion, however, when fully recovered was reposted to their sister battalion: 1/4th.

Most have heard that evocative poem: 'In Flanders Fields', and just to the northwest of Ypres, yet still within the district, they visit the concrete bunker where John McRae served as a doctor/surgeon/ poet, during the horrific 2nd Battle of Ypres, in the spring of 1915. The Canadian officer described his time at this Advanced Dressing Station as: 'Seventeen days of Hades!' There (yes, Hades) he slaved to save the almost conveyor-belt-line of dying, bleeding and suffocating casualties, maimed by bullet, shell, and the new weapon: chlorine gas. During this period, whilst attempting to save the life of a gallant young officer, Lex Helmer, he received the inspiration to write his famous poem.

The pilgrims found the lists of names and the enormity of Ypres' Menin Gate awesome, noting that several etched on a Leicestershire Tablet were comrades of David's grandfather. Again they were deeply moved when at 18.00 hours the traffic was stopped, and buglers played the Last Post in memory of the hundreds of thousands of troops killed-in-action within that scarred Salient.

Loos Cemetery (Dud Corner). On the left is the Memorial Wall where the name of Charles Cavendish is etched. Note the large slagheap in the distance.

The Campavan then travelled south for a few hours to French Flanders where the Battle of the Hohenzollern Redoubt was fought on the 13th October 1915. The 1/4th and 1/5th Battalions took part in this ferocious battle, with the former suffering appalling casualties.

Some time after the Hohenzollern Battle, Charles reappeared, reasonably fit, and returned to the frontline with the 1/4th Battalion.

The pilgrims then trekked the few miles to where personal and family emotions couldn't have been higher: Loos Cemetery (Dud Corner). It was within the confines of this beautiful walled cemetery that a very special wreath was laid below the name of their grandfather. Kay used the very finest of poppies for its construction, it was immaculate, and enclosed a photograph of Charles, taken in 1914. 'IN LOVING MEMORY.'

This was the first time in eighty-seven years that Charles' memory had been honoured in France; the threesome could not leave the cemetery without vowing to return.

David very kindly noted a relative of mine,

Bernard Hatter, whose name also appears on the Memorial Wall. He was killed in the September 1915 Battle of Loos. A Hugglescote man, he was shot in the chest whilst leading his men onto the third line of enemy trenches. My wife, Beryl, and I have prayed at that very spot.

David explained how he was considerably shocked: "*I could not believe that so many soldiers from the coalmines of northwest Leicestershire met their deaths, of all places, amid the coalmines and slagheaps of France!*"

Southwards, onwards and upwards to the heights of Vimy Ridge; once again seeing the remains of old trenches and battle scarred pastures. Our local lads had a severe test on those wintry slopes where mining, shelling, mortaring and gas, challenged pneumonia and 'trench foot' as to who reaped the most casualties.

Further south to the village of Gommecourt, once a citadel on the most northerly aspect of the Somme. It was there, on the 1st July 1916, that Charles was wounded, a piece of shell casing embedding itself into his skull. He was shipped to England for hospitalisation, and during that period heard of the death of both his parents. Additionally, his wife could no longer cope with the stress of supporting five children, and the constant concern about his welfare. The marriage was dissolved—Jane was a victim of the war!

David Cavendish with the specially prepared wreath for his grandfather.

Partial memorial names visible in photo:

BROTHERHOOD, L. E.
BROWN, S. W.
BROWN, W. J. C.
BROWN, L. G.
BROWNLOW, A.
BROWNLOW, A.
BROWNLOW, E.
BUCKINGHAM, S.
BULLOCK, J.
BURTON, A.
BURTON, H.
BURTON, H.

CHAMBERLAIN, F.
CHAMBERS, W.
CHAPMAN, G. H.
CLIBBERY, J.
CLIFF, H. T.
CLIFF, P. W.
CLIFFORD, A.
COLLIER, J. W. T.
COLVER, J. T.
CONCANNON, A.

CROSS, L.
CROSS, R. A.
CURTIS, A.
DAKIN, G.
DALE, A.
DAVIS, F.
DEACON, T. P.
DEACON, S. H.
DEXTER, F.
DODD

ELKIN, C.
ESSEX, A.
FANTOM, W.
FARLEY, W.
FARN, J.
FINCH, H. O.
FINCH, L. A. P.
FIRBAR, G. E.
FLETCHER, G. E.
FLETCHER, H.
FREEMAN, H.
FREEMAN, R.

Kay Elston (nee Cavendish) and her brother, David, at the Clock Tower with the wreath that she made for the Famous Fifty.

David lit his pipe, allowed his shoes to touch the chalky soil of Gommecourt's killing fields, and freed his mind. He pictured the horrendous early morning debacle, when so many troops perished in the enemy machine-gun fire. The bowl of his pipe had long since cooled before he climbed into their vehicle. They headed north, the return 'leg' of their sojourn: walking in grandfather's footsteps.

A stopping point was the St. Elie area in France, not far from Loos. There, on the 21st October 1917, Charles was again wounded, receiving shrapnel wounds to the chest from a bomb dropped by an enemy aircraft.

Upon recovery the brave soldier yet again returned to his unit; they were entrenched within the two villages of Gorre and Essars, near to Bethune, and straggling the canal of the same name. Charles, together with many others was gassed on the 18th June 1918, but after two weeks he recovered sufficiently to return to the same sector. They say old soldiers just fade away, and having used-up more

than his share of lives, a heavy German shell exploded at close proximity. He has no resting place, fading away on the 2nd July 1918!

The approximate location of his death was visited and the threesome said prayers for an exceptionally brave soldier indeed.

It may appear harsh, but soldiers passed fit by medical boards had no option but to return to the frontlines, where the camaraderie was far deeper than brotherly love.

Unlike their grandfather, the pilgrims were free to return to Leicestershire: their memories on videotape, always to appear vivid and unforgettable.

Kay also made a wreath composed of 'Fifty Poppies', a poppy for every member of Coalville's Famous Fifty. On Remembrance Day, 2005, the very special wreath was laid beneath the name of Charles Cavendish by his great grandson, regular soldier, Corporal Mark Cavendish.

Regular soldier, Corporal Mark Cavendish, with the wreath he laid for the Famous Fifty..

ZEPPELIN RAID ON LOUGHBOROUGH

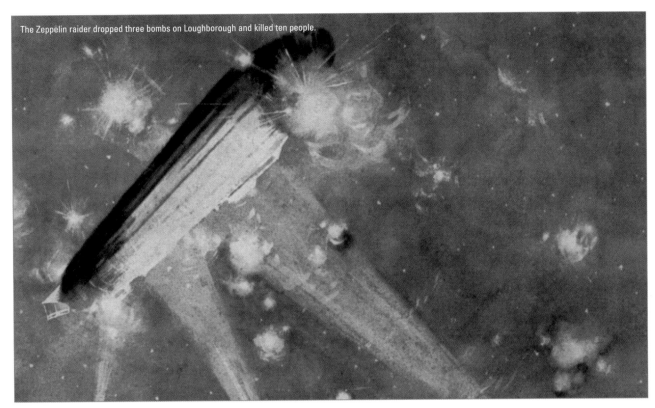

The Zeppelin raider dropped three bombs on Loughborough and killed ten people.

On the night of the 31st January 1916 a Zeppelin Air Ship dropped bombs on the market town of Loughborough in northwest Leicestershire. It is thought that the enemy raider: manned by German sailors, had been blown of course by strong winds and believed they were attacking Sheffield or Liverpool.

Three bombs dropped in all; one fell in the town centre, 'The Rushes' and others on Empress Road and the Morris Crane factory. Historians believe that Loughborough was targeted because blackout precautions had not been taken, and lights could be easily seen at a munitions factory on the Empress Road.

The cylindrical object trailed a railway course from city Leicester:
A gaseous serpent perhaps from the virgin-tended furnaces of Vesta.
Peace, eternal peace, for the ten innocents who rest under God's Light:
They were taken when only a pale moon shone on a cold, demonic night.

The bomb that fell in the town centre killed ten people. They are remembered on a bronze plaque mounted on oak, and it can be seen in the nearby Carillon Tower. It reads as follows:

In memory of our civilian victims of war.

Anne Adcock
Alice Elizabeth Adkin
Joseph Williamson Adkin
Josiah Gilbert
Ethel Alice Higgs
Elsie Page
Joseph Frederick Page
Mary Anne Page
Martha Shipman
Arthur Christian Turnall

Josiah Gilbert was forty-nine years of age, Ethel Higgs twenty-five, Mary Page forty-four, and her children, Elsie sixteen, and Joseph eighteen, Martha Shipman fifty and Arthur Turnall fifty-one.

The above victims were the only Loughborough civilians killed by air raid during both world wars.

In my earlier book about the Famous Fifty, on page 78, a niece of Charles Hatter can distinctly recall seeing a Zeppelin one night over Hugglescote, heading towards Ellistown Colliery, the course seems accurate and was almost certainly the same craft.

SOLDIERS' SILHOUETTES
REMEMBERING THOSE WHO FOUGHT IN WORLD WAR 1

Winter 1916

Dear, dear young souls a marching again into the Devil's fiery hell.
Hungry, weary and with gruesome memories forever unripe to tell.
Onwards, trekking to the front and silhouetted by embers of a setting sun,
As generals worry about death-quotients shocking politicians in London.

Sodden, muddy boots squelch on a defiant Western Front embankment.
Dark frames of brave, dependable men, unknown but eternally magnificent.
I see their reflections in the flooded shell-churned battlefields near to Ypres,
And know soldierly primates will end as soulless images, somewhat deeper!

Sojourners through a dismal, desolate landscape, even birds fight for perches.
Savaged by explosive storms as phosgene gas sinisterly hides in fouled ditches.
Mile follows mile, nothing changes apart from the steamy excesses of decay,
Onwards and onwards, the trenched crossroads of life and death and time to pray.

They're veterans of wilderness years, clawing, clinging to life since early days.
All are young of body, slipping, wading through mud as in their boyish phase.
A wee wag chirps out: "Pack Up Your Troubles" as someone plays a tin whistle,
The song carries across the battle-scarred emptiness to raise many a hair bristle.

Vivid thoughts of family and home bear contrast to this stagnant filthy scene.
If the early moon casts light on metal-helmets then it could appear as a dream.
Nodding, they pass me by in single file, and then fade from view into darkness,
Knowingly, I wish them well, young bodies to become as silhouettes, soul less!

Michael Kendrick.

THE UNKNOWN WARRIOR

Herbert George White, Bert to his mates over in Flanders, knew exactly where he was. It was either France or Belgium, or somewhere like that.

Herbert George White, Harry to his mates back home, knew exactly what time it was. It was 1914 or 1918, or any deathly time between those years.

Lance Corporal Herbert George White, service number 150426, Herbert to his mother and late father, knew exactly what he was doing: he was standing in a shell crater.

About three feet away from him, to his right, he could see Private Ginger Martin's severed left arm. The rest of Ginger was spread all round that side of the crater, like a jigsaw waiting to be pieced together. Bits of bodies—not just Ginger, surrounded him: there were English, Scots, Welsh, French, Belgium, American (not many) and German. He was in the centre of a mass of rotted and rotting flesh, and it stank: the whole putrescent mess stank!

He had seen it all before, many times, he was one of the first soldiers in France; he greeted the first territorial troops, or rather the first body of naïve men and boys who came over eons before: about early 1915; they were worthily entitled the 'Famous Fifty', from Coalville.

Bert whispered to himself: "*I'm getting there, it's no longer 1914, in fact I heard a couple of weeks ago that the war's over; although it doesn't look much like it to me.*" He paused, there wasn't a sound, no wind rustling the leaves, no trees, no birds, no one blaring orders, no comrades calling for assistance, no screaming, no sobbing, no whimpering. "Where is life?" He could hear his own breathing and the steady increase in his heartbeat; he was both frightened and exalted by the total silence. He again spoke to himself: "*Surely nobody has known such silence before: it's so peaceful, even joyous. I want to enter into it, I want to live it, be it. It is almost holy, perhaps it is holy, but what do I know, a simple Lincolnshire farmhand! Yes, what do I know? I can grow and pick spuds and I've been trained to kill my fellowmen, cos I've been told to by all them back there.*"

It was a chilly November day but he felt hot; sweat was trickling down his face and the nape of his neck and his back were sodden, turning his khaki shirt to a dirty green or brown colouring. He took off his helmet to mop his brow, but it felt sticky and cold, very cold, but it made him feel more comfortable, and so he lay down amid the carnage to rest for a while.

Two days pass

Major Peregrine 'Fanny' Featherstonehaugh shouted to Sergeant Mathews: "*There's another godforsaken crater over there, quick about it, see what you can find and then we'll call it a day.*"

Sergeant Mathews never acknowledged, not even a yes-sir, he just ambled to the crater without hope: he'd seen thousands of such holes and there was never anything 'suitable.' He muttered: "*Fancy-dan bleedin' officer, ignorant now, probably forever; just a bloody know-it-all, that prig of a man gets right up my nose.*" Expecting not to find anything he gave a cursory glance, hoping he could report to the jackanapes and say, without a trace of respect, that there was nothing. Just before leaving he spotted, in the corner of his eye, the sleeping Lance Corporal Herbert George White. The sergeant looked intently at the begrimed figure below, and then climbed into the crater and squatted to assess him carefully. After a full five minutes he climbed out and explained in stentorian tones: "*Sir, over here, sah! I may have found what you are looking for.*" He sarcastically muttered: "*Come over here you chinless ponce.*" The officer sighed and made his way: "*Confound it, make it quick, I was looking forward to sharing a bottle of claret with the chaps,*" he garbled. Both figures stared down at the figure. Major Featherstonehaugh suffered a feeling of nausea: vomit and phlegm surge into his throat; but he gulped hard. He had no stomach for close encounters with grotesque wounds. Mathews said: "*There sir, him sah, looks as though there is nothing wrong with him. He may be the 'one'. Take a look sir.*" He hid his contempt while stating that he would value the major's opinion.

Major Featherstonehaugh climbed (almost fell) into the crater. He followed the sergeant's earlier action and squatted down to inspect the find. After checking the lance corporal for a good ten minutes, and only locating a tiny speck of blood, he snapped: "*Sergeant, I do believe I have found our man.*"

The gun carriage bearing the coffin.

Mathews nodded and thought it was a typical affront of the man he despised, yes the major had found the One: not he. "*Yes sir, I do believe you have,*" he sarcastically affirmed.

"*Sergeant Mathews, I can see nothing wrong with him, we'll arrange to take him back to the field hospital for a more detailed inspection.*"

The sergeant muttered to himself: "*We'll arrange. You mean I'll arrange, and then you'll do nothing but wait seventy years to die and live on the reputation of your find!*"

Lance Corporal White then awoke: "*Of course there is nothing wrong with me, now help me up and I will carry on with my duty.*"

Bert was amazed when neither responded to his request and considered that they, no doubt, were suffering from shell blast damage to their ears.

Sergeant Mathews, of course, arranged for Bert's transportation to the field hospital. Soon, they had Bert washed and scrubbed: he looked immaculate, no trace of fleas, clinging trench grime or blood.

He was then prodded and poked by a range of doctors, nurses, orderlies, senior officers and even a few conchies. Bert couldn't understand his numbness: he couldn't feel a thing. They left Bert alone in a room, and various minor processes took place over a period of time. During his stay he attempted to return to that state of holy perfection that he had enjoyed just before he faded into sleep in the crater. A door opened and in strode the senior surgeon and a colonel. "*When we took his helmet off,*" said the surgeon, "*we found a sniper's bullet had penetrated his forehead and trashed his brain. He must have been one of the last soldiers to die. Damn fools, damn wars!*"

"What do we know about the man?" Enquired the colonel. "*Absolutely nothing, no dog tags, no identification; someone must have rifled his body before he was found,*" responded the surgeon.

Bert grumbled to himself: "*They can't be talking about me; all the lads know me; I was at Wipers, Vimy and Paschendaele, I have seen mud, bullets, gore and death, just ask one of the lads.*"

Only one man knew of the tags, Sergeant Mathews, he had taken them and shoved them in his

The Cenotaph shortly after its unveiling.

pocket; something deep inside him made him keep quiet about the issue.

Life became somewhat vague for Bert, but later: days, weeks, or months? He awoke.

The colonel continued: "*He has cleaned up really well, I will get my major to forward him to Boulogne where one of our undertakers can give him the final touches.*" The major in turn ordered Sergeant Mathews to make the arrangements.

On the 9th November 1920 an Army ambulance took Bert from Ypres to Boulogne where he spent the night in the Chateau, guarded by French soldiers.

"*So I am going back to Blighty, I don't suppose they can do much more for me here: they must realise that I am dreadfully paralysed.*"

The following day Bert is taken to the harbour. He awoke to hear the marching of military boots on cobbles and heard someone say that the draped Union Jack was used to cover the coffin of Nurse Cavell. With a great deal of ceremony was put aboard the quarterdeck of the destroyer: H.M.S. '*Verdon*'.

Bert thought: "*What a send off, all this for me. It must be because I was one of the first in and the last one out? I wish I could see more of what is going on though.*" The short journey across the Channel was calm, almost soporific, and he hoped to return to that earlier sate of holy perfection; but he could not.

Perhaps it was the throbbing of the engines or the pleas from the seagulls.

He was placed on a train shortly after arriving at Dover, but saddened not to have had the opportunity of seeing the white cliffs again: he enjoyed their virgin-like beauty when he departed in the summer of 1914.

Bert could not find peace, the train journey to London was noisy, the thrust of the engine and the clickety-click of the wheels as they hit the points.

On 9th November 1920, Sergeant Arthur Mathews made his way to a smallholding just outside of Bourne in Lincolnshire. He knocked on the door of the aged, dilapidated cottage; a careworn woman, looking seventy-five, but actually in her mid-forties answered. He asked her if she was Mrs. White. She nodded and let him in when he said he had news of her son, Herbert. Mrs. Dorothy White sobbed with untold grief at the confirmation of her loss, but filled with pride and joy when told that he would lie with kings. The sergeant, released temporarily from his military mantle, held her gently and they cried in each other's arms.

Wednesday 10th November 1920

Countless people are making their way from various parts of Great Britain to central London, to witness the pomp and ceremony of the empirically acclaimed burial of the UNKNOWN WARRIOR.

Thursday 11th November 1920

Bert feels the roll of the two-wheeled gun carriage, hears the marching of military boots and of people cheering: this continued as he proceeded along a central London route.

"*All this for me, just for me. So they did find out after all, but how? I do like the hymns and the prayers, reminds me of Sundays back home in church. I wish I knew what they meant when they speak of the Cenotaph! I wish I could get up to see the King. The bells of Big Ben, that makes eleven chimes.*" A feeling of deep contentment gradually overcame him and he decided to rest for a while. Steadily, only steadily, he indulged a silence: a perfect peace, a state of permanent holy perfection: he was laid to rest with Kings in Westminster Abbey.

12th November 1920

That evening Dorothy White and Sergeant Arthur Mathews M.M., the only two people who knew of the identity of the Unknown Warrior made a pact never to reveal his identity.

At that very same moment Colonel Featherstonehaugh was in his prestigious West End club, relating for the umpteenth time to his chums as to how he, and he alone, had found the soldier who was to be named the Unknown Warrior.

The Aftermath

A mere ten minutes before Prime Minister, Neville Chamberlain, waved his piece of paper declaring: *'Peace in our time',* a contented Dorothy White waved goodbye to the world as she lost consciousness in her armchair. A photograph of young Herbert holding his father's hand lay on her lap: in her right hand her son's dog tag. World War 2 followed shortly.

Lieutenant Arthur Mathews. M.C. M.M., deeply respected by his men, was shot through the temple by a sniper, dying instantly. The brave officer was commanding his troops in the rearguard at Dunkirk in May 1940. Later some of his men stated that he deserved the top medal for outstanding valour.

Colonel Sir Peregrine Aubrey St. John Featherstonehaugh, knighted for his services to the Pay Corps, died of natural causes at the disappointing, even frustrating age of ninety-eight years. He left a wife, and a son predeceased him.

His obituary in the Daily Telegraph filled almost half a page. In 1938, Jakob Schmidt, (Ex-lance corporal) and specialist sniper who served with the Prussian Guard from 1914-18, was kicked to death by sixteen extremists from the Hitler Youth. His sin: he was "Ein Jude."

Lance Corporal Herbert George White, Harry to his mates, Herbert to his late parents, remains cocooned in a state of holy perfection.

An amazing fictional piece of work written by John Gibbard of Leicester: It truly captures so much of the sadness, pity and apathy of warfare.

My thanks to John for his permission in allowing its publication.

Addition

Bert was sleeping and so did not realise, but on his arrival at Boulogne, he was driven to the fortress overlooking the harbour, and allowed to rest in a small stone room, delicately decorated with autumn's foliage and fitted out as a chapel. Bert was then reverently lowered into a casket and that evening a service was read.

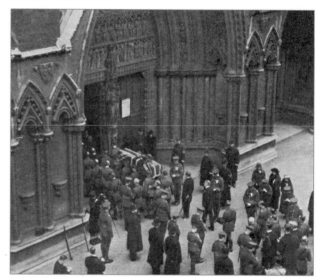

The coffin enters Westminster Abbey.

The casket had been designed in the style of a 16th century treasure chest and made from two-inch English oak. The sides were slightly rounded, as was the lid, and all was finished in a dark wax. It was mounted with four pairs of hammered wrought iron handles and iron bands from head to foot across the shoulder area. The plate was of a 16th century shield design and bore the following description in Old English:

A British Warrior
Who Died
in The Great War
1914-18
for King and Country.

The plate was bolted to the lid over a 16th century Crusader's sword given by His Majesty the King. The ironwork was made in London and finished off at Caernarvon, Wales.

When Bert left Boulogne harbour on 10th November, six British destroyers escorted his ship: three on each side. In the Channel four French destroyers gave a salute and guns also fired from French land forts. At mid Channel the French destroyers departed but not after a further salvo salute.

H.M.S. 'Verdon' arrived at Dover at 15.30 hours, with the hilltop Castle's guns firing a salute. At the jetty massed brass bands played: 'Land of Hope and Glory' and massive crowds cheered the procession to the railways station. The casket was placed in the same railway carriage that once contained the body of Nurse Cavell. Its sides were fitted with latticework intertwined with flowers and banked with laurel and chrysanthemums.

On arrival at Victoria Station the carriage was placed in a special siding and guarded overnight.

On 11th November 1920, huge crowds at Whitehall and Horse Guards witnessed a ceremony during which the Cenotaph was unveiled, and a further salute given to the Unknown Warrior: prior to entombment at Westminster Abbey.

Six Admirals stood to attention on one side of the gun carriage, six generals on the other:

"*We know you well, dear comrade. We know that to you these honours would seem the most gigantic of jokes if they were paid to yourself. Your guffaws would burst a coffin. But you understand us. It is hundreds of thousands we are honouring in your person. Because you are nameless and forgotten we chose you. You represent them all.*"

At the Cenotaph was an assembly representative of the Empire. With the King at the head, all turned to face the body of the Unknown Warrior on the gun carriage.

Behind the King stood the Princess, and a gathering representing the statesmen of England and the Dominions, as well as the Forces and Churches.

Two huge Union Jacks veiled the Cenotaph, with its designer, Sir John Lutyens standing close by. The observing crowd filled every inch of the pavements, packed close and orderly like slates on a roof.

The music stopped and the King stepped forward with a wreath and placed it on the coffin, beside a 'Tommy' steel helmet. The choir sang: '*Oh, God, our help in ages past.*' The Archbishop of

The Stone above the tomb of the Unknown Warrior.

Canterbury then recited the Lord's Prayer, in which the King and the people joined in. This completed, the King touched a mechanism and two huge Union Jacks fell to the ground. The Cenotaph, built in Portland Stone and of a pale lemon colouring rose naked, in a slight mist, before the gathered masses. Its sudden dramatic apparition captured all of the significance of the occasion, itself.

With the final chime of Big Ben's eleven o'clock, everyone could be seen standing with heads bowed: no motion even from the horses that stood with the gun carriage. George V lifted his head and motion was restored to the crowd. The Last Post was sounded. The King and Princes walked to the Abbey immediately behind the gun carriage, followed by statesmen and representatives.

The great masses of crowds then began their pilgrimage, a procession against the Cenotaph. The Victoria Cross holders marched together, naval captains, gunners of the R. F. A., sergeants and soldiers of many foot regiments, side by side with field officers and men in ordinary civilian cloths wearing miniature medals. There were detachments from branches of the Air Services and the Mercantile Marines, also many men in hospital blue, without legs, steering and working their hand tricycles. So many wreaths were left that the Cenotaph appeared to grow out of a wonderful green garden.

Another moving sight was the appearance of six green motor coaches with men in hospital blue, in another coach, men with lost limbs, in another, blinded soldiers, in another, men with such terrible injuries that were incapable of rising to observe the immortal scene.

Other war legacies were in the hearts of the countless women in black who were filing past. The police on horseback directed those with flowers, and so women in the crowd with flowers raised them above their heads, so that they could be helped to join the lengthy procession. All along Whitehall, what was once a mass of black clothing, suddenly bloomed into a startling white blossom: like the hedgerows in April.

Who could deny that perhaps a frail woman by the name of Dorothy White laid flowers on the Cenotaph, arm in arm with a Sergeant Arthur Mathews, who next to the traditional medals was pinned the Military Medal. Who knows?

I thank the detailed records of Mr. Nodes, who in 1920, was President of the National Association of Funeral directors, and who played a major role in returning the Unknown Warrior from France.

FOR THE FALLEN

"They shall grow not old, as we that are left grow old:
Age shall not weary them, nor the years condemn.
At the Going down of the sun and in the morning,
We will remember them."

By Laurence Binyon.

CONCLUSION

With the conclusion of this book, I feel very grateful and content to have had the opportunity to represent some extraordinary brave men who represented King and Country between 1914-18. These men were primarily from northwest Leicestershire, or at the very least spent a considerable amount of their lives in the county: and principally served in the 'Tigers', the (Royal) Leicestershire Regiment.

It is my deepest hope that when people have read my book, they will appreciate that often within the savage realms of warfare there lies the essence of mankind: a God given love to sacrifice a life to save others. If this altruistic seed could grow within the conscience of mankind, then surely the result would be an end to all hostilities: a popular Sixties song, 'Woodstock', suggested that one day mankind might 'get back to the Garden.'

If this is to be my last book on World War 1, then I apologise for all those brave soldiers who have not featured within the pages.

It has been a delight to meet so many wonderful families; by their very desire to enshrine their ancestors' names in black and white exemplifies the love they behold: a great if not greater love.

In the recent past I have volunteered a wealth of information to the computer files of Newarke Museum, Leicester, so that if people do not have the chance to buy this book they will still be able to conduct research.

Finally it is my hope that 'Greater Love' will follow the fortunes of my earlier book: 'Fifty Good Men and True.' In January 2007 I was asked by the National Archives to supply copies to Oxford and Cambridge Universities, Trinity College, Belfast, the National Library of Scotland and the National Library of Wales. Perhaps in one hundred years time caring hands in white gloves will turn the pages of this book.

Thank you for your time.

Michael Kendrick.

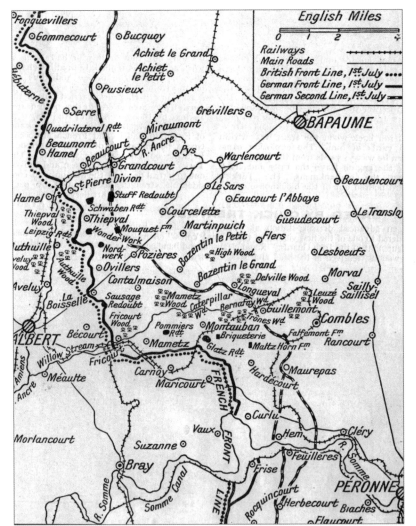

The Somme.

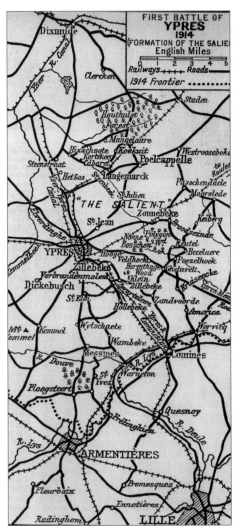

Ypres.

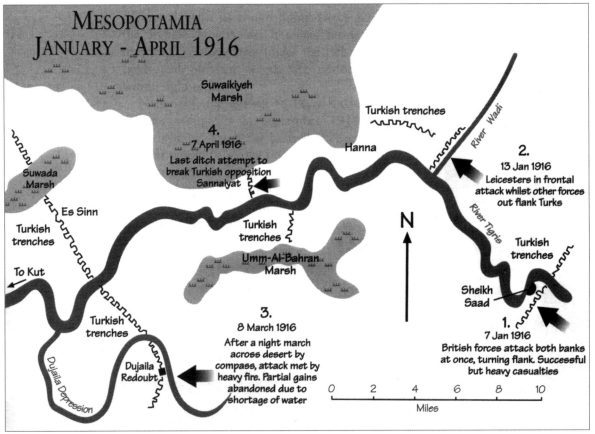

MESOPOTAMIA
JANUARY - APRIL 1916

Suwaikiyeh Marsh

Turkish trenches

River Wadi

4.
7 April 1916
Last ditch attempt to break Turkish opposition
Sannaiyat

Hanna

2.
13 Jan 1916
Leicesters in frontal attack whilst other forces out flank Turks

Suwada Marsh

Es Sinn

Turkish trenches

Turkish trenches

River Tigris

Turkish trenches

N

To Kut

Umm-Al-Bahran Marsh

Turkish trenches

Sheikh Saad

Turkish trenches

3.
8 March 1916
After a night march across desert by compass, attack met by heavy fire. Partial gains abandoned due to shortage of water

Dujaila Depression

Dujaila Redoubt

1.
7 Jan 1916
British forces attack both banks at once, turning flank. Successful but heavy casualties

0   2   4   6   8   10

Miles

Mesopotamia, 1916. Many thanks to Matthew Richardson (Pen & Sword books).